I SHOP, THEREFORE I AM

Ann Marie DaSilva, CSW-
ACSW

I SHOP, THEREFORE I AM

Compulsive Buying and The Search for Self

EDITED BY

April Lane Benson, Ph.D.

JASON ARONSON INC.
Northvale, New Jersey
London

This book was set in 11 pt. Veljovic by Alabama Book Composition of Deatsville, Alabama, and printed and bound by Book-mart Press, Inc. of North Bergen, NJ.

Production Editor: Judith D. Cohen

Library of Congress Cataloging-in-Publication Data

I shop, therefore I am : compulsive buying and the search for self /
    edited by April Lane Benson.
        p.   cm.
    Includes bibliographical references and index.
    ISBN 0–7657–0242–8 (alk. paper)
    1. Compulsive shopping.   I. Benson, April Lane.
RC569.5.S56I12   2000
616.85′84 — dc21   99–43395

Printed in the United States of America on acid-free paper. For information and catalog write to Jason Aronson Inc., 230 Livingston Street, Northvale, NJ 07647-1726, or visit our website: www.aronson.com

To the memory of my father, Edward Lane

The world is too much with us; late and soon
Getting and spending, we lay waste our powers.

—William Wordsworth

CONTENTS

My original interest in the subject of shopping focused on the actualizing possibilities of search — of shopping gone good, if you will, rather than bad. Over a number of years I had become aware of the very important role that a particular store (and my relationships with the people who worked there) played in my life. Recognizing that shopping meant far more to me than its traditional associations with buying or having, I imagined this was true for others as well.

I knew that shopping, undertaken in the spirit of search, could be a constructive process, one that would promote self-definition, self-expression, creativity, even healing. I knew too that it could pose a dangerous threat. I wanted to understand my own experience better and help some of the people I work with transform their relentless pursuit of material goods into a meaningful search for ideas and experiences as well as for things. So I set out to learn, from an academic point of view, what shopping was really about. I began reading from a variety of disciplines about shopping, consumption, the search process, and the meaning of material things.

As I educated myself, the dark side of consumer behavior quickly came into view. As early as 594 B.C., when the first sumptuary laws were enacted in ancient Athens, legislators set prohibitions against excess in consumption. These little-known Athenian laws put restrictions on the cost and number of goods one could buy, confined the wearing of certain colors to the upper classes, and even limited the number of guests at a wedding or the width of decorative trim on a sleeve. Although enacted over time on several continents — the last U.S. sumptuary law was passed in 1800 — such laws were notoriously difficult to enforce. I began to wonder whether the ambivalence so many of us feel about shopping might be a contemporary version of the traditional sumptuary law, legislated now from within.

As I pursued this question, I encountered a persistent trio of myths, half-truths based on the notion of shopping gone bad, that effectively diminish our regard for the entire activity. These half-truths — that shopping is a woman's thing, that shopping is about spending money, that shopping is a meaningless activity — embody vital issues in our culture, from gender differences to handling money to living the unexamined life. Each of them reflects a narrow contextual prejudice and helps to give shopping a bad rap. Together they significantly distort our concept of the shopping process. I hoped that by examining the dark side of shopping I might pry these embedded fictions loose.

So, even as it examines the dark side of consumption, this book represents the seduction of that dark side. I had begun my exploration with a positive spin but have wound up writing — perhaps inevitably — about compulsive buying.

Were it not for my mother, Frances Mehlman, I would not have discovered at a young age both the dark side of shopping and the actualizing possibilities of search. While shopping became the axis around which some of our complicated battles were waged, I have her to thank for nurturing this enduring interest. My early sensitivity to shopping, gone good and bad, eventually led me to write an essay, "When Shopping Heals." That essay in turn became the centerpiece of a workshop I created.

After a story about the workshop appeared in *New York* magazine, I received a call from Wendy Hubbert, an editor at Crown Trade Publications, asking me if I might be interested in elaborating my ideas into a book. While there was no guarantee of a publishing commitment, I liked the idea. Wendy's enthusiastic participation on that leg of the journey gave me the impetus and permission I needed to quiet the individual, familial, and culturally inculcated voices deriding me for an interest in so "superficial" a subject.

Having reined in shame and guilt, I could ride high on curiosity about what I'd see. Thus I set to work on a popular book about the actualizing possibilities of search, after having been "fixed up" with a collaborator, Bernardine Connelly, who would help with the writing. It was one of those rare blind dates that turned into a vision. She put her head and heart into the project, and lent confidence to both me and the work in progress. But in spite of all indications that I would see this work morph into book form, it was not to be at that time. No match for the dark side, the forces of shopping gone good retreated to the back burner.

At this point my longtime friend Joyce Aronson, a natural matchmaker for books, suggested that I join with the dark side and put together an edited collection for the clinician about compulsive buying. For helping me snatch victory from the jaws of defeat, I am grateful to Joyce.

As I set about the job of enlisting contributors, I had the good fortune to find out about and attend a conference on money disorders. It was there that I met and talked with Ronald Faber and Leonard Brazer. Their willingness to write chapters was the reinforcement I needed. As the book unfolded, the graciousness with which each author agreed to serve as docent was truly remarkable. My heartfelt thanks to you all.

Throughout my five-year study of shopping, I've depended on the kindness of others — none of them strangers, some longtime close friends, many also colleagues. My professional home, The Center for the Study of Anorexia and Bulimia (a division of the Institute for Contemporary Psychotherapy), has been a steady source of support and sponsorship. Friends scouted out shopping materials in the popular media, and numerous colleagues shared clinical vignettes, frequently adding their own shopping stories. Several colleagues reviewed the book in progress and made extremely helpful comments or suggestions. Still others unveiled to me the intricacies of craft — and of finding, seeing, and making it. These reinforced my belief in an aesthetic of search, in shopping as a constructive experience in discrimination.

I'm grateful for all of their help. To Beryl Abrams, Sheldon Bach, Jill Edelman Barberie, Roberta Beck, Beatrice Beebe, Barbara Bonventre, Nancy Bravman, Susan Z. Cohen, Caroline Debrovner, Jennifer Dule, Sharon Farber, Augusta Gross, Frank Lachmann,

Lynn Lawrence, Jean Litz, Gerry Lynas, Elisa Michel, Marjorie Nicholson, Judy Rabinor, and Joan Schmidt, thank you. This book would have been but a shadow of the dark side without you.

A special thanks to my friend and neighbor, Morris Holbrook, W. T. Dillard Professor of Marketing at the Graduate School of Business, Columbia University, who willingly invited me into his vast store of knowledge. Morris introduced me to the academic side of consumer behavior, generously allowed me to audit one of his graduate courses, and welcomed me as an interdisciplinary colleague.

The editorial labor of a collection such as this is formidable, and I was fortunate in having great help. Cindy Hyden, formerly of Jason Aronson Inc., assisted in the initial conceptualization and shaping of the book, easing any early doubts that I had. Molly Kovel, Jill-of-all-trades, mistress of many, helped me sew together the chapters that form the quilt of this book, picking up with her delicate hand and tireless attention to detail any dropped stitches or errant threads. Two people, Carol Paradis and my brother, Gary Lane, were enormously helpful with my pieces. And Judy Cohen, Senior Production Editor at Aronson, took great pains at the copy-editing stage to make sure that it was as wrinkle-free as possible.

Three other people deserve special thanks. Whenever I thought I could proofread no longer, my son Corey invited me out to the park for a catch and demanded that I "play [my] heart out"; it was the perfect seventh-inning stretch. My son Eric, always in touch with my emotions, soothed the editorial beast in me with his wonderful jazz piano. And my husband Jim, generous above all, not only tolerated this obsession but supported and embraced it. Bless them for being my angels.

April Lane Benson
March 2000

CONTRIBUTORS

Cecile Andrews, Ed.D.
Community Educator, Seattle, WA
Director, Simplicity Circles Project
Author: *The Circle of Simplicity: Return to the Good Life*

F. Diane Barth, M.S.W., C.S.W.
Faculty, Supervisor, and Training Analyst, The Psychoanalytic Institute of the Postgraduate Center and the National Institute for the Psychotherapies, New York
Faculty, Center for the Study of Anorexia and Bulimia, New York
Private practice of psychotherapy and psychoanalysis, New York, NY
Author: *Daydreaming: Unlock the Creative Power of Your Mind*

Russell Belk, Ph.D.
N. Eldon Tanner Professor of Business Administration, David Eccles School of Business, University of Utah, Salt Lake City, UT
Author: *Collecting in a Consumer Society*
Editor: *Highways and Buyways: Naturalistic Research from the Consumer Behavior Odyssey*
Co-editor: *Marketing and Consumption: Macro Dimensions*

April Lane Benson, Ph.D.
Co-founder, Director of Training, Supervisor, and Faculty, Center for the Study of Anorexia and Bulimia, New York
Private practice of psychotherapy and psychoanalysis, New York, NY

Donald W. Black, M.D.
Professor of Psychiatry, University of Iowa College of Medicine, Iowa City, IA

Author: *Bad Boys, Bad Men — Confronting Antisocial Personality Disorder*

Donna Boundy, M.S.W.
President, Maverick Media Resources, Inc., Woodstock, NY
Author: *When Money Is the Drug: Understanding and Changing Self-Defeating Money Patterns*
Co-author: *Willpower's Not Enough: Why We Don't Succeed at Change*

Leonard Brazer, Ed.S., M.A., C.C.G.C.
Formerly Director and Supervisor, MoneyDisorders/Pathological Gambling Program, Saint Clare's Hospital, Boonton Township, NJ
President, National Council on Spending and Credit Disorders
Private practice of psychotherapy, Denville, NJ

Melissa Burgard, B.A.
Research Coordinator, Neuropsychiatric Research Institute, Fargo, ND

Colin Campbell, B.Sc., Ph.D.
Reader in Sociology and Department Head, University of York, England
Author: *The Romantic Ethic and the Spirit of Modern Consumerism; The Myth of Social Action*
Co-editor: *The Shopping Experience*

Helga Dittmar, D.Phil.
Senior Lecturer in Psychology, Sociology and Social Psychology Subject Group, School of Social Sciences, University of Sussex, England
Author: *The Social Psychology of Material Possessions: To Have Is to Be*

Ronald J. Faber, Ph.D.
Professor of Mass Communications, School of Journalism and Mass Communication, University of Minnesota, Minneapolis, MN
Editor: *Journal of Advertising*

Eve Golden, M.D.
Psychoanalytic Editor and Independent Scholar
Manuscript Editor, 1999 Freud Supplement of the *Journal of the American Psychoanalytic Association*

Ramona Goldman, M.S.W., C.S.W., B.C.D.
Faculty, Continuing Education Program, Postgraduate Center for Mental Health, New York
Supervisor, Psychoanalytic Psychotherapy Study Center, New York
Private practice of psychotherapy, New York, NY

Toby Goldsmith, M.D.
Director, Women's Programs, Psychiatry Specialty Clinics, University of Florida College of Medicine, Gainesville, FL
Clinical Assistant Professor, University of Florida College of Medicine, Gainesville, FL

Bonnie Kellen, Ph.D.
Clinical and Industrial Psychologist
Formerly adjunct faculty, College of New Rochelle, School of New Research, New York, NY
Formerly adjunct faculty, Teachers College, Columbia University, New York, NY
Private practice of psychotherapy and career counseling, New York, NY

David W. Krueger, M.D., F.A.P.A.
Clinical Professor of Psychiatry, Baylor College of Medicine, Houston, TX
Training and Supervising Psychoanalyst, Houston-Galveston Psychoanalytic Institute
Author: *Body Self and Psychological Self: Developmental and Clinical Integration in Disorders of the Self; Emotional Business: Meanings and Mastery of Work, Money and Success*
Editor: *The Last Taboo: Money as Symbol and Reality in Psychotherapy and Psychoanalysis*
Private practice of psychiatry and psychoanalysis, Houston, TX

Betsy Levine, M.S.W., C.S.W.
Community Educator, New York, NY
Private practice of psychotherapy, New York, NY

Karen McCall
Author: *The Financial Recovery Workbook; You and Your Money:
   Planning Your Way to Peace of Mind* (forthcoming)
Financial Recovery Trainer
Private practice of Financial Recovery Counseling,
   San Anselmo, CA

Susan L. McElroy, M.D.
Director, Biological Psychiatry Program, University of Cincinnati
   Medical School, Cincinnati, OH
Professor of Psychiatry, University of Cincinnati Medical School,
   Cincinnati, OH

Mary Ann McGrath, Ph.D.
Associate Professor of Marketing, School of Business
   Administration, Loyola University Chicago, Chicago, IL
Co-editor: Issue on Consumer Rituals, *Journal of Ritual Studies*

Olivia Mellan, M.S.
Private practice, Washington Therapy Guild, Washington, DC
Author: *Overcoming Overspending: A Winning Plan for Spenders
   and their Partners; Money Harmony: Resolving Money Conflicts in
   Your Life and Relationships*

James E. Mitchell, M.D.
President and Scientific Director, Neuropsychiatric Research
   Institute, Fargo, ND
Professor and Chairman, Department of Neurosciences,
   University of North Dakota School of Medicine and Health
   Sciences, Fargo, ND
Author: *Bulimia Nervosa; Elements of Clinical Research in
   Psychiatry*
Editor: *Eating Disorders: Diagnosis and Treatment*

Werner Muensterberger, M.D.
Retired Associate Professor of Psychiatry, State University of
   New York, Brooklyn, NY

Former Editor-in-Chief: *The Psychoanalytic Study of Society*
Author: *Collecting: An Unruly Passion; The Personality of the Forger*
  (forthcoming)
Co-editor: *Between Reality and Fantasy: Transitional Objects and
  Phenomena*
Private practice of psychotherapy and psychoanalysis,
  New York, NY

Arlene Kramer Richards, Ed.D.
Training and Supervising Analyst, New York Freudian Society,
  New York, NY
Fellow, Institute for Psychoanalytic Training and Research,
  New York, NY
Co-editor: *The Spectrum of Psychoanalysis: Essays in Honor of
  Martin Bergmann*
Private practice of psychotherapy and psychoanalysis,
  New York, NY

BACKGROUND

Compulsive shopping is finally coming out of the closet. First described by Kraepelin in 1915 and then by Bleuler in 1924 (they labeled it *oniomania* from the Greek *oniomai*, to buy, and included it among other pathological and reactive impulses), it went largely ignored for the next sixty years. Only in the last decade have we seen specific and persistent inquiry into the disorder — in the psychiatric literature, in studies of consumer behavior and marketing, and in the popular press. And although the study of compulsive buying is still in relative infancy compared with some of its psychological siblings — alcoholism, for example, or eating disorders or drug abuse — there is more and more evidence, both research and anecdotal, that it poses a serious and worsening problem, one with significant emotional, social, occupational, and financial consequences.

How many people are we talking about? Estimates vary. According to Faber and O'Guinn (1992), somewhere between 1 and 6 percent of the population may be full-fledged compulsive buyers. The American Psychological Association's *Monitor* (Mjoseth 1997) agrees, reporting that perhaps 15 million Americans have little control over how much they spend or what they buy. Estimates in the popular literature go higher; they see a full 10 percent of the population, perhaps 28 million Americans, as problem buyers (Trachtenberg 1988). And nonpathological compulsive buying — a compelling need to purchase that is not self-destructive but may become so — could exist in as many as a quarter of us (Nataraajan and Goff 1992). Richard Elliot (1994), who has written about the relationship between addictive consumption and the postmodern condition, suggests that as incomes rise and shopping becomes a leisure pursuit, more and more addictive shoppers will emerge. The same possibility is envisaged by Scherhorn and colleagues (1990). No surprise, then, that diagnostic criteria for compulsive buying are being proposed to the American Psychiatric Association for possible inclusion in the next revision of the *Diagnostic and Statistical Manual*.

The present collection focuses a wide-angle lens on the many issues and aspects that surround this multidetermined disorder. Individual contributions approach the subject from the fields of sociology, marketing, consumer behavior, and community education, as well as those of psychology and psychiatry; they address the biological, sociological, psychological, and spiritual issues that are bound up with compulsive buying. This disorder is often linked to emotional deprivations in childhood, an inability to tolerate negative feelings, the need to fill an internal void, excitement seeking, excessive dependency, approval seeking, perfectionism, general impulsiveness and compulsiveness, and the need to gain control (DeSarbo and Edwards 1996, Faber et al. 1987). There is a clear correlation between addictive consumption tendencies and the extent to which people perceive that the shopping experience and the goods purchased can make them feel and appear more socially desirable. Said simply, compulsive buying seems to represent a desperate search for self in people whose identity is neither firmly felt nor dependable.

As you will read, most shopaholics try to counteract feelings of low self-esteem through the emotional lift and momentary euphoria provided by compulsive shopping. These shoppers, who also experience a higher than normal rate of associated disorders — depression, anxiety, substance abuse, eating disorders, and impulse-control disorders — may be using their symptom to self-medicate.

Underlying (or at least intensifying) the deeply felt need of problem shoppers is our nationwide outbreak of "affluenza," the modern American plague of materialism and overconsumption. This addiction to affluence and all its trappings underscores the reality that for every voice echoing Thoreau's famous plea, "Simplify, simplify," a hundred others cry, "Amplify, amplify!" (Sanders

1998). And amplify we do. The kind and number of shopping sites proliferates, and the gap between what we have and what we want grows ever wider. In addition to stores, still the most frequent sites by far, catalogue shopping, television shopping, cybershopping, and perhaps even online trading are becoming fertile grounds for the growth of compulsive purchase.

A particular media focus has been the fetching eye candy displayed by Internet auction sites, the newest temptation in the compulsive buyer's Garden of Eden. *USA Today* summed up the attraction: "Take the thrill of gambling, the excitement of computer games, the enjoyment of collecting, and the desire to get a good deal, and sprinkle it with a little of the old hunter–gatherer instinct. Suddenly, you've got several million people hooked on on-line auctions" (Weise 1999). Although mental health professionals, addiction support groups, and researchers are just beginning to see cases of what might be called auction addiction, we can expect the numbers to increase sharply. For the susceptible shopper or buyer, these sites have a hypnotic pull.

As always, shopping jokes and bumper stickers are ubiquitous. Thus the "smiled upon addiction," as Catalano and Sonenberg have called it (1993), is smiled upon in two senses: it is at once a source of wry humor and at the same time a behavior much inflamed by our ever-present marketing machinery. As a result, compulsive shopping may be an even greater source of guilt and shame than alcoholism or drug abuse. Those disorders are commonly thought of as diseases, or at least recognized as serious problems requiring treatment. Compulsive buyers, who are often quite secretive about their habit, worry that they will be considered simply materialistic and vacuous — judgments that likely reflect their self-perceptions.

In my clinical experience and that of most of my colleagues, it is still unusual for a patient to refer him- or herself for treatment for a compulsive buying problem. If compulsive shopping is a presenting problem, the patient has typically been referred by a financial counselor, lawyer, law enforcement officer, family member, or spouse. Much more frequently, a compulsive buying problem reveals itself in the course of ongoing psychotherapy. As treatment progresses, some patients begin to talk openly about the problem; with others it emerges in the context of financial independence and responsibility issues, relationship problems, difficulties at work, or parenting problems. Compulsive buying may also present itself indirectly in therapy: a patient may wear something new or different to every session, or arrive with shopping bags week after week, or repeatedly give gifts to the therapist, or fall behind in paying the bill. Often a patient will enact several of these behaviors simultaneously.

TOWARD A DEFINITIVE DIAGNOSTIC TERM

As the study of what was once called *oniomania* evolves, we move semantically back toward the Greek root. In both popular and professional literature, the terms *compulsive shopping, compulsive buying,* and *compulsive spending* are often used interchangeably, but the behaviors they represent are in fact distinctly different (Nataraajan and Goff 1992). One may buy, after all, without shopping, or shop without buying. Because progress in understanding this disorder must in part depend on thinking and speaking clearly about it, most current researchers use the term *compulsive buying* and subscribe to an exceptionally specific definition proposed by McElroy and her colleagues (1994).

Their choice of *buying* rather than *shopping* reflects the difference between a relatively narrow act — taking possession of something — and a far broader one. Shopping, the broader act, is largely the province of consumer behaviorists and retailers, who have evolved their study of it from an early emphasis on rational choice to today's focus on its experiential aspects. Their several concepts of shopping include a type of generalized search behavior (Hawkins, et al. 1989), a hedonic recreation (Holbrook and Hirshmann 1982), and a way to "spend" discretionary time (Arndt and Gronmo 1977). Viewed thus, as a kind of consumer ritual that enables the shopper to gather information for immediate or future use, shopping can be a way to satisfy many nonpurchase motives (Nataraajan and Goff 1992).

Even *spending*, though closer to *buying* than *shopping* is, need not be synonymous with acquisition. Spending bespeaks the action of relinquishing funds rather than the gathering of material objects. Nataraajan and Goff (1992) observe that it may occur without either shopping or buying (except in a vicarious or surrogate sense), as when a parent gives money to children. In one solidly middle-income family I know of, the parents, in a desperate attempt to be loved, gave enough to their adult children that they literally bankrupted themselves.

These distinctions amount to more than hairsplitting. Semantic confusion can proliferate into typological and methodological errors, so it is essential that we speak with clarity when we consider the problem of compulsive buying. The most widely used definitional criteria (McElroy et al. 1994) define the disorder, in essence, as a maladaptive preoccupation with buying or shopping, whether impulses or behavior, that either (1) is experienced as irresistible, intrusive, and/or senseless or (2) results in frequent buying of more than can be afforded or of items that are not needed, or shopping for longer periods of time than intended. The buying preoccupations, impulses, or behaviors cause marked distress, are time consuming, significantly interfere with social or occupational functioning, or result in financial problems, and they do not occur exclusively during periods of hypomania or mania. In short, the compulsive buyer is a person who allows shopping to destructively deflect resources — whether of time, energy, or money — from the fabrication of everyday life.

The "Typical" Compulsive Buyer

We don't yet know very much about the "typical" compulsive buyer. To be sure, several research studies support the popular stereotype, pinpointing a thirtysomething female who experiences irresistible urges, uncontrollable needs, or mounting tension that can be relieved only by the compulsive buying of clothing, jewelry, and cosmetics, and who has been buying compulsively since her late teens or early twenties (Black et al. 1997, Christenson et al. 1994, Scherhorn et al. 1990). But there are serious methodological questions about these studies, which tend to rely on self-selected subjects. More likely, the spectrum of compulsive buyers is wide, reflecting a set of people who differ from one another in age and gender, in socioeconomic status, in patterns of buying, in the intensity of their compulsion, and in underlying motivation. This diversity suggests that efforts to capture the essence of the archetypal consumer are likely to be fruitless.

Thus, for every well-known name in the "Who's Who of Chronic Shoppers" — Princess Diana, Jacqueline Kennedy Onassis, Imelda Marcos, and even Mary Todd Lincoln (who needed eighty-four pairs of gloves before she could move into the White House) — there are dozens or hundreds of unknowns. And the disorder is not restricted to women. No less a personage than George Washington was reported to have had a "consuming passion" for shopping, a habit that he tried (but failed) to support by consigning his tobacco or other cash crops to his creditors. And Abraham Lincoln (even before he met Mary Todd) referred to himself as an "insolvent debtor" (Catalano and Sonenberg 1993, Seelye 1998, Wesson 1990). Male or female, rich or poor, famous or not, youthful or middle-aged — there is no convenient identifying demographic.

Until recently, most of the literature on compulsive buying adopted a simple, dichotomous classification; an individual either was or was not afflicted (DeSarbo and Edwards 1996). Now we are beginning to take a closer look. Investigators are differentiating among such patterns of behavior as compulsive daily shopping, occasional but consequential shopping "binges," compulsive collecting, image spending, bulimic spending, codependent spending, buying multiples of each item, compulsive bargain-hunting, compulsive hoarding, and ceaseless buy–return cycles. As yet, however, there is little or no empirical data about these patterns.

Somewhat more has been done to investigate the compulsive buying continuum and the psychological subtypes of buyers. Providing theoretical constructs for the empirical work that followed, Albanese (1988) proposed a consumption continuum ranging from the stable and consistent consumer to the compulsive, addictive, and irrational consumer, based on Kernberg's (1976) object relations theory of personality. And although they did not test it empirically, Valence and colleagues (1988) created a typology of compulsive buyers that includes the emotionally reactive consumer, the impulsive consumer, the fanatical consumer, and the compulsive consumer. The researchers differentiated these types by the particular combination of psychological forces — such as strong emotional activation, high cognitive control, and high reactivity — that inform the compulsive buying act.

Edwards, in a series of published and working papers (1993, 1994a,b), has developed a measure of the severity of buying behavior. Scores on Edwards's compulsive buying scale (1993) place consumers along a continuum from the normal or noncompulsive buyer, who is assumed to shop and spend mainly out of necessity, all the way to the addicted buyer, who buys primarily to relieve anxiety and whose buying creates a dysfunctional lifestyle. Between these poles lie the recreational buyer, who occasionally uses shopping and spending to relieve stress or to celebrate; the borderline compulsive buyer, whose spending habits fall somewhere between the recreational and the compulsive; and the compulsive buyer, who buys mostly to relieve anxiety, though without yet strongly disrupting his/her life.

In the only empirical research to date that has examined heterogeneity in compulsive buying, DeSarbo and Edwards (1996) hypothesized that there may be more than one path to the behavior, or more than one manifestation of it, each with distinct motivations and tendencies. They tested this hypothesis by separating the predispositional and circumstantial antecedents of compulsive buying and found two psychologically distinct clusters. For the first group, compulsive buying appears driven by feelings of low self-esteem, dependency, and anxiety. Such individuals attempt to build esteem via the (temporary) sense of worth, power, and control they achieve in shopping excessively. This cluster has a higher proclivity for compulsive buying than the second, and is more likely to seek treatment or self-help. Individuals in the second cluster appear influenced more by their circumstances than by psychological motivations or basic personality traits. These subjects seem to act as they do out of simple materialism or social isolation or avoidance; they shop simply to acquire, to escape from loneliness, or to flee from stress.

Both of the DeSarbo/Edwards groups are markedly impulsive, but the relationship of impulse buying to compulsive buying remains uncertain. D'Astous and colleagues (1990) argue that the two lie on a continuum, with the former, of course, closer to normal shopping. O'Guinn and Faber (1989) suggest that compulsive buying is, by definition, a chronic state, while impulse purchasing is an acute behavior. Edwards (1993, 1994a) suggests that impulse buying, which she defines as the unplanned purchase of generally inexpensive items, occurs when an external trigger, a product, stimulates the individual to make a purchase. Compulsive buying, in contrast, is motivated by an internal trigger, anxiety, from which shopping and spending is an escape.

While we still have much to learn about compulsive shopping, we have begun making inroads. As the problem gains wider recognition and more focused attention, as the routes into the terrain of compulsive shopping are gradually mapped, answers to many of our questions will emerge. My hope for the present collection is that it will serve as a provisional guide, highlighting established landmarks and suggesting promising but uncharted new paths.

THE PLAN OF THIS BOOK

The book is divided into seven thematically organized sections. The first three deal with backgrounds and special issues in compulsive buying. The last four focus on practical approaches to the clinical treatment of the disorder.

Part I, "An Overview," begins with Donna Boundy's introduction to this disorder and its various faces. Boundy carves out clinical profiles of the different types of compulsive shoppers and identifies the behavioral indicators of a compulsive shopping problem. Her subgroups are differentiated from one another on the basis of what the spender seeks, consciously or unconsciously, from his/her spending. Some, Boundy learned, spend to fulfill fantasies of themselves as successful; others spend to get rid of their money, because they feel more comfortable being broke. Still others shop to distract themselves from unwanted feelings, or spend on partners or children in a never-ending attempt to buy love. The chapter closes with a discussion of the cultivation of true wealth, a theme I revisit in the final chapter of the book.

Providing research support for much of Boundy's material, Ronald Faber chronicles the results of his more than twelve years' pioneering experimental research into the demography, phenomenology, prevalence, etiology, and causal mechanisms of compulsive buying. Based on their initial examination of this problem, Faber and his colleagues defined compulsive buying as chronic, repetitive purchasing that becomes a primary response to negative feelings, providing immediate short-term gratification but ultimately causing harm to the individual and/or others (O'Guinn and Faber 1989). Their subsequent work has generally been driven by three basic research questions that Faber investigates in the chapter: "What drives or motivates compulsive buying behavior?" "Why does this problem affect some people but not others?" "Why do some people turn to buying, rather than some other behavior or substance?" As you read through the book, you will notice that almost every other author refers to Faber's work, which will continue to serve as a touchstone for research and study in this field.

Part II, "Shopping, Buying, and Selfhood," features four chapters that examine, each very differently, the relationship between possessions and the sense of self. Whenever the topic of compulsive buying is mentioned, assumptions about gender rise to the surface. Why is it that this seems predominantly a woman's problem — and is it really? Colin Campbell's chapter, "Shopaholics, Spendaholics, and the Question of Gender," takes up the gauntlet of this complex question, suggesting that the two genders apply a very different calculus when it comes to the value of the shopping process. Men, he finds, adapt the activity of shopping to a work frame; women, in contrast, fit it to a leisure frame. Having built this foundation, Campbell also considers the question of how individuals make the transition from shopaholic (or more controlled recreational shopper) to spendaholic.

Regardless of who does the shopping and what the activity looks like, there is an object to the hunt. Russ Belk's seminal paper, "Possessions and the Extended Self" (1988), has been revised, updated, and expanded for the current volume; it surveys the meanings that consumers attach to possessions, which then serve as reflections of the individual's extended self. Belk considers the evidence that possessions are important components of the sense of self, describes the processes by which possessions become self-extensions, considers the functions of possessions over the course of the life cycle, and addresses the question, "What are the functions of the extended self ?"

Clearly, defining ourselves by our possessions can contribute to feelings of well-being, even if those feelings are fleeting. Having conducted to my knowledge the only empirical research into the relationship between self-image and compulsive buying, Helga Dittmar is in a unique position to report that there are underlying social psychological mechanisms centered on consumers' self-concepts, and that these mechanisms play a role in both ordinary and excessive impulse buying. What differentiates the two populations, Dittmar finds, is the significantly greater degree to which compulsive buyers believe that consumer goods are an important route toward success, identity, and happiness. She argues that problem buyers purchase goods to bolster their self-image, drawing on the symbolic meanings of products in an attempt to bridge gaps between the way they see themselves, the way they wish to be, and the way they wish to be seen.

Fashionable clothing is the highest frequency purchase for the particular subgroup of compulsive shoppers reported on most often in the professional literature, that "thirtysomething female" referred to above. In her chapter, "Clothes, Inside Out," Eve Golden weaves a beautiful tapestry, using the psychological meanings, roles, and function of clothes as the warp and the sociological literature on adornment as the weft; she strategically shuttles literary and artistic threads throughout her essay.

Picking up some very different threads, Part III, "Special Issues in Compulsive Buying," includes two chapters that highlight a pair of quite disparate subgroups of compulsive buyers. Werner Muensterberger writes about the compulsive collector, who is neither thirtysomething nor typically female. In the case of compulsive collecting, he finds, the passion that is normally the wellspring of collecting becomes an obsessive attempt to master and rework childhood trauma. Muensterberger provides rich illustrations of compulsive collecting from his extensive clinical experience as well as from history.

The other special issue explored in this section is compulsive gift-giving, which has received no formal attention until now. Mary Ann McGrath's "Giving until It Hurts" is an in-depth study of two individuals, one male and one female, who feel they cannot give enough while consistently giving too much. Her chapter, which represents a first attempt to merge the academic findings of gift-giving behavior with the clinical concerns of mental health professionals, casts light on a dark side of this activity.

The remainder of the book, Parts IV through VII, offers concrete, practical help to the clinician who wants to learn more about evaluation and treatment of this disorder. These sections address compulsive buying from a number of vantage points: psychiatric considerations, psychodynamic thinking and therapy, couples and group treatment, and financial counseling and self-help.

What distinguishes pathological from nonpathological buying behavior? The external criterion is whether or not such behavior is causing significant disruption or impairment in an individual's social, occupational, financial, or marital functioning. Internally, however, the situation is much less clear. Part IV offers two looks at the complex psychiatric considerations involved in assessing, diagnosing, and treating compulsive buying. These include establishing a definition of pathological buying behavior based solidly on valid and reliable research data, and looking hard at the nosological dimensions of the disorder, particularly at whether compulsive buying is controllable and whether it is ego-syntonic or ego-dystonic. These questions bear directly on diagnosis and treatment, and answers to them may be different for different sufferers. Some compulsive buyers, not unlike the ritual handwasher, take neither pleasure nor release from their uncontrollable and unwanted buying; these appear obsessive-compulsive. Others, apparently impulse driven, can exert some finite, albeit varying, control over buying behavior. These buyers often feel intense gratification: "I felt high," "It was like being on a drug."

Donald Black, in the first chapter of this section, looks carefully at a number of clinical screeners currently in use, as well as several other important assessment techniques. He describes, compares, and contrasts these assessment procedures and offers commentary on how to create an effective and informative assessment battery. In the second chapter, Toby Goldsmith and Susan McElroy propose a definition of compulsive buying based on their own empirical findings (as well as those of other researchers). They also address the important issue of comorbidity and compare the findings of the three major research studies that have explored the relationship between compulsive buying and other disorders. Their chapter includes a discussion of the findings from drug studies that have been undertaken with this population and offers suggestions for future research.

In the two chapters that begin Part V, "Psychodynamic Theory and Technique," a pair of issues raised in the previous section are explored in detail. First, Ramona Goldman examines compulsive shopping as an addiction, continuing the broadening of a concept once used only with reference to drugs or alcohol. Goldman surveys the relevant literature on addiction as well as the empirical research that has been done on the relationship between addictive behavior and compulsive buying. After describing her work with two different types of addictive buyers, she discusses the treatment implications of viewing this disorder as an addiction.

Eating disorders, which can also be viewed as addictions, are often associated with compulsive buying (Faber et al. 1995, McElroy et al. 1995). In her chapter, "When Eating and Shopping Are Companion Disorders," Diane Barth looks at the relationship between these two consumptive feeding frenzies, describing the way that both are used to regulate and process overwhelming feelings that can't be put into words.

David Krueger, whose case material confirms the frequent coincidence of eating and shopping disorders, writes about compulsive buying as an action symptom. He sees it as a story with its own developmental history and psychodynamic scenario, one that includes both defensive and developmentally reparative intentions. Krueger's theoretical view of the disorder richly informs his therapeutic technique.

In the final chapter of this section, "Clothes and the Couch," Arlene Kramer Richards considers clothes shopping in the context of a psychoanalytic understanding of women's interest in dress. She discusses the development of shopping compulsions, suggests what they can mean, and provides clinical material to illustrate four different manifestations of this symptom. Richards demonstrates how shopping for clothes, touching as it does on so many issues of sexuality, narcissism, safety, and power, can become a natural venue for symptomatology.

We move from individual treatment to other therapeutic modalities in Part VI, which includes chapters on couples and group treatment. In "Overcoming Overspending in Couples," Olivia Mellan guides us through the different money types commonly found in polarized couples with an overspending partner. The core of her "money harmony" work is individual self-awareness, which she tries to promote through experiential techniques. These include asking her patients to write a money dialogue and to practice the nonhabitual by "taking a walk in each other's shoes." Mellan's focus in treatment is on helping overspending couples learn to communicate better about money. To accomplish this goal, she exposes several myths that impede couples' healing, outlines what a spender needs to do to change, and suggests how the non-overspending partner can help.

I have had the good fortune to learn of not one but two highly structured, comprehensive group treatment programs for compulsive shoppers. The two have significant areas of overlap as well as significant areas of difference. Melissa Burgard and James Mitchell have adapted a highly successful cognitive-behavioral group treatment model for eating disorders to the treatment of compulsive shopping. Their chapter identifies the unique features of the program, which include helping a patient identify and restructure dysfunctional thoughts and requiring the periodic participation in the group of his or her support system. Leonard Brazer's money disorders program, which combines psychoeducational lectures and structured dynamic group therapy, seems particularly suitable for compulsive buyers who are also compulsive debtors; participation in Debtors Anonymous is an integral part of the program. In his chapter he details the content of both the lecture portion and the structured group format that follows each lecture.

Part VII, "Treatment Adjuncts," begins with a thorough investigation of Debtors Anonymous, a twelve step recovery program, yet another type of support system. In "Debtors Anonymous and Psychotherapy," Betsy Levine and Bonnie Kellen, specialists in money issues and compulsive behaviors, walk us up the steps and into the meetings that make up the work of Debtors Anonymous. Cataloging the usefulness of D.A. for patients with compulsive buying problems, they illustrate the integration of D.A. and ongoing therapy in three case vignettes. As a preemptive closing gift, they alert us to some potential problems in treating compulsive buyers who also participate in Debtors Anonymous.

At this point in the book the reader will have become familiar with the terms *spending plan* and *shopping diary*. Nowhere are they more central than in financial recovery counseling work as practiced by Karen McCall. McCall's method, detailed in her chapter, is essentially holistic: while supplying the tools and teaching the skills clients need for managing their money effectively, she also addresses the underlying family-of-origin and spiritual issues that have helped to shape, and may continue to fuel, a client's money behaviors. This chapter introduces the richness and breadth of financial recovery counseling, describes the method, and illustrates the integration of the financial recovery process with psychotherapy and other support services.

Simultaneous with the decade's heightened awareness of compulsive buying has been the development of voluntary simplicity. This grassroots movement turns away from activities that have failed to deliver satisfaction and contentment — shopping, for example, or scrambling up the career ladder — and embraces instead the joys of creativity, community, and the celebration of daily life. One of the leading proponents of voluntary simplicity is Cecile Andrews, who for some time has been leading simplicity circles, a form of adult education and social change that helps people in their quest for meaning. In her chapter Andrews describes the history of these circles and explains their three basic elements and format. She discusses the outcomes that are generated and, in citing general observations and a member's specific story, suggests how simplicity circles could help a compulsive buyer.

The final frontier of this book is the space created when we let go of an antishopping mythology, the set of artful half-truths that obscure the possibility of self-definition, self-expression, creativity, and healing that are embedded in shopping. In "What Are We Shopping For?" I explore such questions as "Is Shop a Four-Letter Word?" "Can Shopping Ever Really Matter?" "Is Selfhood for Sale?" and "Are Consumer and Culture Codependent?" I attempt here to disengage *shopping* from *buying*, to reframe it as a vital and innate motivation for search. I hope to free shopping from the codependence of consumer and culture, and validate it as a quest for identity and meaning.

I invite you to shop this book as you would a store, feeling free to pick and choose, return or exchange, gather information on anything you wish. My hope is that it will serve as both source and stimulus, promoting your interest in this problem and helping you foster change when you work with compulsive buyers. May they no longer lay waste their powers, getting and spending.

REFERENCES

Albanese, P. J. (1988). The intimate relations of the consistent consumer: psychoanalytic object relations theory applied to economics. In *Psychological Foundations of Economic Behavior*, ed. P. J. Albanese, pp. 59–79. New York: Praeger.

Arndt, J., and Gronmo, S. (1977). The time dimension of shopping behavior: some empirical findings. *Advances in Consumer Research* 4:230–235.

Belk, R. (1988). Possessions and the extended self. *Journal of Consumer Research* 15:139–168.

Black, D. W., Gabel, J., and Schlosser, S. (1997). Urge to splurge. *American Journal of Psychiatry* 154 (11): 1630–1631.

Bleuler, E. (1924). *Textbook of Psychiatry*. New York: Macmillan.

Catalano, E., and Sonenberg, N. (1993). *Consuming Passions: Help for Compulsive Shoppers*. Oakland, CA: New Harbinger.

Christenson, G., Faber, R. J., de Zwaan, M., et al. (1994). Compulsive buying: descriptive characteristics and psychiatric comorbidity. *Journal of Clinical Psychiatry* 55 (1): 5–11.

d'Astous, A., Maltais, J., and Roberge, C. (1990). Compulsive buying tendencies of adolescent consumers. *Advances in Consumer Research* 17:306–313.

DeSarbo, W. S., and Edwards, E. A. (1996). Typologies of compulsive buying behavior: a constrained cluster-wise regression approach. *Journal of Consumer Psychology* 5:231–252.

Edwards, E. A. (1993). Development of a new scale for measuring compulsive buying behavior. *Financial Counseling and Planning* 4:67–84.

—— (1994a). *Development and test of a theory of compulsive buying*. Unpublished paper. Ypsilanti: Eastern Michigan University.

—— (1994b). *Models for defining a continuum of compulsive buying behavior*. Unpublished paper. Ypsilanti: Eastern Michigan University.

Elliot, R. (1994). Addictive consumption: function and fragmentation in postmodernity. *Journal of Consumer Policy* 17:159–179.

Faber, R. J., Christenson, G. A., de Zwaan, M., and Mitchell, J. (1995). Two forms of compulsive consumption: Comorbidity of compulsive buying and binge eating. *Journal of Consumer Research* 22:296–304.

Faber, R. J., and O'Guinn, T. C. (1992). A clinical screener for compulsive buying. *Journal of Consumer Research*. 19:459–469.

Faber, R. J., O'Guinn, T. C., and Krych, R. (1987). Compulsive consumption. *Advances in Consumer Research* 14:132–135.

Hawkins, D. I., Best, R. J., and Coney, K. A. (1989). *Consumer Behavior: Implications for Marketing Strategy*, 4th ed. Homewood, IL: BPI.

Holbrook, M., and Hirschmann, E. (1982). The experiential aspects of consumption: consumer fantasies, feelings and fun. *Journal of Consumer Research* 9:132–140.

Kernberg, O. (1976). *Object Relations Theory and Clinical Psychoanalysis.* New York: Jason Aronson.

Kraepelin, E. (1915). *Psychiatrie* 8th ed. Leipzig: Verlag Von Johann Ambrosius Barth.

McElroy, S., Keck, P., and Phillips, K. (1995). Kleptomania, compulsive buying, and binge-eating disorder. *Journal of Clinical Psychiatry* 56:14–26.

McElroy, S. L., Phillips, K. A., and Keck, P. E., Jr. (1994). Obsessive compulsive spectrum disorder. *Journal of Clinical Psychiatry* 55(10, suppl): 33–51.

Mjoseth, J. (1997). What triggers our penchant for overzealous shopping? *Monitor*, December, p. 13.

Nataraajan, R., and Goff, B. (1992). Manifestations of compulsiveness in the consumer-marketplace domain. *Psychology and Marketing* 9 (1): 31–44.

O'Guinn, T. C., and Faber, R. T. (1989). Compulsive buying: a phenomenological explanation. *Journal of Consumer Research* 16:147–157.

Sanders, S. (1998). The stuff of life. *Utne Reader*, November–December, pp. 47–49.

Scherhorn, G., Reisch, L. A., and Raab, G. (1990). Addictive buying in West Germany: An empirical investigation. *Journal of Consumer Policy* 13:355–387.

Seelye, K. (1998). Abraham Lincoln, deadbeat. *The New York Times*, June 14, Section 4, p. 2.

Trachtenberg, J. (1988). Shop until you drop? *Forbes*, January 11, p. 40.

Valence, G., d'Astous, A., and Fortier, L. (1988). Compulsive buying: concept and measurement. *Journal of Clinical Policy* 11: 419–433.

Weise, E. (1999). Internet auctions can fulfill passions. *USA Today*, Mar. 10, p. 01A.

Wesson, C. (1990). *Women Who Shop Too Much.* New York: St. Martin's.

I

An Overview

1

When Money Is the Drug

Donna Boundy

> The consumer of commodities is invited to a meal with-
> out passion, a consumption that leads to neither satiation
> nor fire . . . and he is hungry at the end of the meal,
> depressed and weary as we all feel when lust has dragged
> us from the house and led us to nothing.
> — Lewis Hyde, *The Gift* (1983)

Normally, people spend money to acquire the goods and services that they need or want — and that they can afford. But
when a person is *driven*, when he "has to" buy it, do it, spend
it — regardless of resources — his spending is compulsive, placing
an impossible burden on the economic dimension of his life. For a
considerable number of psychotherapy clients today, money and
things have become an almost constant focus, overshadowing
other life goals such as the pursuit of creative interests, satisfying
relationships, and peace of mind. Have material things — or shopping and spending itself — become the drug of choice for our time?

Whether someone is a compulsive spender has little to do with
the actual numbers involved. A person can spend one dollar or a
million dollars compulsively. It's not the amount of money someone earns, spends, or borrows that makes him compulsive, but the

way it is used and the effect it has on his life. A client's spending is compulsive if it causes negative consequences in his life — yet he or she keeps repeating the same pattern anyway.

It is often thought that most compulsive spenders are women (and that men just pay their bills), but this is not true. Though compulsive clothes-shoppers tend more often to be women (although the number of men is increasing), men spend compulsively on big-ticket items, from electronic toys to sporting goods and vehicles. And a high proportion of money-related crime is committed by men trying to get more money to spend. Spending is an equal opportunity mood-changer.

I first began to suspect there was something "driven" or compulsive about my own spending habits in my early thirties when, despite a graduate degree in social work and a professional career, certain negative money patterns had become repetitive: my credit cards were perpetually maxed-out, bounced check notices were so frequent that I recognized the envelopes they came in, and my savings account held steady at a zero balance.

By this time in my life I'd already completed a five-year course of psychotherapy. Yet, oddly enough, my therapist and I had never once discussed money. I'd managed to bounce only one or two checks to him, and pretended I'd made an error in my math. I didn't want to alert him to this secret of mine, and he didn't pursue the subject. Until recently, few clinicians had much awareness of money disorders. Besides, we live in a culture that, by and large, accepts compulsive spending and the resulting debt as normal.

Because I found virtually nothing that helped me understand my money pattern and how to change it, I determined to research the subject and interview as many people as I could about their spending habits. I came to believe that just as some people develop dysfunctional ways of eating and are said to have eating disorders, others seem to develop dysfunctional ways of using money, a phenomenon I began to call *money disorders*.

I came to believe that all compulsive habits are more alike than they are different, that they are all different expressions of the same addictive disease. Our growing vulnerability to addictive behaviors of all kinds — from chemical addiction to eating and money disorders, codependency, and workaholism — is the result of living in a culture that is failing to meet legitimate human needs, needs for self-esteem, empowerment, community, creativity, and meaning. Our craving for various mood-changers is the natural result of chronic negative mood states arising from these unmet needs. We are becoming more vulnerable to using anything as a mood-changer, including spending and buying.

PROFILES OF COMPULSIVE SPENDERS

Compulsive spenders typically cluster into five subgroups: image spenders, bargain hunters, compulsive shoppers, codependent spenders, and bulimic spenders (who spend to stay broke). Mostly they differ in what the person seeks, consciously or unconsciously, from his or her spending. Some spend to fulfill fantasies of themselves as successful, others for the thrill of "getting a steal." Some spend to get rid of their money because they feel more comfortable being broke. Still others shop to distract themselves from unwanted feelings, or spend on others in a fruitless attempt to buy love. Many develop yet another problem in the course of their spending: chronic debt.

Image Spending

This type of compulsive spender uses money in a highly visible way, always picking up the tab, driving expensive cars, living well, even when the money's not there to cover it. The image spender is driven by an insatiable need to be admired and to appear important and powerful, even if he or she has to be deep in debt and dodging creditors to do it.

Because it is important to image spenders to be among the elite, they crave preferential treatment, whether it's getting the best table in the restaurant, flying first class, or staying in luxury suites.

And they are particularly vulnerable to any marketing pitch that plays on this.

Image spenders define themselves by their lifestyle. In a sense they believe that "you are what you spend." They figure that if they look successful — have the right house, car, and clothes–they *are* successful. Because their self-esteem hinges on this fantasy, they are driven to keep up appearances no matter what. Image spenders will often overextend themselves with prestige purchases, taking on huge debt to buy impressive homes, fancy cars, gleaming jewelry — anything that people will admire. In opening a new business, they may prematurely sink money into such things as luxurious offices at an impressive address, three-color brochures, company cars, and expense accounts. Then they're surprised when the books show they're not able to sustain such expenses. They make excuses: it's the times, or bad business advice. It's never their fault.

For image spenders, it is very important to be seen as generous. To be considered cheap would be humiliating. Consequently, they tend to pick up the tab in restaurants whether or not they can afford it, give lavish gifts, and lend money to virtual strangers even if they owe others. And they will keep lending money even when there's evidence that it won't be paid back.

For Michael, a business owner now gaining insight through psychotherapy, this pattern is all too familiar: "For fifteen years I grabbed every check in a restaurant or bar. That was my identity, the 'successful guy.' And I'm very competitive, so it was my way of showing others that only *I* could afford to do this. I also drove a Lexus and lived in a river-view mansion, regardless of the fact that I went bankrupt twice."

Bargain Hunting

Other compulsive spenders are in it for the hunt, gaining an inordinate sense of victory from finding bargains. This is not the client who shops wisely for the best price, but the person who spends lots of time (and money) buying things just because he or she can get them cheaply. Often the bargainer can well afford to pay full price but gets specific satisfaction from talking the seller down.

Nola, an admitted bargainer, explains the appeal it had for her: "For me, it was my victory. I'd say, 'Look at this shirt I got for $2. It was a steal!' Getting over, finding something dirt cheap, making a killing, that was my rush, my drug. It was me in the jungle, beating the odds and surviving. It gave me this sense of prowess, like I was a victorious hunter."

Note the multiple references Nola makes to aggression, power, and control. To the bargain hunter it's not the article itself that matters so much as the act of getting a steal, of getting the best of the seller.

According to psychoanalyst Edmund Bergler in *Money and Emotional Conflicts* (1985), the seller represents the withholding parent of childhood, and the bargainer sets out to finally get something by outsmarting him or her with aggressive bargaining. First, the bargainer devalues the article by pointing out its defects. Then, if he or she can't get it for the desired price, the bargainer rejects it and walks away. These bargainers are in control because they don't really care whether they get the object.

The fact remains that the compulsive bargainer's behavior is self-defeating. He spends a lot of time and energy tracking down these bargains. And because the real purpose is to outsmart the seller, he often doesn't even care that much about the item. So although the compulsive bargain hunter thinks he's saving money or getting the best of someone, he is actually only fooling himself. As Bergler puts it, he has "purchased a defense mechanism." And he's spent a good deal of time and money doing so.

Compulsive Shopping

For compulsive shoppers the main (unconscious) purpose is using the stimulation and distraction of shopping to avoid unwanted feelings. "When the going gets tough," as the saying goes, "the tough go shopping." Without thinking it through, any unwanted feelings of depression, anger, fear, loneliness, or boredom get translated into the urge to shop. Once at the mall or department store, or tuned into the Home Shopping Channel, they lose themselves in the appealing merchandise, the visual distractions, the fantasies of what this coat or those shoes will do for them. While numbing out unwanted feelings, shopping simultaneously provides enough stimulation to allow the person to feel "alive."

While in the act, the compulsive shopper often feels a sense of well-being, excitement, and control. But after the spree, as this woman drives home or puts away the goods, she begins to feel anxious and guilty about how much she's spent, confused about her loss of control, vaguely let down that the new items aren't magically transforming her moods or life, and ashamed that she can't seem to get her spending under control. In short, she emerges from the experience "spent." Her cravings to shop are then fanned by this complex of uncomfortable feelings, and thus the cycle perpetuates itself.

One of the most common rationales for a shopping binge is the feeling that "I deserve it." That's because compulsive shopping often comes on the heels of stress buildup and feelings of deprivation. The compulsive shopper can see shopping as a reward for putting up with an otherwise stressful, dull, or ungratifying life. Not having what he or she wants in life (or even knowing what that is), the compulsive shopper tries to compensate for this nagging lack of fulfillment by shopping. Shopping becomes a sort of pseudopleasure.

The shopping binge can also be a way of acting out anger. Ian's mother died when he was 14 years old, and at 16 he was sent to live on his own while his well-to-do father went off to Europe with a new wife. Ian was given rent money and his father's American Express card. He looks back on that first year on his own, and how his deep resentment expressed itself through spending: "I had no regard for money whatsoever. If I saw the sign that said, 'We take American Express,' I'd rush into that store and buy something. I figured, 'Hey, my dad's out there having a good time. I'm here busting my butt just to get by, so I'm going to stick it to him with the credit card bills. I'm going to have what I want.'"

Ian felt understandably deprived of the nurturing he needed from his father. Such a sense of deprivation is usually a core issue for compulsive shoppers. Because he harbors such feelings of deprivation, he may feel he deserves his indulgences.

Pamela, an incest survivor, suffers from extremely low self-esteem. She shops most when she fears being judged and rejected. When she gets into a new love affair, or is going to visit family or friends, she is compelled to splurge on all the right clothes and accessories to present herself to them — whether she can afford it or not. She poignantly describes how she always tried to get her self-worth from clothes: "Before I left the house I would literally total up how much the clothes and jewelry I was wearing were worth, and sort of 'put that on' as my value for the day. I knew it was crazy, but I couldn't help doing it in my head. Because I had no sense of intrinsic value, I looked to clothes for my sense of worth, because price is a measurable thing."

Now that Pamela has been attending Debtors Anonymous for over a year, she is starting to be able to recognize this syndrome of fear and anxiety before it turns into the urge to splurge. She picks up the phone and talks to someone about it, so she's not so likely to act out.

Because the compulsive shopper is often more invested in the act of shopping than in the details of what she buys, clothes may hang in the closet with their tags on, and recreational equipment can sit in the garage after one or two uses. She didn't really need the items; she just needed to shop.

Some compulsive shoppers describe having had a shopping "blackout," a kind of altered state during which they don't remember what they've bought. As Lisa describes: "One night, I went to the mall and bought a new pair of Reeboks, among other things. When I got home and I went to put them away, I found an identical pair of Reeboks in a bag in my bedroom; I'd apparently bought them the night before. I didn't have the faintest memory of buying them, but there they were, with my signature on the charge slip. This happened a few times. It was pretty scary."

Codependent Spending

People who are codependent spenders are usually driven to spend on others in an effort to win approval, companionship, loyalty, or love — at any cost. They often spend lavishly on others, yet may neglect their own financial needs. The codependent spender looks generous, but her giving may actually be a way of trying to control a relationship. She feels more comfortable in the role of "rescuer" than in the give-and-take of real intimacy. By making herself needed, she hopes to stave off rejection or abandonment. She doesn't believe she is worth someone's love and loyalty just for her own sake.

A money codependent gives not from her fullness but from her neediness, in an effort to control the relationship with the gift recipient. Healthy giving energizes the giver, resulting in feelings of vitality, fullness, gratification. Codependent giving depletes the giver, resulting in feelings of resentment and exhaustion. Healthy giving also enriches and empowers the recipient, making him feel loved and cared for. Codependent giving is an "investment" that seeks a certain return — approval, gratitude, cooperation, or control. It eventually cripples the recipient, creating feelings in him of confusion, depression, ambivalence, and/or resentment.

Both men and women can be codependent spenders, though women are perhaps more vulnerable, since they are often trained to take care of others at their own expense. But the provider role that men have grown up with can also be a setup for money codependency. Some men feel that to be adequate providers they must never say no, even though they resent it and give with strings attached.

Eric, a 28-year-old insurance salesman, has noticed a pattern in himself. He spends the most, he says, when he's afraid that someone is mad at him, or is going to reject him. He especially tries to avoid conflict. Rather than dealing with uncomfortable feelings, he says, "I just go out and buy her something. I figure if she's getting enough out of it, maybe she won't leave me." He bought the girl he's dating an audio system for her car last month, even though they'd just begun seeing each other. "I know that blew her away," he says, unable to conceal his pride. "But still, I wish I'd meet someone who would return the favors a little too."

Sometimes people behave codependently with money because they feel guilty about something else and think they have to make up for it financially. Larry, a recovering alcoholic, says that he spent lavishly on his kids, rarely saying no to them, because he felt guilty about his drinking. "I failed them in so many ways. I felt I had to make it up to them somehow, so I gave them whatever they wanted." Other money codependents are terrified of conflict and spend to keep peace at any cost.

Because of her inability to set financial boundaries, the codependent spender is likely to be broke a lot. That's the only way she feels she can legitimately say no. To have boundaries means you have to disappoint others sometimes, and the codependent isn't willing to pay that price. She'd rather stay broke and deprive herself if necessary, just to avoid an emotional dilemma. If she doesn't have anything, she can't be expected to give it. Therefore she doesn't have to suffer the discomfort of trying to set boundaries, or the pain of failing to.

Holidays are a particularly dangerous time for the codependent spender. She doesn't feel she can decide what to buy on the basis of her resources, but is driven to please others, no matter what it takes.

At the core of codependent spending, behind the need to control and the fear of abandonment, is the devastating belief, "I am not enough." The money codependent doesn't feel deserving to receive just as she is. She believes that people who love her will surely withdraw once they find out how inadequate she really is. She doesn't feel entitled to unconditional love, but settles for feeling needed, asking for as little as possible for herself.

Bulimic Spending

Some people spend compulsively for the main (unconscious) purpose of getting rid of their money. Whether they have $5 or $5,000 in their checking account, they spend it as quickly as possible in order to get back to broke. I term this *bulimic spending* because, like the bulimic eater, the bulimic spender may allow herself to take in a lot of money so she may be a good earner. But she "vomits" it right back up, by spending it, so in the end is always broke.

Brian won several hundred thousand dollars in a lottery at the age of 29. Three years later he had nothing to show for it. He threw a few outrageous parties, bought a couple of fancy cars, and gave some away to friends and family. But he didn't save or invest a penny. "I just wanted to get rid of it as soon as possible and get back to normal," he says.

For the bulimic spender, having money creates an inner tension that isn't relieved until the balance reads zero again. Getting back to being broke gave Brian a sense of limits again: "It's a terrible feeling, really, to spend money in the extreme. It's like I have no controls inside, which is a scary thing. It's excess all the way, then horrible feelings of guilt and shame afterward that I've done this. I think that's why I got rid of the money as fast as I did, so I could feel back in control again. At least if I'm broke, I can't spend like crazy and put myself through that. There's some built-in control there."

Someone who grew up in a cold, loveless environment but later comes into an inheritance may get rid of it as quickly and as foolishly as possible to send a message to the dead parent: "I don't want your stinking money." Forty-five-year-old Amy relates to this: "My father's been dead now for four and a half years, and I've managed to spend a lot of my inheritance in this time. It's been like an ongoing drive to get rid of the money. It's like I'm still paying my father back in a way, because nothing would be more disturbing to him than my pissing away his money. That's how to get back at him."

Once she is "spent," the bulimic spender often feels profound guilt and shame that she didn't handle the money better. During the boom in real estate in the early '80s, Fran sold a co-op in New York City for ten times the purchase price. Suddenly she had $400,000. Over the course of the next three years she frittered it all away, without generating any new income. At the time she couldn't seem to control it, but when it was over, she was left with tremendous shame and remorse: "I felt so ashamed that I didn't do something better with that money. Like here I had all this money and couldn't make use of it properly. That's how I've been all my life. I always end up feeling like a bad little girl."

Perhaps feeling bad is what the bulimic spender is driven to seek.

Chronic Debt

So many compulsive spenders wind up in a pattern of chronic debt that it is worth mentioning here. Driven as he is to spend money for any one of the above reasons, the compulsive spender often seeks repeated loans and credit in order to maintain his spending "fix." Rather than saying, "I can't afford it," he puts it on his credit card. Rather than face a creditor, he borrows from one line of credit to pay another. He relies on credit to buy another impressive toy, more gifts for others, or to pick up the tab and appear important.

The aggressive marketing of credit in America over the past thirty years has fed this compulsion. And the cost to the person who gets in chronic debt is high: stress illnesses, strained relationships, insomnia, loss of job freedom, longer working hours, depression, anxiety — even suicide. Perhaps the worst consequence suffered by the compulsive debtor is the loss of a light heart. Harangued by creditors, yet still driven to spend money, the compulsive spender in debt finds it increasingly difficult to enjoy the simple pleasures of life.

INFLUENCES ON COMPULSIVE SPENDING

Family Influences

In many cases compulsive spending is "inherited." Using shopping as a distraction from uncomfortable feelings, for instance, is often learned at home as a child. Whatever compulsive money patterns are displayed by parents, their offspring will tend to either repeat it, marry someone with that pattern, or strive rigidly to be the "opposite" of a parent.

In today's families, money and material goods are frequently used to reward children for good behavior: "If you're good, I'll buy you a toy." Children who are rewarded with things often develop a pattern of rewarding themselves as adults with material things when they feel down or stressed out.

In many families children are indulged but not enriched; they are provided for materially as a substitute for being given adult time, love, attention, and affection. A parent who is often away on business may try to assuage his guilt by buying his teenage son or daughter a new car, for instance. Children in such a family end up feeling like "poor little rich kids." They have little true wealth in their lives, and on some level they know it. But because they have access to money, everyone around them says they're lucky. The result can be pretty confusing. Such children want the cars, toys and other things, but suspect deep down that they are being bought off, and deeply resent it.

Without help, children who are given so much materially, yet malnourished emotionally, can grow up confusing emotional needs with financial needs. Money, spending, gifts, and material things can come to represent love and emotional support. When they're feeling emotionally needy, they will indulge themselves materially, which provides only temporary relief. Or they suffer with the feeling that if only they had more money to buy things, all would be well.

Societal Influences

It is impossible to separate our individual spending patterns from the messages received at the societal level. We live in a pervasive spending-addicted culture in which (over the past fifty years) there has been a steady shift away from the values of conservation and thrift in favor of consumerism: buying, using up, discarding, and buying more. In the shift of our identity from that of citizens to that of consumers, our collective money behavior entered the realm of addiction. If we aren't fulfilled, rather than question the premise that consumerism is the ticket to happiness, we assume that we simply don't have enough money or possessions yet to purchase that all-important ticket.

For many compulsive spenders money and material goods have replaced the church, community, and family as the entity around which life is organized. The mall has become a temple to be visited almost daily, and shopping a comforting ritual. Many clients will endure considerable hardships in their worship of the "Almighty" dollar, including fourteen-hour workdays, long-distance commutes, and loss of leisure. Perhaps they are willing to do all this because, in the secular worship of money, "not measuring up" financially is considered *the* cardinal sin.

Ironically, however, all this spending hasn't made us more content. According to surveys, the percentage of the U.S. population that reported being "very happy" peaked in 1957 (Schor 1991). And surveys have found that beyond the attainment of a basic standard of living above the poverty level, material riches have little bearing on one's experience of happiness (Freedman 1978). Like a dog chasing its tail, we can never quite get where we want to go. "Enough," as Paul Wachtel observes in *The Poverty of Affluence*, "is always just over the horizon" (1983, p. 17). Our average income is sixty-five times the average income of the poorest half of the world's population, and well over a million Americans are millionaires. Yet only 0.005 percent of us consider ourselves "rich" (Harper's Index 1992, Phillips 1990, Schor 1991, *World Development Report* 1991).

Wachtel (1983) sheds some light on what has gone wrong and why our intense focus on the material hasn't brought us satisfaction:

> Our economic system and our relation with nature have gone haywire because we have lost track of what we really need. Increasing numbers of middle-class Americans are feeling pressed and deprived not because of their economic situation *per se* — we remain an extraordinarily affluent society — but because we have placed an impossible burden on the economic dimension of our lives. [p. 2]

Compulsive spenders are trying to use shopping and acquiring to meet nonfinancial needs for self-esteem, personal potency, and community. But if one looks to material goods for self-esteem, one can never get enough or spend enough to feel good about oneself. Likewise, if one's sense of power is based on conspicuous material goods, one will always crave more. When what one wants (money and stuff) is different from what one needs (self-esteem, a sense of belonging, true personal empowerment), there is never enough. It's not actual poverty that drives the money addict then, but inner poverty — a condition of emotional, spiritual, creative, and social impoverishment.

THE "CHARGE" THAT MONEY (AND CREDIT CARDS IN PARTICULAR) CARRIES

One reason money has become a vehicle for compulsive behavior is that money, no less than food and sex, is a powerful symbol in our psyche, loaded with unconscious meaning. To some people, money represents the security they can't find in intimate relations; to others, money feels magical, and credit cards give instant access to a world of fantasy. And in a society where more and more people feel powerless over conditions in their lives, money represents some source of control or power.

Credit cards, for example, because they give the illusion of unlimited possibility, have the potential to cast us quite literally under a spell. It's easy to believe that they bestow on us their magic power. Eighteen-year-old Ian describes how he felt when he got his first credit card: "I'm walking around the store thinking, 'I can buy whatever I want! I can buy this whole store! I don't have to think about it right now, I can just *have* it.'" Advertisers capitalize on our belief in material magic by leading us to believe that this item or that one can transform us magically into someone more attractive, younger, more powerful. A person who feels insecure about his or her own personal potency, his or her ability to have an effect on the world, will be all the more concerned with gaining access to the magic of money.

In a society that awards the most clout and respect to those with money, money is also associated with power. The problem is, some people have come to believe in money and things as the source of power rather than as a channel through which it is accessed. And because they mistake money as the source, they think that if they get enough money, *they* will have that power, *they* will be the "power-full."

This overemphasis on money as the source of power causes people in its thrall to forgo other pleasures and stifle other faculties that could ultimately be enriching. They fail to develop other aspects of their lives — creative interests, relationships, service, to name a few — then come to therapy reporting feelings of emptiness.

It is precisely because money is so psychically loaded that people with money disorders have such difficulty acting rationally in relation to it. One compulsive spender, when confronted by his wife with their ailing checkbook, vowed not to spend any more money on "nonessentials" that month. He voluntarily handed over his credit cards to his spouse for safekeeping, and she thought she'd finally gotten through to him with reason, that he was responding rationally. Then, much to her dismay, the husband brought home an antique rug three days later. When questioned, he admitted that he charged it by retrieving the account number from the file. His behavior was not rational; it was driven by an inner mandate much more powerful than reason or even intention.

INDICATIONS OF COMPULSIVE SPENDING

A Penny Earned Is a Penny Spent

The compulsive spender typically spends whatever he has, whether that's $10 or $10,000. There's not a point at which his urge to buy something is satisfied and he relaxes into enjoying what he has. As his income goes up, so does his spending. It's as if he's trying not to have any money left over by the end of the month. He spends on things he doesn't really need, and he spends regardless of whether he has the money to pay for them. Splurging on nightly dinners out and deluxe vacations, the spender can seem self-indulgent. But he often neglects his more basic needs, like paying the rent, or saving the down payment for a house.

Says Steve, a dancer, musician, and compulsive spender: "Whatever I get is gone; $800 can go in twenty-four hours. It's like I'm hemorrhaging money. If I've got money in my hand, I never think about saving it for next month's bills. I think, 'What can I buy?' The notion of spending less than you earn is a total revelation to me. I always assumed that whatever you had was what you spent."

Some compulsive spenders assume that all they need to do to get out of their financial squeeze is generate more income. But the fact is, when compulsive spenders do get more money, they tend to deal with it exactly as they did less money: they spend everything they have coming in, and then some.

Inability to Tolerate Frustration and Accept Limits

The compulsive spender has trouble accepting limits. If he sees something he wants in a catalog or a store, he feels as if he has to have it, immediately, even though he's gotten along without it until now. Things that other people (even people with more money) may consider luxuries, the compulsive spender experiences as necessities. He *has* to have that new cell phone, the latest golf clubs, or the big screen TV.

Tracy was astounded when her compulsive spender husband came home with a new toaster recently. Only days earlier he had agreed not to charge anything else. When Tracy asked, "What about our agreement?" he replied with all sincerity, "But this is an emergency!" "A toaster — an emergency?" Tracy repeated, incredulous. To him it was. He couldn't stand to want something and not have it. That was the emergency.

One reason the spender has trouble with limits is that he hates feeling uncomfortable or frustrated and wants to do something about it right away. Once a craving to spend is triggered, a compulsive spender has great difficulty not gratifying it. Even if he manages to walk away, he often comes back soon afterward and buys the item that acted as trigger.

Amy describes what happened to her recently once the urge to splurge was triggered:

> The other day while waiting for a friend, I was looking in the window of this antique shop. I wanted to buy my son and daughter-in-law a silver frame for the picture of their first baby, and I saw one in the window, a beautiful silver frame. But it had a pricetag on it of $350. I said, "Oh, I just can't do this anymore. I can't do it!" So I walked away, didn't even go into the store. But I was still waiting for my friend, so I walked across the street into an antique jewelry shop. And within three minutes I bought myself a pair of earrings — for $350.

Compulsive Energy

Some spenders describe a vague, uncomfortable awareness of being out of control when they're spending. They know what they're doing is crazy, but they can't control it. Rosalyn describes it as "compulsive energy," a feeling of being "driven":

> It's something inside that starts to drive me. It's a sense that if I just do this or get that, I'll find relief, I'll be happy. I've been like this since I was a kid. I can feel this thing on a cellular level, like it's imprinted in my cells. It's a feeling that I *have to* buy this stuff, or fly to the Virgin Islands, or whatever. I have to, have to. I think this compulsive energy clicks in whenever I'm uncomfortable with things as they are, when I'm feeling not in control, especially of my feelings. Keeping down the feelings must be what I experience as compulsive energy.

This compulsive energy can be exhausting, she adds. "There's a speediness to it, an aggression. It gets really tiring. I mean, you blow yourself out after awhile."

Vagueness

The compulsive spender avoids any clear thinking that might interfere with her spending. She doesn't keep her checkbook tallied, and is usually unclear about how much she is spending. Says Polly, "I blank out, go into vagueness. If I'm clear, I'm afraid I won't get what I want. If I stay in denial, I won't have to take responsibility. Something powerful in me resists knowing."

Spending Most When They Have Least

Compulsive shoppers tend to spend more when they are feeling hopeless and powerless. So ironically, when their finances are in the worst shape, they tend to spend more, as Deborah describes: "Inevitably, I fritter away the most money when I'm in the biggest hole, tottering on the edge of financial disaster. When I have money, I guess I feel some sense of control over my life, more hopeful, and so I spend less."

Short-Lived Satisfaction

Satisfaction from a purchase never lasts long. Shortly after buying the cross-country skis, the compulsive shopper's interest shifts to motorcycles, or video cameras. Perhaps that's because much of his spending feeds fantasies he has about himself. He harbors some vague hope that the next purchase is going to change his life, make him more interesting, fulfilled, but it never does. As soon as the high wears off, another craving sets in.

Often Spends More than Planned

The compulsive spender pays very little attention to budgets or spending plans. Michael went out to buy an area rug for his living room, roughly figuring he'd spend one or two hundred dollars.

Instead, he came home with a thousand-dollar rug. "I don't know what it is," he said afterward. "I would never dream of saying, 'I can't have that one because it costs more than I planned to spend.' If I see it, and I want it, I have to have it." That would be all right if Michael had the money to pay for it, but he doesn't.

Spends Not Just Earnings, but Savings and Capital

The compulsive spender tends to regard all resources — income *and* capital — as "spending money." If he comes into a windfall — an inheritance, royalty check, lottery winnings — he spends it rather than reserving it for investment or a cushion. When the compulsive spender does manage to get some money into a savings account, it eats away at her. Usually she'll be able to keep it there for only a short time, then uses the money for something. Deborah: "Every year when I get my income tax return, I open a savings account. And each time, it's gone within a month. I use up all my withdrawal slips and still have all the deposit slips."

Compulsively Spends Time and Energy Too

According to Ernest Borneman in *The Psychoanalysis of Money* (1976), spenders actually get some creative enjoyment from "expelling" (spending), which is probably why they tend to also expel (spend) time, energy, and sexuality more freely than other people do. Conserving is just not their thing. According to Borneman, such people tend to experience spending as a creative achievement rather than a loss.

Angry If Confronted about Spending

The compulsive spender erects a wall of denial around himself and tends to get irritated if anyone tries to dismantle it. Doris's husband, Leo, is building a house for them that is turning out to be three times the size of the original plan. They're now $200,000 in debt, with little income to offset it. Whenever Doris tries to question what he is doing, Leo verbally attacks her: "He gets angry if I question the spending, even though we're approaching bankruptcy at this point. As soon as I say something, he snaps 'You're just like your mother. You're just tight, money-grubbing.' Then I think, 'Maybe he's right. I should stop bugging him.'"

Gets a Special "Charge" out of Spending on Credit

For compulsive spenders, credit cards provide constant access to their drug supply — money for spending. Lisa, a secretary who accrued $35,000 in debt by age 25, once had a contest going with a friend to see who could qualify for the most credit cards: "I had 32 of them, and he only had 30. I'd call him whenever a new card came in, saying, 'Guess what they sent me,' like I'd won a prize. When a new card came, it meant I could go out for dinner, go shopping, or plan some exotic vacation. I thought of it as free money, not like I'd ever have to pay it back." Lisa declared bankruptcy at age 26.

Pays Only the Minimum on Credit Cards

Because the spender wants to have as much available for spending as possible, she often pays only the minimum due on her credit card bills. To her, that's being current. Of course, the bank doesn't mind, because they make a tremendous profit on the interest. According to Eisenson and colleagues (1998), if a person with $3,500 on her credit card pays only the monthly minimum due, she will eventually pay a whopping $11,162.

Protects His Access to Some Credit Cards

Just as the alcoholic tries to control his drinking so that he never has to give up alcohol, the compulsive spender often pays selectively on some accounts so that he always has one or two credit cards still under their limits, maintaining his access to spending.

Wants Take Precedence Over Needs

The compulsive spender operates on the principle that he should spend what he wants, then pay his bills with what's left. You may recall a TV commercial some years ago featuring a pubescent Brooke Shields in Calvin Klein jeans, lying on the floor in a provocative pose. "I'm saving my money for more Calvins," she cooed intimately to the camera. "And if I have anything left over, I'll pay the rent." That's exactly how the compulsive spender thinks, that he shouldn't let details like rent interfere with having the things he wants. Ken, a compulsive spender and debtor, remembers that commercial well: "That's exactly how I used to live, only my 'designer jeans' was eating out in fancy restaurants seven nights a week. I put that before paying the rent or going to the dentist. It didn't matter if the money was there or not, there was just a voice in me that said, 'Do it.' The question, 'What can you afford?' never occurred to me. I just did it."

RECOVERING FROM COMPULSIVE SPENDING

Like the Buddhist notion of Right Livelihood, I believe there is such a thing as the "Right Use of Money," which leads to the cultivation of true wealth. Rightly used, money enriches our lives: it allows us to take care of our material needs, maintain our health, accomplish our life goals, nurture our families and communities, improve ourselves with education and travel. It is a source of enrichment. Addictively used, money impoverishes us. It drains meaning and purpose from our lives, objectifies our relationships, causes us to neglect our children, steals our leisure, undermines our communities and our environment, and contributes to isolation. It is a source of impoverishment.

A word about the challenge of recovery from spending disorders: alcoholics recover by not taking a drink one day at a time. As incredibly challenging as this is, it is at least clear what must be done. But clients with spending disorders can't stop spending money altogether. They can't simply be instructed to avoid "people, places, and things" associated with spending. Indeed, they have to continue to live in a society that revolves around money. That's why connecting them with some support group that addresses spending disorders, such as a twelve-step money recovery group or a psychotherapy group for compulsive spenders, is crucial. In addition, the following are some supplemental steps that can aid clients in recovery from compulsive spending. I will only list them here as keeping a spending diary, developing strategies to ride out cravings to spend, working with irrational thoughts, preparing for the feelings that surface when they stop spending compulsively, learning to spend on basic needs first, and increasing knowledge about the "cost" of credit. They are all described in more detail in my book, *When Money Is the Drug: Understanding and Changing Self-Defeating Money Patterns*, and many are addressed in the remainder of this volume.

THE CONCEPT AND CULTIVATION OF "TRUE WEALTH"

I first came across the term "true wealth" in a book of that name written by Paul Hwoschinsky (1992). According to Hwoschinsky, "Money is just one part of the total system that produces a feeling of well-being. The challenge is earning money to live life rather than living to earn money" (p. xii). Wealth, according to this philosophy, is something we experience rather than possess. "Having money is not at all bad," writes Hwoschinsky, "it simply is not 'it'" (p. 2).

Money is just a convenience. It can help us get where we want to go, but it can't provide the gratification. I can pay for an elaborate all-day beauty treatment and still not feel beautiful; I can spend on a vacation but the money spent does not ensure a happy time. More money is not the key to enrichment anymore than

more sex is the key to sexual fulfillment or more church attendance is the ticket to spiritual enlightenment.

Nonfinancial assets, which are different things for different
people but might include education, talents, creativity, friends,
family, community, self-esteem, health, are those aspects of life
that contribute to our overall well-being, even to our ability to earn
money. Because a sense of inner poverty, emotional and spiritual,
is at the core of most compulsive spending, clients must build real
gratification into their lives as part of recovery.

As Lao-tzu wrote, "He who knows he has enough is rich" (1972,
No. 33). It's the *knowing* that is key. If a client has "enough" but
doesn't know it, he's not rich. It's as simple as that. We have enough
when we know that we do. This doesn't mean that one should
never take steps to increase income, make sound investments, or
otherwise enhance access to resources. It simply means that an
inner state of satisfaction can exist independent of outer conditions. Prosperity, it turns out, is not reached once a certain amount
of "stuff" is accumulated. It's a state of mind and an approach to
resources that can be cultivated at any income bracket.

Some Jungians believe that money and material goods serve as
a modern day "talisman of the self" (Lockart 1982, p. 21) onto
which current psychic conflicts are projected and played out. If
indeed this is true, then psychotherapists need to pay close attention to the communications present in a client's financial beliefs,
wishes, and patterns. Seizing the opportunity to help clients unveil
and verbalize their spending and debt conflicts can be crucial in
helping them create and build greater gratification in their lives.
For just as the realms of work and love can be disabled by money
disorders, so too can they be enhanced by financial recovery.

REFERENCES

Bergler, E. (1985). *Money and Emotional Conflicts*. New York: Inter-
national Universities Press.
Borneman, E. (1976). *The Psychoanalysis of Money*. New York:
Urizen.

Boundy, D. (1993). *When Money Is the Drug: Understanding and Changing Self-Defeating Money Patterns*. Woodstock, NY: Maverick Media Resources.

Eisenson, M., Detweiler, G., and Castleman, N. (1998). *Invest in Yourself*. New York: Wiley.

Freedman, J. (1978). *Happy People*. New York: Harcourt Brace Jovanovich.

Harper's index (1992). *Harper's*, February, p. 11.

Hwoschinsky, P. (1992). *True Wealth*. Berkeley, CA: Ten Speed Press.

Lao-tzu (1972). *Tao-te Ching*, trans. G. Feng and J. English. New York: Vintage.

Lockart, R. A. (1982). Coins and psychological change. In *Soul and Money*. Dallas, TX: Spring Publications.

Phillips, K. C. (1990). *The Politics of Rich and Poor*. New York: HarperCollins.

Schor, J. (1991). *Overworked American*. New York: Basic Books.

Wachtel, P. (1983). *The Poverty of Affluence: A Psychological Portrait of the American Way of Life*. New York: Free Press.

World Development Report. (1991). Washington, DC: World Bank.

2

A Systematic Investigation into Compulsive Buying

Ronald J. Faber

For the past twelve years my colleagues and I have been engaged in the study of compulsive buying. When we first began this investigation we had little idea of what compulsive buying was all about. However, over the years we have found it to be a compelling topic that drove our research interest and one that needs to be better understood.

Consumer behavior researchers have long been interested in how people develop their buying beliefs, attitudes, and behaviors. This is studied under the rubric of consumer socialization, which is often defined as the study of how people learn to be good consumers (Ward 1974). Yet years of experience researching this topic indicate that many people never learn to be "good" consumers; rather, they develop bad habits and behaviors. Until recently, this "dark side" of consumer behavior was not discussed in the literature. It was an interest in examining the causes of dysfunctional consumer behavior that led my colleagues and me to first examine the problem of compulsive buying.

Initially we believed compulsive buyers might have high desire for goods and low willpower to resist buying more than they could afford. We felt this might be a result of watching television and using other media where people tend to see images of others who have lots of nice things, are able to travel, and seem to have no financial concerns. We originally thought that seeing a world in which others have everything they want might lead some viewers to feel that they should have these things as well. They might thus develop financial problems because they do not have large enough incomes to meet their desire for purchases or the willpower to delay or deny themselves these items.

However, after observing a few self-help groups and conducting some interviews with compulsive buyers, we quickly realized that compulsive buying was a very different phenomenon from what we had originally conceived. For example, income did not seem to be a factor that led to compulsive buying problems. Compulsive buyers appear to come from all income groups (Faber et al. 1987), and later studies comparing the household income of compulsive buyers with other consumers have supported the belief that there are no significant differences among these groups (Christenson et al. 1994, O'Guinn and Faber 1989, Scherhorn et al. 1990).

From our initial set of interviews and observations we came to believe that compulsive buying was a problem that was not about a choice or decision to buy, but was the result of strong, uncontrollable urges to buy. Rather than enjoying the items they bought, compulsive buyers often spoke of hiding their purchases, or of never even taking them out of the bag they came in. Thus it seemed that the behavior had more to do with the act of buying than with desiring or gaining pleasure from the item purchased. Buying was generally viewed as a way of coping with unpleasant feelings, and over time became the primary response people had when faced with negative emotions. This could be clearly seen in the responses we got to a sentence that we asked compulsive buyers to complete as part of our initial investigation (Faber et al. 1987). The sentence fragment read, "I am most likely to buy myself something when . . ." Among the respondents, 73.9 percent mentioned some type of negative emotion in their answer. In a study that did not involve compulsive buyers, Belk (1985) found that only 20 percent responded to this same sentence fragment with any type of emotional response (either positive or negative). However, while buying appeared to be a way of coping with negative emotions, most people eventually experienced pain or harm from their buying behavior. This included family arguments, financial problems, and even the breakup of marriages and severe legal consequences.

Based on our initial examination of this problem, we defined compulsive buying as chronic, repetitive purchasing that becomes a primary response to negative feelings and that provides immediate short-term gratification, but that ultimately causes harm to the individual and/or others (O'Guinn and Faber 1989). A key element of this definition is that the behavior is highly repetitive. Interviews with compulsive buyers revealed that many go shopping every day. These people report feeling anxious on days they don't go shopping. For others, shopping is their primary response when confronted with negative life events or feelings. Shopping becomes their initial reaction because they find that it temporarily makes them feel better, but ultimately it leads to more negative feelings and additional consequences.

A FRAMEWORK FOR THE RESEARCH AGENDA

Our initial investigation allowed us to develop a definition of compulsive buying and provided us with a more reasonable sense of what this problematic behavior was like. Having achieved this, our work since that time has generally been driven by three basic research questions. The investigation of these questions also provides a framework for the rest of this chapter. The first question elaborates on some points already discussed: "What drives or motivates compulsive buying behavior?" In other words, "Why do people become compulsive buyers?" and "What, if any, needs does it meet for them?"

Our research suggested that the answer to the first question characterized a potentially large group of people. Not all of these people become compulsive buyers. Therefore, the second question that needed to be answered was, "Why does this problem affect some people, but not others?" The answer to this question suggests there may be a number of factors that interact in causing someone to become a compulsive buyer.

Finally, our search for the answer to the second question led us to realize that there were a number of similarities between compulsive buying and other disorders including alcoholism, substance abuse, eating disorders, pathological gambling, and other impulse control disorders. This led to our third driving question, "Why do some people turn to buying rather than some other behavior or substance?"

WHAT DRIVES OR MOTIVATES PEOPLE TO BECOME COMPULSIVE BUYERS?

When we initially heard about the problem of compulsive buying, we thought that it might simply be an extreme form of impulse buying. Some researchers had characterized impulse buying as arising from a momentary struggle in which desire overcomes willpower (Hoch and Loewenstein 1987). While impulse buying is concerned with single episodes of buying, compulsive buyers repeatedly engaged in this behavior. Thus it would seem that these people must have a high desire for many things and accordingly may be particularly materialistic.

Authors examining impulse buying conceptualized it as a desire for a specific item (Hoch and Loewenstein 1987, Rook 1987). However, our initial research with compulsive buyers had indicated that many of them do not have a great deal of interest in items after they are purchased, and often never used them or even took them out of their original bags or boxes (Faber et al. 1987). While this did not rule out the fact that compulsive buyers had a great desire for products prior to their purchase, it did make us question how much of the behavior was due to a desire to own or possess an item. As a result, one of our early studies looked to see if compulsive buyers were either particularly possessive or highly materialistic.

To do this we sent questionnaires to a large number of self-identified compulsive buyers. These people had heard about one of the first self-help groups developed for this problem from various interviews and articles in newspapers and magazines, and on radio and television, and had written to the director of this group. In the six months prior to our study, the self-help organization had received approximately 1,400 letters from around the country. We read and reviewed the letters, eliminating any that did not indicate the letter writer had a personal buying problem. We then took a sample from the remaining letter writers and mailed out approximately 800 questionnaires. A total of 386 self-identified compulsive buyers returned completed questionnaires, yielding a response rate of 47.8 percent.

To serve as a comparison for the compulsive buyers' responses, we sent questionnaires to a general population sample from Illinois. We sent out 800 questionnaires to this sample and received 250 completed questionnaires back for a response rate of 31.3 percent.

One section of the questionnaire included a number of items designed to measure materialism (Belk 1985). Previous research had found that the materialism scale was composed of three separate subscales: possessiveness, nongenerosity, and envy. The results of this study showed that compulsive buyers did score significantly higher on the overall materialism scale than did general consumers (see Table 2–1). However, when the three subscales are examined separately, it becomes apparent that the greater level of materialism found among the compulsive buyers is due not to a greater desire to own or possess things, but rather to differing levels of envy and nongenerosity. Envy and nongenerosity may be viewed as representing more interpersonal elements of materialism rather than a desire for acquisitions. It seems then that interpersonal feelings may play a greater role in driving compulsive buying than a desire to have specific things.

A further indication of this (i.e., that the greater level of materialism found among the compulsive buyers is not due to a greater desire to own or possess things, but rather to differing levels of envy and non-generosity) was shown in a series of motivational questions regarding buying that were part of this

TABLE 2–1. Difference in Materialism among Compulsive Buyers and General Consumers

Scale	Mean of Compulsive Buyers	Mean of General Consumers	F-value	p <
Total Materialism	39.27	34.97	36.20	.001
Possessiveness	14.16	13.75	1.47	n.s.
Envy	12.50	9.98	55.87	.001
Nongenerosity	12.69	11.27	15.76	.001

study. One set of items tapped respondents' desire for the object as a reason for buying and might be considered indicative of possessiveness. Interestingly, the comparison sample scored significantly higher on this measure than did the compulsive buyers. This again suggests that possessiveness is not what leads people to become compulsive buyers.

Qualitative data from depth interviews with compulsive buyers further supported the notion that buying had less to do with the specific items acquired and more to do with self-feelings and interpersonal relationships. The lack of importance in the item purchased could be seen in informants' comments such as these:

"I couldn't tell you what I bought or where I bought it. It was like I was on automatic." (F, 40)

"I really think it's the spending. It's not that I want it, because sometimes, I'll just buy it and I'll think, 'Ugh, another sweatshirt.'" (M, 30)

Another place this could be observed was when we asked people to tell us about something they bought that they really liked. We were surprised to find that several compulsive buyers stopped and thought about this question, but said they couldn't think of anything. When people did give us an answer, it was frequently similar to the following response:

"You know, of all the possessions, of all the things that I have gotten and obtained in various ways, I'm not proud,

proud of any of them. I suppose my favorite possession is
something that my husband bought me and paid cash for;
it's a very inexpensive nightgown." (F, 35)

Although asked about something bought while on a shopping
binge, compulsive buyers often named items they themselves had
not bought, but rather items given to them by significant others.
This is one way in which it became apparent to us how important
others are to compulsive buyers.

Another way in which the importance of interpersonal relations emerged was in the buying of items for others. Some compulsive buyers bought almost exclusively for other people. These gifts
seemed to be used as a means of maintaining or deepening interpersonal relationships. The desire for attention and communications with others emerged in another surprising way. Several
informants talked about store personnel or delivery people as
being important to them and in some cases the reason why they
bought things.

"I have literally spent thousands at L. L. Bean, literally
thousands, and it's because even over the telephone I
feel like I know those people very, very well. They are so
kind." (F, 35)

"The attention I got in there was incredible. She waited
on me very nicely, making sure it would fit and if it didn't
they would do this and that; and I guess I enjoyed being
on the other end of that. I had no idea how I was going to
pay for it. I never do." (F, 35)

"I know the UPS drivers in my neighborhood real well.
They all wave and say hello by first name." (F, 28)

The responses of the informants coupled with the survey data
suggest that compulsive buying is not the result of a great desire for
things, but rather driven by a desire to be noticed and appreciated.
This is an important way in which people can feel better about
themselves.

Enhanced self-feelings can also arise internally without interaction with other people. Compulsive buying allows some people
to derive more positive self-feelings because when buying they can

imagine themselves to be more important or more powerful than they otherwise do. As one informant described how she felt when using her credit card:

"I got this great high. It was like you couldn't have given
me more of a rush just for the power of having that card."
(F, 35)

Indeed, the key factor that seems to motivate the behavior for compulsive buyers is mood enhancement. We examined this more directly in a more recent study (Faber and Christenson 1996). In this study twenty-four compulsive buyers were compared with a matched control group. We asked people how frequently they experienced a number of different mood states both prior to and during shopping. These moods included both positive moods (e.g., happy, excited, proud) and negative mood states (e.g., sad/depressed, angry, anxious, hurt, bored). If one factor that causes people to engage in compulsive buying is that they are trying to improve their negative affective state, then we might expect that compulsive buyers will more frequently state they are in a negative mood state prior to shopping than will the control sample. As it turned out, the compulsive buyers reported experience all of the moods, both positive and negative, more frequently prior to shopping than did the control sample. However, the differences among the groups were far more noticeable for the negative mood states. Among nine mood states examined (three positive and six negative), only two were reported as sometimes or often experienced by at least half of the control group. Both were positive moods (91.6 percent were happy and 75 percent felt excited at least some of the time prior to shopping). A majority of the compulsive buyers reported experiencing each of the nine mood states at least some of the time before shopping. Three moods were reported as often experienced by at least a third of the compulsive buyers. All were negative mood states: bored (47.8 percent), sad/depressed (39.1 percent), and anxious (34.8 percent). Thus it seems that the decision to go shopping is more likely to occur for compulsive buyers feeling in a negative mood than for other shoppers.

When the frequency of experiencing mood states during shopping was examined, the three positive moods were the ones most frequently reported as being experienced at least some of the time by the compulsive buyers (happy, 91.7 percent; excited, 91.7 percent and powerful, 73.9 percent). Only one negative mood was reported as being experienced this often by as many compulsive buyers (anxious, 73.9 percent). Among the comparison sample, happy was the only mood reported by at least half the sample as sometimes or often experienced while shopping.

Given the level of measurement used here, direct comparisons of the frequency of experiencing specific moods before and during shopping is problematic. However, in another question, respondents were asked if their mood changed after making a purchase and, if so, how. Only 29.2 percent of the comparison sample said buying something changed their mood state. Compulsive buyers, on the other hand, were far more likely to report that buying changed their mood (95.8 percent). Additionally, among those who report a change in the control sample, 66.7 percent reported that the change was in a positive direction. An even greater percentage of the compulsive buyers reported that this change was in a positive direction (83.3 percent). These results are consistent with a belief that the motivating force behind compulsive buying is a desire to improve mood state and feel better about oneself.

A different way of examining the impact of mood and emotions as a factor that drives this behavior is by studying the cues that trigger episodes of compulsive buying. Thus, in another study, we attempted to determine what intrapersonal or environmental factors compulsive buyers thought increased their urge or desire to buy (Faber et al. 1996). Compulsive buyers were asked to examine a list of over 400 items and to circle all of the items that worsened their compulsive buying problem by increasing their desire to buy something or reduced their willpower to avoid shopping or buying. The items on the list represented five categories of stimuli that might increase a person's desire to buy. These included locations, activities, feeling states, objects, and circumstances. Thirty-three different locations were examined, including places such as closets, supermarkets, shopping malls, department stores, garage sales, and casinos. A total of eighty-six activities were included.

Among these were shopping, getting out of bed, collecting things, weighing yourself, taking an examination, and leaving home. By far the largest category was objects, with 213 items listed. These included specific kinds of products such as clothes, stereo equipment, candy, antiques, leather goods and gadgets; buying/selling related objects such as advertisements, money, sales personnel, and credit cards; and other potentially less directly relevant objects and people (e.g., cigarettes, specific numbers, police, mother, father). The smallest category was feeling states, with twenty-three items listed. These included both positive feelings (e.g., happy, elated) and negative feelings (e.g., angry, depressed, bored, feeling trapped). Finally, forty-six items represented circumstances or events such as being late, being wrong, being alone, specific smells, birthdays, and Christmas.

The compulsive buyers who filled out the cue checklist were free to circle as few or as many items as they felt influenced them. The range of items circled went from a low of zero to a high of 139. Twenty-three items were picked by at least a third of the respondents. Virtually everyone (95.8 percent) indicated that Christmas was an event that made their buying problems worse. While it may not be surprising that Christmas would heighten compulsive buying problems, there are several different reasons for this. Some people buy predominantly for others and Christmas is a time when they may overindulge in this practice. Alternatively, it may be that buying for others during the Christmas season reduces inhibitions about buying for oneself. A third alternative is that the level of excitement and activities in stores is heightened during Christmas and that it is this heightened state of arousal that leads to buying problems. Finally, holidays, especially Christmas, can be stressful and depressing times for many people. It may be that it is this stress or negative mood state that triggers the actual compulsive buying episodes.

Birthdays were another event/circumstance cited by a sizable percentage of compulsive buyers (45.8 percent) as a cue that triggered buying episodes. Again, like Christmas, there may be several reasons for this. These may include feeling particularly lonely on one's birthday, feeling depressed about aging, or feeling that one deserves to get treats on this day, thereby reducing willpower or restraint in buying.

The remaining cues mentioned frequently by compulsive consumers can generally be divided into two major categories (see Table 2–2). The first are items related to shopping or buying, including places people shop, seeing sales or bargains, having a desire for an item, and symbols of payment such as money or credit cards. The second set of items were negative emotional states. Along with these were a couple of items dealing with weight and feeling fat. This again suggests that a key motivation for compulsive buying may well be to overcome negative emotions

TABLE 2–2. Most Frequently Endorsed Cues

Cues	Percent Mentioning
Items on sale	58.3
Shopping malls	58.3
Department stores	54.2
Shopping	54.2
Having money	50.0
Credit cards	45.8
Wanting something	45.8
A bargain	41.7
Money	41.7
Collecting things	37.5
Feeling overweight	66.7
Feeling fat	58.3
Feeling bored	58.3
Feeling stressed	54.2
Feeling depressed	50.0
Feeling angry	41.7
Feeling hurt	33.3
Feeling irritable	33.3
Weighing yourself	33.3

and try to temporarily feel better. Thus, looking at the issue of what seems to drive compulsive buying from several different perspectives seems to yield a common finding: negative emotions are an important reason for engaging in this behavior.

WHY DO SOME PEOPLE BECOME COMPULSIVE BUYERS, BUT NOT OTHERS?

Many people like to go shopping to cheer themselves up or to feel better. However the majority of these people do not become compulsive buyers. Therefore we must ask the question, "Why do some people become compulsive buyers, but most do not?" This is very much like asking, "Why do some people who drink become alcoholics?" The key to answering these questions is not in the behavior itself, but rather in other factors that predispose someone to potentially develop a problem with the behavior. As has been found with many other forms of impulse control behaviors and addictions, no one factor causes problematic consumption behavior; rather, numerous factors may play a part. These are often discussed as part of a "biopsychosocial" model that includes biological, psychological, and sociological factors (Donovan 1988, Faber 1992).

Over the years, our research has focused primarily on looking at psychological factors that may be related to compulsive buying. One factor found to be associated with a number of addiction and compulsive consumption disorders is low self-esteem. In our large-scale survey we compared compulsive buyers and the comparison sample on a five-item scale of self-esteem. The results showed that the compulsive buyers had significantly lower levels of self-esteem (O'Guinn and Faber 1989). Similar findings have been reported by several other researchers (d'Astous et al. 1990, Elliott 1994, Hanley and Wilhelm 1992, Scherhorn et al. 1990).

Low levels of self-esteem were also apparent in several comments informants made in the depth interviews. Several expressed low opinions of themselves or felt others saw them this way.

"So I never really know who I was or how people really liked me because I've never been fully represented." (F, 35)

"I always refer to myself as being very shallow and superficial. I don't feel there's much more behind me than what you see." (M, 30)

Low self-esteem was particularly apparent when respondents compared themselves to their siblings. For example, one informant stated:

"I have a brother who is now a dentist, who is everything Mother and Dad ever wanted without question. He was bright and he was very engaging and he's very well to do and all of that. And then there's me, and my mother did my schoolwork ever since I was in fifth grade. She did all of my schoolwork, even my college papers. It's not much to be proud of." (F, 35)

People with low self-esteem may be particularly susceptible to developing a compulsive buying disorder since buying serves as a way of temporarily overcoming this poor self-image. Another factor, which may help allow this to occur, is the ability to imagine oneself differently. Put another way, people more prone to become compulsive buyers may be particularly good at fantasizing. To test this we developed a short three-item measure to assess people's propensity to fantasize. This was administered to both compulsive buyers and a general population sample. As expected, compulsive buyers scored significantly higher on this measure.

Other psychological characteristics we have found to be related to compulsive buying are depression and anxiety. Compulsive buyers score significantly higher on measures of depression, as well as on both state and trait anxiety scales (Christenson et al. 1994, O'Guinn and Faber 1989). Other researchers examining compulsive buying have reported similar results (Lejoyeux et al. 1996, Scherhorn et al. 1990, Valence et al. 1988).

A chance event led us to consider another possible factor that might be important in explaining why some people became compulsive buyers and others didn't. Early in our research efforts we were observing a self-help group in California when one member of the group arrived late. This woman was in obviously good spirits when she arrived, smiling and with a bounce to her step. Another member of the group noticed her upbeat mood and asked about it. She replied, "I guess I am in a good mood. I was late tonight so I was speeding down the highway to get here and driving fast always makes me feel good." As she finished this last statement, there was an audible "yeah" from the group, indicating they too experienced this feeling. At the end of the group meeting we were talking to the members and commented about the fact that many of them seemed to enjoy driving fast. One man in front, however, vigorously shook his head no. Since his action was impossible to miss, we said, "So you don't like to drive fast?" He responded, "No, it doesn't do anything for me. . . . Skydiving that's what I like." From this interaction we began to think that perhaps there was some element of a need for arousal that was important in determining who might be most likely to develop a compulsive buying disorder.

Reviewing the literature on other forms of compulsive consumption behaviors revealed that other authors had hypothesized the importance of arousal in the development of these behaviors. For example, Jacobs (1989) has developed a general model of addiction in which arousal plays a major role. He believes that those people who are likely to become addicted to a particular substance or activity have a physiological resting state that is aversive to them. They desire either a heightened or reduced level of arousal, and are predisposed to become addicted to activities or substances that can help them achieve a more desirable arousal state. Similar viewpoints have been expressed by a number of other researchers as well (Barnes 1983, Kuley and Jacobs 1988, Zuckerman 1979).

In our survey data we asked compulsive buyers and other shoppers to indicate to what degree they felt high while shopping and depressed after shopping. We found that compulsive buyers were significantly more likely to report feeling high when shopping and to experience depression after shopping.

Some support for the role of arousal can also be found in the mood study previously discussed (Faber and Christensen 1996). In the open-ended questions we looked at the way they described their mood while buying. The comparison group tended to talk about positive emotions such as feeling pride over finding a good deal, being happy they could afford something, or feeling joy in giving a gift. While these are positive emotions, they are not ones with a particularly high level of arousal. In contrast, compulsive buyers tended to describe their buying moods with terms such as *high, powerful, excited,* and *elated.* Similarly, negative terms used to describe how they felt when buying — *angry* and *out of control* — were also highly laden with arousal.

Finally, the depth interviews provide a clearer indication that buying is associated with a high level of arousal for compulsive buyers and is often used to overcome a less desirable level of arousal. For example, in response to a question about whether there were certain events that made the informant want to buy, compulsive buyers responded in the following ways:

"Not that I'd recognize, no. If anything, boredom. When I don't have anything else to do or I want something exciting to do. Maybe that's it more. When I want something exciting to do that's what usually comes to mind." (F, 49)

"There's times when I'm depressed or bored or something. I just want something new and I'll just go and feel like buying and it makes me feel good. I feel different, excited, happy and I'm ready to go on with other boring things." (F, 21)

In some cases the level of excitement and arousal was clearly captured in the informants' description.

"It was like, it was like my heart was palpitating. I couldn't wait to get in to see what was there. It was such a sensation. In the store, the lights, the people; they were playing Christmas music. I was hyperventilating and my hands were starting to sweat, and all of a sudden I was touching sweaters and the whole feel of it was just beckoning to me." (F, 40)

The role of arousal here suggests that it is not just psychological, but perhaps also physiological or biological factors that contribute to becoming a compulsive buyer. The role of biological factors has also been suggested by research reports of the successful treatment of some compulsive buyers with drugs that affect neurotransmission (Black et al. 1997, McElroy et al. 1991a). When these drugs are administered, the urges to buy are reportedly diminished. When the treatment is stopped, the urges return.

In the case of other compulsive consumption disorders such as alcoholism, researchers have found that people from families with a history of a problem behavior are more at risk to develop the disorder (Donovan 1988). For example, studies of the sons of alcoholic fathers find that they are four times more likely to become alcoholic even when they are reared apart from their biological fathers (Collins 1985, Goodwin 1984). This suggests a biological linkage that may be passed genetically. Researchers studying different disorders have also found that people with one form of impulse control disorder are more likely to develop other disorders (Lesieur et al. 1986, McElroy et al. 1991a).

In our research we have looked to determine if compulsive buyers are more likely than other people to have had other forms of impulse control disorders (Christenson et al. 1994, Faber et al. 1995). In one study twenty-four compulsive buyers were compared with a matched sample of normal buyers (see Table 2–3). Psychiatric interviews indicated that the compulsive buyers were significantly more likely than the normal buyers to have had a history of eating disorders, alcohol dependence, and other impulse control disorder.

TABLE 2–3. Psychiatric Comorbidity

Disorder	Compulsive Buyers (N = 24)	Normal Buyers (N=24)	P<
Eating disorder	20.8%	4.2%	.05
Alcohol depend.	45.8%	12.5%	.05
Impulse control	20.8%	4.2%	.05

Over the years we came to recognize that there are many similarities between compulsive buyers and people with binge eating disorder. Therefore we decided to examine the potential of a relationship between these two disorders in greater depth (Faber et al. 1995). In an initial study we looked to see if people with binge eating disorder were more likely to be compulsive buyers than nonbinge eaters of a similar weight. To do this volunteers in a treatment program for binge eating and a matched control sample were tested. All participants were women, and all were at least 50 pounds above standard body weight for their height and age.

Each subject filled out the compulsive buying scale (CBS) questionnaire (Faber and O'Guinn 1992). The CBS is an empirically developed, seven-item scale used to assess compulsive buying. It was developed by having self-identified compulsive buyers and a more general population of consumers respond to twenty-nine items thought to represent important elements of compulsive buying. These items were chosen based on earlier research with compulsive buyers. The responses were entered into a logistic regression analysis to find those items that best predicted if a person was a compulsive buyer. The analysis yielded seven items that significantly contributed to the regression analysis. These items assessed the frequency with which people:

1. Bought things even though they couldn't afford them
2. Felt others would be horrified if they knew of their spending habits
3. Wrote a check when they knew they didn't have enough money in the bank to cover it
4. If they had any money left at the end of a pay period, felt they just had to spend it
5. Made only the minimum payments on their credit card
6. Felt anxious or nervous on days they didn't go shopping
7. Bought something to make themselves feel better

A formula was developed to weight each item to create an overall score for any individual, and a cut-point was determined to classify a person as a compulsive buyer. The scale and scoring formula can be found in this book in Table 1, Chapter 9, by Donald Black (also see Faber and O'Guinn [1992] for more details regarding this scale).

To determine if there was significant comorbidity between compulsive buying and binge eating, the scores on the CBS scale of the binge eaters and similar-weight nonbinge eaters were compared. In general, the binge eating group scored higher on the compulsive buying scale than did the nonbinge eaters. To more fully assess the relationship of these two disorders, the percentage of each group that would be classified as actually being compulsive buyers was compared. Using the most conservative classification criteria, 15 percent of the binge eating group was assessed as being compulsive buyers compared to just 4.4 percent of the similar-weight nonbinge eaters.

After observing that binge eaters were more likely to also be compulsive buyers, we devised a second study to see if the opposite was also true. Were compulsive buyers more likely to engage in binge eating behaviors? This study showed that compulsive buyers were more likely than a matched comparison sample to engage in behaviors associated with binge eating disorder (e.g., consuming large amounts in a short period of time; eating very rapidly; feeling out of control when eating).

Taken together, these studies suggest that compulsive buyers are more likely than other people to also suffer from other related disorders including eating disorders, alcohol dependency, and impulse control disorders. It is unclear from our data alone whether this is due to common biological abnormalities or if it results from shared psychological characteristics (for more information on the comorbidity of eating and shopping disorders, see Chapter 12 by Barth, this volume). Either way, however, if compulsive buying is a result of a set of common biological or psychological characteristics, it raises the final question driving our research: Why do some people develop compulsive buying disorder rather than some other type of disorder?

WHY COMPULSIVE BUYING
AND NOT SOME OTHER DISORDER?

Our research has suggested that compulsive buying is not just an extreme desire for things, but rather a psychological disorder with much in common with many other impulse control and addiction disorders such as pathological gambling, substance abuse, alcoholism, and eating disorders. Similar views have been expressed by other research groups (McElroy et al. 1991b, Schlosser et al. 1994). Why, then, do some people develop one form of disorder rather than another? The most likely answer is that it has a lot to do with socialization and chance occurrence.

In an initial effort to explore the question of how socialization may relate to the development of compulsive buying, we examined retrospective perceptions of childhood interactions with parents (Faber and O'Guinn 1988). Parents can influence their children's consumer values and behaviors in several ways: through direct modeling of parents' behaviors, through the reward and punishment given to children, and through parental discussions with children. Thus we attempted to explore the role various types of parent–child interactions and monetary behaviors may play in fostering compulsive buying.

To accomplish the goals of this study, we used two different methodologies: (1) a mail survey administered to a group of compulsive buyers and a comparative group of more typical consumers, and (2) in-depth clinical interviews with self-identified compulsive consumers.

Quantitative data looking at direct modeling of parental behaviors showed no significant differences between the compulsive buyers' parents and those of the general consumer sample in regard to their spending or saving habits, level of debt incurred, or general extravagance. However, the compulsive buyers did report a significantly greater frequency of parents who used money and gifts as rewards for the child's behavior. For compulsive consumers this form of reward may replace or compensate for the absence of other signs of caring. Thus, for them, buying may become a method of gaining feelings of affection.

Family discussions also differed among the two groups. For example, encouragement to save money was reported to have been significantly less frequent among parents of the compulsive buyers. Family communication patterns were also found to vary among the two groups of consumers. As hypothesized, compulsive consumers came from families that placed a greater emphasis on socio-oriented communication, an effort of parents to foster harmonious social relations and produce deference in children. Children in socio-oriented families are taught to avoid controversy by repressing their true feelings in order to avoid offending others. Compulsive consumers also came from families that placed less emphasis on concept-oriented communication, a form of communication that encourages children to form and express their own opinions and logically think through positions on issues. Thus compulsive consumers were more likely to be socialized to appear to get along with others and to give in to other people's desires rather than to express their own opinion.

Finally, support was found for the belief that parents contribute to compulsive buying through fostering low self-esteem and feelings of inadequacy. This occurred especially when parents were perceived to be inequitable in the way they treated siblings. This showed up in the interviews with several compulsive buyers.

> "My other sister has never grown up. She's 36 years old and my father is still supporting her. They live very close by. They baby-sit her children all the time. They never did that for me. They give her things. They never did that for me. So my sister was given everything. Both of them [sisters] were given help and my brothers too. And I was given nothing." (F, 40)

The qualitative data indicate that compulsive buyers saw themselves as trying to live up to their parents' role expectations, but received little reward or recognition for this. "Because you're the oldest you're supposed to be the good little person. I was always trying to win their [parents] approval, but couldn't. You know you could have stood on your head and turned blue and it wouldn't matter. I got straight A's and all kinds of honors and it never mattered. That's probably why I went out and bought all of that stuff for my kids because I was reliving in my own mind, this is what I should have had." (F, 40)

"I was trying to show my parents, 'Yes, you do have to worry about me. I am not perfect.'" (F, 28)

Quantitative data supported these findings by indicating that compulsive buyers had received less verbal approval from parents than other consumers did.

Another example of the potential impact of socialization comes from the gender difference found among compulsive buyers. This is one of the most striking findings in the study of compulsive buyers. In all of our research projects, between 85 and 95 percent of self-identified compulsive buyers are women. Other researchers have noted similar gender disparaties (Christenson et al. 1994, Elliott 1994, Scherhorn et al. 1990). Chapter 3 by Colin Campbell in this volume more specifically addresses the issue of gender differences.

There may be various explanations for this gender imbalance. For example, women are more likely to seek help for psychological disorders and are more likely to volunteer to participate in research. However, even considering this, women seem far more likely than men to develop compulsive buying problems. This gender inequity is similar to the one found with eating disorders such as anorexia and bulimia. Historically, however, men have been more likely to develop problems such as alcoholism, substance abuse, and pathological gambling, although the gender disparity is diminishing. The reason for these gender differences is most likely socialization.

In most societies men and women are socialized to behave differently. In many Western nations, women are socialized to be more concerned about their looks and weight than men are. It is therefore not surprising that they are more likely to develop eating disorders that revolve around body image and thinness. Similarly, women in these nations are generally expected to do most of the shopping and are taught at a young age that shopping and buying are enjoyable activities. Additionally, socialization often teaches women that shopping is something to do to feel better about oneself or when one is bored. As a result, women are more likely to engage in this behavior when in negative mood states. Some women who are predisposed to problem behaviors because of biological and/or psychological characteristics may learn that buying is a behavior that temporarily makes them feel better. As this is repeated, it becomes a learned response to negative mood states or life events. Thus, to develop this disorder requires being predisposed to it, plus having sufficient chance experiences to learn that it can relieve negative feelings.

WHERE DO WE GO FROM HERE?

Our program of research over the past dozen years has helped to shed some light on the problem of compulsive buying. However, there is still a great deal more to learn. The future agenda of research in this area may take many different forms and address a number of different issues. For example, we still don't know how prevalent a problem compulsive buying is. A better indication of the prevalence of compulsive buying may help to publicize this disorder and help it gain attention in the research and therapeutic communities. Thus a true prevalence estimate is one important step needed in future research on compulsive buying.

In developing our screening instrument we tried to apply the CBS to the general population sample we studied in order to get some indication of how common this problem may be (Faber and O'Guinn 1992). Based on this group and using conservative criteria, we estimated the prevalence to be 1.8 percent of the population. However, this is only a vague approximation. The sample we used was far too small and incomplete to allow for a true population estimate.

There is also some concern about the adequacy of using the CBS as a measure to assess a prevalence estimate. Although we (and others) have demonstrated the validity of this scale (Christenson et al. 1994, Cole and Sherrell 1995, Faber and O'Guinn 1992), the measurement scale used may be subject to changes over time due to economic conditions (Faber et al. 1995). Thus it may be desirable to try to develop a better and more stable measure prior to doing a large-scale epidemiological study. This might attempt to utilize the items from our original scale, but to measure them with more precise and objective indicators.

Another potentially productive area for future research would be to expand our understanding of the factors associated with compulsive buying. This might be done in several different ways. First, additional psychological constructs are likely to be associated with compulsive buying. One thing we have noted in several of our studies is that compulsive buyers tend to see themselves as perfectionists. This focus on perfectionism along with a desire to please others may be important elements in this disorder. Other personality factors may also be related to this disorder.

Another area of fruitful exploration might be in the early experiences of compulsive buyers. Most compulsive buyers pinpoint the beginning of their problem to their late teens or early twenties. However, this is partially due to the fact that it isn't until this time of life that they have sufficient money, credit, and/or autonomy to be able to get into obvious buying problems. An alternative possibility is that the roots of this problem started much earlier in life with interactions with parents and other family members and with the way that money and goods were used to express emotions. Although we attempted one study to begin to explore this issue (Faber and O'Guinn 1988), greater investigation of early childhood experiences is needed and may lead to some important findings regarding the nature and development of compulsive buying.

Finally, it may be worthwhile to examine some of the differences that exist among compulsive buyers. For example, we have interviewed some buyers who buy almost exclusively for others, while most compulsive buyers buy predominantly for themselves. Some buyers need to shop every day and feel anxious when they don't go shopping. Others binge only on occasion, typically set off by some negative event in their life. Some buyers shop exclusively in stores, while others prefer catalogue or home shopping programs on television. Finally, some buyers enjoy interpersonal interactions with sales personnel, while others report disliking such interactions. An attempt to develop typologies of different forms of compulsive buying to see if they differ in other important ways as well has begun (DeSarbo and Edwards 1996).

It is also hoped that the research agenda in the coming years may be partially shaped by the needs of therapeutic intervention programs. One goal of research on compulsive buying is to provide help and relief for those people who are suffering from this disorder. Most intervention efforts are still in the early stages of development, often borrowing from what has worked with other types of disorders. As these programs grow, there will be more need for specific types of research to help shape and guide these therapeutic programs.

Research suggests the need to focus recovery programs on improving low self-esteem and overcoming depression. Finding alternative ways of increasing positive self-feelings is necessary if people are going to be able to replace their need for buying. The importance of interpersonal interactions for many compulsive buyers also suggests that any efforts to stop compulsive buying must consider how powerful praise and respect from others appears to be in the promulgation of this behavior. For some compulsive buyers improved self-esteem may have to come from external sources rather than generated internally.

The findings regarding arousal also suggest that some way of meeting this need may also be an important component of a successful treatment program. This might be accomplished through drug treatment to alter arousal level to a more comfortable point, or it may be done in the choice of activities used to replace buying.

It is unrealistic to assume that people can stay away from buying situations. The nature of life requires people to buy some things. Thus any treatment program must keep this in mind and change the nature of the buying situation and replace its function, rather than use discipline to avoid such situations. Again, research may be helpful in providing guidance in how this can best be done.

REFERENCES

Barnes, G. (1983). Clinical and pre-alcoholic personality characteristics. In *The Pathogenesis of Alcoholism*, vol. 6, ed. B. Kissin and
H. Begleiter. New York: Plenum.

Belk, R.W. (1985). Materialism: trait aspects of living in the material world. *Journal of Consumer Research* 12:265–280.

Black, D.W., Monahan, P., and Gabel, J. (1997). Fluvoxamine in the
treatment of compulsive buying. *Journal of Clinical Psychiatry*
58:159–163.

Christenson, G. A., Faber, R. J., de Zwaan, M., et al. (1994).
Compulsive buying: descriptive characteristics and psychiatric
comorbidity. *Journal of Clinical Psychiatry* 55:5–11.

Cole, L., and Sherrell, D. (1995). Comparing scales to measure
compulsive buying: an exploration of their dimensionality.
Advances in Consumer Research 22:419–427.

Collins, A. C. (1985). Inheriting addictions: a genetic perspective
with emphasis on alcohol and nicotine. In *The Addictions:
Multidisciplinary Perspectives and Treatment*, ed. H. B. Milkman
and H. J. Shaffer, pp. 3–10. Lexington, MA: D. C. Heath.

d'Astous, A., Maltais, J., and Roberge, C. (1990). Compulsive buying tendencies of adolescent consumers. *Advances in Consumer
Research* 17:306–313.

DeSarbo, W. S., and Edwards, E. A. (1996). Typologies of compulsive buying behavior: a constrained clusterwise regression
approach. *Journal of Consumer Psychology*, 5:231–262.

Donovan, D. M. (1988). Assessment of addictive behaviors: implications of an emerging biopsychosocial model. In *Assessment of
Addiction Behaviors*, ed. D. M. Donovan and G. A. Marlatt, pp.
3–48. New York: Guilford.

Elliott, R. (1994). Addictive consumption: function and fragmentation in postmodernity. *Journal of Consumer Policy* 17:159–179.

Faber, R. J. (1992). Money changes everything: compulsive buying
from a biopsychosocial perspective. *American Behavioral Scientist* 35:809–819.

Faber, R. J., and Christenson, G. A. (1996). In the mood to buy:
differences in the mood states experienced by compulsive

buyers and other consumers. *Psychology and Marketing* 13:803–820.

Faber, R. J., Christenson, G. A., de Zwaan, M., and Mitchell, J. E. (1995). Two forms of compulsive consumption: comorbidity of compulsive buying and binge eating. *Journal of Consumer Research* 22:296–304.

Faber, R. J., and O'Guinn, T. C. (1988). Dysfunctional consumer socialization: a search for the roots of compulsive buying. In *Psychology in Micro and Macro Economics*, vol. 1, ed. P. Vanden Abeele. Leuven, Belgium: International Association for Research in Economic Psychology.

—— (1992). A clinical screener for compulsive buying. *Journal of Consumer Research* 19:459–469.

Faber, R. J., O'Guinn, T. C., and Krych, R. (1987). Compulsive consumption. In *Advances in Consumer Research*, vol. 14, ed. M. Wallendorf and P. Anderson, pp. 132–135.

Faber, R. J., Ristvedt, S. L., Mackenzie, T. B., and Christenson, G. A. (1996). *Cues that trigger compulsive buying*. Paper presented at the Association for Consumer Research Conference, Tucson, AZ, October.

Goodwin, D. W. (1984). Studies of familial alcoholism: a review. *Journal of Clinical Psychiatry* 45:14–17.

Hanley, A., and Wilhelm, M. S. (1992). Compulsive buying: an exploration into self-esteem and money attitudes. *Journal of Economic Psychology* 13:5–18.

Hoch, S. J., and Loewenstein, G. F. (1987). *A theory of impulse buying*. Unpublished paper, Graduate School of Business, University of Chicago, Chicago.

Jacobs, D. F. (1989). A general theory of addictions: rationale for and evidence supporting a new approach for understanding and treating addictive behaviors. In *Compulsive Gambling: Theory, Research and Practice*, ed. H. J. Shaffer, S. A. Stein, B. Gambino, and T. N. Cummings, pp. 35–64. Lexington, MA: D. C. Heath.

Kuley, N. B., and Jacobs, D. F. (1988). The relationship between dissociative-like experiences and sensation seeking among social and problem gamblers. *Journal of Gambling Behavior* 4:197–207.

Lejoyeux, M., Ades, J., Tassain, V., and Solomon, J. (1996). Phenomenology and psychopathology of uncontrolled buying. *American Journal of Psychiatry* 153:1524–1529.

Lesieur, H. R., Blume, S. B., and Zoppa, R. M. (1986). Alcoholism, drug abuse and gambling. *Alcoholism: Clinical and Experimental Research* 10:33–38.

McElroy, S. L., Pope, H. G., Hudson, J. I., et al. (1991a). Kleptomania: a report of 20 cases. *American Journal of Psychiatry* 148:652–657.

McElroy, S. L., Satlin, A., Pope, H. G., et al. (1991b). Treatment of compulsive shopping with antidepressants: a report of three cases. *Annals of Clinical Psychiatry* 3:199–204.

O'Guinn, T. C., and Faber, R. J. (1989). Compulsive buying: a phenomenological exploration. *Journal of Consumer Research* 16:147–157.

Rook, D. (1987). The buying impulse. *Journal of Consumer Research* 14:189–199.

Scherhorn, G., Reisch, L. A., and Raab, G. (1990). Addictive buying in West Germany: an empirical study. *Journal of Consumer Policy* 13:355–387.

Schlosser, S., Black, D. W., Repertinger, S., and Freet, D. (1994). Compulsive buying: demography, phenomenology, and comorbidity in 46 subjects. *General Hospital Psychiatry* 16:205–212.

Valence, G., d'Astous, A., and Fortier, L. (1988). Compulsive buying: concept and measurement. *Journal of Consumer Policy* 11:419–433.

Ward, S. (1974). Consumer socialization. *Journal of Consumer Research* 1:1–14.

Zuckerman, M. (1979). *Sensation Seeking: Beyond the Optimal Level of Arousal.* Hillsdale, NJ: Lawrence Erlbaum.

II | *Shopping, Buying, and Selfhood*

3

Shopaholics, Spendaholics, and the Question of Gender

Colin Campbell

In recent years psychologists have come to recognize that shopping addiction is a disorder similar to compulsive gambling and alcoholism. It is "a syndrome of behavior involving loss of control over shopping which is very similar to other forms of addiction. It is largely, overwhelmingly indeed, seen in women, and it is usually carried out in secret" (Mihill 1994, p. 10). Mihill's comment raises the obvious question of why it is "overwhelmingly" women who are prone to this particular syndrome. While it could be that this is simply a consequence of their greater exposure to risk, given that studies show that women actually engage in more shopping activity than do men (Gronmo and Lavik 1988), this seems an unconvincing argument. Women are also more exposed than men to other activities, such as vacuuming or ironing clothes, and there is little evidence to suggest any frequent "loss of control" in relation to these activities. The obvious explanation is that shopping differs from these in that it is typically experienced by women as pleasurable, and any activity that yields pleasure has the potential to become the focus of an addiction. It is for this reason that we are not surprised to discover that there are shopping addicts or shopaholics — individuals who are dependent on the activity and must repeat it regularly or experience psychological distress. The question I consider in this chapter is why it is more common for women than men to find shopping pleasurable, and whether this relates to the markedly different incidence of shopping addiction identified by Mihill above.

I would also like to consider two seemingly different forms of shopping addiction. One I will call a *shopaholic* disorder; the other I will call a *spendaholic* disorder. *Shopaholics* are those people who seem to be addicted to the activity of shopping itself, unrelated to the buying or the having of an object; *spendaholics* are people who are addicted to spending and for whom the shopping activity is usually quite secondary. What are the differences between these two disorders, and what is the relationship between them? I will address these questions as well.[1]

GENDER AND SHOPPING

Virtually all adults have some experience of shopping and hence can be expected to express an attitude toward the activity. However, research has revealed a wide variation in the degree to which individuals judge this activity to be enjoyable; the range extends from those who describe shopping as a source of almost ecstatic

---

1. A variety of terms can be used to describe a pattern of behavior that an individual repeats more often than is necessary or warranted by his or her circumstances. Such a pattern could be said to be compulsive (arising perhaps from a mental obsession) or, where the conduct in question yields pleasure, addictive (or more correctly, indicating the existence of dependence). The term *compulsive* is not preferred here because the repeated pattern of activity discussed does not seem — at least in most cases — to arise from a mental obsession with the idea of shopping. Rather, it would seem that the element of compulsion is associated with the desire to engage in the activity in question. In this respect the pattern discussed seems closer to those associated with genuine drug dependency (such as alcohol or stimulants), arising from either an eagerness to experience pleasurable effects or a need to avoid the aversive consequences produced by the absence of these effects.

pleasure to those who express a fierce dislike of it.[2] For a surprising number of people shopping is regarded as a very disagreeable activity. One man described going shopping for clothes with his wife as the pits; another said that he hates going shopping in town; another that he can't stand it. Others describe shopping as very tedious, an ordeal, or boring. Another respondent said he would be ecstatic if someone else could do all his shopping for him because he considered it a chore, something done purely out of necessity and which he hoped to complete as soon as possible. Still another asserted that he "wouldn't do any shopping if I didn't have to. I hate shopping for anything, even buying clothes. I'd much rather sit on a settee and go through the *Next* directory. Shopping, I just can't be bothered . . . I can always think of something better to do."

At the other extreme were those respondents for whom all kinds of shopping were regarded as a source of pleasure and enjoyment. Pat, for example, declared that she loved "all types of shopping," indeed she "likes shopping for anything." Margaret also "loves shopping; shopping for anything." There are many people, of course, between these extremes, those who can take it or leave it or who don't mind it and who consequently reject the extreme attitudes expressed above.

These reports suggest that women are much more likely than men to express positive attitudes toward shopping and, conversely, that men are more likely than women to express negative attitudes toward shopping. Furthermore, women are far more likely than men to express a stronger positive attitude toward shopping, that is, to say that they "love" shopping rather than that they merely "like" it. Correspondingly, men are far more likely to express a stronger negative attitude, that is, they "hate" it rather than merely

---

2. The following discussion is based on an analysis of data obtained through focus group interviews with men and women between the ages of 25 and 45 and drawn from socioeconomic groups whose heads of households range from higher managerial, administrative, or professional occupations through semiskilled and unskilled workers. They took place on the premises of a market research agency in Leeds (England) between October 1991 and May 1992. Some eighty individuals took part.

"dislike" it. In addition, women are more prone to express positive attitudes toward a range of different kinds of shopping, while when males express a positive attitude it is more likely to be toward a very product-specific form of shopping (for example, shopping for CDs, computers, or electrical goods). Women are also much more likely than men to express a preference for shopping above other forms of leisure-time activity, such as watching a film or eating a meal in a restaurant.

These data reaffirm the suggestion that shopping in a modern, industrialized, Western society is a thoroughly "gendered" activity (Lunt and Livingstone 1992, Oakley 1976) that is widely perceived as closely linked with the female role and thus seen in some degree as a "feminine" activity. This is congruent with the data on shopping behavior that show, as noted above, that not only do women constitute a majority of shoppers, spending more time shopping than men, but that they also generally visit more retail outlets and purchase more products (Gronmo and Lavik 1988). Since it has been suggested that at root the male–female dichotomy in modern societies is little more than a direct correlate of the more general contrast between production and consumption (as Gardner and Sheppard [1989] put it, "traditional wisdom has it that men produced whilst women consumed" [p. 46]), the feminine nature of shopping could be seen as a special instance of that equation. In reality such a claim seems overgeneralized; notions of masculinity and femininity would appear to be defined in terms of differences that apply to the spheres of both production and consumption. What one can state with confidence, however, is that there is a marked difference in those predominant activities that typify each gender's preferred pattern of consumption. Thus, while drinking and watching sports constitute popular male forms of consumption, it would seem that shopping is the preferred female mode of consumption (Campbell 1998).

It is important to enter a caveat at this point. For although it is clear that men and women commonly articulate very different attitudes toward shopping, their actual behavior may not correlate very closely with the opinions and attitudes that they express. Apart from the fact that a considerable literature in the social sciences suggests that there is commonly a gulf between accounts and actions (see Gilbert and Mulkay 1984, Heritage 1983), evidence also suggests that the contrast in male and female shopping activity is not actually as marked as the expressed attitudes would lead us to believe. Among the evidence for this is the fact that men often exclude purchasing a major item like a car or a boat from their interpretation of the term *shopping*. They also fail to equate the considerable time they spend browsing in bookshops and music or computer stores with the time women spend browsing in clothes shops.

One way of looking at the marked gender difference in attitudes toward shopping is to regard males as associating shopping with a work frame while females associate it with a leisure frame. Males (either because of their socialization or because of their traditional greater involvement in the world of paid work) are predisposed to see shopping as an activity that falls under the general heading of work even if in their eyes this is qualified by the addition of the adjective *women's*. Consequently, they do not expect it to be recreational. They also presume that the appropriate standards for evaluating it are those typically applied in the world of work, that is, rationality and efficiency. This leads to men's tendency to clearly define a need, identify an appropriate retail outlet where this need can be satisfied through purchase, then expend as little effort and money as possible in finding and purchasing the item.

In contrast, women tend to apply a leisure frame when viewing shopping, especially clothes shopping. They regard this as essentially recreation, sharply distinguishing it from work of either the paid or "house" varieties. It follows that women are necessarily inclined to define the activity as enjoyable and to reject any purely instrumental or utilitarian frame of reference. Like all recreation, the values they assume are those of enjoyment and the indulgence of wants and desires in the legitimate pursuit of pleasure (Campbell 1998).

It seems probable that this close identification of shopping with one gender explains why the men in our sample were much less enthusiastic than the women about the activity. If they perceived shopping to be a female activity, then they would have a good reason to refrain from endorsing it; they might feel that to do so could put their own masculinity in question. Other evidence suggests that many men do indeed perceive shopping to be effeminate. As Oakley (1974) noted, "There are husbands who will not go in shops, [and] husbands who will go in shops but who will not carry the shopping bag for fear of being labeled 'effeminate'" (p. 93). Comments from our interviewees also suggest that some men, if they admit to enjoying shopping when in the company of other men, seem to feel the need to accompany such a declaration with a disclaimer of some kind. Indeed, it is possible that, for some men at least, this public expression of distaste for the activity is seen as a confirmation of their manhood. However, it is clearly not sufficient to suggest that women are more likely than men to find shopping pleasurable simply because that activity has traditionally been defined as part of a woman's role. Hence, there must be factors involved other than socialization and the successful identification with stereotypical gender roles. To gain an understanding of what these might be it is first necessary to refine the concept of shopping.

Shopping is not an undifferentiated activity. While there is more than one way to subdivide this single overall category, the most common and significant one by far for both men and women — and one that relates to important differences in attitude — is the distinction between food and nonfood shopping. Shopping for food is regular and local, while nonfood shopping is less frequent and usually involves taking a shopping trip, that is, journeying to a city center, shopping mall, or galleria. The precise terminology here varies, but the former is generally described in terms of the type of products being purchased (i.e., food shopping, grocery shopping, etc.). Or because these tend to be household items that need regular replacement, the shopping may be defined by that very regularity, for example, the weekly shopping or the Saturday shopping. This form of shopping may also be described in terms of the regular retail outlet at which it occurs; for example, the Safeway shopping or simply the supermarket shopping. While all these alternatives are commonly encountered, the term most often used is still simply *food shopping*.

In contrast to this general agreement on terms, respondents found it difficult to find a suitable term to describe the remaining "other" category. They frequently described it by negation, referring to it as "anything other than food shopping." When it is positively described, it is most often referred to as *clothes shopping*, or *clothes and shoes shopping*, although it is not restricted to these items but may include anything from birthday cards to plants or cushions. Since it often occurs in a different retail locality from the regular grocery store, it is also sometimes defined in those terms; for example, "going shopping in town" or, since it is also often distinguished by the number of outlets visited, as going to "the stores." It is not unusual for this kind of shopping to be described in terms of the amount of time devoted to it. Hence it may be referred to as a day's shopping or a day out. This last phrase directs attention to the fact that this form of shopping is also often described as a shopping trip (or even an expedition), something indicative not only of the scale of the activity involved, but also of the attitude of those who undertake it. Another revealing phrase is the reference to "going round the shops," or "looking around the shops." This also implies the notion of a trip, language that suggests the close association between this kind of shopping and other recreational and leisure-time pursuits.[3]

Now although it should be noted that a small number of women confessed to liking all forms of shopping, it was far more common for women to state that they liked (or even loved) the kind of recreational, nonfood, clothes shopping, better than grocery shopping. Indeed, they often admitted to having an aversion to the

---

3. However, these two categories do not cover all shopping. There remains an important category that does not fit into either. It is variously described by men as "electronics, computers, and things" "technology," or "anything electrical." Women commonly refer to it as "do-it-yourself shopping" or "car shopping." Perhaps a suitable general term for this category would be *technology shopping*, since this is its main item, although it also includes books, CDs, and videos.

latter. As Joanne says, "I don't like shopping for food but I like shopping for clothes." Linda agreed that she "feels excited" when about to go clothes shopping, but dreads grocery shopping, seeing it as something to get over and done with as quickly as possible. Pat declared that while she doesn't mind food shopping, she is "obsessed" by clothes shopping. The combination of an aversion to food shopping with an enthusiasm for clothes shopping was a common pattern among the women interviewed. Women typically obtain pleasure from shopping that is closely associated with a particular category of products; this suggests that the pleasure gained from shopping is connected with leisure and recreation rather than with economic transactions. This is something that social scientists and market researchers have only lately come to recognize.

Ever since the mid-1950s, social scientists and market researchers have sought to develop and refine taxonomic schemes for studying shoppers and shopper orientations. Gregory Stone (1954), the acknowledged pioneer in this field, interviewed over one hundred women about their attitudes toward shopping, focusing on their reasons for choosing one kind of retail outlet rather than another. Stone then used the answers to these questions on retail patronage to identify four basic orientations toward shopping: the "economic" shopper whose primary considerations are price and quality; the "personalizing" shopper to whom economic criteria are of secondary importance when compared to the opportunity for interaction that the shopping experience offers; the "ethical" shopper who claims to employ moral considerations in the choice of retail outlet; and the "apathetic" shopper who conducts this activity simply out of necessity. This typology has had a significant influence on subsequent research on shopping (see Westbrook and Black [1985] for a review of this literature).

Not surprisingly, given the historical importance of economic theory to marketing research, the category of economic shopper (together with the subcategory of convenience shopper) has been prominent in the consumer behavior literature. At the same time there has been a marked trend in consumer and marketing research in recent years toward greater recognition of the noneconomic and more distinctly experiential features of consumption activity (Hirschman and Holbrook 1982, Holbrook 1986, Holbrook and Hirschman 1982). This research has led to greater recognition of the importance of the nonpurchasing, browsing, or recreational category of shopper (Bellenger and Korgaonkar 1980, Bellenger et al. 1977, Bloch et al. 1989). This is a highly pertinent observation in this context because of the presumption — present in much of the literature on compulsive and addictive shopping — that the activity of shopping must equate with that of buying. In other words, it is almost always assumed that the compulsive shopper is, in effect, a compulsive buyer.

Recognizing the importance of recreational shopping raises the possibility that some individuals might be addicted less to the purchase of goods than to the practice of shopping. How should we interpret the comments of Linda, quoted above, who said she felt better when clothes shopping, or admitted to feeling excited at the prospect, while Pat confessed to being obsessed by the very idea? Should we assume, in line with the traditional image of the shopaholic, that their pleasure and excitement derives from the actual and anticipated purchase of goods? Or is it possible that some part of this strong positive feeling derives merely from the activity of browsing or window-shopping, irrespective of whether purchases are made?

What is interesting is that the female respondents who reported gaining the most pleasure from the activity of shopping were also those who were most likely to stress the pleasures of browsing. The exact nature of this latter activity was rarely specified precisely, but it did seem to possess three clear characteristics. First, it involved looking, that is, scanning and scrutinizing both the retail environment itself and the wide variety of goods on display. Second, such visual scanning occurred in the absence of a need to make any particular purchase. Third, it involved looking around in the absence of any pressing time constraint. Charlotta expressed the pleasure of browsing: "It's fun to go round the shops during the lunch-break, since you've got time to spend." Rochelle also expresses it: "I don't really ever go to town with the intention of buying anything. I just go to town and if I see something I like, then I buy it, but it doesn't bother me, just window-shopping." Susan describes how she just likes browsing and going to look at different things, not having anything in mind that she's gone in to buy. She likes to make it an afternoon and enjoy it. Or as Penny says: "I love town. I think the thing is just to have a day and be able to wander and just look at things. I don't even have to buy them often, I could just wander all day just looking at everything." As Heidi expresses it: "I like to browse, yes. Even if I'm not buying I do like to look around clothes shops, big stores especially. Especially at Christmas; I can't get away from them."

Some men speak of the pleasures of browsing in a similar manner, although less often. Mike says that he "could spend hours, going from one place to another"; Kevin states that he "could spend hours browsing if I've got the time. I'm quite happy to just browse round." For the men this activity is far more likely to take place within one retail outlet, such as a music or bookshop, or a computer store, while for the women the pleasures of browsing seem almost always to encompass moving between shops. In general, however, men are far less likely than women to describe browsing as pleasurable. Indeed, they are more likely to identify browsing — that is, the explicitly nonpurposive "just looking" that accompanies meandering around and between shops — as something they explicitly dislike about nonfood shopping. This contrast in attitudes would seem to stem from the endorsement of fundamentally different ideologies of shopping by the two genders.

Men and women employ a rather different calculus when it comes to judging the value of the activity of shopping in terms of the expenditure of time, energy, and money. The male view of shopping is typically, as described above, one in which a need is identified, an appropriate retail outlet is visited, and a suitable item purchased, after which the shopper returns home. As one of the interviewees expressed it, men like to "go in, buy it, and come out." It follows that browsing is not usually viewed as having an essential part to play in this process, being seen as a waste of the precious commodity of time while adding little or nothing to the success of the activity itself. Male shoppers do not claim to be indifferent to price, and some do indeed look for bargains. However, there is a sense in which the male philosophy can lead to a higher value being placed on time than money (as we saw above, men "can always think of something better to do" with their time). Consequently if "shopping around" means literally visiting many retail outlets, then it may well be rejected in favor of paying a higher price in order to keep the overall shopping time to a minimum. In this respect the male ideology more closely resembles that of the convenience shoppers, first identified by Stone (1954; see also Bellenger and Korgaonkar 1980).

The female view, by contrast, regards browsing as an essential part of the activity of shopping, whether undertaken within or between retail outlets. It is seen as essential, not just because it is the only means of obtaining information about the full range of items available for purchase, but also because it is through direct exposure to the items for sale that the women are more likely to experience the pleasure that can be gained from the activity of shopping (whether or not any purchases are made). They refer, for example, to the pleasure found in just looking around or in being able to wander and look at things. This reinforces the suggestion (made previously) that a fundamentally aesthetic and expressive gratification is involved; women are much more likely than men to refer to shopping in terms that imply an enjoyable leisure-time activity in its own right, a recreation. Consequently, women often look forward to going shopping, and in sharp contrast to men often embark on a trip without any specific idea of what they intend to buy. This distinction may explain why men typically refer to the need to go shopping for X, while women simply say they are going shopping. Women are more likely than men to combine a shopping trip with other pleasurable activities such as "having a chat" with a friend, or having coffee or a meal. Since for them the activity has its own intrinsic satisfactions, women spend time and effort shopping around in the direct physical sense, visiting a range of retail outlets. Women are effectively acquiring information about products, prices, and retail outlets as a mere by-product of enjoying their leisure time. By contrast, for those men who dislike the activity of shopping, acquiring such information is possible only at considerable cost and effort (Campbell 1998).

*   *   *

In our attempt to come closer to an understanding of why women are more prone to the "syndrome" of compulsive or addictive shopping, we have noted that (1) in general, women tend to find shopping more pleasurable than men; (2) the focus of their pleasure tends to be nonfood shopping (clothes, etc.); and (3) the pleasure they derive from this activity is associated with the activity of browsing and is not necessarily equated with purchasing. We have also noted that while women's "ideology" of shopping legitimates such browsing, the male ideology does not, being more clearly instrumentalist in character. With this framework clearly in mind we can now move closer to an explanation of the link between gender and compulsive shopping activity. First, however, we need to distinguish between the spendaholic and the shopaholic syndrome, often referred to by other authors as compulsive spending and compulsive shopping, respectively.

SPENDAHOLICS AND SHOPAHOLICS

The person who is conventionally termed *shopaholic* (what I call *spendaholic*) is actually a compulsive (or addictive) spender. As Diane, a reformed shopaholic, confessed:

> The joy was the act of buying itself. Often, I wouldn't bother to try things on — I'd look at the price tag and think, "I've got to have this," especially if I thought it was a "bargain" I might not see again. More often than not, when I got my booty home, I'd never even hang it up; it would sit in the carrier bag or the shoebox under the bed. It didn't matter *what* I bought; it still wouldn't have satisfied the continual, gnawing desire for more. [*Clothes Show*, 1994, p. 30]

It is clear from this that the traditional shopaholic is actually a compulsive purchaser, someone who is focused on the buying itself rather than on the general process of shopping. The high that is associated with the addictive form of this behavior tends to coincide with the moment of purchase, while the goods them-selves often remain unused, often not even unwrapped. According to Belk (1995), it is the fact that the goods remain unused that distinguishes the shopaholic (or, in my terms, the *spendaholic*) from the compulsive acquirer or collector. Compulsive spenders are rarely browsers since the compulsion is to move to the moment of purchase as quickly as possible. In addition, such individuals are often compulsive purchasers of particular kinds of goods (such as Imelda Marcos and her shoes) and thus tend to head straight to the nearest shoe shop, jewelry shop, or whatever location best suits their particular compulsion. Women who resembled this type — if in less extreme form — were found among our sample of respon-dents, and included women who declared that they found a special pleasure in purchasing only such distinct categories of product as dresses, skirts, shoes, jewelry, flowers, or perfume.

It is important to stress that the compulsive spender is unlikely to be a compulsive browser. Indeed, there is clearly a tension between the two impulses, since browsing involves spending time rather than money. The spendaholic generally knows exactly which retail outlet to go to in order to indulge the need to purchase, and consequently has no special need to tour a number of outlets. In this age of catalogue shopping, teleshopping, and Internet shopping, the spendaholic does not even need to visit a retail outlet to indulge the compulsion.

The fact that there is another form of aberrant consumption behavior, which I refer to as *shopaholic*, that is, someone who is not a compulsive spender but is rather addicted to the recreational activity of shopping, is suggested by the comments of two re-spondents who talked about their relationship to this activity in language directly parallel to that used by those who are drug dependent. One respondent described how she got the shakes if she was deprived of the opportunity of shopping because she was on holiday in a remote location, while another described the pleasure associated with extended clothes-shopping as being like having an injection. One form of compulsive recreational shop-ping combines the pleasures of compulsive spending with none of its obvious drawbacks. This is the buy-and-return form of shopping that, in Britain at least, is classically practiced by some customers of Marks and Spencers. This chain has a widely publicized policy of allowing customers to return any product that, for any reason, they do not wish to keep. This means that a customer may buy any number of items one day, take them home and try them on, and take them all back to the store. Then, provided that she has the necessary receipts, she has the choice of exchanging them for yet more items or receiving her money back. Such a buy-and-return form of shopping allows the compulsive recreational shopper to act like a compulsive purchase shopper in actually experiencing the high of purchase, without incurring the (literally) very high price paid by the spendaholic. Indeed, since the need to return the goods — which in all probability the shopper never intended to keep in the first place — provides the ideal excuse for yet another shopping trip, the purchasing may well have been prompted in part by the compulsion that drives what I call the shopaholic, or compulsive browser.

Although the two forms of compulsive or addictive shopping are distinct from each other, they both seem to be effectively legitimated by the same ideology of shopping outlined previously: that is, that shopping for women is thought of as recreation and desire-filling. These beliefs and values provide ideal justification not only for spending large amounts of time and/or money on the activity of shopping but also for the practice of visiting many retail outlets, regardless of whether it is primarily to browse or to buy. Hence they can serve to legitimate both addictive recreational shopping and spendaholicism. In so far as "good" shopping requires a complete knowledge of the market — the full range of products of a particular kind that are available for purchase — and of course the variation in their price, it follows that all relevant retail outlets should be visited, and visited often. This outlook not only requires shopping to continue beyond the point at which a suitable product at an appropriate price has been located, but it also justifies both extended and repeated shopping activity, independent of the existence of any particular need. By contrast, the male ideology of shopping, since it does not legitimate browsing to anything like the same extent, cannot be said to provide a framework of legitimacy for conduct conducive to shopaholism or spend-aholism.

How individuals might make the transition from the status of shopaholic (or indeed, mere controlled recreational shopper) to spendaholic is not clear, nor do we know whether being addicted to browsing makes it more or less likely that one will become a compulsive spender. It is at this point that individual personality variables rather than social or cultural conditions probably become crucial.

Although appreciating the significance that women typically attach to browsing and recreational shopping helps to suggest why they are more prone than men to fall victim to compulsive urges, it still does not fully explain the gender differential. After all, men do browse sometimes; it would be wrong to give the impression that they never engage in this activity. However, they tend to browse in a very different environment and for very different items. As suggested earlier, their preference is to browse in com-puter stores, electrical goods showrooms, car accessory stores, do-it-yourself stores, and the like. A critical point here is that, in accord with the two genders' contrasting ideologies, when men browse, the browsing is conceived of as principally information-gathering rather than as an exercise that involves aesthetic discernment. Expressed simplistically, one could say that the items men browse are the ones that are judged in terms of their instrumental capac-ity — what they can *do* — while the women's are judged first and foremost in terms of their aesthetic qualities — or what they *are*. Hence the men are primarily involved in making a technical judgment (many of them are indeed self-confessed technophiles interested in new developments) while the women are primarily involved in making a judgment of taste.

A spendaholic syndrome is far more likely to develop in a context in which purchase is directed at satisfying desires than in one in which purchase occurs in order to meet a specified need. This is not to suggest that male shoppers do not indulge in desire-prompted purchase. In fact, there is evidence to suggest that males are probably more likely than females to indulge their desires when shopping for food or drink, typically spending considerable time selecting wine, for example, or desserts. The opportunities for this to occur, however, are more limited than they would be for a female shopper who sees browsing as recreation. Desire when manifest in this rather direct gustatory sense of taste is rather different from taste as a faculty for aesthetic discernment, and men typically limit their exposure to contexts in which it is necessary to exercise the latter definition of taste. It is this (coupled with their preference for presuming that purchases should be made on the basis of an instrumental judgment of need rather than an expressive judgment of liking) that may serve to protect men (to some extent) from developing the spendaholic syndrome with respect to aesthetically significant products. What it does not protect them against, of course, is the possibility of developing either the compulsion to consume gustatory pleasurable products, which might lead to alcoholism, or the compulsion to acquire products that are perceived as part of a purposeful constructive endeavor (as Belk [1995] suggests is the case with compulsive collecting). In both of these activity syndromes males tend to outnumber females.

CONCLUSION

It is clear that modern consumer society is organized in ways that facilitate both compulsive spending and compulsive shopping. Just as saturation advertising and the easy availability of credit creates the ideal environment for the compulsive purchaser, so too is the retail world organized to provide the ideal circumstances for the compulsive recreational shopper. Twenty-four-hour television, catalogue and Internet shopping, as well as the steady increase in shopping centers, malls, and gallerias, all cater to the recreational shopper. More and more recreational sites of all kinds (such as museums, art galleries, zoos, and theme parks) now come complete with one or more shops, places that are often more crowded with customers than the associated attractions. Of course, the key point about obsessive (or addictive) shopping, when compared with obsessive spending, is that it is a largely invisible phenomenon. Since it is not directly equated with buying, it does not lead to the serious, sometimes calamitous, financial consequences that a spendaholic pattern of conduct, no matter how secretively undertaken, eventually reveals. Visiting the shops every single day, for hours at a time, may have some visible negative consequences (for example, housework may be left undone, job responsibilities may be shirked, and children may even be neglected), but on the whole it is a pattern of conduct that is neither dysfunctional in itself nor obviously dysfunctional in its consequences. What is more, it is possible that the two patterns of compulsive conduct may stem from differing motives, since although both could be regarded as responses to some kind of mental disturbance, or even possibly the alienation or inner emptiness that some writers see as characteristic of modern life (Lasch 1978), there are possible differences between them. Aggressive spending may be prompted by a desire (conscious or subconscious) to run up debt (such as to spend one's partner's money as a means of revenge for some perceived hurt or insult), or to enhance status, or to impress others — motives that relate to the ownership of things. On the other hand, compulsive recreational shopping is more likely to stem from a desire to get out of the house, to alleviate loneliness, or to experience sensory stimulation — motives that do not involve issues of ownership.

The term *shopaholic* has to date been rather misapplied. Those people to whom this label has been attached would be more accurately described as *spendaholics* since their compulsive behavior concerns the purchasing of goods rather than shopping per se. This distinction is important since investigations reveal the existence of a large body of shoppers for whom activities other than purchase are judged to be of value in themselves. This activity is commonly described as *browsing*, that is, the scrutinizing and scanning of products offered for sale and the exploration of the retail environment more generally. Those who enjoy browsing are identified as recreational shoppers and may include within their ranks individuals who have become dependent on the pleasures associated with these activities. So it is these who truly deserve to be labeled *shopaholics*. One intriguing issue — clearly a priority for further research — concerns the relationship between these two forms of compulsion — whether or not, for example, a spendaholic pattern of behavior develops only out of a context in which a shopaholic pattern already exists. Whatever the relationship, however, we can say that it is the distinctive female ideology of shopping that provides the key to explaining why an overwhelming majority of both shopaholics and spendaholics are women.

REFERENCES

Belk, R. W. (1995). *Collecting in a Consumer Society*. London: Routledge.

Bellenger, D. N., and Korgaonkar, P. K. (1980). Profiling the recreational shopper. *Journal of Retailing* 56:3:77–92.

Bellenger, D. N., Robertson, D. H., and Greenberg, B. A. (1977). Shopping center patronage motives. *Journal of Retailing* 53:29–38.

Bloch, P. H., Ridgway, N. M., and Sherrell, D. L. (1989). Extending the concept of shopping: an investigation of browsing activity. *Journal of the Academy of Marketing Science* 17 (1):13–21.

Campbell, C. (1998). Shopping, pleasure and the sex war. In *The Shopping Experience*, ed. P. Falk and C. Campbell, pp. 166–176. London: Sage.

Clothes Show (1994). The high price of being a shopaholic, June, pp. 30–32.

Gardner, C., and Sheppard, J., (1989). *Consuming Passion: The Rise of Retail Culture* London: Hyman.

Gilbert, G. N., and Mulkay, M. (1984). *Opening Pandora's Box: A Sociological Analysis of Scientists' Discourse*. Cambridge: Cambridge University Press.

Gronmo, S., and Lavik, R. (1988). Shopping behaviour and social interaction: an analysis of Norwegian time budget data. In *The Sociology of Consumption: An Anthology*, ed. P. Otnes, pp. 101–118. Oslo: Solum Forlag A/S.

Heritage, J. (1983). Accounts in action. In *Accounts and Action: Surrey Conferences on Sociological Theory and Methods*, ed. G. N. Gilbert and P. Abell, pp. 117-131. Aldershot, UK: Gower.

Hirschman, E. C., and Holbrook, M. B. (1982). Hedonic consumption: emerging concepts, methods and propositions. *Journal of Marketing* 46:92–101.

Holbrook, M. (1986). Emotion in the consumption experience: toward a new model of the human consumer. In *The Role of Affect in Consumer Behavior: Emerging Theories and Applications*, ed. R. Peterson, W. Hoyer, and W. Wilson, pp. 17–52. Lexington, MA: D.C. Heath.

Holbrook, M., and Hirschman, E. (1982). The experiential aspects of consumption: consumer fantasies, feelings, and fun. *Journal of Consumer Research* 9:132–140.

Lasch, C. (1978). *The Culture of Narcissism*. New York: Norton.

Lunt, P. K., and Livingstone, S. M. (1992). *Mass Consumption and Personal Identity*. Buckingham, UK: Open University Press.

Mihill, C. (1994). Compulsive shopping: real illness. *The Guardian*, October 6, p. 10.

Oakley, A. (1976). *Housewife*. Harmondsworth, UK: Penguin.

Stone, G. P. (1954). "City shoppers and urban identification: observations on the social psychology of city life. *American Journal of Sociology* 60:36–45.

Westbrook, R. A., and Black, W. C. (1985). A motivation-based shopper typology. *Journal of Retailing* 61 (1):78–103.

4

Are We What We Own?*

Russell Belk

We cannot hope to gain a comprehensive understanding of compulsive buying without first gaining some understanding of the meanings that consumers attach to possessions. A key to understanding what possessions mean is recognizing that, knowingly or unknowingly, intentionally or unintentionally, we regard our possessions as parts of ourselves (Belk 1988). We are what we have and possess. This is perhaps the most basic and powerful fact of consumer behavior.

Treating possessions as extensions of ourselves is not a new phenomenon. William James (1890) observed that:

> a man's Self is the sum total of all that he CAN call his, not only his body and his psychic powers, but his clothes and his house, his wife and children, his ancestors and friends, his reputation and works, his lands, and yacht and bank-account. All these things give him the same emotions. If they wax and prosper,

*I would like to thank April Benson for her kind help in extracting pertinent material from my previously published article, for allowing me to update this material by inviting this chapter, and for her help in securing reference material during a year I spent in Zimbabwe enlarging my extended self.

> he feels triumphant; if they dwindle and die away, he feels cast
> down, — not necessarily in the same degree for each thing, but
> in much the same way for all. [pp. 291–292]

James stipulates that there is also a nonmaterial self, but that a substantial part of who we are is composed of the things we call ours.

The purpose of this chapter is to examine the relationship between possessions and our sense of who we are. This relationship is of importance not only for understanding our behavior as consumers but, more important, for understanding how consumption relates to our broader projects in life (Belk 1987a). Defining ourselves by our possessions can contribute to feelings of well-being as well as feelings of emptiness and vulnerability if we believe that we are nothing more than what we own. Overreliance on possessions for self-definition may be manifested in how we shop, how we care for the things we acquire, and the degree to which we cling to our possessions rather than discard them.

A key concept linking the extended self to compulsive shopping is that of materialism. Materialism has been defined as "the importance a consumer attaches to worldly possessions. At the highest levels of materialism, such possessions assume a central place in a person's life and are believed to provide the greatest sources of satisfaction" (Belk 1985, p. 265). For the highly materialistic consumer, purchases are potential panaceas for all manners of dissatisfactions with self and with life generally. O'Guinn and Faber (1989) found some aspects of materialism to be related to compulsive shopping tendencies, and Dittmar (1992) found even stronger evidence of such a relationship. To the highly materialistic person, purchases of consumer goods offer the potential for magical transformation of self (Belk 1991a). Buying becomes a transformative ritual intended to precipitate a totally new life; it is an attempt to replay the romantic rebirth of the Cinderella story.

The first section of the material that follows considers evidence that possessions are an important component of the sense of self. The most direct form of evidence is found in the nature of self-perceptions. The second section addresses the question of what functions the extended self serves for us. It begins with a brief review of the basic states of our existence: having, doing, and being. These states are each potentially critical to self-definition, but for the materialist having becomes all important. Next, the functions of possessions in human development are considered. A central function considered in this section is the role of possessions in creating or maintaining a sense of past.

A third section examines how material objects become a part of the self. A key process in this involves the initial incorporation of objects into our extended selves. A number of incorporation processes are discussed, not all of which involve possession in the sense of individual ownership. A final section discusses the implications that the extended-self construct has for further research on compulsive buying. It briefly reviews the construct of the extended self and offers conclusions.

POSSESSIONS IN SELF-PERCEPTION RESEARCH

Possession as Parts of Self

Rochberg-Halton (1984) specifies the role of possessions in the project of self-construction: "Valued material possessions . . . act as signs of the self that are essential in their own right for its continued cultivation, and hence the world of meaning that we create for ourselves, and that creates our selves, extends literally into the objective surroundings" (p. 335).

In DeLillo's (1985) postmodern novel *White Noise* it is suggested that while life is brief, the extended self may survive the body:

> The dead have faces, automobiles. If you don't know a name, you know a street name, a dog's name, "He drove an orange Mazda." You know a couple of useless things about a person that become major facts of identification and cosmic placement when he dies suddenly, after a short illness, in his own

bed with a comforter and matching pillows, on a rainy Wednesday afternoon, feverish, a little congested in the sinuses and chest, thinking about his dry cleaning. [p. 293]

The conflation of person and possessions is even stronger among the living, as James (1890) notes:

> It is clear that between what a man calls me and what he simply calls mine the line is difficult to draw. We feel and act about certain things that are ours very much as we feel and act about ourselves. Our fame, our children, the work of our hands, may be as dear to us as our bodies are, and arouse the same feelings and the same acts of reprisal if attacked. And our bodies themselves, are they simply ours, or are they *us*? Certainly men have been ready to disown their very bodies and to regard them as mere vestures, or even as prisons of clay from which they should some day be glad to escape. [p. 291]

Research that has addressed the "things" that are viewed to constitute self (McClelland 1951, Prelinger 1959) has generally found that possessions are second only to body parts and mind in their centrality to self. The particular possessions we see as most a part of ourselves (Belk 1987b) also show a close relationship to the objects we see as most magical, and include perfume, jewelry, clothing, foods, transitional objects, homes, vehicles, pets, religious icons, drugs, gifts, heirlooms, antiques, photographs, souvenirs, and collections (Belk 1991a). McCarthy (1984) concludes that such objects act as reminders and confirmers of our identity, and that this identity may often reside more in these objects than it does in the individual.

In claiming that something is "mine," we also come to believe that the object is "me." How can we explain the particular choice of possessions deemed most critical to self-definition? Besides magical efficacy, control has been suggested to be the critical determinant of feelings of possession (Furby 1978, Tuan 1984). That is, the more we believe we possess or are possessed by an object, the more a part of self it becomes. There is some evidence that men are more likely than women to value objects for the sense of control that they provide (Lunt and Livingstone 1992). Where men tend to value possessions for self-focused and instrumental reasons, women tend to emphasize expressive and other-oriented reasons for feeling attachment to possessions (Dittmar 1992, Kamptner 1989, Wallendorf and Arnould 1988).

Age is another factor affecting the nature of our attachment to possessions. In a three-generational study of favorite possessions, Rochberg-Halton (1984, 1986, Csikszentmihalyi and Rochberg-Halton 1981) found that as we age the possessions we cite as "special" tend increasingly to be those that symbolize other people (e.g., gifts from people, photographs of people). They interpret these findings to suggest an age-related widening of the boundaries of self (Rochberg-Halton 1984). These findings may suggest that possessions are not only regarded as a part of self, they may also be instrumental to the "development" of our sense of self. Research on the role that special possessions may play in easing life transitions suggests that possessions can be instrumental to the maintenance of self-concept (e.g., Anderson 1985, McCracken 1987, Nemy 1986). One instance in which possessions provide such a sense of self-continuity is seen in the careful packing, transport, and redeployment of treasured possessions when we move from one locale to another (Belk 1992).

Investing Self in Objects

The idea that we make things a part of self by creating or altering them appears to be a universal human belief. Csikszentmihalyi and Rochberg-Halton (1981) provide a more psychological explanation in suggesting that we invest "psychic energy" in an object to which we have directed our labor, time, and attention. This energy and its products are regarded as a part of self because they have grown or emerged from the self. Purchasing objects offers another means for investing self (in this case more symbolically) in possessions.

Ames (1984) records feelings attached to a nineteenth-century purchase of a parlor organ:

> Buying a prominent object like a parlor organ might initiate a new chapter in a set of lives, not only by providing a new way to use time but also a new tool to measure time. In later years the object would serve to remind its owners of the day it first entered their home and of the time that had passed since then. It would not only structure their present but also their perceptions of their own past. They knew from experience that purchasing a major object could be a significant and momentous occasion in itself, a time of heightened positive emotions and feelings of well-being and importance . . . a major purchase would transform them in their own eyes and in the eyes of others. They would become worth more . . . and acquire greater status. By so doing they would receive more respect and deference from others which would, in turn, make them feel better about themselves. Buying a parlor organ would make them something they were not before. [pp. 30–31]

In this example we see an instance in which a family possession rather than a personal possession contributes to sense of self. In other cases, such as monuments and landmarks, entire communities or even nations may share these objects as parts of extended self.

The feeling of identity invested in material objects can be extraordinarily high. One of the modern equivalents of the parlor organ, in terms of impact on extended self, is the automobile (Bloch 1981, Myers 1985, Stone 1966, Weiland 1955). Niederland and Sholevar (1981) suggest that for many young American males in particular, the automobile is a part of their ego ideals. A shiny new car is experienced very much as a shiny new self. This view is supported by consumer self-concept research (e.g., Bloch 1982, Grubb and Hupp 1968, Jacobson and Kossoff 1963, Munson and Spivey 1980, Ross 1971, Wright et al. 1992). The processes of creating and nurturing extended self through an automobile may also be seen in customizing (personalizing) the car and in lavishing great care on its maintenance. When such a car is damaged, the owners react as if their own bodies had been injured. Consider the sense of personal injury described by Bellow (1975) when a treasured car is assaulted: "Someone had done to my car as rats, I had heard, did when they raced through warehouses by the thousands and tore open sacks of flour for the hell of it. I felt a similar rip at my heart . . . I had allowed the car to become an extension of my own self . . . , so that an attack on it was an attack on myself. It was a moment terribly fertile in reactions" (p. 36).

Furthermore, the possessors of such damaged treasures are anxious to either restore the auto to its former perfection or replace it with a more perfect substitute. These reactions reflect the desire to restore the damaged sense of (extended) self caused by the injury to the automobile. The owner of an expensive Porsche described his attachment in this way:

> Sometimes I test myself. We have an ancient battered Peugeot, and I drive it for a week. It rarely breaks, and it gets great mileage. But when I pull up next to a beautiful woman, I am still the geek with the glasses.
>
> Then I get back into the Porsche. It roars and tugs to get moving. It accelerates even going uphill at 80. It leadeth trashy women . . . to make pouting looks at me at stoplights. It makes me feel like a tomcat on the prowl. . . .
>
> . . . Nothing else in my life compares — except driving along Sunset at night in the 928, with the sodium-vapor lamps reflecting off the wine-red finish, with the air inside reeking of tan glove-leather upholstery and the . . . Blaupunkt playing the Shirelles so loud it makes my hair vibrate. And with the girls I will never see again pulling up next to me, giving the car a once-over, and looking at me as if I were a cool guy, not a worried, overextended 40-year-old schnook writer. [Stein 1985, p. 30]

As these examples suggest, the degree to which self becomes extended into possessions can be great (Belk 1988).

FUNCTIONS OF EXTENDED SELF

Having, Doing, and Being

Objects in our possession can literally extend self, as when a tool or weapon allows us to do things of which we would otherwise be incapable. Possessions can also symbolically extend self, as when a uniform or trophy allows us to convince ourselves (and perhaps others) that we can be a different person than we would be without them. Tanay (1976) offers an example of the latter type of self-extension in suggesting that handguns represent a symbolic penis for their owners. However, Kates and Varzos (1987) challenge this interpretation and instead emphasize the instrumental rather than symbolic power given by guns. It was this sense of enhancement of personal power that reputedly made the six-gun the "equalizer" in American Western lore. Whereas Tanay's symbolic interpretation is focused on the sense of "being" presumably provided by such a weapon, this alternative interpretation maintains that it is what one can "do" with a gun that contributes to sense of self. Having possessions can thus contribute to our capabilities for either doing or being.

The relationships between having, doing, and being are strong and have been most fully explored by Jean-Paul Sartre. In *Being and Nothingness*, Sartre (1956) suggests that doing is merely a transitional state or a manifestation of the more fundamental desires to have or to be. Further, Sartre maintains that the only reason we want to have something is to enlarge our sense of self, and that the only way we can know who we are is by observing what we have. In other words, having and being are distinct but inseparable. When an object becomes a possession, what were once self and not-self are synthesized, and having and being merge. Thus, according to Sartre, possessions are all-important to knowing who we are. We seek, express, confirm, and ascertain our sense of being through what we have.

Other people also affect the relationships between our having, doing, and being, according to Sartre. Besides others sometimes serving in an object capacity as possessions, others are an important mirror through which we may see ourselves. These others first come to associate possessions with possessor and then, depending upon which is known best, infer the traits of one from the other. Belk (1978, 1988), Belk and colleagues (1982), and Holman (1981), review abundant buyer behavior literature supporting this view.

Contrasting Sartre's view that having and being are the central modes of existence is Karl Marx's view that doing, and particularly working, is central to existence and self-worth. The problem with having, in Marx's view, is that it produces a false path to happiness through "commodity fetishism" (Marx 1867). In commodity fetishism goods are worshipped by consumers and believed to have magical powers to bring happiness, provoking a pervasive expectation that happiness lies in the next purchase, or, "I would be happy if I could just have . . ." The idea noted earlier of magical transformation via consumer purchases is evident here as well. Both the compulsive consumption and the self-gift literatures (e.g., Mick 1996, Mick and DeMoss 1990, O'Guinn and Faber 1989, Sherry et al. 1995) find goods such as clothing and jewelry to be common foci of compulsive purchases to self and others. Notably, both are worn close to the body and promise potential magical transformation of self. Fairytales are full of magical rings, magical shoes, and other items of adornment that transform their wearers (Belk 1991a). The branded magic of Nike, Armani, and Tiffany represent a highly polished extension of these tales of magic.

While Sartre saw *having* as the dominant mode of existence and Marx saw certain forms of *doing* (through meaningful and properly rewarded work [Marx 1842]) as the dominant mode of existence, a third view explicated by Fromm (1976) completes the possibilities by advocating *being* as the preeminent form of existence. Like Marx, Fromm attacks "radical hedonism," or the concentration on having, as being unrewarding. He suggests that this view promotes a having mode of existence that views things, experience, time, and life itself as possessions to be acquired and retained. In the alternate *being* mode of existence that Fromm proposes, this orientation is rejected in favor of an opposing orientation to share, to give, and to sacrifice. The outcome of practicing this *being* mode of existence, according to Fromm, is to realize one's identity without the threat of losing it inherent in the having mode — for which he asks, "If I am what I have and if what I have is lost, who then am I?" (Fromm 1976, p. 76).

The views of Sartre, Marx, and Fromm on having, doing, and being present significant philosophical alternatives that it is not necessary or possible to resolve here. All three agree, however, that having possessions functions to create and maintain a sense of self-definition and that having, doing, and being are integrally related. Furthermore, various disciplines share the notion of fetishism as involving an essentially unhealthy investment of self in possessions. As Ellen (1988) argues, Marxist economic's commodity fetishism, anthropology's religious fetishism, and Freudian psychology's sexual fetishism have more commonalties than differences.

Mastery of Possessions and Human Development

Developmental evidence suggests that the identification with our things begins quite early in life when as an infant we learn to distinguish self from environment and then from others who may envy our possessions. Emphasis on material possessions tends to decrease with age, but remains high throughout life as we seek to express ourselves through possessions and use material possessions to seek happiness, remind ourselves of experiences, accomplishments, and other people in our lives, and even create a sense of life after death. Our accumulation of possessions provides a sense of past and tells us who we are, where we have come from, and perhaps where we are going.

Self versus Environment

The functions that possessions fulfill in our lives are not constant over our life spans. In infancy the distinction between self and not-self emerges as a result of the contingency and kinesthetic feedback produced by the infant's actions (Lewis and Brooks 1978,

Seligman 1975). That is, as the infant's motor skills develop, those objects that can be controlled come to be seen as self and those objects that cannot be controlled come to be seen as environment.

According to Isaacs (1933), the mother's caregiving also produces the first sentiments of ownership: "In the case of the infant at the breast, to *have* is literally and simply to take into oneself, into one's mouth. The nipple is only *here* at all when it is in my mouth, when it is (in feeling) a part of *me*. And to bite and swallow a thing is for long the only sure way of retaining it. . . . This is the ultimate form of ownership, from which all others are derived" (p. 226).

Even though the mother provides care, nourishment, and security, her lack of perfect responsiveness to the infant's desires makes it likely that she is the first object that comes to be regarded as not-self. It is also the separation from mother that has led others to suggest that the "security blanket" serves as a transitional object, helping the child to feel the security of the mother through an object that symbolizes her (e.g., Furby and Wilke 1982, Passman 1976, Passman and Halonen 1979, Weisberg and Russell 1971, Winnicott 1953).

If the early changes in person–object relationships may be described as moving from being one with the environment to having objects that aid in the transition to a world where self is distinct from the environment, the next changes may be characterized as moving from having transitional objects to doing things with or to the environment. This motivation has been labeled *competence* (Furby 1980), *mastery*, (White 1959), or *efficacy motivation* (Lichtenberg 1989). This concept has been expanded by Furby (1980), who suggests that we develop a stronger sense of self by learning to actively control objects in our environment rather than feeling controlled by them.

Self versus Others

Data from Kline and France (1899) and Isaacs (1935) suggest that the relationship between a person and an object is never as simple as a person–thing bond, however, because other people often seek to control these objects: "A great part of the value of those things which little children want to own is far from intrinsic. It arises directly from the fact that others have or want the object. And thus we enter the open field of rivalry. Not to have what others have, or to have less than they, is to feel shut out from the love and regard of the person giving. It is to be treated as not loveworthy." (Isaacs 1935, p. 74).

In this sense relationships with objects are always three-way (person–thing–person) relationships. This brings forth a "meum et tuum" concern with object ownership (Beaglehole 1932).

The rivalry aspects of possession seem clear among young children. Horney (1937) suggests that such competitiveness, along with other evidence of lack of affection from parents or peers, leads the child to compensate as an adult through neurotic strivings for power, prestige, and possessions — a pattern that may become manifest in compulsive shopping. Muensterberger (1994; Chapter 7, this volume) finds a similar connection between a felt lack of parental love and compulsive collecting. Whether or not this is a complete explanation of these adult traits, it seems a more plausible basis for adult orientations toward possessions than are explanations via Freudian oral and anal fixations (Belk 1982a). Freud himself was an avid collector of antiquities, but did not apply such explanations to his own or others' collecting activity (Belk 1995).

Although receiving material objects may convey a sense of love and worth to a child, from the parents' point of view control of their children's material possessions as rewards or punishments offers a means of bringing about desired behaviors. The way that parents use such resource-mediated behavioral modification may not only affect behaviors (both those concerning possessions and other behaviors), it may also create new attitudes toward the possessions used as reinforcements. For example, if sweets are withheld or withdrawn, or if threats to do so are made, these actions may simultaneously enhance the value of sweets, encourage the delay of gratifications until unpleasant tasks are completed, or instill an attitude that good performance should be followed by indulgence. The potential effects of such socialization on adult lifestyles are easily envisioned.

Adolescence and Adulthood

Erikson (1959) suggested that adolescents predictably undergo an "identity crisis." One element of this search is that adolescents at this stage increasingly seek identity through acquiring and accumulating selected consumption objects. A study of 8- to 30-year-old Chicagoans by Csikszentmihalyi and Rochberg-Halton (1981) found that this generation was more likely than its parents and grandparents to cite as favorite possessions those that either reflect skills in use (e.g., athletic equipment) or that the possessor can manipulate or control (e.g., music instruments, stereo, pets).

Csikszentmihalyi and Rochberg-Halton (1981) found that during preretirement adulthood, emphasis shifts from defining oneself by what one does to defining self through what one has. Furby (1978) found that 40- to 50-year-olds were the most likely of all age groups to cite social power and status as reasons to own personal possessions. Csikszentmihalyi (1982) explains:

> A person who owns a nice home, a new car, good furniture, the latest appliances, is recognized by others as having passed the test of personhood in our society . . . the objects we possess and consume are . . . wanted because . . . they tell us things about ourselves that we need to hear in order to keep ourselves from falling apart. This information includes the social recognition that follows upon the display of status symbols, but it includes also the much more private feedback provided by special household objects that objectify a person's past, present, and future, as well as his or her close relationships. [pp. 5–6]

Olson (1981, 1985) found that young couples cited as favorite objects in the home those that reflected their future plans and goals, while older couples cited objects related to their experiences together as a couple. Cameron (1977) conducted a series of experiments suggesting that having children is a key life event that causes the parents to become less self-focused and more focused on children. Feibleman (1975) notes the emergence by late middle age of a tendency to live vicariously through one's children. Children at this point represent an extension of self, but not to the exclusion of material possessions. In fact, Belk (1985) found parents to be more materialistic and possessive than their children and their own parents. Because of accumulated possessions, well-developed skills, possession of both a past and a future, and parenthood, the middle years of life are also likely to involve the most extended concept of self.

Old Age

If the young are future-oriented, the old are past-oriented. Csikszentmihalyi and Rochberg-Halton (1981) found that for their Chicago sample such possessions as photographs, athletic trophies, and mementos are most treasured by grandparents. The reason most often cited for possessions being treasured by this group was their ability to symbolize others, often because they were gifts from these important others. Sherman and Newman (1977) found that postretirement-age persons who possessed such remembrances were happier than those who did not. Places especially relevant to one's past have also been found to be particularly valued by the old because of the memories they stir (Howell 1983, Lowenthal 1975).

During old age the sense of one's own mortality also becomes more and more undeniable. With decreasing future years, declining skills and abilities, and a shrinking network of old friends, it might be imagined that sense of self contracts as well. However, this is not necessarily the case. In fact, some seek to assure that their self will extend beyond their death. Lifton (1973) suggests five ways in which this may be attempted: (1) through one's children, (2) through belief in a life after death, (3) through one's works, (4) through identification with nature (which will continue), and (5) through experiential transcendence (e.g., absorption in music may allow the person to transcend the world of here and now and symbolically be reborn). A sixth way that is not listed is to have one's possessions (especially those in collections one has created) "live on" through heirs or museums (Belk 1991b, Rigby and Rigby 1949).

Possessions and the Sense of Past

A general function of possessions across the age continuum is to provide us with a concrete sense of our past. Overall, Csikszentmihalyi and Rochberg-Halton (1981) found that the three types of possessions most frequently treasured by the 315 Chicago families they interviewed were furniture, visual art (including that created by family and friends), and photographs. In each case the most frequently given explanation for valuing these objects was the memories they called forth of other people, occasions, and relationships. These reasons overshadowed both functional explanations for attachments to furniture and aesthetic reasons for valuing art objects and photographs.

Integral to a sense of who we are is a sense of our past. Possessions are a convenient means of storing the memories and feelings that evoke our sense of past. A souvenir may make tangible some otherwise intangible travel experience. An heirloom may record and recall family heritage. And a historic monument may help to create a sense of a nation's past.

The desire to know one's individual past can explain the retention of personal memorabilia, just as the desire to remember family heritage can explain retention of family heirlooms, and the desire to appreciate national history and achievements can explain museum patronage and visits to historic sites. But what can explain the desire to acquire and collect antiques and antiquities from another time, place, and family? Clearly it is not a claimable sense of past that is achieved at any except the broadest level of identity. Part of the answer lies in the desire to identify with an era, place, or person in which we believe a desirable set of traits or values inhere. At a national level neoclassical architecture seems to have this objective. At a more personal level owning artifacts that once belonged to a famous historical figure seems to share this objective (Rigby and Rigby 1949, Wallendorf and Belk 1987). In each case there appears to be a desire to bask in the glory of the past in the hope that some of it will magically rub off—a form of positive contagious magic (Levi-Strauss 1962/1963). Another reason for the accumulation of antiquities that are found or acquired (rather than inherited or claimed on the basis of more direct linkage to the extended self) is that they are necessarily rare and therefore potentially serve as symbols of status or as "status markers" (Douglas and Isherwood 1981).

We can summarize then the functions that possessions play in the extended self as involving the creation, enhancement, and preservation of a sense of identity. Possessions help us at all ages to know who we are. This does not imply, however, that we are always active in selecting the possessions that we see as a part of our selves. As the next section discusses, passive receipt of objects into the extended self also occurs (Belk 1988).

PROCESSES OF SELF-EXTENSION

Ways of Incorporating Possessions into the Extended Self

Sartre (1943) suggests three primary ways through which we may come to regard an object as a part of self. One way is through appropriating or controlling an object for our own personal use, a view similar to McClelland's (1951) hypothesis that objects are experienced as part of self to the extent that we can exercise power and control over them. Sartre also holds that we can appropriate intangible or nonownable objects by overcoming, conquering, or mastering them. Thus climbing a mountain or living in a city can make these "nonobjects" feel a part of us. And it is only through learning to ride a first bicycle, manipulating a new computer system, driving a first car, or successfully negotiating rapids in a new kayak that these objects really become parts of the extended self. This is an important point, for it provides an explanation of how nondurable products or services and public property or events may come to be viewed as possessions and thereby potentially contribute to sense of self. A related way of appropriating a second-hand durable possession like a home or an automobile is through cleaning it, and in so doing symbolically removing any contagious traces of former owners. McCracken (1988) describes such cleansing as a possession ritual.

A second way of coming to own an object and incorporating it into self is by creating it — a view echoing anthropological findings and Locke's (1690) labor theory of property — that ownership comes through transformation. Whether the thing created is a material object or an abstract thought, the creator retains an identity in the object as long as it retains a mark or some other association with the person who brought it into existence. This identity is sometimes codified through copyrights, patents, and scientific citations that preserve associations between people and their mental creations.

The third way in which objects may become a part of self is by *knowing* them (in the biblical sense). Whether the object known is a person, place, or thing, Sartre maintains that the relationship in knowing the object is inspired by a carnal and sexual desire to have the object. Likewise, as Beaglehole (1932) observed, it is our intimate knowledge of a community, store, or book that makes it not only "ours" but also a part of self. It is only when the object is known passionately that it becomes subject rather than object. One way of passionately knowing an object is through collecting it. The cultivation of a collection is a purposeful, self-defining act (Belk 1995). While the collections of both humans and animals were once primarily assemblages of necessities stored in order to be more secure in satisfying future needs, collections today are made of luxuries assembled in order to seek distinction and self-definition (Belk 1982b). As Rigby and Rigby (1949) insightfully observed: "From the small boy to the connoisseur, the joy of standing before one's accumulated pile and being able to say 'this belongs to me' is the culmination of that feeling that begins with ownership of the first item . . . they become us" (p. 35).

Rather than representing a fourth way of bonding oneself with objects, Sartre believed that buying an object is merely another way of creating the object. For some people money is too abstract, invisible, or "commoditized" (Kopytoff 1986) to become a part of extended self. Nevertheless, money is a highly charged and magical symbol for many people (Belk 1999). If the desire is to extend self through having, then using the money to buy more tangible, visible would-be extensions of self is more likely for such people (Wright et al. 1992). The latent buying power of money can also contribute to sense of self. As Marx (1844) proclaimed, "that which exists for me through the medium of money, that which I can pay for, i.e., which money can buy, that am I, the possessor of money" (p. 377). In this sense we may suppose that money enlarges our sense of self because it enlarges our imagination of all that we might have and do. Money also gives us the power to selectively acquire or reject purchasable objects, thereby more selectively shaping our extended selves. Sartre also sees giving possessions to others as a means to extend self. In giving an object as a gift it will continue to be associated with the giver so that the giver's identity will have been extended to include the recipient.

All three means of making objects a part of extended self outlined by Sartre (control/mastery, creation, and knowledge) are active and intentional ways of self-extension. Clothing (Solomon 1986), housing (Jaeger 1985), and automobiles are all acquired as a "second skin" that others often use to make inferences about us. Objects such as land to the farmer, crafts pieces to the craftsperson, and artworks to the artist may become a part of extended self because we have intentionally worked on or created these things, investing both energy and self in them. These are clearly all active processes. But objects like household furnishings may also become a part of us through the knowledge that comes with habituation — they have become part of our familiar interior landscape, have been the setting for numerous special as well as ordinary occurrences in our lives, and often have received the same amount of care and attention that we lavish upon ourselves and immediate family members. During their tenure with us, a great many memories are likely to have accreted in these objects. Thus not all forms of self-extension are active and intentional. Self-extension can also come about through the gradual accommodation of objects in our lives and the slow accretion of meaning in objects that have taken their place with us.

CONCLUSIONS: IMPLICATIONS FOR COMPULSIVE CONSUMPTION RESEARCH

The possessions incorporated in extended self serve valuable functions for healthy personalities. One such function is acting as an objective manifestation of self: an exterior representation of our interior structures. As Douglas and Isherwood (1979) note, such possessions are "good for thinking." They help us manipulate our possibilities and present the self to others in a way that is able to garner feedback from those who are reluctant to respond so openly to the unextended self.

The possessions in our extended self also give us a personal archive or museum that allows us to reflect on our histories and see how we have changed. Through heirlooms, the family is able to build a similar archive and allow individual family members to gain a sense of permanence and place in the world that extends beyond their own lives and accomplishments. Communities, nations, and other group levels of self are similarly constituted via monuments, buildings, books, music, and other created works. The association of these artifacts with various group levels of self provides a sense of community that is essential to group harmony, spirit, and cooperation. In addition, natural wonders can be incorporated into extended self in such a way that we have an even greater feeling of immortality and place in the world.

This is not to suggest that extending self into material possessions has only positive effects. Research on materialism reveals some of the negative consequences of relying on possessions to provide meaning in life (e.g., Dittmar 1992). Money can be expulsively and wastefully spent on consumer goods, sometimes because we feel we do not deserve to have wealth (Belk 1991a; Boundy, Chapter 1, this volume). However, it is likely that attempted self-enlargement or compensation for a diminished sense of self motivates compulsive consumption more than does the wish to rid ourselves of money. The materialist has a magical, optimistic belief in the efficacy of consumer goods to bring about a total transformation of current life to one that is far, far better — a romantic belief in a fairy tale of transcendent consumption. This magical and unrealistic belief seems more intimately connected to compulsive consumption than does the self-punitive waste of money. Whatever the motivation for compulsive consumption, there can be extremely negative consequences to building a sense of self that is externally manifest, because the inner core self is likely to feel more and more empty and more vulnerable as this process continues over a lifetime. Moreover, when attempts to enhance self through accumulating possessions results in the compulsive acquisition of consumer goods, using purchasing as an intended mood enhancer and possessions to compensate for a lack of significant others in our lives, more psychological harm than good may result.

This does not mean that compulsive consumption is caused only by the desire for contributing to our extended self through ownership of possessions. The process of acquisition may be more likely than the process of possession to be the main source of gratification in compulsive buying. But whether or not this is the case may depend upon the degree of compulsion, as Schor (1998) argues:

> Using the same test [as Faber and O'Guinn 1992] on a group of mostly college students in Arizona, Allison Magee [1994] esti-mated 15–16 percent [are compulsive buyers]. (We know the tendency is greater among youth.) On the other hand, clini-cally defined compulsives may not be fundamentally different from "normal" consumers. They're just the extreme cases. Millions of ordinary people also exhibit high "generalized urges to buy." Indeed, an innocuous form of compulsive buy-ing appears to afflict one-quarter of us. This should probably come as no surprise in a country [the U.S.A.] where 41 percent of the population age 22–61 (and nearly half of all young

adults) say that "shopping makes me feel good" [Farkas and Johnson 1997, p. 159]

The more generous estimates of compulsive buying here are based on Natarajan and Goff (1991), who suggest that as many as one-fourth of Americans indulge in a relatively innocuous form of compulsive buying. These estimates are also consistent with others who view compulsive buying and normal buying as lying on a continuum rather than forming discrete categories (e.g., d'Astous 1990, Edwards 1993, Valence et al. 1988). Even more inclusively Frank (1999) concludes: "Fearing they will gamble too much, many people limit the amount of cash they take to Atlantic City. Fearing they will stay up too late watching TV, they move the television out of the bedroom. In varying degrees, Ainslie (1992) argues, we are all addicts of a sort, battling food, cigarettes, alcohol, TV sportscasts, detective novels, and a host of other seductive activities." [p. 185]

With such a view in mind, Lunt and Livingstone (1992) characterize the credit card-aided purchase of luxury goods as a seduction that makes self-discipline extremely difficult. Similar to the resistance tactics noted by Frank (1999), they identify a number of coping strategies by which consumers seek to impose a degree of self-control on their buying activities (Livingstone and Lunt 1992, Lunt and Livingstone 1992).

Still, certainly not all consumer buying or even all consumer buying that is intended to enlarge the extended self can be considered compulsive. Context is important. Sometimes the factor that motivates a compulsive purchase is a feeling of entitlement (Belk 1987b). But perhaps the most common situational condition that may shift a given purchase into a compulsive action is a sense of emptiness in the self, or what Wicklund and Gollwitzer (1982) characterize as the drive for symbolic self-completion. Ironically, as noted above, the greater the tendency for the person to rely on material possessions to constitute self, the greater the emptiness in sense of self that a compulsive shopper is likely to feel. This in turn is likely to stimulate further efforts to fill the void with attractive material goods, and the vicious cycle continues.

REFERENCES

Ainslie, G. (1992). *Picoeconomics*. New York: Cambridge University Press.

Ames, K. L. (1984). Material culture as nonverbal communication: a historical case study. In *American Material Culture: The Shape of Things Around Us*, ed. Edith Mayo, pp. 25–47. Bowling Green, OH: Bowling Green University Popular Press.

Anderson, L. J. (1985). The pet in the military family at transfer time: it is no small matter. In *Pets and the Family*, ed. M. B. Sussman, pp. 205–222. New York: Haworth.

Beaglehole, E. (1932). *Property: A Study in Social Psychology*. New York: Macmillan.

Belk, R. W. (1978). Assessing the effects of visible consumption on impression formation. In *Advances in Consumer Research*, vol. 5, ed. H. K. Hunt, pp. 39–47. Ann Arbor, MI: Association for Consumer Research.

—— (1982a). Acquisitiveness and possessiveness: criticisms and issues. In *Proceedings of the 1982 Convention of the American Psychological Association*, ed. M. B. Mazis, pp. 70–73. Washington, DC: Division 23, American Psychological Association.

—— (1982b). Acquiring, possessing, and collecting: fundamental processes in consumer behavior. In *Marketing Theory: Philosophy of Science Perspectives*, ed. R. F. Bush and S. D. Hunt, pp. 185–190. Chicago: American Marketing Association.

—— (1985). Materialism: trait aspects of living in the material world. *Journal of Consumer Research* 12:265–280.

—— (1987a). Identity and the relevance of market, personal, and community objects. In *Marketing and Semiotics: New Directions in the Study of Signs for Sale*, ed. J. Sebeok, pp. 151–164. Berlin: Mouton de Gruyter.

—— (1987b). Presidential address: happy thought. In *Advances in Consumer Research*, vol. 14, ed. M. Wallendorf and P. Anderson, pp. 1–4. Provo, UT: Association for Consumer Research.

—— (1988). Possessions and the extended self. *Journal of Consumer Research* 15 (2):139–168.

—— (1991a). Possessions and the sense of past. In *Highways and Buyways: Naturalistic Research from the Consumer Behavior Odyssey*, ed. R. W. Belk, pp. 114–130. Provo, UT: Association for Consumer Research.

—— (1991b). The ineluctable mysteries of possessions. *Journal of Social Behavior and Personality* 6 (6):17–55.

—— (1992). Moving possessions: an analysis based on personal documents from the 1847–1869 Mormon migration. *Journal of Consumer Research* 19:339–361.

—— (1995). *Collecting in a Consumer Society*. London: Routledge.

—— (1999). Money. In *The Elgar Companion to Consumer Research and Economic Psychology*, ed. P. Earl and S. Kemp, pp. 383–388. Aldershot, UK: Edward Elgar Publishing.

Belk, R. W., Bahn, K., and Mayer, R. (1982). Developmental recognition of consumption symbolism. *Journal of Consumer Research* 9:4–17.

Bellow, S. (1975). *Humboldt's Gift*. New York: Viking.

Bloch, P. (1981). An exploration into the scaling of consumers' involvement with a product class. In *Advances in Consumer Research*, vol. 8, ed. K. B. Monroe, pp. 637–641. Ann Arbor, MI: Association for Consumer Research.

—— (1982). Involvement beyond the purchase process: conceptual issues and empirical investigation. In *Advances in Consumer Research*, vol. 9, ed. A. Mitchell, pp. 413–417. Ann Arbor, MI: Association for Consumer Research.

Cameron, P. (1977). *The Life Cycle: Perspective and Commentary*. Oceanside, NY: Dabor Science Publications.

Csikszentmihalyi, M. (1982). *The symbolic function of possessions: towards a psychology of materialism*. Paper presented at 90th Annual Convention of the American Psychological Association, Washington, DC, August.

Csikszentmihalyi, M., and Rochberg-Halton, E. (1981). *The Meaning of Things: Domestic Symbols and the Self*. Cambridge: Cambridge University Press.

d'Astous, A. (1990). An inquiry into the compulsive side of "normal" consumers. *Journal of Consumer Policy* 13:15–31.

DeLillo, D. (1985). *White Noise.* New York: Viking Penguin.

Dittmar, H. (1992). *The Social Psychology of Material Possessions,* New York: St. Martin's Press.

Douglas, M. and Isherwood, B. (1979). *The World of Goods: Towards an Anthropology of Consumption.* New York: Norton.

Edwards, E. A. (1993). Development of a new scale for measuring compulsive buying behavior. *Financial Counseling and Planning* 4:67–84.

Ellen, R. (1988). Fetishism. *Man,* June, pp. 213–235.

Erikson, E. (1959). Identity and the Life Cycle. *Psychological Issues* 1:1–171.

Faber, R. J., and O'Guinn, T. C. (1992). A clinical screener for compulsive buying. *Journal of Consumer Research* 19:459–469.

Farkas, S., and Johnson, J. (1997). *Miles to Go: A Status Report on Americans' Plans for Retirement.* New York: Public Agenda Foundation.

Feibleman, J. K. (1975). *The Stages of Human Life: A Biography of Entire Man.* The Hague: Martinus Nijhoff.

Frank, R. H. (1999). *Luxury Fever: Why Money Fails to Satisfy in an Era of Excess.* New York: Free Press.

Fromm, E. (1976). *To Have or To Be.* New York: Harper & Row.

Furby, L. (1978). Sharing: decisions and moral judgments about letting others use one's possessions. *Psychological Reports* 43: 595–609.

—— (1980). The origins and early development of possessive behavior. *Political Psychology* 2:30–42.

Furby, L., and Wilke, M. (1982). Some characteristics of infants' preferred toys. *Journal of Genetic Psychology* 140:207–219.

Grubb, E. L., and Hupp, G. (1968). Perception of self, generalized stereotypes, and brand selection. *Journal of Marketing Research* 5:58–63.

Holman, R. (1981). Product use as communication. In *Review of Marketing,* ed. B. M. Enis and K. J. Roering, pp. 106–119. Chicago: American Marketing Association.

Horney, K. (1937). *The Neurotic Personality of Our Time.* New York: Norton, 1964.

Howell, S. C. (1983). The meaning of place in old age. In *Aging and*

Milieu: Environmental Perspectives on Growing Old, ed. G. D. Rowles and R. J. Ohta, pp. 97–107. New York: Academic Press.

Isaacs, S. (1933). *Social Development in Young Children*. London: Routledge.

—— (1935). Property and possessiveness. *British Journal of Medical Psychology* 15:69–78.

Jacobson, E., and Kossoff, J. (1963). Self-percept and consumer attitudes toward small cars. *Journal of Applied Psychology* 47: 242–245.

Jaeger, B. (1983). Body, house, city or the intertwinings of embodiment. In *The Changing Reality of Modern Man*, ed. D. Kruger, pp. 51–59. Pittsburgh: Duquesne University Press.

James, W. (1890). *The Principles of Psychology*, vol. 1. New York: Henry Holt.

Kamptner, N. L. (1989). Personal possessions and their meaning in old age. In *The Social Psychology of Aging*, ed. S. Spacapan and S. Oskamp, pp. 165–196. Newbury Park, CA: Sage.

Kates, D. B., Jr., and Varzos, N. (1987). *Aspects of the priapic theory of gun ownership*. Paper presented at the 1987 Popular Culture Association Meetings. Montreal, March.

Kline, L. W., and France, C. J. (1899). The psychology of ownership. *Pedagogical Seminary* 6 (4):421–470.

Kopytoff, I. (1986). The cultural biography of things: commoditization as process. In *The Social Life of Things: Commodities in Cultural Perspective*, ed. A. Appadurai, pp. 64–91. Cambridge: Cambridge University Press.

Levi-Strauss, C. (1962/1963). *Totemism*. Boston: Beacon.

Lewis, M., and Brooks, J. (1978). Self, other, and fear: infants' reactions to people. In *The Origins of Fear*, ed. M. Lewis and L. A. Rosenbaum, pp. 165–194. New York: Wiley.

Lichtenberg, J. (1989). *Psychoanalysis and Motivation*. Hillsdale, NJ: Analytic Press.

Lifton, R. J. (1973). The sense of immortality: on death and the continuity of life. *American Journal of Psychoanalysis* 33(1):3–15.

Livingstone, M. S., and Lunt, P. K. (1992). Everyday conceptions of necessities and luxuries: problems of cultural relativity and moral judgment. In *New Directions in Economic Psychology: Theory, Experiment and Application*, ed. S. E. G. Lea, P. Webley, and B. Young, pp. 28–48. Aldershot, UK: Edward Elgar.

Locke, J. (1690). *Two Treatises of Government*. Oxford: Oxford University Press.

Lowenthal, D. (1975). Past time, present place: landscape and memory. *Geographical Review* 65 (1):1–36.

Lunt, P. K., and Livingstone, S. M. (1992). *Mass Consumption and Personal Identity: Everyday Economic Experience*. Buckingham, UK: Open University Press.

Magee, A. (1994). Compulsive buying tendency as a predictor of attitudes and perceptions. *Advances in Consumer Research*, vol. 21, pp. 590–594. Provo, UT: Association for Consumer Research.

Marx, K. (1842). The centralization question. In *Writings of the Young Marx on Philosophy and Society*, ed. and trans. L. D. Easton and K. Guddat, pp. 106–108. Garden City, NY: Anchor Books, 1967.

—— (1844). Critique of Hegelian philosophy of the right — introduction. *Deutsch-französische Jahrbücher/ Karl Marx: Early Writings*. New York: Vantage, 1975.

—— (1867). *Capital: A Critique of Political Economy*, vol. 1, trans. B. Fawkes. Harmondsworth, UK: Penguin. 1978.

McCarthy, E. D. (1984). Toward a sociology of the physical world: George Herbert Mead on physical objects. In *Studies in Symbolic Interaction*, vol. 5, ed. N. K. Denzen, pp. 105–121. Greenwich, CT: JAI Press.

McClelland, D. (1951). *Personality*. New York: Holt, Rinehart, and Winston.

McCracken, G. (1987). Culture and consumption among the elderly: three research objectives in an emerging field. *Aging and Society* 7 (2):203–224.

—— (1988). *Culture and Consumption: New Approaches to the Symbolism of Consumer Goods and Activities*. Bloomington, IN: Indiana University Press.

Mick, D. G. (1996). Self-gifts. In *Gift Giving: A Research Anthology*, ed. C. Otnes and R. F. Beltramini, pp. 99–116. Bowling Green, OH: Bowling Green University Popular Press.

Mick, D. G., and DeMoss, M. (1990). Self-Gifts: phenomenological insights from four contexts. *Journal of Consumer Research* 17: 322–332.

Muensterberger, W. (1994). *Collecting: The Unruly Passion*. Princeton, NJ: Princeton University Press.

Munson, J. M., and Spivey, W. A. (1980). Assessing self-concept. In *Advances in Consumer Research*, vol. 7, ed. J. C. Olson, pp. 598–603. Ann Arbor, MI: Association for Consumer Research.

Myers, E. (1985). Phenomenological analysis of the importance of special possessions: an exploratory study. In *Advances in Consumer Research*, vol. 12, ed. E. C. Hirschman and M. B. Holbrook, pp. 560–565. Provo, UT: Association for Consumer Research.

Nataraajan, R., and Goff, B. G. (1991). Compulsive buying: towards a reconceptualization. *Journal of Social Behavior and Personality* 6(6):307–328.

Nemy, E. (1986). Security blankets never really vanish. *New York Times Magazine*, February 16, p. 73.

Niederland, W. G., and Sholevar, B. (1981). The creative process—a psychoanalytic discussion. *The Arts in Psychotherapy* 8:71–101.

O'Guinn, T. C., and Faber, R. J. (1989). Compulsive buying: a phenomenological exploration. *Journal of Consumer Research* 16:147–157.

Olson, C. D. (1981). *Artifacts in the home and relational communication: a preliminary report*. Unpublished master's thesis, University of Utah Department of Psychology.

—— (1985). Materialism in the home: the impact of artifacts on dyadic communication. In *Advances in Consumer Research*, vol. 12, ed. E. Hirschman and M. Holbrook, pp. 388–393.

Passman, R. H. (1976). Arousal reducing properties of attachment objects: testing the functional limits of the security blanket relative to the mother. *Developmental Psychology* 12:468–469.

Passman, R. H., and Halonen, J. S. (1979). A developmental survey of young children's attachments to inanimate objects. *Journal of Genetic Psychology* 134:165–178.

Prelinger, E. (1959). Extension and structure of the self. *Journal of Psychology* 47:13–23.

Rigby, D., and Rigby, E. (1949). *Lock, Stock and Barrel: The Story of Collecting*, Philadelphia: Lippincott.

Rochberg-Halton, E. (1984). Object relations, role models, and cultivation of the self. *Environment and Behavior* 16 (3):335–368.

——— (1986). *Meaning and Modernity.* Chicago: University of Chicago Press.

Ross, I. (1971). Self-concept and brand preference. *Journal of Business* 44:38–50.

Sartre, J. P. (1956). *Being and Nothingness: A Phenomenological Essay on Ontology.* New York: Philosophical Library.

Schor, J. B. (1998). *The Overspent American: Upscaling, Downshifting, and the New Consumer.* New York: Basic Books.

Seligman, M. E. P. (1975). *Helplessness: Depression, Death and Development.* San Francisco: Freeman.

Sherman, E., and Newman, E. S. (1977). The meaning of cherished personal possessions for the elderly. *International Journal of Aging and Human Development* 8 (2):181–192.

Sherry, J. F., Jr., McGrath, M. A., and Levy, S. J. (1995). Egocentric consumption: anatomy of gifts given to the self. In *Contemporary Marketing and Consumer Behavior: An Anthropological Sourcebook.* Thousand Oaks, CA: Sage.

Solomon, M. (1986). Deep-seated materialism: the case of Levi's 501 jeans. In *Advances in Consumer Research*, vol. 13, ed. R. J. Lutz, pp. 520–521. Provo, UT: Association for Consumer Research.

Stein, B. (1985). The machine makes this man. *Wall Street Journal*, June 13, p. 30.

Stone, H. S., Jr. (1966). Youth and motorcycles. In *The Man Made Objects*, ed. G. Kepes, pp. 172–185. Los Angeles: Studio Vista Publishers.

Tanay, E., with Freeman, L. (1976). *The Murderers.* Indianapolis, IN: Bobbs-Merrill.

Tuan, Y-F. (1984). *Dominance and Affection: The Making of Pets.* New Haven, CT: Yale University Press.

Valence, G., d'Astous, A., and Fortier, L. (1988). Compulsive buying: concept and measurement. *Journal of Consumer Policy* 11:419–433.

Wallendorf, M. and Arnould, E. (1988). My favorite things: a cross-cultural inquiry into object attachment, possessiveness and social linkage. *Journal of Consumer Research* 14:531–547.

Wallendorf, M., and Belk, R. (1987). Deep meaning in possessions, video. Cambridge, MA: Marketing Science Institute.

Weiland, J. H. (1955). The adolescent and the automobile. *Chicago Review* 9:61–64.

Weisberg, P., and Russell, J. E. (1971). Proximity and interactional behavior of young children to their "security" blankets. *Child Development* 42:1575–1579.

White, R. W. (1959). Motivation reconsidered: the concept competence. *Psychological Review* 66:313–324.

Wicklund, R. A., and Gollwitzer, P. M. (1982). *Symbolic Self Completion*. Hillsdale, NJ: Lawrence Erlbaum.

Winnicott, D. W. (1953). Transitional objects and transitional phenomena. *International Journal of Psychoanalysis* 34:89–97.

Wright, N. D., Clairborne, C. B., and. Sirgy, M. J. (1992). The effects of product symbolism on consumer self-concept. *Advances in Consumer Research* 19:311–318.

5

The Role of Self-Image in Excessive Buying[1]

Helga Dittmar

OVERVIEW

Thus far, the main perspective on compulsive buying or shopping addiction has been a clinical model that treats excessive buying as similar to other types of psychiatric disorders (e.g., impulse control disorders, compulsive-obsessive disorders). This assumes that excessive buying is a deviant activity, qualitatively distinct from ordinary consumer behavior. In contrast, this chapter proposes that there are underlying social psychological mechanisms centered on consumers' self-concept that play a role in *both* ordinary and excessive impulse buying. From this perspective, excessive (or

1. The research summarized in this chapter was supported by Economic and Social Research Council grant L122251012 as part of the Economic Beliefs and Behavior Program. Special thanks go to Susanne Friese who worked as a research assistant on the project, to Rod Bond for his help with the discounting data analysis, and to Peter Taylor-Gooby for his support and help as program director. I would particularly like to acknowledge the invaluable contribution of Jane Beattie (co-grant holder), who worked with me on all aspects of the research reported until her tragic death shortly before the project ended.

"compulsive") buyers have two main characteristics. They believe that consumer goods are an important route toward success, identity, and happiness, and they purchase these goods to bolster their self-image, drawing on the symbolic meanings associated with products in an attempt to bridge gaps between how they see themselves (actual self), how they wish to be (ideal self), and how they wish to be seen (ideal self). This model is intended to complement existing theories rather than replace them, because excessive buying is most likely multidetermined. The claim that the motivation to bolster self-image is a significant — if not the only — factor in excessive buying was examined in a series of studies that use different methodologies — including questionnaires, shopping diaries, and in-depth interviews. The findings provide support for the social psychological model proposed and have implications for treatment of the "compulsion" to buy excessively.

Excessive buying is used in this chapter, because it seems preferable to the terms *compulsive buying* or *shopping addiction* used more commonly. It avoids the assumption, built into the term *compulsive* buying, that consumers experience shopping as an activity over which they have absolutely no control and which has only negative emotional aspects. This notion of an involuntary and unenjoyable habit sits uneasily with frequent reports from excessive buyers that they experience an emotional high when shopping. Excessive buying is also useful in that it does not assume that this behavior is best conceived of as an addiction. Some perspectives on addiction as a temporary relief from anxiety, stress, and/or low self-esteem would support this view, but others would prefer to see the term reserved for chemical substance abuse with a directly discernible physiological dependence.

SELF-IMAGE — IS IT IN THE BAG?

Both excessive buyers and normal buyers often purchase goods that they believe will enhance their self-image. This can be seen in the interview excerpt given below, in which an excessive buyer describes the relationship between her impulse purchases and her identity. She tried to use expensive consumer goods to move closer to an ideal self-image, in the eyes of both others and herself:

> I felt really depressed about myself. And when I've analyzed it now, I think I probably wanted to make myself feel that I was something better than I was. And so to do that, I bought expensive clothes, expensive make-up, expensive perfumes and things. Got it all on the store cards from a big department store. 'Cause I used to dress up really smart and I used to think, "Oh, the shop assistants probably think I've got loads of money and I'm this sort of person," and I enjoyed getting them because of that really. [*Interviewer*: What kind of person?] I think it was kind of a smartly dressed, young, trendy woman that you see around the places, who can afford to wear designer labels and show them off and have Chanel make-up and that kind of thing. The sort of image that they portray in the make-up stalls in the big department store. And the way the girls are always so nice to you, and all around there's the pictures and the images. And seeing those started me off. It was the make-up I started off in first and then went on to the clothes. And the clothes I chose were like the clothes that were in the make-up adverts. [Dittmar and Drury, in press]

Rather than being read only as the personal account of an individual suffering from compulsive buying, this narrative needs to be understood in the context of profound social and cultural changes in developed Western economies over the last two decades. These changes have transformed shopping — in the United States maybe even more strongly than in Europe. Alongside developments in "modern" consumer spending, such as marked increases in personal disposable incomes and mushrooming credit facilities, there are important shifts in the significance of, and motivations for, buying consumer goods. Consumption has come to play an increasingly stronger psychological role in people's lives (Dittmar and Beattie 1998).

These changes may help explain why shopping now seems to have an increasing potential to become dysfunctional for consumers. "Pathological" buying is not an altogether new phenomenon, but it has reached proportions as a widespread problem only recently. Empirical studies on shopping addiction or compulsive buying have been carried out in the last ten years in the U.S. (Hanley and Wilhelm 1992, O'Guinn and Faber, 1989), Canada (Valence et al. 1988), Germany (Scherhorn et al. 1990), Belgium (Vlerick, personal communication 1998), and the U.K. (Elliott 1994). None of these are prevalence studies, but their findings suggest that such extreme buying behavior is on the increase. The one prevalence study that exists (Faber and O'Guinn 1992) suggests that extreme buying behavior may affect an estimated 2 to 5 percent of adults in developed Western economies. To give a concrete example, even if the more conservative 2 percent estimate is used, when turned into actual numbers, this implies that more than five million adults in the U.S. could be affected.

A consideration of the cultural context of shopping and the social psychological functions consumer goods fulfill for people can help in developing a new perspective on excessive buying (Dittmar et al. 1996). Shopping is changing in nature in Britain, the United States, and the rest of the advanced Western economies. A former focus on buying provisions to satisfy the physical needs of oneself and one's family has shifted toward using consumer goods as a modern means of acquiring and expressing a sense of self-identity (Dittmar 1992a), regulating emotions (Elliott 1994) or gaining social status (McCracken 1990). Shopping has thus changed for a substantial segment of consumers from the acquisition of necessities to a major leisure and lifestyle activity. Americans now spend more time in the shopping mall than at any other single location besides work and home (Bloch et al. 1991), and an English survey identified 25 percent of their sample as predominantly leisure buyers (as opposed, for example, to thrifty or routine buyers), who buy goods as rewards for self and others, and buy on impulse (Lunt and Livingstone 1992).

Social psychological research on the meanings and functions of personal possessions converges with this literature in asserting that material goods can and do function as symbols of self. Belk (1988; Chapter 4, this volume) demonstrates that people perceive a whole range of material objects as an actual part of their self, and concludes that material objects can be viewed as self-extensions. Dittmar's reviews of this literature and her own empirical studies show that material possessions are intimately involved in the expression of one's own self-identity as well as in perceptions and judgments about other people's self-identity (Dittmar 1989, 1991, 1992a,b, 1994, Dittmar et al. 1996). The argument that consumer goods can and do function as material symbols of who a person is and who they would like to be is the central tenet of the social psychological perspective introduced in this chapter.

CLINICAL MODELS AND A NEW SOCIAL PSYCHOLOGICAL PERSPECTIVE

Models of impulsive and excessive buying can be found in economics, consumer research, and psychology, but they are disjointed theoretically and methodologically (Dittmar et al. 1995, 1996). These models are discussed elsewhere with particular reference to impulse buying (Dittmar, in press), while this chapter focuses on a brief consideration of clinical perspectives on excessive buying, including consumer research literature that takes a clinically informed approach.

Compulsive buying is not listed (as yet) as a psychiatric disorder in its own right in the current diagnostic manual used by clinicians, the *DSM-IV* (American Psychiatric Association 1994) — but it is included in the category "impulse control disorders not otherwise specified." In the mainstream clinical perspective, excessive buying is seen as closely linked with, or similar to, one or more general psychiatric disorders, including impulse control disorders and compulsions or addictions (Black et al. 1998, McElroy et al. 1994). A recent American clinical study reports that 95.8 percent of sufferers described buying that resembled an impulse control disorder (Christenson et al. 1994), while work in Germany proposes that the shopping high reported by sufferers can be better understood in an addiction framework (Scherhorn et al. 1990). Other clinical research argues that excessive buying should be treated as a distinct psychiatric disorder, but one that has high

comorbidity with other disorders, such as mood, anxiety, substance use, eating, or personality disorders (Black 1998, Schlosser
et al. 1994). In more phenomenologically oriented consumer research, compulsive shopping is described as an inability to control
an overpowering impulse to buy (O'Guinn and Faber 1989) or as
excessive impulsive consumption (Faber et al. 1987).

This approach assumes that excessive buying is a deviant
activity, qualitatively distinct from ordinary consumer behavior,
without considering that there may be underlying social psychological mechanisms related to consumers' self-concept that play a
role in *both* ordinary and excessive impulse buying. Although
many of these studies report that excessive buyers purchase certain types of goods much more frequently than others, this tends to
be treated as an incidental finding rather than as a central characteristic requiring explanation. There seems to be a common assumption that the purchase activity is more important to excessive
buyers than the goods obtained, which is implicit in the psychiatric
literature and explicit in some of the consumer research literature.
For instance, O'Guinn and Faber (1989) found that compulsive
buyers scored no higher on possessiveness measures than a "normal" comparison sample. On the basis of this particular finding,
notwithstanding that compulsive buyers were higher on an overall
measure of materialism, they claim that "the desire to own products is not a primary motivation behind this behavioral problem"
(p. 155). In summary, clinical models and clinically oriented consumer research cannot explain a striking feature of excessive
buying: why it is that some types of consumer goods are common
favorites for excessive buyers (e.g., fashionable clothes) while
others hardly ever inspire an irresistible urge to buy (e.g., basic
kitchen equipment).

A New Social Psychological Model

Taking into account the changed context of buying behavior and
the social psychological functions that consumer goods fulfill for
people leads to a new perspective in which goods are linked to

consumers' self-concept because they function as important material symbols of personal and social identity (Dittmar 1992a,b, 1996). Buying goods to bolster one's self-image is probably a motivation that plays a role in most buying behavior, but I propose here that it is particularly important when people engage in impulse buying — in spur of the moment purchases not thought through and planned for. Symbolic self-completion theory (Wicklund and Gollwitzer 1982) proposes that perceiving shortcomings in oneself produces a motivation to compensate. Among diverse strategies this can involve acquiring and using material symbols that are relevant to those aspects of self that are felt to be lacking. For instance, by displaying a recognized masculine symbol, such as wearing a black leather motorcycle suit, a young man can compensate for not feeling masculine enough through using the object to tell both himself and others that he is indeed masculine. To determine whether an individual uses consumption as a symbolic self-completion strategy rather than for filling an actual need, the studies used here drew on Richins and Dawson's (1992) conceptualization of materialism. They see this characteristic as an individual value orientation where the acquisition of material goods is a central life goal, prime indicator of success, and key to happiness and self-definition. We also used Higgins's (1987) conceptualization of self-discrepancies between actual self (how an individual sees her- or himself) and ideal self (how he or she would ideally wish to be). Since our research is the first application of self-discrepancies to buying behavior, we designed our own measure for the project.

Our theoretical model is described in more detail elsewhere (Dittmar et al. 1996, Dittmar and Beattie 1998), but it can be presented schematically as in Figure 5–1, where arrows present causal links. In other words, according to this figure, if an individual is high in self-discrepancies *and* is prone to use material goods as compensation, then he or she should buy a lot on impulse, be motivated by mood and self-image buying considerations, and should have high excessive-buying tendencies. It is important to emphasize at this point that we do not propose that self-discrepancies are the *only* reason for impulsive and excessive buying, rather they are multidetermined. However, we do propose that a conjunction of high self-discrepancies and materialism will lead to such buying behavior.

The main objective of the research project was to develop and test a social psychological model of impulse buying behavior in ordinary and excessive ("compulsive") buyers. This model proposes that buying consumer goods can be understood as an attempt to bolster self-image and personal identity. Several general hypotheses can be derived from this model for empirical study:

- Some consumer goods make more likely impulse buys than others.
- When consumers buy on impulse and excessively, having the goods is as important to them as the shopping experience.
- Self-image concerns are a particularly important motivation in impulsive and excessive buying.
- Systematic differences exist between excessive and ordinary consumers in impulse buying, self-concept, and consumption values, and buying behavior can be predicted from a person's self-discrepancies if they hold materialistic values.

QUANTITATIVE AND QUALITATIVE RESEARCH METHODS

These hypotheses were tested in three linked studies that drew on different methodological approaches (this description has appeared previously in Dittmar, in press). Derived from experimental decision-making methodology, we developed a computer-run study on discount rates for different consumer goods (this is reported in Dittmar and Bond 1999). A postal survey was used to collect questionnaire measures of planned and impulsive buying behavior, buying motivations, shopping attitudes, and self-concept. We also carried out qualitative research on impulse buying by using in-depth interviews and shopping diaries. These quantitative and qualitative methods should produce convergent data on the hypotheses under consideration.

FIGURE 5–1.

Social psychological model of impulsive and excessive buying

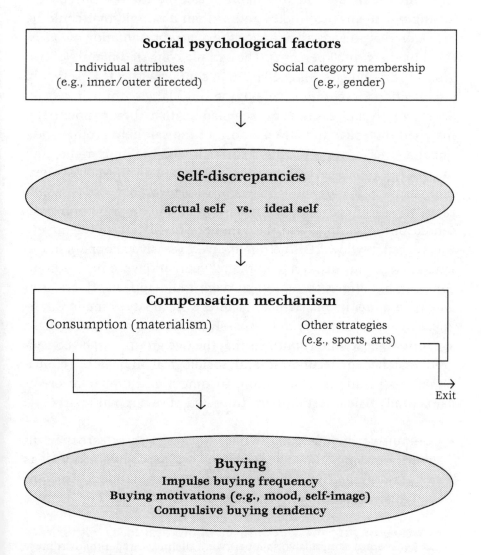

Reprinted from "Objects, Decision Considerations and Self-Image in Men's and Women's Impulse Purchases," *Acta Psychologica* (1996) 93: 192, by H. Dittmar, J. Beattie, and S. Friese, by permission of Elsevier Science B. V. Publishers.

Postal survey. The final sample of the mail survey consisted of 331 respondents, who were classified as either ordinary (n=236) or excessive (n=95) buyers. Our strategy of contacting respondents was aimed explicitly at producing a sample for the purpose of testing our theoretical model rather than a sample that could be considered representative (hence the overrepresentation of excessive buyers with 29 percent). The sample consisted mainly of two groups: respondents who had been in contact with a U.K. self-help organization for "compulsive" buying and a larger group of respondents whose addresses were selected so that they residentially matched (by town and street) those of the self-help group. Additional addresses were obtained through "snowballing," radio, and newspaper appeals. The overall response rate for this postal questionnaire was 56 percent, which compares favorably with standard rates of around 30 to 40 percent. Women buyers are overrepresented in the sample, and the number of male excessive buyers was regrettably low. (Of the ninety-five excessive shoppers in the mail survey, only sixteen [less than 20 percent] were men despite considerable efforts to recruit through radio appeals, flyers, and advertisements in magazines.) There were no systematic differences between ordinary and excessive buyers apart from a slight age difference,[2] which confirms that the two groups can be considered matched on economic and sociological indicators (educational qualifications, occupation, income, and number of credit cards used). The questionnaire consisted of seven main parts:

- Compulsive buying scale, which was used as a "screener" to divide the sample into excessive and ordinary buyers as well as to gain a graded measure of an individual's tendency toward compulsive shopping (d'Astous et al. 1990)

---

2. On average, compulsive shoppers were slightly younger than ordinary shoppers, which is consistent with the claim that excessive buying has become more common only recently and therefore would be more likely found among younger consumers. Age was not consistently related to any of the dependent variables of interest.

- Rated frequency of buying nine types of durable consumer goods as planned purchases (including, clothes or kitchen equipment)
- Buying motivations for planned purchases (including functional, mood-related, and self-image motivations)
- Self-discrepancy measure (developed for this project). This consisted of respondents completing the sentence *"I am . . . . , but I would like to be . . . . . ."* repeatedly, and then rating the size and salience of each self-discrepancy
- Frequency of buying the same nine types of goods as impulse purchases
- Buying motivations for impulse purchases
- Materialism scale, used as a proxy measure for the extent to which an individual uses consumption as a compensation strategy (Richins and Dawson 1992). An example item is "Some of the most important achievements in life include acquiring material possessions."

Respondents in the mail survey were asked whether they were willing to participate in follow-up studies, and the final sample for the qualitative studies consisted of sixty-one respondents. The number of compulsive male buyers in these follow-up studies was so small that they were excluded from analysis, and systematic comparisons were therefore made between three buyer groups: excessive women buyers, ordinary women buyers, and ordinary men buyers.

Qualitative studies. These consisted of respondents keeping a shopping diary and being interviewed in depth. In the diary they recorded each impulse purchase of durable consumer goods over a period of four weeks, including information about:

- Item bought
- Global evaluation of how good or bad they felt about themselves during three phases of their shopping trip (just before purchase, just after, after getting home)
- Open-ended accounts of their thoughts and feelings during the same three phases

The format for reporting thoughts and feelings was unstructured, chosen with the explicit rationale that respondents would be more likely to record those concerns most salient to them than when prompted by constructs developed by the researchers. In-depth interviews were carried out with respondents when the completed shopping diary was collected. (For some of the respondents farthest away from where the research was conducted, shopping diaries were returned by mail and the interview was carried out over the telephone to economize on traveling costs.) Ten interviews each with "ordinary" women and men buyers, and ten interviews with women excessive buyers were selected for in-depth thematic analysis (reported in more detail in Dittmar and Drury, in press). Three themes are of central interest for this chapter:

- Respondents' own understanding and experience of impulse and planned buying
- Features of a typical impulse buying episode (including motivations, situational influences, consumer goods bought, method of payment, and the act of buying)
- Relationship of shopping to self (including self-image and self-discrepancies)

Main findings. The main findings of the research project are presented here under four headings, drawing on the survey and qualitative studies together, rather than discussing results from each study in turn. These findings have previously been presented in Dittmar (in press) and in Dittmar and Drury (in press).

TYPES OF CONSUMER GOODS AND IMPULSE BUYING

When examining whether some types of consumer goods make more likely impulse purchases than others, it is important to take into account not only how often an item is bought on impulse, but also how often it is a planned purchase. For instance, if a consumer buys an item very frequently indeed — but as a planned rather than an impulse purchase — taking only the raw impulse buying frequency would be misleading. From the buying frequencies reported in the mail survey, we therefore constructed an *impulsivity index*, which allows us to ascertain which goods are most likely to be bought on impulse, relative to their planned purchasing frequency. It can vary between −1.0 (the item is always bought in a planned fashion and never on impulse) and +1.0 (the item is bought exclusively on impulse and never planned). If an item is bought equally frequently on impulse and planned, then the impulsivity index is zero.

The types of goods that make the two most likely impulse buys — clothes and jewelry — seem closely linked to self-image and appearance, in contrast to the two types of goods least likely to be bought on impulse — practical footwear and body care products. Means for ordinary and excessive buyers are shown in Figure 5–2. With one exception these are negative, indicating that most goods are bought slightly more often planned than on impulse, but there are clear relative differences between types of consumer goods. Excessive buyers do more (proportional) impulse buying than ordinary buyers overall, but the difference is greater on the high-impulse goods (clothes and jewelry).

In addition to differences between ordinary and excessive buyers, there were also differences between women and men, confirming that gender influences which types of goods are bought on impulse (Dittmar and Beattie 1998).

The approach taken in the mail survey — asking respondents to report buying frequencies (as well as buying motivations) separately when purchasing goods planned and on impulse — assumes (1) that consumers are able to draw a clear distinction between planned and impulse buying, and (2) that their behavior is actually organized in terms of these two distinct modes of buying. Are these two types of buying actually distinct activities that can be meaningfully contrasted in terms of underlying motivations — as we assumed — or do most purchase decisions involve both planning and impulse to some extent? For instance, the decision to buy oneself some appearance booster (such as clothes or jewelry) involves some intention to purchase a particular category of con-

FIGURE 5–2.

Excessive and ordinary buyers' impulse buying of four types of
goods (two highest and two lowest on impulsivity index)

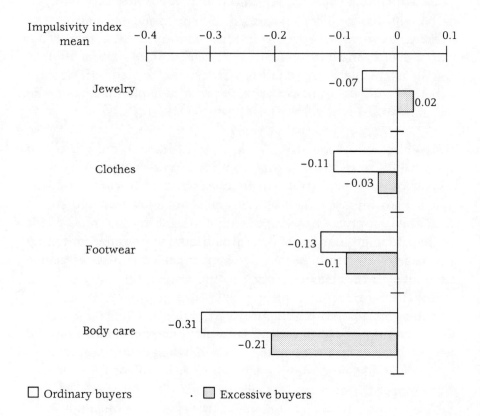

☐ Ordinary buyers   · ☐ Excessive buyers

Reprinted from "Impulse Buying in Ordinary and 'Compulsive' Consumers,"
in *Conflict and Tradeoffs in Decision-Making*, by H. Dittmar; volume edited by
J. Baron, G. Loomes, and E. Weber (in press), by permission of Cambridge
University Press.

sumer product, although the exact item or shop is not planned in
advance. The in-depth interviews were used to check the validity
of our approach by eliciting spontaneous commonsense definitions of impulse versus planned buying. Responses in the interviews confirmed a consensus among both ordinary and excessive
buyers that planned buying is clearly distinguished from impulse

buying: consumers act like rational decision-makers — they shop around and choose the best value within their financial constraints. This consensus is typified in this excerpt:

> Well, it's in the process of home-making or home-improvement that my wife and I set out to look for a particular piece of furniture, or when we're replacing kitchen units and kitchen flooring or whatever, we then go out week after week looking and researching that. Looking at prices, comparing articles and finding the right colors. A planned expedition. [*Male ordinary buyer*]

Definitions of impulse buying were more diverse but characterized by little deliberation; psychological motivations (desire, treat, thrill) overtook financial considerations. Women emphasize emotional aspects of impulse buying more than men, and the lack of regard for financial consequences becomes extreme for excessive buyers who find the urge to buy irresistible. This response gives a flavor of the experience of impulse buying:

> It's some kind of excitement. You give yourself a little thrill as if you were younger, when you were a child or a teenager having a ride at one of those merry-go-rounds at the fair. It's sort of a little bit like that. It can be exhilarating. [*Woman ordinary buyer*]

The commonsense understanding and experience of impulse buying is clearly a far cry from the definitions of planned buying, validating the conceptualization of pure impulse and pure planned buying as opposite extremes of consumer behavior.

The shopping diaries enabled a comparison between the self-report ratings in the mail survey and actual impulse buying behavior. Clothes and accessories (e.g., handbags) were the most frequent impulse buys, constituting more than a third of all reported purchases. In contrast, kitchen items were hardly reported at all. Although the impulsivity rank order of consumer goods in the diary study does not exactly match the impulsivity index derived from the mail survey, there is considerable agreement on which items make more and less likely impulse purchases. Impulse-buy frequency differed between the buyer groups, with excessive women buyers reporting a higher number of impulse purchases per month than ordinary buyers. Thus the diary findings replicate and support the results from the mail survey.

CONSUMER GOODS BOUGHT
VERSUS THE SHOPPING EXPERIENCE

An important issue in impulse buying concerns the relative importance of the shopping experience compared to the acquisition of particular goods. In clinical and clinically informed consumer research perspectives on shopping addiction or compulsive buying, sufferers are often portrayed as hooked on the thrill of the shopping experience and spending money, and as less concerned with the actual goods they obtain (O'Guinn and Faber 1989). In contrast, our social psychological model suggests that the goods bought are equally important, if not more so, because goods typically bought on impulse are those that are particularly relevant to self-presentation and self-image. In the in-depth interview study, respondents were asked directly which was more important for them, the actual buying process or having the goods. Three types of responses were identified, as illustrated below with verbatim quotes.

First, there was a clear consensus among male buyers, and most of them were explicit in stating that having the goods is more important to them than the shopping experience: "I like shopping, but having the goods is most important" [*Male ordinary buyer*].

Second, women buyers gave rather different and more elaborated responses. It became clear that they like the actual buying, the shopping experience, but having the goods is also seen as important: "I like going out and buying the things, but I think probably actually having the end product is more important. That's the reason for going out now; certainly nowadays my reason for going out shopping is to buy something and so it's once I've actually bought the product that I'm happiest" [*Ordinary woman buyer*].

Third, the narratives of excessive women buyers are more diverse. Over half answered similarly to ordinary women buyers, by emphasizing that both the goods and the shopping experience are important. However, three mentioned that the act of buying itself gave a high like a drug, and this is typified in this response:

> It's like a taste in my mouth, a dry mouth, a ringing in my ears, believe it or not. Sometimes my vision will . . . I'll be swaying a bit, I'll have to reach out for something to steady myself. And I've often thought I'm having an attack, an anxiety attack or whatever, but it can't be, because it seems to be every time I'm going in to spend money. And then when I've spent the money, I start to come down a bit. [*Excessive woman buyer*]

The preceding quote supports the clinical perspective, but it appears to apply to a minority of excessive women buyers interviewed. However, given the small sample size, this finding must be regarded as speculative. Perhaps a related finding is more important: even when an excessive buyer talked this way, there is evidence that she would not buy just anything.

Thus, in support of the social psychological model presented here, the actual goods bought are seen as important as, or even more important than, the shopping experience itself. Only a minority of women excessive buyers reported that the buying activity itself was more important, and even then there was a clear indication that certain types of goods were nevertheless selected.

This qualitative finding is validated and supported further by quantitative results from the mail survey. In the questionnaire respondents were not asked directly for a decision about which of these two aspects of impulse buying (the activity and the goods bought) was more important to them. Instead, they responded on two independent rating scales, one asking them to indicate the extent to which they got enjoyment from goods bought, the other about enjoyment from the shopping experience. There was a systematic difference between ordinary and excessive buyers in the sense that excessive buyers gave higher ratings for *both* enjoyment from goods and enjoyment from the shopping experience. However, the main finding, again in support of the social psychological model presented, was that all buyers — ordinary and excessive, women and men — reported getting significantly more enjoyment out of the products they bought rather than out of the shopping atmosphere and experience.

UNDERLYING MOTIVATIONS IN IMPULSE BUYING

Findings from the mail survey confirm that high-impulse goods (such as clothes and jewelry) are bought for different reasons than low-impulse goods (such as practical footwear and body care products). For the latter, functional motivations were rated most important: consumers are concerned with whether the purchase is a good value for the money and whether it is practical or useful. In other words, they behave like rational decision-makers. For high-impulse goods, however, psychological buying motivations became more powerful than price and usefulness. Consumers buy because the purchase "puts me in a better mood," "makes me feel more like the person I want to be," and "expresses what is unique about me." Intending to bolster one's self-image and mood thus were rated as particularly salient in impulse buying.

The importance of self-image gains was confirmed in the open-ended accounts of impulse purchases given in the shopping diary. Four different buying motivations were mentioned often enough to be coded,[3] that is, subjects reported it for at least a quarter of their impulse buys. Those four were mood improvement (20 percent), self-image gain (52 percent), usefulness (48 percent), and good value for the money (52 percent). These are not mutually exclusive as respondents could, and often did, state more than one motivation for an impulse purchase. Thus, while func-

---

3. The coding system developed for the diaries showed excellent inter-rater reliability: the mean agreement per category was 93 percent.

tional concerns (usefulness and price) clearly were important motivations in impulse buying, self-image gains were reported to play an equally strong role as an anticipated benefit. Mood change appeared comparatively less important.

In the survey the differences between buying motivations for goods often bought on impulse compared to goods hardly ever bought on impulse were similar for ordinary and excessive buyers: functional concerns decrease, psychological concerns increase. However, the relative importance of different types of buying motivations diverges for these two groups of consumers. Referring to high-impulse goods, Figure 5–3 shows these differences for three types of decision considerations: functional ("good value for

FIGURE 5–3.

Excessive and ordinary buyers' motivations
when buying high-impulse goods

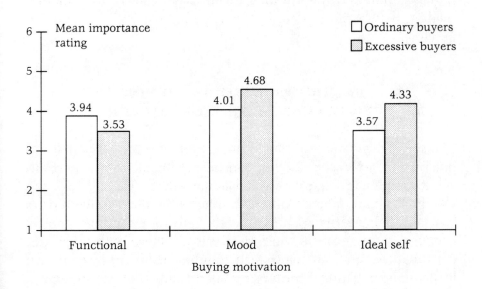

Reprinted from "Impulse Buying in Ordinary and 'Compulsive' Consumers," in *Conflict and Tradeoffs in Decision-Making,* by H. Dittmar; volume edited by J. Barton, G. Loomes, and E. Weber (in press), by permission of Cambridge University Press.

the money," "useful"), mood ("puts me in a better mood"), and ideal self ("makes me feel more like the person I want to be").

Differences between the two buyer groups are significant for each of these buying motivations. Functional considerations are relatively less important for excessive than for ordinary buyers, and the psychological considerations are more important. The largest difference occurs in the category of buying in order to feel "more like the person I want to be," that is, to move closer to their ideal self. Excessive buyers were much more likely to be motivated by this than were ordinary buyers.

The aim of improving self-image is not always achieved, as shown by findings from the shopping diaries. Reported self-image gains were coded both as a motivation before purchase and a descriptor afterwards (with the criterion that self-image had been stated for at least a quarter of the purchases). Patterns over time are especially interesting here. Only 18 percent of excessive women buyers reported actual self-image gains after getting the purchase home, while self-image gains were clearly a strong motivation before the purchase, stated by almost half of them (46 percent).

PREDICTING EXCESSIVE BUYING
FROM CONSUMERS' SELF-CONCEPT

The social psychological model presented here proposes that impulsive and excessive buying can be predicted from a person's self-discrepancies, "gaps" between actual and ideal self, if he or she has highly materialistic values. In other words, excessive buyers typically believe that material goods help them compensate by bringing them closer to their ideal selves. Those with large self-discrepancies but low materialistic tendencies might instead turn to alcoholism, eating disorders, or "sports addiction" as compensation strategies.

In support of this model excessive buyers reported that buying to bolster their self-image was a more important decision consideration than ordinary buyers (as described in the previous section). Moreover, they held stronger materialistic values. In the survey the mean rating of ordinary buyers (3.15) fell below the midpoint of the materialism scale (3.50), whereas the mean rating of excessive buyers (3.90) fell above the midpoint, a highly significant difference. Thus it seems that excessive buyers believe much more strongly than ordinary buyers do that acquiring consumer goods is an important route to success, happiness, and a sense of identity.

In terms of discrepancies in consumers' self-concept, we constructed a single quantitative index for each respondent on the basis of their indications for each self-discrepancy of how far they felt they were away from their ideal self (size of discrepancy) and how much they worry about it (importance of discrepancy), summing these and dividing them by the number of discrepancies listed (Dittmar et al. 1996). The extent and salience of self-discrepancies were measured separately because they can be independent of each other. For instance, there may be a large discrepancy—a person wanting to be thin rather than heavily overweight—but they may never worry about it. The possible range of the self-discrepancy index is 1–36, and excessive buyers had a much higher mean score (16.0) compared to ordinary buyers (10.5). Thus excessive buyers reported greater and more psychologically salient self-discrepancies than ordinary buyers.

One of the most central concerns of the research project was the question of whether impulsive and excessive buying can be predicted directly from an individual's self-discrepancies and materialistic values. Hierarchical multiple regression analyses were carried out to address this question, for which individuals were classified as either low or high in materialism, while the self-discrepancy index was treated as a continuous variable.

Interaction variables were created by multiplying personal self-discrepancies with (1) level of materialism, (2) gender, and (3) both gender and materialism. The first step of this analysis consisted of a main-effects-only model, in which level of materialism, gender, and self-discrepancy were entered as predictors. In the second step the two-way interaction terms were added as further predictors, and the three-way interaction term was added in a third step to assess the presence, strength, and nature of any interactions between materialism, self-discrepancy, and possibly gender.

One of the most important variables to be predicted was an individual's tendency toward compulsive buying, as measured by the screener questionnaire developed by d'Astous et al. (1990). Self-discrepancies should be linked to excessive buying tendencies only when consumers make use of consumption as a compensatory strategy. Thus our model predicts that the relationship between self-discrepancy and tendency toward excessive buying should be small or absent when a person's materialism is low, but that this relationship should be present when their materialism is high.

The model predicted best for women buyers, for whom large self-discrepancies in combination with materialistic values were a powerful predictor of proneness to become an excessive buyer. There was no relationship between the self-discrepancy index and excessive buying tendency for women low in materialist values ($r=0.16$; non-significant). In contrast, for women consumers high in materialist values this relationship was strong ($r=0.49$; $p < .001$). The predictions did not work as well for male consumers, which might be in part a reflection of the small sample of excessive male buyers. Alternatively, the fact that links were stronger for women than men might suggest that shopping still constitutes a more culturally available and socially acceptable activity for women. For instance, a recent UK survey found that women were still most often responsible for shopping for households, while men tended to express a dislike for shopping as a nonmasculine activity (Lunt and Livingstone 1992). Other compensation strategies, such as excessive sports or becoming a "workaholic," may be more available and socially sanctioned for men. This interpretation is strengthened by (1) the finding that a respondent classified as an excessive shopper in the mail survey was over 2.5 times more likely to be a woman and by (2) our difficulties in finding male excessive buyers to take part in the project. This gender imbalance is slightly lower than findings from various clinical and community samples in the U.S., which report that 80 to 90 percent of excessive buyers are women (Black 1996).

It is important to emphasize that the gender explanation given here should not be misunderstood as an essentialist account of differences between male and female consumers. Rather, we are putting forward the argument that shopping will remain gendered in the way described only as long as cultural norms and social representations (Moscovici 1988) continue to frame shopping as closely linked to women's social, personal, and gender identities. In addition, social constraints may make shopping self-completion a more likely compensation strategy for women than for men, who might have better opportunities for engaging in different activities, such as excessive sports or going out for a drink. For instance, primary caregivers and homemakers, still predominantly women, may be able to bring their children along on shopping trips, but not on excursions to the gym. However, with changes in the occupational and domestic roles of women and men, and the recent, increasing emphasis on appearance, body image, and consumption of goods also for men (Dittmar and Morse 1997), it seems likely that excessive buying may become more common in men.

CONCLUSION AND IMPLICATIONS

The findings reported suggest a theoretical basis for therapeutic intervention, given that self-discrepancies have been identified as one important underlying motivation for excessive buying. Self-help organizations for shopping addiction, or counseling services for debt management, tend to concentrate on aiding clients in developing realistic budget plans and strategies for long-term debt reduction. While such aid is vital, their clients' concerns with self-image are likely to remain unaddressed. Current medical treatment for "compulsive" buying often entails the use of anti-depressant drugs (Black et al. 1997), such as Prozac, or behavioral therapies. These forms of treatment can successfully reduce the number of shopping episodes, but buying tends to increase again after the end of treatment. From the perspective developed in this chapter, this implies that treatment should focus on underlying motivations for shopping rather than on alleviating symptoms.

The issues of self-discrepancies and materialism need to be addressed, either by aiding clients in changing aspects of their self-concept or finding different, more positive, and less costly avenues for self-completion.

We do not want to claim that "compulsive" buyers are only, or even mainly, excessive impulse purchasers who are propelled by strong self-discrepancies. However, it appears that excessive impulse purchasers constitute at least one subpopulation of compulsive buyers. The psychiatric and clinically informed consumer research literature has tended to focus on very extreme buying behavior. For instance, some studies used patients who were hospitalized or in treatment for diverse clinical conditions (McElroy et al. 1994), and even in community samples there is a tendency to select the most extreme excessive buyers, those whose lives are very much impaired. It is therefore not surprising that a number of studies have found that individuals who suffer from excessive buying also present other psychiatric conditions, such as eating disorders (Faber et al. 1995) or pathological gambling (Black and Moyer 1998). However, a substantial proportion of excessive buyers are without psychiatric comorbidity and may well lead fairly "normal" and reasonably successful lives apart from their buying behavior. It is probably safest to conclude at this stage that excessive buyers are not a homogeneous group but a collection of subpopulations with different pathways into shopping addiction. This argument is in line with a recent paper offering different typologies of "compulsive" buying behavior with different "drivers" (DeSarbo and Edwards 1996). A recent review by a clinician also concluded that "subtypes need better exploration, not only by looking at buyer types, but at those with and without psychiatric co-morbidity" (Black 1996, p. 54).

This social psychological model may be particularly useful for a subpopulation of excessive buyers, young professionals who are both consumption-oriented and extreme impulse buyers. Most likely, they would be seen from a clinical perspective as having a comparatively mild illness (Black 1996) because they may not suffer from psychiatric comorbidity. However, even for severe sufferers, the model presented here may present a more precise unpacking of the low self-esteem and depression commonly reported by excessive buyers through proposing that it is the conjunction of two factors — self-discrepancies and materialistic values — that ties self-concept deficits into shopping rather than a different way of trying to find psychological relief. In conclusion, the aim of the model presented in this chapter is to complement, rather than challenge outright, existing clinical models of compulsive buying through conceptualizing impulsive and excessive buying as based, at least in part and for more materialistic consumers, on the social psychological motivation of bolstering one's self-image.

REFERENCES

American Psychiatric Association (1994). *Diagnostic and Statistical Manual of Mental Disorders, 4th ed. (DSM-IV)*. Washington, DC: American Psychiatric Association.

Belk, R. (1988). Possessions and the extended self. *Journal of Consumer Research* 15:139–168.

Black, D. W. (1996). Compulsive buying: a review. *Journal of Clinical Psychiatry* 57 (suppl. 8) 50–55.

—— (1998). Recognition and treatment of obsessive-compulsive spectrum disorders. In *Obsessive-Compulsive Disorder: Theory, Research and Treatment*, ed. R. P. Swinson, M. M. Antony et al., pp. 426–457. New York: Guilford.

Black, D. W., Monahan, P., and Gabel, J. (1997). Fluvoxamine in the treatment of compulsive buying. *Journal of Clinical Psychiatry* 58:159–163.

Black, D. W., and Moyer, T. (1998). Clinical features and psychiatric comorbidity of subjects with pathological gambling behavior. *Psychiatric Services* 49:1434–1439.

Black, D. W., Repertinger, S., Gaffney, G. R., and Gabel, J. (1998). Family history and psychiatric comorbidity in persons with compulsive buying. *American Journal of Psychiatry* 155:960–963.

Bloch, P. H., Ridgeway, N. M., and Nelson, J. E. (1991). Leisure and the shopping mall. *Advances in Consumer Research*. 18:445–452.

Christenson, G. A., Faber, R. J., de Zwaan, M., and Raymond, N. C. (1994). Compulsive buying: descriptive characteristics and psychiatric co-morbidity. *Journal of Clinical Psychiatry* 55:5–11.

d'Astous, A., Maltais, J., and Roberge, C. (1990). Compulsive buying tendencies of adolescent consumers. *Advances in Consumer Research* 17:306–313.

DeSarbo, W. S., and Edwards, E. A. (1996). Typologies of compulsive buying behavior: a constrained clusterwise regression approach. *Journal of Consumer Psychology* 5:231–262.

Dittmar, H. (1989). Gender-identity-related meanings of personal possessions. *British Journal of Social Psychology* 28:159–171.

—— (1991). Meanings of material possessions as reflections of identity: gender and social-material position in society. *Journal of Social Behavior and Personality* 6(6):165–186.

—— (1992a). *The Social Psychology of Material Possessions: To Have Is To Be*. Hemel Hempstead: Harvester Wheatsheaf; New York: St. Martin's Press.

—— (1992b). Perceived material wealth and first impressions. *British Journal of Social Psychology* 31:379–392.

—— (1994). Material possessions as stereotypes: material images of different socio-economic groups. *Journal of Economic Psychology* 15:561–585.

—— (1996). The social psychology of economic and consumer behavior. In *Applied Social Psychology*, ed. G. R. Semin and K. Fiedler, pp. 145–172. London: Sage.

—— (in press). Impulse buying in ordinary and "compulsive" consumers. In *Conflict and Tradeoffs in Decision-Making*, ed. J. Baron, G. Loomes, and E. Weber, Cambridge: Cambridge University Press.

Dittmar, H., and Beattie, J. (1998). Impulsive and excessive buying behavior. In *Choice and Public Policy: Limits of Welfare Markets*, ed. P. Taylor-Gooby, pp. 123–144. London: Macmillan.

Dittmar, H., Beattie, J., and Friese, S. (1995). Gender identity and material symbols: objects and decision considerations in impulse purchases. *Journal of Economic Psychology* 15:391–511.

—— (1996). Objects, decision considerations and self-image in men's and women's impulse purchases. *Acta Psychologica* 93: 187–206.

Dittmar, H., and Bond, R. (1999). *I want it and I want it now: temporal discounting of different consumer goods in normal and "compulsive" buyers.* Unpublished manuscript, University of Sussex, England.

Dittmar, H., and Drury, J. (in press). Self-image — is it in the bag? A qualitative comparison between "ordinary" and "excessive" consumers. *Journal of Economic Psychology.*

Dittmar, H., and Morse, E. (1997). *The effect of exposure to attractive male media images on the self- and body-esteem of young hetero- and homosexual men.* Paper presented at the British Psychological Association Social Section Conference, Brighton, UK, March.

Elliott, R. (1994). Addictive consumption: function and fragmentation in postmodernity. *Journal of Consumer Policy* 17:159–179.

Faber, R. J., Christenson, G. A., de Zwaan, M., and Mitchell, J. (1995). Two forms of compulsive consumption: comorbidity of compulsive buying and binge eating. *Journal of Consumer Research* 22:296–304.

Faber, R. J., and O'Guinn, T. C. (1992). A clinical screener for compulsive buying. *Journal of Consumer Research* 19:459–469.

Faber, R. J., O'Guinn, T. C., and Krych, R. (1987). Compulsive consumption. *Advances in Consumer Research* 14:132–135.

Hanley, A., and Wilhelm, M. S. (1992). Compulsive buying: an exploration into self-esteem and money attitudes. *Journal of Economic Psychology,* 13:5–18.

Higgins, T. (1987). Self-discrepancy: a theory relating self to affect. *Psychological Review* 94:319–340.

Lunt, P. K., and Livingstone, S. M. (1992). *Mass Consumption and Personal Identity: Everyday Economic Experience.* Buckingham, UK: Open University Press.

McCracken, G. (1990). *Culture and Consumption.* Indianapolis: Indiana University Press.

McElroy, S. L., Keck, P. E., Harrison, G., et al. (1994). Compulsive buying: a report of 20 cases. *Journal of Clinical Psychiatry* 55:242–248.

Moscovici, S. (1988). Some notes on social representations. *European Journal of Social Psychology* 18:211–250.

O'Guinn, T. C., and Faber, R. J. (1989). Compulsive buying: a phenomenological exploration. *Journal of Consumer Research* 16:147–157.

Richins, M., and Dawson, S. (1992). Materialism as a consumer value: measure development and validation. *Journal of Consumer Research* 19:303–316.

Scherhorn, G., Reisch, L. A., and Raab, L. A. (1990). Addictive buying in West Germany: an empirical investigation. *Journal of Consumer Policy* 13:155–189.

Schlosser, S., Black, D. W., Repertinger, S., and Freet, D. (1994). Compulsive buying: demography, phenomenology, and comorbidity in 46 subjects. *General Hospital Psychiatry* 16:205–212.

Valence, G., d'Astous, A., and Fortier, L. (1988). Compulsive buying: concept and measurement. *Journal of Consumer Policy* 11:419–433.

Wicklund, R. A., and Gollwitzer, P. M. (1982). *Symbolic Self-Completion*. Hillsdale, NJ: Lawrence Erlbaum.

6

Clothes, Inside Out

Eve Golden

In *Seeing through Clothes*, art historian Anne Hollander (1978) says that "all nudes in art since modern fashion began are wearing the ghosts of absent clothes. . . . People without clothes are still likely to behave as if they wore them. . . . Clothes, even when omitted, cannot be escaped" (p. 86).

The development of dress was a great cultural achievement. Like cooking, clothing transformed crude necessity into expressive art. But it has shaped us as irrevocably as we have shaped it. (Anyone who doubts this, or thinks clothes trivial among our lofty concerns, can turn for enlightenment to Thomas Carlyle's 1833 *Sartor Resartus*, a satirical "spiritual biography" constructed metaphorically upon a Philosophy (the capitals are Carlyle's) of Clothes. This is among other things a bravura display of the symbolic richness of clothing, and of the depth and pervasiveness of the psychological experience of Dress.) Clothing by now is much more for us than a simple response to cold or sunburn, as food is more than a response to hunger. It is more even than a way to "express ourselves," honestly or not, to other people. It is a reservoir of accumulated cultural, social, and personal meaning. I will limit my discussion to clothes in our own postindustrial Western society, and offer some ideas about how they work in and on us, along with an assortment of illustrations. I will point to important references where they seem appropriate in the hope that they will compensate in part for necessary omissions and facilitate further exploration. Finally, I will consider briefly some possible links between clothing and obsessional symptomatology.

My topic is clothing as a concept — the *idea* of clothes — distinct from the particulars of what any person chooses to wear. *Fashion* by definition is ever-changing. But although dress varies, "clothes" are a psychological constant, stable and relatively independent of style.

HISTORICAL VIEWS OF CLOTHES

The origins, forms, and "purposes" of clothes have been debated for centuries. The first two of these lie outside my brief, and I will ignore them. The third has not always been handled with much psychological sophistication, and the resulting explanations are mostly too general to be satisfying. Still, some of them have been important historically and some are useful descriptively, so I will survey them here.

Until the mid-nineteenth century, literal and figurative interpretations of *Genesis* had established "modesty" as the primary "reason" for clothes. James Laver (1969), an eminent British historian of fashion, defined modesty as "the enemy . . . of Swagger and Seduction" (p. 13). (He noted sardonically that moralists have usually been alert for offenses against the latter "sin" in women and against the former in men.) Victorian commentators speak of "hygiene" as a fundamental concern in dress; this austere assumption of restrained healthfulness is the one that was politically correct when Freud came along.

J. C. Flügel in 1930 was the first psychoanalytic thinker to attempt a systematic study of clothing. He concluded that its purposes were decoration, modesty, and protection, and that these were interrelated in complex and ambivalent ways; his work was very influential and still attracts interest. Laver (1969) proposed three "purposes" for clothes, which he called principles: utility, hierarchy (or dominance), and seduction. Hollander (1994) elaborated them this way: "We put on clothing for some of the same reasons that we speak: to make living and working easier and more comfortable, to proclaim (or disguise) our identities and to attract erotic attention" (p. 27). This last, the seduction theory, remains popular, although some follow Laver in the belief that women have traditionally dressed for seduction and men for dominance, because those reflect their respective chief values as mates. But recent theoreticians of clothing, Hollander and Valerie Steele among them, have challenged the seduction theory. Hollander thinks that the rules that govern the other visual arts also govern dress — in other words, clothes are primarily a way of experiencing form. Steele, in her 1985 *Fashion and Eroticism*, takes a parallel but more psychological approach, believing that people strive for beauty rather than seduction in their dress.

CLOTHING AS INTERFACE

For psychologists these explanations oversimplify the complexities of motivation and awareness that exist in real people. They also fail to address the essential fact that clothing — "so different from flesh but so necessary to it" (Hollander 1994, p. 85) — shapes our psychology as much as it reflects it. It influences how we see ourselves, and it serves as an active interface between ourselves and the non-self world — a membrane regulating what we allow in and out.

Concretely, for instance, a fur coat contains body heat within it, and simultaneously keeps cold without. Psychologically, the same coat may help contain the insecurities of an impoverished childhood and ward off disrespect from others. One person may feel that fur attracts (lets in) too much anger, or displays (lets out) too much arrogance, and therefore reject it. But someone who relishes a rumble and thinks any attention is better than none can flaunt the coat and let the devil take the hindmost.

Clothing contributes to the language of imagery by which we think of and speak to ourselves. When we picture (imagine) ourselves as sexy, businesslike, or healthy, or as mother, lover, or violinist, we generally distinguish one "me" from all the others by the way we dress the image. Because of its intimate association with all aspects of our lives, clothing carries great symbolic and metaphoric weight.

Clothing has a paradoxical quality that runs very deep. Clothes are elective, in that we choose what we wear, but they are also compulsory, in that we have no choice but to wear something. Clothes are concrete physical objects, yet endlessly plastic in their psychological uses. Above all, although clothing never becomes physically part of us the way food does, we know ourselves to be incomplete without it. We feel ourselves so strongly as dressed beings that the moments when we don't wear clothes are the ones when we are most aware of them. (We don't yet have a study of how this comes to pass in children, but it does come to pass. A friend of mine objects: How about nudists? I think that nudists know better than anyone the depth of the conviction they challenge.)

Thus clothing functions psychologically both as artifact and as idea. As artifact—that is, in its material form as garment—it protects and delineates. As idea—as inner artifact, if you will—it expands our symbolic representations of ourselves and serves, like all ideas, as the raw material for art and imagination. We wear the thing, but the idea shapes our thinking about ourselves and about others.

Clothing is different from all our other devices in that we experience it as self and as not-self at the same time. Some people feel closer to their clothes than to their dreams and fantasies (in which we are almost always dressed). This built-in ambiguity makes clothing an elegant device for modulating the tensions between us and the world "outside." Separation and merger, inclusion and exclusion, conformity and individuality, closeness and distance, concealment and display, truth and fiction: clothing helps us keep these adjusted to tolerable levels.

THE TRANSITIONAL NATURE OF CLOTHES

Because of its curious self/not-self status, the psychological home of clothing is neither the inner nor the outer world, but what

Winnicott (1971) called the potential space: "the area of experiencing, to which inner reality and external life both contribute" (p. 2). In this, clothes have much in common with the transitional phenomena of infancy, in which "[use is made of] objects that are not part of the infant's body yet are not fully recognized as belonging to the external world" (1958, p. 230). Like teddy bears and security blankets, clothes protect us from the full impact of a frustrating environment, and increase our capacity to take care of ourselves. Also like blankets, they have no psychological value (however elegant they may look in Bloomingdale's) until we pick them out; but as they become ours, we invest them with meaning and power.

Unlike the temporary transitional objects of infancy, however, clothes need never be given up; on the contrary, they become ever more acceptable and validated as a permanent aspect of ourselves. Consider this statement from the *World Book Encyclopedia* (1959): Although other land animals depend on body hair to keep them warm, the *World Book* says, "we do not need hair because we wear clothes. Neither do whales because they have blubber" (p. 8729). This is a clear, if befuddled, demonstration of how deeply we feel clothing as intrinsic, and how uneasily we balance it between "self" and "not-self." It also shows why the question Winnicott (1971) raised about transitional objects — "Did you conceive of this or was it presented to you from without?" (p. 12) — is the question that drives a psychological study of clothes.

I emphasize this because transitional phenomena (the abstract kind as well as teddy bears) are very important in the development of the capacity to reflect upon, rather than just undergo, internal and external experience. To be able to reflect, one must be able to imagine, and retain the imagination of experience in symbolic form. Ultimately, the confidence that one will be able to reflect upon and contain what one feels allows risk-taking in the object world. But that confidence requires ability to recognize and tolerate the separateness of self and other, the limits of personal omnipotence, and the reality of emotional ambivalence, because those abilities underlie imagination.

Transitional objects are a means by which a baby explores

(some say "denies" [Muensterberger 1994, p. 3], but I think it is not only that) these elements of separation: the borders of self and other, the distribution of power, and the toleration of intense affect. The baby allocates comforting not-me attributes to an object that he can control. This allows him to experiment with separation more safely than he could with an independent other person; see Winnicott (1958, 1971) for more on this. Clothes resemble a baby's blanket in being what Winnicott considered half-discovered and half-created: that is, the physical garment is already there, but it has no psychological potency until its wearer invests (a clothing metaphor) meaning in it. Clothing has great potential as a more or less permanent transitional object because it is always available to us (unlike a teddy bear, it never needs to be "outgrown"), and because society actively encourages its use as an artificial reinforcement or extension of the boundaries of the self. The psychological importance of clothing is invented by the individual wearer in the service of safe exploration of the self and not-self worlds. Correspondingly, when this sense of safety is inadequate for any reason, clothes may be enlisted to try to compensate for it (see also Muensterberger 1994).[1]

For convenience I will divide this study into the primarily external and the primarily internal manifestations of what clothes "mean." But however clothes manifest themselves (in cotton, in fantasies, in paintings), I hope to show that their roots remain permanently in the area of transition between the "me" and the "not-me."

---

1. A brief detour: Anne Hollander's *Seeing through Clothes* (1978) is an important study of clothing in art. Hollander looks at how representations of form in art and fashion interact with self-image, and are then acted upon by it. Although she doesn't put it like this, she provides an intensive exploration of the area of interaction between self and not-self — of Winnicott's potential space. *Seeing through Clothes* contains much of value for the study of transitional phenomena and the nature of visual and symbolic representation.

CLOTHING AS GUARDIAN OF BOUNDARIES

Clothes in the outer world delineate and maintain boundaries: bodily ones for physical protection and psychic ones for safety in relationship. Many students of fashion dismiss physical protection as a matter of no importance, believing that this primitive function has long since been superseded by the more sophisticated ones that have accrued over the centuries. (What! says Carlyle [1833]. "Hast thou always worn [clothes] perforce, and as a consequence of Man's Fall; never rejoiced in them as in a warm movable house, a Body round thy Body, wherein that strange THEE of thine sat snug, defying all variations of Climate?" [Book I, chapter ix]). But psychologists know that primitiveness is no guarantee of irrele-vance — quite the contrary — and that the persistence of archaic needs is a testament to their strength. Hollander (1994) says correctly that it is Nature herself who "ordains that human beings be completed by clothing, not left bare in their own insufficient skins" (p. 5).

> A clinical example attests to the psychological vitality of the issue: A young woman feared and dreaded winter, and would stay inside, isolated and depressed, once it got cold. She expected herself to be absolutely self-reliant, and knew that she succeeded poorly in this. Her mother had preached an idealized and moralistic asceticism, and had discouraged her children's attempts at self-soothing, which she considered regressive. The daughter became aware in her analysis that she did not dress warmly enough, and in this was acting out guilt over and anger at too-harsh standards. Her chattering teeth and blue lips exposed her mother's Spartan approach as unrealistic; at the same time her cowardice in avoiding the cold, and her suffering when out in it, were reasons and a way to punish herself for both her weakness and her rage. When she finally began to challenge her unattainable standards, she acquired a warm coat and scarf and boots that didn't leak, and winter lost its terrors. It was the work on the symptomatic

denial of her need to keep warm that eventually gave access to the deeper problems of separation.

So our wardrobes are compulsory, however carefully they may also be chosen. I am reminded of the outburst of Hobbes the tiger when Calvin wonders why people are never content with what they have. "Are you kidding?" cries Hobbes. "Your fingernails are a joke, you've got no fangs, you can't see at night, your pink hides are ridiculous, your reflexes are nil, and you don't even have tails! . . . Now if *tigers* weren't content, that would be something to wonder about" (Watterson 1966, p. 157). Hobbes, from the superior vantage point of tigerhood, has no problem recognizing what we usually deny — that we want because we don't have. Our skins are so insufficient that we are driven to supplement them. The attention we focus on what to wear distracts us from the humiliating knowledge that in a world of poison ivy, wind-chill factor, and UV rays we alone among animals must wear something. The lack of distinction between fur and clothing in the *World Book* quotation above illustrates this denial perfectly.

Clothes provide nonphysical protections, too. The lover's sweater, the mirrored shades, the athlete's lucky shorts, and the currently talismanic "power suit" provide a psychological safety that we all understand. They also make clear that the wish for more potent sartorial magic (like seven-league boots) is alive and well (Lurie 1981). ("Air" would have been nothing without 'em, says my brother the sports fiend, of the lucky shorts without which Michael Jordan was famous for never playing a game.)

Dress designer Elizabeth Hawes (1942) thought that we also use clothes to protect ourselves against "what we conceive to be moral danger" (p. 38) — perhaps the danger of too much exhibitionism. This is not to say that we can't exhibit ourselves even as we hide — in translucent negligees, for example, or the short face veils of the '40s — for clothing is nonpareil at this sort of paradox. But whatever the threat may be, clothes, simultaneously, both demonstrate and remediate our vulnerability. And they do it tactfully, without ever asking Winnicott's numinous question about where the protective power lies, in us or in them.

CLOTHING AS DELINEATOR OF BOUNDARIES

Clothes delineate boundaries among and within groups, and among and within individuals. They are very effective in this, allowing quick, broad identifications from a great distance, and very fine ones from closer in. They let us distinguish among groups while both integrating and differentiating ourselves within them. (Army uniforms are a stylized example.) This is not a minor matter; we place great reliance on such information. That is why we condemn an enemy who attacks us in his own guise much less harshly than we do one who disguises (dresses) himself to conform with a group not his own in order to attack it from within. One is an enemy, who may still be treated with honor; the other is a spy or traitor.

This gate-keeping aspect of clothing can be seen at extremes among those groups of teenagers, say, for whom an uncool brand of sneakers spells ostracism and catastrophe. But any person who doubts his welcome in a desired group may turn to clothes both to prove he belongs and to hide that he doesn't. The Duchess of Windsor (1956), a compulsive clothes buyer by her own account, seems to have operated like this. (Cultural anthropologist Ted Polhemus's *StreetStyle* (1994) is a wonderful guide to the group — styletribe, he calls it — dynamics for clothes. Polhemus traces the rise and fall of urban cultural groups by the development of their garb, documenting their life cycles in clothing. The photographs are a treasure trove for anyone interested in clothing as a communicative display.)

What an individual does with the group's basic uniform provides still more information. Hollander points out that clothes address simultaneously the need to belong and the need to be separate. They help us balance the safety of conformity with the risks and pleasures of individual notice. In *Gone with the Wind*, Scarlett O'Hara pushed the envelope on purpose, to make sure she was seen; her mother's elegance transcended conformity and dictated the rules; her father tried to conform but never quite could, which his friends found delightful and his wife contemptible. Melanie actively valued conformity, both as a shy person and as a traditionalist; her brother Charles hadn't the imagination for anything else. Ashley could imagine, but not act. Hollander (1994) reminds us that "the social laws that govern choice in fashion are both unwritten and slippery, and wearing the right thing requires the right instinct and judgment instead of plain obedience to the rules of custom" (p. 20). The green silk bonnet that Scarlett did not dye black was the first real step toward her rejection by "genteel" Atlanta; it proved that she was not truly one of the group, however expert her disguise.

Endless variations of this kind show how sensitively dress can reflect fine degrees of merger and separation. It can also enforce those degrees, actively influencing the distance that we experience between ourselves and others. Concretely it interposes layers of matter between people (rubber gloves and johnnies in the examining room); metaphorically it sends signals (the flannel nightgown instead of the silk one). Above all, it gives us alternative sets of boundaries that we can take up and put aside as we need them, in most cases so automatically that we never even have to notice that we are enlisting auxiliary troops at all. Thus Sinatra, when someone tried to move him over a bit on a crowded podium: "Hands off the threads, creep!" Ordinarily we say, "Don't touch me," or "Keep your hands to yourself," but Sinatra's extreme, if apocryphal, verbal separation of himself from his clothes apparently gave him a sense of space that he needed right then.

Biographer Marian Fowler offers detailed studies of five great "dressers" in her intriguing but disappointingly documented work of "fashion biography" *The Way She Looks Tonight* (1996). One of these is Jacqueline Kennedy Onassis, whose use of clothing Fowler considers to have been an incomparably successful device to regulate distance. Fowler believes that Onassis developed a style of dress tailored (another clothing metaphor — they are extremely common) to her needs with such perfection that, by itself, it managed to garner for her both the notice she craved and the distance she needed. It riveted the attention of others on her clothes and away from herself in a kind of sartorial bait-and-switch.

Fowler thinks that Onassis's clothes combined impersonal drama with the obscuring of personal cues: they concealed her eyes, for example, with veils and sunglasses, and the lines of her body with stiff fabrics — what Hawes (1942) called "hiding behind clothes." This balance bound so much anxiety, if Fowler's sources can be believed, that Jackie preferred acquiring clothes to wearing them, and was driven to near disgrace by smuggling Paris originals into the White House when she was supposed to be wearing only American-made clothes. ("'Jesus, Jackie,' yelled Jack. 'The New Frontier is going to be sabotaged by a bunch of goddamned French couturiers!'" [p. 257]). In contrast with Marlene Dietrich's "generous desire to fully gratify, or even satiate, the eye," Fowler understands Jackie's clothing as austere and unwelcoming, as if to say: "Look at me! But don't get too close" (p. 276).

CONCEALMENT AND REVELATION

After the need to fit in, which we take so much for granted that we usually are not aware of it, most of us care very much about how we are seen. Manipulations of distance tend to be unconscious, but we think consciously about pride and shame, hiding and showing, truth and disguise. (Of course, we also *don't* think about them. Both show in our dress.) This dialectic, including as it does the great sexual tension between the wish to expose and the wish to hide, is the subject that until recently has most exercised psychoanalysts and historians. It is therefore also the one that has accumulated the wildest collection of interpretations (shoes as phallic symbols, and so on).

The main thing about exposure and concealment in clothes is that it's hard to tell them apart. The fig leaf is a fitting symbol because, as has often been pointed out, it draws attention to the sexual organs by the very act of covering them. Clothing always hides, and it always reveals — frequently the same things, and always at the same time. To reveal one thing is to conceal another, and vice versa. Layers of dissimulation lie (and lie) beneath the surface of any array of "manifest clothes."

Just as psychoanalytic theory gradually and fruitfully extended early concrete observations about sexuality to include abstract aspects of desire and need, we can extend the fig-leaf metaphor beyond the actual sexual organs to the body and then to the self. This makes the ambiguous connection between hidden and exposed even more acute, and not only in the sexual arena.

Flügel (1930) commented epigrammatically that "the very word 'personality' . . . implies a 'mask (persona=mask)' which is itself an article of clothing" (p. 16). When the boundaries between personality and clothes are so fluid, how can we know which characteristics belong to the clothes and which to the person? It is the baby's use of a blanket for soothing, not, of course, the blanket itself, that ultimately effects change in his psychic structure. But for the baby who has attributed power to a particular blanket, that blanket has to be there for the change to happen. A scared medical intern derives confidence from his first white jacket; his use of it changes him. Where, in those first weeks, did his confidence reside? Not in himself, not in the jacket, but in his use of the jacket. We can ask, with Winnicott, "Did you conceive of this, or was it presented to you from without?" (This use of clothing as talisman is very common and may be an aspect of compulsive clothes-seeking.)

Flügel (1930) points out another paradox: "When we wear a mask, we cease, to some extent, to be ourselves; we conceal from others both our identity and the natural expression of our emotions, and, in consequence, we do not feel the same responsibility as when our faces are uncovered. . . . The masked person is, therefore, apt to be freer and less inhibited . . . and can do things from which he might otherwise be impeded by fear or shame" (p. 51). So when we are masked, says Flügel, we are both more and less ourselves. At the same time, only when masked are we fully ourselves.

Obviously "mask" is a metaphor for clothing; garments not only cover us but also provide alternate facades with readable meanings of their own (Lurie 1981; see also extended examples in Fowler 1996). The disguise may not necessarily be known to its wearer. Hollander (1994) quipped that "the famous messages of dress, the well-known language of clothes, is very often not doing any communicating at all; a good deal of it is a form of private muttering" (p.

189). Helen K. Golden, Ph.D. (personal communication), comments that the common experience of buying something and then finding it so "not right" as to be unwearable is a variety of this private muttering. She adds that it shows not only how intimately we identify with our removable skin, but also how greatly our interaction with it instructs us about our internal selves. (People who know themselves poorly may shop desperately and unsuccessfully for clothes, hoping to learn to recognize themselves.)

A great deal has been made of the disingenuous aspects of dress. But most of us know from experience how limited in fact are the powers of clothes to transform — sometimes to our relief, and sometimes to our dismay (see Richards, Chapter 14, this volume, for example). They must always reveal even while they conceal. Hollander (1978) reminds us that in any case clothes are not primarily aimed at the outside world. "Clothes cannot be altogether dramatic or theatrical because people are not always acting or performing, even though they are always appearing. It is the inner theater that is costumed by the choice in clothes, and this is not always under conscious management. The public may not always be intended, much less able, to get the picture" (p. 451). Hardheaded Hawes (1954) addresses the same question with her usual brutal practicality: "You, too, can learn to use your dressing for play-acting, but in my opinion it gets to be a bore" (p. 199).

CLOTHES AND SEXUALITY

Theoreticians seem to agree that there is something intrinsically sexual in the experience of wearing clothes. This can be allowed, I think, even if one rejects the reductionism of the clothes-as-seduction theory. Steele (1985) says simply that "because clothing is so intimately associated with the physical body, at the deepest level all clothing is erotic" (p. 9), and Hollander (1994) agrees that "clothes address the personal self first of all, and only afterwards the world" (p. 6). The autoerotic, and not the seductive aspects of clothing lie deepest. Hawes (1954), no theoretician, takes this as a matter of course: "There is, of course, plenty of pleasure to be derived from looking decorative in the bedroom even if no one else is about. I doubt if even those psychologists who dub this kind of pleasure narcissistic and, in their opinions, bad, would deny that the pleasure of finding one's self pleasing to look at is real" (p. 24). (Hawes is alone in reliably distinguishing between dressing to attract and dressing for display, while Steele reliably distinguishes between the desire for beauty and sexual desire.)

The seduction, or attraction, theory of clothes is usually attributed to Flügel (see above). His work has a great deal of charm although it is slightly dated by its very early Freudian point of view. But Flügel himself was considerably more subtle a thinker than he has sometimes appeared in the interpretations of his psychologically inexpert followers. He knew ambivalence to be more a weighing of risks than a simple power struggle, and he didn't consider clothing the passive result of ambivalence but rather an active contribution that we ourselves make to the resolution of conflict: "an ingenious device for the establishment of some degree of harmony between conflicting interests" (p. 20). He understood very well that modesty and exhibitionism transcend the sexual, and he believed that the autoerotic aspects of clothing are rooted in the confusion of the sense of self with the physical object.

So we can extend the fig-leaf metaphor yet another degree. Steele (1985) paraphrases Flügel: "The unconscious conflict between exhibitionism and modesty is displaced from the naked body onto clothing, which then functions as a 'compromise,' since it both covers the body and attracts attention to it" (p. 25). This same conflict holds true in all areas where exhibitionism and modesty coexist: the social, the artistic, the intellectual — in short, wherever people maintain narcissistic investment in themselves. And in these conflicts, too, clothing can function as a compromise. (People who feel narcissistically deficient may seek clothes as a way to make good the lack, relying on them at once for proud display and for concealment of shame.)

A last comment on this: clothing is erotic in part because it arouses curiosity, which is one result of the conceal-and-reveal counterpoise. Some people consider fashion a device to nurture curiosity. Endless change constantly restores the jaded eye and causes it to look again, keeping curiosity and engagement high. As Hollander (1994) puts it: "One basic modern need is to escape the feeling that desire has gone stale. Fashion therefore depends on managing the maintenance of desire, which must be satisfied, but never for too long" (p. 49). Steele's book, *Fashion and Eroticism*, is an intricate and extensive study of this subject. Having said that, I will leave it to her, and turn from the internal reflections of external clothes to the outward manifestations of clothing-as-idea.

CLOTHES AS CONCEPT

Clothes-the-idea is an imaginative enrichment of the conception of the self. (*Sartor Resartus* is not to be missed in this regard.) In most of our experience of life we are clothed; the concept of clothing seems to have grown nearly inseparable from the concept of self in the mind's representational machinery.

These representations, our "imaginings" of ourselves — the making of ourselves into images — are the means by which we picture ourselves in our own thoughts. They have two primary uses: to portray ourselves to ourselves (for instance in psychic structure and in fantasy); and to portray ourselves to others (for instance in art).

INTERNAL REPRESENTATIONS

Selfobject Functions

Kohut (1971, 1977) pointed out that infants depend on other people for the restoration of narcissistic equilibrium, the elusive state of psychological well-being that people of all ages desire, but which is all too easily lost under stress. Kohut called the internal representations of such restorative experiences archaic or transitional selfobjects, and he considered them precursors of psychic structure. His idea of selfobject experience shares three characteristics with

Winnicott's idea of transitional phenomena: they are both efforts to maintain psychic equilibrium; they are both temporary functional fusions of the self with an object not fully differentiated from it; and they both require the child's investment of his own psychic powers in the object. In both cases the result is a strengthening of the experience and boundaries of the self rather than a "relationship" with an object.

Older people use related techniques for pulling themselves together when they fall apart (Kohut calls this a restoration of the cohesiveness of the fragmented self); but as we mature we tend to seek out nonhuman sources of such selfobject functions, among other reasons because they are convenient and because we can control them. Food and sleep are commonly used in this way; I wish I could remember who once wrote about baths as selfobject phenomena. Any sufficiently steadying and reorganizing experience (gardening, running, shopping, listening to music) can serve, and people establish their own preferred techniques. The need for selfobjects is common to everyone and not pathological in itself. But when narcissistic vulnerability is especially great, the need for restoration is more frequent and feels more desperate. Very vulnerable people may therefore seek selfobject support from things, which are safe and predictable, rather than from people or experiences, which may not be. Muensterberger (1994; Chapter 7, this volume) addresses this theme specifically.

It seems to me that clothes by nature possess extremely powerful, near-universal selfobject potential. Although we keep the idea of clothing very close to the idea of self, clothes themselves are immune to the psychic fragmentation that selves undergo; as concrete matter they possess a permanent cohesiveness that the self in need can draw upon. This is the vision behind the expression "coming apart at the seams." In a beloved hymn the poet John Greenleaf Whittier prayed God to "reclothe us in our rightful minds," an exquisite illustration of the metaphor of clothing-as-cohesive-self. A third variation on the theme is the frequently cited (but provenance unclear) aphorism that "the consciousness of being perfectly well dressed may bestow a peace such as religion cannot give." My own clinical experience leads me to think that much clothes-related psychopathology can be understood as extensive dependency on clothes as selfobject. Krueger and Muensterberger (Chapters 13 and 7, respectively, this volume) have much more to say on this subject.

INTERNAL REPRESENTATIONS

Fantasy

The same conflation of idea-of-self with idea-of-clothing means that clothing appears in almost all of our fantasies and dreams. People in them are conceived to be dressed. Even if it is not worthy of note or recollection, the conceptual presence of clothing is demonstrated by our reaction to its absence. The rarity of dreams of nakedness, and the dismay and mortification that they cause us, betray how strongly we feel our inner selves as clothed. And because clothing is conceptually present in all our experiences (including — probably especially — those for which we take it off), it has associative attachments to everything in our lives.

This is remarkable. Try to think of any single other not-self element, however important, that is present in virtually all dreams. Or for that matter in virtually all encounters, virtually all activities, virtually all locales, virtually all fantasies. I can't. Richards (Chapter 14, this volume) further demonstrates the flexibility and vitality of clothing as symbol and metaphor in fantasy.

The fundamental psychological "fact" of clothing, therefore, is that clothes and the representation of the self can *never* be definitively separated. Like language, its only rival in this, clothing is an ever-present lens through which we see ourselves: more, by whose devices we learn to see ourselves in the first place. Clothes and self form each other in an invisible and eternal spiral. "In human life the dressed state, though it may be a lower condition than theoretical ideal nudity, is also the best emblem of corporeal existence. . . . Clothes stand for knowledge and language, art and love, time and death — the creative, struggling state of man" (Hollander 1978, p. 448).

EXTERNAL REPRESENTATIONS

Clothes and Art

Elizabeth Hawes was a radical dress designer of the 1930s who wrote eccentric but perceptive books on the relationships of people (both sexes — she really was a radical) with their clothes. She was a tough-minded pragmatist as well as an artist in clothing, and she had a rude but canny grasp of psychology where it intersected with her own medium.

Hawes thought that most people get little pleasure and a lot of grief from their clothes. Influenced by Flügel's psychoanalytic theories, but possessed of a practical understanding of clothing-as-artifact that he didn't have, she tried to bring the notion of what clothes "mean" down to earth. She considered the act of dressing a route to self-awareness, and she agreed with Carlyle (1833) that "the beginning of all Wisdom is to look fixedly on Clothes . . . till they become *transparent*" (Book I, chapter x) — an ambiguous statement if ever there was one. She concluded that the confusion of boundary between self and other is what clothes and art have in common. (I can't say much about this contention here. Hollander's *Seeing through Clothes* is an admirable and exhaustive study of the relationship of clothes to other visual arts for those who are interested in clothing at its highest level of abstraction.)

One further twist in the helical relationship between ourselves and our clothes, and, incidentally, a confirmation of Hawes's idea, is illustrated in a passage from *The Seduction of the Minotaur*, by Anaïs Nin (1961):

> She no longer sat before an easel, but before a dressing table. . . . Sometimes her dress seemed painted with large brushstrokes, sometimes roughly dyed like the costumes of

the poor. Other times she wore what looked like fragments of ancient Mayan murals, bold symmetrical designs in charcoal outlines with the colors dissolved by age. Heavy earrings of Aztec warriors, necklaces and bracelets of shell, gold and silver medallions . . . all these caught the light as she moved. It was her extreme liveliness that may have prevented her from working upon a painting, and turned a passion for color and textures upon her own body. [p. 33]

Like Nin's imaginary woman, there are real people for whom the act of dressing is a deliberate personal art. Fowler (1996) provides extended studies of several of these (in this context see especially the chapter on Marlene Dietrich). Both Nin and Fowler, I think, validate Hawes, and illustrate Hollander's provocative statement that mirrors let us see the self as a picture. Valerie Steele, who tends to be more interested than Hollander in the experienced (as opposed to the perceived) meaning of clothes, notes that the eyes as well as the skin are a primary erogenous zone. The experience of seeing the self as a picture adds yet another dimension to the endless interplay between self and not-self that is the hallmark of everything having to do with clothes.

Whether we do it deliberately or not, we are constantly making what Hollander calls visual fictions of ourselves. Every time we get dressed we create images that represent us to the outside world and also to ourselves. These images not only reflect our inner representations of ourselves, but inform them as well, in an infinitely recursive process. The wearing of clothing both demonstrates and undermines the truth of ourselves as we know it, and at the same time it constructs new fictions and new truths. Any of these can be used internally as self-knowledge or externally as art.

CONCLUSION: CLOTHES AND COMPULSION

Why are clothes, like food, gambling, and drugs, such a common object of obsession? In themselves they are fascinating, and one way or another they address a wide variety of human needs. But most clothes-hungry people are not compulsive. When people *are* compulsive, the cause — poor affect tolerance, narcissistic depletion, and so on — generally has little to do with clothing per se. This raises questions: Under what conditions do ordinary interests in clothes become compulsive? And what is it about clothes that makes them such a potent magnet for compulsions when they do arise?

I think the answer lies in their transitional nature. Winnicott (1971) believed that the use of the "potential space" between self and other evolved with maturation away from the magical and toward the purely symbolic. The "space" itself retains forever the uniqueness of its intermediary position, but as the boundaries of the self strengthen, it becomes increasingly the venue of what he called "play": the symbolic ideation that allows us to see and reflect upon inner experience and to act with awareness in the outside world.

When symbolic capacity is limited for any reason, its precursors (one of which is compulsive ideation) may be enlisted to contain anxiety. Clothes lend themselves to compulsive scenarios because of their metaphoric richness, their unsurpassed selfobject potential, and their conceptual location in the same transitional area in which the vicissitudes of magical thinking occur. In addition, they can to some degree substitute concretely for unreliable internal resources — for instance, provide a look of self-confidence for a person who cannot feel it — and so they offer a kind of tempting transitional mimicry when the need arises. (See also Muensterberger [1994] for an extensive study of acquisition and transitional phenomena, and Barth, Chapter 12, this volume.)

In short, compulsions are external reflections of pressing inner needs and conflicts. Clothes, as Hollander (1978) has said, "give a visual aspect to consciousness itself. . . . They produce its look as seen from within" (p. 451). Both compulsions and clothes therefore enable the outward staging of interior dramas. They are natural partners when complex feelings cannot be contained internally and spill over into action. When we can't see ourselves in our imaginations, we turn to clothes to show us ourselves. That's what they do.

REFERENCES

Carlyle, T. (1833). *Sartor Resartus*. New York: Holt, 1970.

Flügel, J. C. (1930). *The Psychology of Clothes*. London: Hogarth.

Fowler, M. (1996). *The Way She Looks Tonight*. New York: St Martins Press.

Hawes, E. (1942). *Why Is a Dress?* New York: Viking.

—— (1954). *It's Still Spinach*. Boston: Little, Brown.

Hollander, A. (1978). *Seeing through Clothes*. New York: Viking.

—— (1994). *Sex and Suits*. New York: Knopf.

Kohut, H. (1971). *The Analysis of the Self*. New York: International Universities Press.

—— (1977). *The Restoration of the Self*. New York: International Universities Press.

Laver, J. (1969). *Modesty in Dress*. Boston: Houghton Mifflin.

Lurie, A. (1981). *The Language of Clothes*. New York: Random House.

Muensterberger, W. (1994). *Collecting: An Unruly Passion*. Princeton, NJ: Princeton University Press.

Nin, A. (1961). *The Seduction of the Minotaur*. Chicago: Swallow Press.

Polhemus, T. (1994). *StreetStyle*. New York: Thames & Hudson.

Steele, V. (1985). *Fashion and Eroticism*. New York: Oxford University Press.

—— (1996). *Fetish*. New York: Oxford University Press.

Watterson, B. (1966). *There's Treasure Everywhere: A Calvin and Hobbes Collection*. Kansas City, MO: Andrews and Michael.

Windsor, W. (1956). *The Heart Has Its Reasons: The Memoirs of the Duchess of Windsor*. New York: D. McKay.

Winnicott, D. W. (1958). *Through Paediatrics to Psycho-Analysis*. London: Tavistock.

—— (1971). *Playing and Reality*. London: Tavistock.

World Book Encyclopedia (1959). Chicago: Field Enterprises Educational Corporation.

III Special Issues in Compulsive Buying

7

Collecting as Reparation

Werner Muensterberger

One form of compulsive shopping and spending that is not only condoned but has gained an aura of status in our culture today is collecting. Collecting is one of those aspects of human conduct that seem at first glance not at all exceptional or mysterious. Yet on closer inspection we see that it can be quite perplexing and not easily understood. Collectors themselves — dedicated, serious, infatuated, beset — cannot explain or understand this often all-consuming drive, nor can they call a halt to their habit, despite the fact that it is often accompanied by serious negative social, vocational, or material consequences. Many are aware of a chronic restiveness that can be curbed only by more finds or by yet another acquisition. A recent discovery or another purchase may assuage the hunger, but it never seems to fully satisfy it.

Is it an obsession? An addiction? Is it a passion or urge, or perhaps a need to hold, to possess, to accumulate? Is it more like an unquenchable thirst? Even a very serious and reflective collector is hard put to offer a clear and convincing explanation of his or her "drivenness" or the intense emotion that occasionally occurs in the process of obtaining an object.

The aim of this chapter is to throw some light on the habits of collectors and to explore the deeper emotional and experiential conditions that provide the underlying impingements leading to this kind of craving. In order to do this, I shall first offer a definition of what I consider collecting. I define *collecting* simply as the selecting, gathering, and keeping of objects of subjective value. Note that I emphasize the subjective aspect of collecting because the emotion and often the ardor attached to the collected object or objects is not necessarily commensurate with its specialness or commercial value, nor does it relate to any kind of usefulness.

Observing collectors, one soon discovers an unrelenting need, even a hunger, for acquisitions. This ongoing search is a core element of their personality, evidently linked to far deeper roots. It turns out to be a tendency that derives from a not immediately discernible sense memory of deprivation, loss, or a feeling of aloneness in childhood, and a subsequent longing for substitution, closely allied with moodiness and depressive leanings.

Collectors share a sense of specialness, of not having received satisfying love or attention, or of having been hurt or unfairly treated in infancy. Their possessions have an inherently magical function serving as a restitutive defense. At one and the same time the collector's possessions are part of the collector's internal and external world. The overt attitude of collectors may range from ostentation to apparent modesty or occasionally even secretiveness (which after all is often a covert form of exhibitionism). But most characteristically, there is always an addictive component — a potential, but always present, unconscious modality of affect linked to a powerful reparative need.

Due to this ever-present affect-laden core, the challenge of reassertion by means of more or less constant replenishment is the most conspicuous feature of habitual collection. The replenishment manifests itself as the gathering of what are in essence reparative substitutes of the primary (i.e., maternal) object. All sorts of presumably magical objects provide a feeling of contentment because they defuse, albeit temporarily, the reemergence of traumatic anxiety.

Provoked by early unfavorable conditions or by the lack of emotional closeness on the part of not-good-enough care or mothering, the child's attempt toward self-preservation quickly turns to some substitute to cling to. This is a condition that, depending on circumstances, may also lead to addiction. Thus he or she has a need for compensatory objects of one kind or another in the case of the collector; drugs, alcohol, or gambling for the addict. This can also be interpreted as a self-healing attempt.

To put it another way: such a person requires symbolic substitutes to cope with a world he or she regards as basically unfriendly or even hazardous. So long as he or she can touch, hold, possess, and, most important, replenish these surrogates, they constitute a guarantee of emotional support.

Irrespective of what kind of objects collectors choose to assemble, there are clues that help us understand their behavior and the nature of their passion. They are often marked by feelings of exhilaration and states of transport, but are also found in moments of tension, sensations of distress, or restless nights, and sometimes are seen in harrowing doubt. Often the very process of acquisition is a transparent source of excitement, although it may simultaneously prompt stirrings of guilt and dis-ease. If one observes collectors in pursuit of an object, one quickly recognizes conspicuous and telling individual attributes — the different ways by which they go about acquiring a new object, how they express their craving, or how they transmit overwhelming feelings of pleasure. On the other hand, after obtaining an object, they may maltreat themselves with bouts of remorse and self-reproach, quite incomprehensible to the noncollector. The following vignette of an unmarried lady in her late twenties should help depict the emotional history of such a constellation.

> Louise was referred to me by her physician. He suggested a few talks with me because of her intermittent depression, which he saw as an outcome of her not very satisfying life. She was engaged in work of her own choosing but described her personal life as emotionally impoverished. She had few friends and spent most of her free time with her cat, her books, and, as it gradually turned out, with the well-chosen objects of her collection.
>
> She is a rather tall and not unattractive woman who tried to talk of her background as if it were a prepared biographical

sketch; clearly avoiding any reference to her internal, reflective existence. She was an only child of parents who had met
in college and married in their early twenties, a fact her father
regretted in his more mature years. He talked to her once she
was about 15 or 16 about the circumstances of his marriage to
her mother. She was born toward the end of her parents' third
year of marriage. She had a clearer and in fact more positive
image of her nanny, a warm English girl, than of her mother.
"Mother was always busy — mostly golf or bridge; always
'bourgeois correct,'" she commented. Her sense of deprivation was evident.

She spoke of these details rather early in her analysis. She
had a tendency to gloss over facts that were related to more
profound and hurtful emotions. She liked her nanny. But her
unconflicted feelings belonged to her paternal grandmother
who stayed with her whenever the nanny had her day off.
Grandma used to tell stories and gave her a bath that Louise
fondly remembered. It was in this connection that she recalled Sunday evenings with Daddy who, when he was home,
gave her a bath and while drying her, rubbed her quite
vigorously, "especially between the thighs." It turned out to be
a highly vested memory that came back to her after a dream
about swimming in the Mediterranean. She was afraid of
drowning when a giant of a man came to her rescue and
gently carried her to the beach. She wanted to talk to him and
express her gratitude. But he did not speak English nor did she
understand his native tongue.

She enjoyed those Sundays when her father was home. He
allowed her to sit on his lap while he was reading or making
notes or telephoning. She wanted to be close to him but was
too much in awe to express what she really felt. On the other
hand, she saw her mother as immature and with few ambitions or interests, a fact of which she became more aware
once her nanny had left and she started in a private grade
school. Most of what I have said so far points to Louise's inner
loneliness. While there was much hidden admiration for her
father and warm feelings for his mother, the love shown by

both of them did not constitute continuous presence. It was not available when she felt in need.

It was shortly before her ninth birthday when one day after returning from school her mother greeted her crying incessantly. She told her that Dad had gone on one of his frequent business trips but he would not come home. Louise did not quite understand and only gradually realized that her father wanted to leave them. Suddenly her world seemed to change. It was a moment of distress and confusion for both mother and daughter. Louise remembered how much she felt abandoned and unwanted.

It was about twenty years after this incident that she consulted me. Her mother had moved to Florida. Her father had died about three years before, a few months after a severe car accident. Louise was still mourning, for after her college graduation she had "found" her father again, and by that she meant that they had a good mature relationship. He had remarried, and had achieved much success in his professional endeavors and provided generously for his daughter.

In fact, when she came for treatment, Louise was working for a foundation that she had established with the inheritance from her father. In addition, she found an "ideal" intellectual pursuit in studying and collecting early ceramics. She read extensively, visited museums, approached other collectors, and acquired, according to her description, a goodly number of rare or significant specimens. These were good enough to be recognized by connoisseurs and professional specialists. Both her collecting and the genre of what she collected turned out to be quite significant, something that surfaced in the analysis.

A day or so after her mother presented her with the fact of her father's departure, Louise went or sneaked (she could not remember) into her father's room, sat at his desk, and thought of the good times when she felt close to him. Before leaving his desk she grabbed a small ceramic ashtray he had used and, in her subjective experience, thievishly appropriated it.

The specific episode had long been forgotten. She recalled

it in the course of associating to the dream about her swim in the Mediterranean, her rescue by a gigantic man, and her father bathing and drying her. She then added: "Oh yes, I took the ashtray to bed." It is a habit I have seen in quite a number of collectors, which gives a rather convincing indication that the collectibles have a fetishistic value (see Winnicott 1975). It was this incident that a decade or so later widened out, opening the realm of collecting for a young woman who was on the way to becoming a spinster. The ashtray was not a functional object but a fetishistic, almost sensuous device of enormous inner meaning because it provided comfort and contact with the father of her childhood.

Without any conscious awareness, these were the circumstances that encouraged both her scholarly interest in ancient ceramics and, after her father's death, the careful selection of ceramic bowls and vases. Consciously, she used them for aesthetic enjoyment as well as a delight in fine shapes. Unconsciously, the affective meaning of these objects was that they were a way she had of keeping in touch with the father who tended to touch her after having given the Sunday evening baths.

Here the analysis revealed what preceded her desire for her particular choice as well as the repetitive thrill of obtainment. What she obtained was not at all incidental because all her collected objects echoed the first item she had secured for herself — Dad's ashtray.

While the response to ownership, the love of one's possessions, the inner pressure for more and more acquisitions, and the manner of giving expression to owning the objects, among other things, exist in all collectors, neither personal style nor circumstances are ever identical. Rather, they differ according to the confluence of inner causes and external circumstances, or what one might describe as the particular individual's collecting sentiments.

It is of course a given that whatever is collected is of particular significance to the individual collector. Each single item in a collection usually has a distinct meaning for the owner, and this meaning is inevitably determined by a great many external and experiential factors. Thus, while two collectors may crave the same object (think of several bidders for a specimen at an auction), their causal reasons for desiring it, and the ways they may go about obtaining it, may be, and usually are, entirely different. What drives them depends on their personality, on particular sociocultural conditions, and, in a deeper sense, on the nature of their antecedent emotional experience, as the case of Louise reveals.

What concerns us here is the question of the causality of the drive to collect. This can be understood only if one is aware of certain underlying factors, the most important of which is the constant search for new objects, new additions or acquisitions. My emphasis is on the overwhelming significance of objects to the collector.

Observing dedicated collectors in their often-consuming pursuits, one can detect an overmastering search for objects. Paying attention to certain people as they browse through flea markets, one has here and there a chance to recognize a kind of persistence behind which seems to lie a compulsive preoccupation. Like all compulsive action, this is molded by reactive factors, factors that stem from a range of historical circumstances. These circumstances may be concrete incidents such as physical hurt, emotional trauma, or actual neglect, or they may be more or less tangible states of alarm and anxiety, particularly when experienced when no real help or comfort was instantly forthcoming.

In some cases collecting can become an all-consuming passion, not unlike the dedication of a compulsive gambler to the gaming table, to the point where it can affect a person's life and become the paramount concern in his or her pursuit, overshadowing all else: work, family, social obligations, and responsibilities. I know of numerous cases in which moral standards, legal considerations, and societal taboos have been disregarded in the passion to collect.

In one case I encountered a collector of bells of all sorts, from cowbells from the Swiss Alps to Tibetan prayer bells and Chinese temple bells. I soon learned that the man had been brought up in a Catholic missionary orphanage under conditions that seemed pitifully grim and depressing. Only the sound of the bells of the little mission church had seemed to provide some source of comfort. Other considerations may have motivated this man, but there is much empirical evidence to indicate how crucial such childhood experiences are.

> The well-known case of Sir Thomas Phillipps (1792–1872), the man who wanted "a copy of every book," is a good example of an obsessional monomaniac who started out as a lonely and probably confused illegitimate son of an aging nouveau riche bachelor and his housemaid who was about thirty years younger. Phillipps's history provides us with many essentials to explore the generative conditions leading up to a collector's obsessional infatuation with particular objects. The maid was sent away. Young Thomas remained with his difficult and hardly caring father until he joined a private school where he did poorly. His only interest was collecting church records, deeds, gravestone inscriptions, and related documents from the vicinity of Middle Hill in Gloucestershire, clearly an extension of an illegitimate and lonely boy's need for discovering his own identity.
>
> These were the beginnings of what became the largest collection of books at the time, including manuscripts, old drawings, Babylonian seals, and other related items. Everything was sacrificed for Phillipps's collection. He ran up debts. He did not pay his servants' salaries or the butcher's bills. His first wife died out of sheer distress for him, and, as he was an incredible miser for everything besides his collection, he allowed her to suffer physically and mentally because his interest was focused exclusively on obtaining more and more books and manuscripts. Phillipps gives us a clear example of an obsessional collector who sets all social conventions aside for the sake of his needful and eroticized habit.

In doing clinical work it is important to explore the generative conditions leading up to the cause of the collector's obsessional infatuation with the objects. This obsessional infatuation reduces, for a period, an inner longing or, in psychoanalytic terms, the tension between id and ego. Inner longing and external representation achieve a temporary balance. Anyone acquainted with habitual collectors is well aware of how much of their time and effort is absorbed by their hobby and how the never-ending search for yet another acquisition generates excitement, anxious expectations, and thrills. Also generated, almost unavoidably, is hesitation, and (as I have observed quite frequently), suspicion bordering on paranoia. This kind of involvement is usually determined by unconscious concerns that serve as a device to screen off and master deeper doubts and ambiguities.

The significance of early events like these lies in the fact that they may establish a disposition for special techniques to alleviate the lingering dread of a repetition of exposure to trauma. Child observation shows us that the infant may look to alternative solutions for dealing with the anticipation of vulnerability, aloneness, and anxiety. The infant often will be looking for a tangible object like a comforter, a cushiony doll, or the proverbial security blanket to provide momentary freedom from anxiety, to give solace that was not forthcoming, and to allow the child a sense of not being alone. Thus, the collector, not unlike the religious believer, assigns power and value to these objects because their presence and possession seems to have a modifying, usually pleasure-giving, function in the owner's mental state. From this point of view objects of this kind serve as a powerful help in keeping anxiety or uncertainty under control. Their history, as in the case of Louise's collection, shows clearly that every new addition is a reaffirmation of one's ability to undo anxiety or hurt, or the dread of aloneness.

Favoring things instead of people may be one of several solutions for dealing with emotions that echo old traumata and uncertainties. Many observers have pointed out how one or the other kind of fear or anxiety can invoke a wide array of precautionary measures. Giving a doll or some other object a "soul" or a name is one telling example. This is a phenomenon anthropologists are long acquainted with. It is known as *animism*. In psychological terms it has been described as *attachment*, or *clinging response*, not only among children but in adults as well. Having discovered the palliative effect of her doll or his teddy bear, the infant soon tends to credit these first possessions with magical power. Affection becomes attached to these material objects, which in the eyes of the beholder can become animatized like the amulets and fetishes of preliterate humankind or like the holy relics of the religionist.

The concrete manifestations vary. Some people remember a favorite toy; others recall the first attempts at collecting baseball cards or campaign buttons, or perhaps going in search of shells or minerals. Despite all possible variations, there is reason to believe that the true source of the habit is the emotional state leading to a more or less perpetual attempt to surround oneself with magically potent objects.

Objects in the collector's experience allow for a magical escape into a remote and private world. This is perhaps the most intriguing aspect in any collector's scenario. But it is not enough to escape to this world only once, or even from time to time. Since it represents an experience of triumph in defense against anxiety and the fear of loss, the return must be effected over and over again. The obsessional collector's need shows a resemblance to the recurring state of hunger and the periodic need for replenishment. Regardless of how often and how much one ingests, within a few hours hunger returns and one must eat again.

Over many decades I have encountered all kinds of collectors from all walks of life, of all different ages ranging from children to octogenarians. Some of them recalled childhood events of a clearly circumscribed kind that caused anxiety — a parent's suicide, prolonged illness, physical handicaps, death of a sibling, war scenes and revolutionary turmoil, or simply not-good-enough early care. Whatever the motivation, there is little question that collecting is much more than the simple experience of pleasure. If that were the case, one butterfly or one painting would be enough. Instead, repetition is mandatory. Repeated acquisitions serve as a vehicle to cope with inner uncertainty, a way of dealing with the dread of renewed anxiety, with confusing problems of need and longing. The sense following the acquisition is usually that of blissful satisfaction and excitement, at times accompanied by flagrantly exhibitionistic elation, all of which is usually short-lived.

While collectors use their objects for inner security and quite often for outer applause, their deep inner function is to screen off self-doubt and unassimilated memories. The roots of their passion can almost always be traced back to their formative years, often hidden from their conscious awareness. In the light of these personal histories, we see how collecting has become an almost magical means for undoing strains and stresses a child felt unable to cope with.

REFERENCES

Winnicott, D. (1975). *Through Paediatrics to Psycho-Analysis*. New York: Basic Books.

8

Giving until It Hurts

Mary Ann McGrath

G iving and receiving gifts is deeply ingrained in both the culture and psyche of U.S. society. The internal psychological
phenomenon merges both with a behavioral process and with the
ritual responses of individuals in a sociological context. Gifts are
used to complete celebratory occasions and to note rites of passage. In addition, they may be given "just because" to reinforce or
build relationships. Under most circumstances gifts explicitly de-
note and symbolically connote generosity, selflessness and caring
on the part of the giver, and gratitude on the part of the recipient.
This chapter, however, explores gift giving in the extreme. Studying in-depth two individuals who feel that they cannot give
enough, while consistently giving too much, contributes to the
understanding of compulsive behaviors in general and begins to
illuminate the dark side of gift giving itself. Compulsive gift giving
has been given no formal attention to date. This represents a first
attempt to merge findings of consumer behavior with clinical
concerns of mental health professionals.

THEORIES OF GIFT GIVING

The exchange paradigm is traditionally favored in the various
explanations of the process and nature of gift giving (Belk 1979,

Mauss 1954, Sherry 1983). A person gives a gift with the expectation that something will be given in return. In addition, recent work has proposed a second paradigm, that of agapic or selfless love as motivation for giving gifts (Belk and Coon 1993, Sherry and McGrath 1989). Most current research on gift exchanges within the discipline of consumer behavior has been motivated by Sherry's (1983) three-stage characterization of the gift exchange process. The first stage is *Gestation*, and includes planning, search, gift choice, and wrapping. The second stage, *Presentation*, is the actual presentation of the gift to its recipient. The final stage is *Reformulation*, the postpresentation period during which the personal relationship may be altered and the receiver's relationship with the gift object itself may be developed or diminished. Aspects of compulsive gift giving impact each of these three stages.

In addition to the exchange and the agapic paradigms, a third and newer perspective on this traditionally positive and celebratory behavior has explored the darker side of gift exchanges (McGrath et al. 1993, Sherry et al. 1992a,b). It is in this venue that compulsive gift giving behavior resides, although the other two perspectives serve to contribute to understanding gift giving at its extreme.

The Exchange Perspective

From a social exchange perspective, gift giving involves reciprocity. The obligations to give, receive, and reciprocate are considered paramount (Belk 1976, Mauss 1954, Schieffelin 1980).

When explaining this exchange-centered view of gift giving, researchers have focused primarily on the social, personal, and economic aspects of the situation (Belk 1976, Sherry 1983). The social aspects emphasize the nature and importance of the relationship between the giver and receiver of the gift. Gifts tend to be symbolic and expressive gestures reflecting the importance of this social relationship. Thus a husband giving his wife a piece of jewelry, worn publicly as a "beacon" to attest to the importance of the relationship, differs dramatically from the symbolism of the gift of an appliance, used privately in the home to prepare a meal. Through gifts a giver partakes "in a recipient's tribulations and joys, despite the presence of an ulterior motive" (Sherry 1983, p. 157). Thus givers hope to please, but also hope to be pleased themselves as they receive a gift in return. Related to these interpersonal and kinship exchanges, Cheal (1986) points out that gifts enhance social bonds, but do not change the economic balance between the giver and the receiver.

The personal model refers to the giving of gifts as an exercise in the preservation and possible enhancement of the self-concept. Gifts are metaphors. Once an object is deemed a gift, in a sense it takes on a life of its own. It is encoded with meaning and attempts to communicate to both the giver and the receiver the unique nature of their relationship and their perceptions about themselves and others (Belk 1976). At the same time the gift reflects the giver. Thus "good" gifts may be thought to come from sensitive, generous, thoughtful givers, while "bad" gifts are the product of givers lacking those characteristics.

The economic model looks at gift giving from an equity perspective, the attempt to keep the exchange balanced over the long term. To do this involves factors beyond the momentary gift exchange at hand. Rather, this is influenced by the availability of money and time, the specific gift occasion and its appropriate rituals, and the history of the gift exchange relationship between these two people. While exchanging gifts is seemingly not obligatory, receiving a gift is often viewed as "an implicit recognition of dependence on the giver" (Belk 1976, p. 155). The perceived material value given to the recipient tends to be a primary factor in reciprocating the gift. Within the American context research suggests that equality of exchange is considered important by both the giver and the recipient (Cancian 1966).

A significant amount of a household's budget in the U.S. goes toward gift buying. According to a recent study of Christmas spending by the Conference Board (Christmas Spending 1998) the average U.S. household spends approximately $500 on Christmas gifts, and significantly more yearly on gifts overall. Thus it is not surprising that economic theories are frequently employed to explain gift exchange behavior. Garner and Wagner (1991) used Becker's (1974) theory of social interaction to evaluate the economic variables crucial to understanding expenditures incurred on gifts given outside the immediate household. Combining economic theory with social exchange theories, they correlated the expenditures on gift giving with socioeconomic variables. In addition to the intuitive finding that lower income households were less likely to give outside the immediate family, they found evidence that the social need for equality encouraged reciprocity even when recipients lacked resources. Individual motivations, demographics, and psychographic characteristics have also been deemed to influence the giver's behavior.

Alternatives to Reciprocity

Even though the social, personal, and economic models capture distinct dimensions of gift giving behavior, the holistic process and contexts of gift giving is not fully understood. We realize that gifts involve symbolic communication and reciprocity. In addition, it is clear that the three dimensions do not operate independently. For example, using the social exchange model, an investment by the giver and receiver cannot be fully explained without an understanding of the personal dimension, since members of the dyad also communicate their personal identities, put themselves on the line so to speak, through a gift exchange.

Otnes and colleagues (1993) note that social exchange theories neither address nor explain the process from the recipient's perspective. As an alternative, they offer a role theory perspective to explain gift giving. They conclude that givers can become like chameleons who can change to assume alternative roles of pleaser, provider, compensator, socializer, acknowledger, and avoider while selecting gifts for different recipients. Thus a parent, when selecting an educational toy for a child, could be a pleaser (given that the child wanted the toy) and a socializer (due to the learning function of the toy). Similarly, when a friend replaces another's lost wallet, the giver is acting as a compensator. Providers may choose utilitarian gifts such as socks and underwear. Acknowledgers give token gifts, while avoiders do not give in an attempt (often unsuccessful) to end the exchange process. Otnes and colleagues (1993) further note that the nature of the relationship between the giver and the receiver often dictates the role that the giver will assume in a certain gift-giving context. Sherry and colleagues (1992a) echo this view from the perspective of the recipient. Their research in the disposition of the gift indicates that gifts from children to parents are guaranteed to be enjoyed, while gifts from in-laws are frequent sources of angst and disappointment.

The paradigm of agapic or selfless love has been proposed by Sherry and McGrath (1989) and Belk and Coon (1993). This type of giving is nonobligatory, yet distinct from altruistic giving in more familiar philanthropic contexts in which prestige may be a motive. Agapic gifts spring from an emotional motive — the giver's love for the receiver. This type of giving is on the extreme positive end of an altruistic-agnostic continuum proposed by Sherry (1983). Beatty and colleagues (1993) note that individual personal values are of significance when examining gift giving across cultures, primarily in instances involving the giving of nonobligatory gifts. When focused on gifts given "just because" and for no apparent reason, these findings suggest that personal values and emotional involvement provide strong motivation to give a nonobligatory gift. The giving of gifts may spring from self-satisfaction, a sense of belonging, passion, and the extension of friendship and warmth to others.

The Dark Side of Gift Giving

Sherry and colleagues (1992a,b) have proposed and explored the "dark side" perspective to the study of gift giving. Although it is not socially acceptable for a person to admit to being a reluctant giver or an ungrateful recipient, several instances of negativity emerged in this stream of research. This sensitive data was accumulated through the use of projective techniques rather than direct questioning. The respondents described how "others" would react to various scenarios, indirectly giving insights into their own thoughts. In one particularly enlightening analysis, we found that certain types of relationships lend themselves to unpleasant exchanges. Table 8–1 examines the relative value of a gift, labeled *substance*, and the closeness and importance of the relationship, labeled *sentiment*.

TABLE 8–1. Relative value of a gift

	High Sentiment	Low Sentiment
High Substance	Gifts to spouse	Forced gifts to in-laws or other relatives
Low Substance	Handmade gifts from child to parent	Grab bag gifts blindly given and received

The greatest outpouring of negativity was expressed in situations that involved low sentiment and high substance. It is in these exchange relationships that reluctant givers may feel forced to give gifts of significant value to individuals for whom they feel little attachment. In these studies informants characterized "the perfect gift" as the handmade gift of a child, although it was also clear that such handmade gifts could come *only* from a child. Other adult givers may have to infuse more resources into a gift for it to be viewed as successful by its recipient.

Disappointment was also voiced in situations in which the substance of the gift did not match the importance of the relationship. In general, expensive and publicly displayed items were deemed appropriate as gifts between spouses. The study was restricted to women, who indicated that jewelry was an appropriate and favored gift from a significant other. Jewelry can be symbolically displayed to make a public statement about the importance and depth of the marital relationship. This spoke not only to their need for recognition from their husbands in the form of gifts, but also to the consumption values they have adopted in their own gift-giving behavior.

EMPIRICAL EVIDENCE OF
COMPULSIVE GIFT-GIVING BEHAVIOR

In the course of my studies of gift giving and receiving, I have interviewed many individuals about their feelings, heuristics, and behaviors relating to gift exchange in specific contexts and related to various types of relationships. From this extensive collection of data two individuals were selected for study because they fit what appeared to be the description of compulsive gift givers. Both tend to agonize over their gift choices, generally overbuy, engage in uneven exchanges, and often indicate feelings of regret and guilt after a gift exchange transaction.

Following is a summary description of each person, along with some details of their compulsive gift-giving behavior. The focal individuals and their spouses were interviewed by me on several occasions. I have been familiar with these people for several years. Their cooperation and candor were motivated both by their elevated interest in gift giving in general and by their continued interest in my research in this area. As much as possible I have attempted to capture and express their stories in their own words, although I have interjected descriptions where appropriate and have altered specific descriptive details to protect their anonymity. The descriptions were read by each of the informants, altered when deemed appropriate by them, and given final approval by each individual involved.

Case Study I

Donald McCoy is a successful 53-year-old investment banker. He has been married to his wife, Emma, a computer consultant, for twenty-seven years. The couple has three children, all unmarried and in their twenties. They live an upper-middle-class lifestyle, belong to a country club, and have a large home in a prestigious suburban location. Donald appears to be a well-adjusted professional with manifold discretionary resources. His gifts to community organizations and charities give him elevated status and are known among his peers. He also gives extravagant gifts to his wife on various occasions. Emma possesses an impressive collection of jewelry, all gifts from her husband. Interviews with the couple shed some light on their motivations and personal reactions to such gift giving.

Donald describes his own situation regarding the giving of gifts:

> I give really great gifts. I think about what I'm going to give family members for Christmas all year long. In fact, I bought my wife her twenty-fifth wedding anniversary gift almost three years before our anniversary. I planned her fiftieth birthday party and gift for over a year. But I never get anything I like from anyone. Do you think anyone would pick up on the hints that I give when I want something special? I start hinting for Christmas months in advance, and no one ever pays attention or remembers.

Donald retains salient memories of disappointments with gifts during his childhood: "It was the same when I was a child. My brother and I are very close in age, and he liked trains. Everyone assumed that I did too, so all our gifts were additions to our train set. I never played with it, and yet no one noticed. They kept giving us train pieces. I used to dread Christmas. And all summer, when my brother played with the trains, I used to read. I hated those trains."

In a sense, he is the man who has everything, yet his sensitivity and attention to gift giving appear to bring him pain and frustration when he is cast in the role of recipient. He articulates what Sherry and colleagues (1997) found in their study of gifts to self—the object may be perfect, but without another person to choose it, the self-gift falls short. As Donald says, "I'm always disappointed with the gifts that people give me. Really, I realize that I don't want anything from anyone. I would rather pick things out myself. Of course, if someone *really* knew me, they would be able to pick out something I would really like. But that will never happen."

In addition, Donald gives extravagant Christmas gifts to an extended list of current, potential, and former clients. These are always sent from Tiffany's, because he says that the impact of the blue box wrapped with red satin ribbon is important to the overall impression of the gift. He generally spends between $7,000 and $8,000 to send these gifts to his "short list" of sixty to seventy people. "The impact is worth the money. People are stunned when they receive these gifts. The store always makes sure that they arrive around December 23, so that there's no time for them [recipients] to send me a gift in return. I'm guaranteed to be one-up for the holiday season."

Donald expressed some of the dark-side motivations for his extravagance in an unexpected moment of candor. Part of his motivation to give an extravagant or unexpected gift is the sense of power and control that he feels after the exchange. But similar to many addictive behaviors, it is a short-lived fix, followed by feelings of remorse and lowered self-esteem as he sees the behavior as a reflection of his own inadequacy.

> I really like the feeling I get when I've given a really great gift to someone, and they don't even know how to re-spond. They feel awkward, uncomfortable, and usually embarrassed, because they don't have such a great gift to give back to me. That makes me feel really powerful, at least for the moment. I know that I'm really successful, and that such success brings money that can be used to control people. But then afterward, I regret doing that. I regret putting them in such an awkward, uncomfortable situation.

An interview with Donald's wife, Emma, sheds another perspective on his gift giving. She has been the recipient of many of Donald's extravagant and often publicly presented gifts. In addition, she is the unwitting recipient of the credit and attention he receives due to his generosity to various charities. She also expresses her own frustrations with the process of trying to give Donald gifts that please him.

> I love my husband, but giving gifts to him drives me crazy. I can never meet his expectations. Nothing is ever good enough, special enough. He spends a tremendous amount of thought, time, and money choosing gifts for me, for family members, for clients, and even for charities. I think he's often thinking of things he would like for himself, and he's hoping we can figure this out and produce it for him. But I'm not a mind reader, and neither are our children. We always disappoint him.

Emma expresses a perspective on gifts and on spending money in general that is the polar opposite of the approach taken by Donald. Their early socialization and childhood histories appear to contribute to these differences. Emma says, "One problem for me is simply that I'm not extravagant. My family never gave expensive gifts, mostly because we couldn't afford it. Actually, I tend to be a minimalist. I really don't want to own a lot of things — it's just more to take care of. Now that we have the money, I still can't bring myself to buy expensive gifts, especially when I've learned that Don won't really like anything."

Emma details one gift-giving success. Her husband appeared surprised by a prestigious item in short supply: "I did manage to delight him once, ironically by doing something more illegal than expensive. I gave him ten Cuban cigars that I asked a friend to bring me from London. He was thrilled, and, to my embarrassment, told everyone about this."

Emma understands that because she and Donald are a couple, both his gift choices and his gift-giving style are attributed to her. Although she claims that his extravagance and need for recognition would not be her chosen actions, she appears to make no effort to correct this misconception.

I prefer to be low-profile in giving gifts to friends as well as in making charitable donations. Don, however, always studies the donor categories and always gives amounts that will be recognized. He does include me as giving these gifts; he always lists us as "Mr. Donald and Mrs. Emma McCoy." I've never seen the cards, but even his clients seem to think that their Christmas gifts from Tiffany's come from both of us. They write gushing notes of thanks. I've often wondered if this happens because they think of women as shoppers and gift givers and they cannot imagine that a man would put so much effort into gift giving. They obviously don't know Don.

Case Study II

Jane Zeller is a 37-year-old retail employee. She and her husband, Greg, a fireman, have been married for eleven years and have no children. Jane is a high school graduate who did not attend college, and her husband completed his bachelor's degree on a part-time basis after they were married. They live in a small house in a middle-class suburb, and both admit that they never have enough money and that Jane "has a problem" with managing her spending in general, and controlling her gift-giving behavior in particular.

In the following perspective on her consumer behavior in general, Jane indicates an elevated interest in the marketplace and a compulsive tendency toward acquiring new objects: "My spending money has always been a problem in our relationship. I don't know what it is, but I need to go shopping at least once a week. I just need to see if there's anything new or different in my favorite stores. And when I see something I like, I just *have* to have it. I can't think about the price or about how I'll pay for it; I just have to buy it."

Impression management has a strong influence on Jane's gift-giving practices. Gifts have the power to enhance or deflate her image in the eyes of receivers. Thus she anthropomorphizes the gift as an extension of herself. She also obsesses over what she finds to be a poor gift from another, and tends to project that behavior onto the recipients of her own gifts.

> And with gifts it's even worse. I know how I feel when someone gives me something that's cheap or tacky. I would be embarrassed to give someone something that I wouldn't want [to receive] myself. I remember gifts [I received] for a long time. The bad ones really stay with me. I think other people do the same thing and it's like I think they'll hold it against me. I would be embarrassed to face them if I gave them something cheesy.

Similar to the musings of Donald, Jane relates her strong feelings about gifts to childhood disappointments. Such memories appear not to be aberrant, but the intensity to which both informants cling to them tends to be more extreme than other people I have interviewed on this topic.

> I always got terrible gifts for Christmas when I was little. People had no idea what I liked. I would never even show my friends what I got for Christmas. Once I remember that I got this terrible sweater from my parents. My mother wanted me to wear it, and I kept making excuses. Finally I put it on once and got some mustard on the front on purpose because I knew it would stain and I would never have to wear it again.

Jane describes a process that she and her husband appear to repeat each Christmas. In a sense the couple becomes trapped in both compulsive debting and a codependency with money, both concepts explicated by Boundy (1993; Chapter 1, this volume). In the latter case the codependency is an attempt to buy relationships with money and goods. It is transitory at best, and in Jane's case leads to the temporary, but predictable, erosion of her important relationship with her husband. "Christmas is a really hard time for me. I know I overspend, and I know that Greg and I are going to fight when the bills come in, but I have to give good gifts. I can't give that up. It's like, well, my reputation. So I pick out what I think works, and then I brace myself for the big explosion when we have to try to pay our charge cards."

Jane's husband Greg expresses that he understands that his wife's behavior is extreme and somewhat compulsive, but neither member of the couple has made any attempt to seek help or counseling outside their family unit. He speaks as a long-suffering, loving husband who vacillates between indulgence in and anger at his wife's behavior.

> If there's anything that will drive Jane and me apart, it's her spending. She has always worked in retail, so she seems to know about and want all kinds of new things. I don't care most of the time, but there have to be some limits. A few times we've agreed to put away the credit cards and only use cash for purchases. We did that last Christmas, and I thought that would keep her spending to what we could afford. But she wrote checks for everything, and in the end we didn't have the money for our mortgage and utilities. I'm a pretty controlled guy, but I really lost it at this point. I mean, I don't care if she spends what she makes, but she can't spend all the household money . . . my check . . . on Christmas.

Both Jane's gift giving to others and her general tendency to overspend influence her husband's gift giving to her. He is uninvolved in the choice of gifts that are chosen by her, but given from the couple. Like Emma, Greg in a sense receives credit for Jane's gift choices and extravagance. By not articulating concern during the overspending process of which he seems aware, Greg provides silent permission for Jane's behavior. Greg is subsequently caught in a dilemma as to how much more of the family's resources to devote to gift giving when it is time to give his wife a gift. "Money is always a problem with us. We never have enough. I don't know what we would do if we had kids. And at Christmas it gets to the point that I know she's spent so much, I don't want to spend any more on her gift. But in the end, she tells me what she wants and I buy it."

Both Donald and Jane do not represent the norm in their gift-giving practices and were selected from a myriad of people whom I have met in the course of my studies of gift giving precisely because they exhibited compulsive characteristics. It was the subsequent willingness of their spouses to discuss their own and their partner's gift practices that made these couples appropriate subjects for this study. Based on this relatively small sample, the following are some cautious attempts to generalize this phenomenon about which there has been no formal study to date.

WHAT ARE THE COMMON CHARACTERISTICS OF COMPULSIVE GIFT GIVERS?

When examining characteristics common to those who tend toward compulsive gift giving, it is important, yet difficult, to distinguish the external symptoms from the underlying causes that contribute to these symptoms. While psychologists are generally more interested in understanding, and possibly treating, the underlying causes, consumer researchers focus on both aspects, and may take more interest in overt behaviors. In the following discussion the common behavioral and motivational characteristics of these two individuals are enumerated and discussed. At this early stage of investigation it seemed prudent not to discount any notable insights so that others may accept the challenge to further clarify this unexplored area.

BEHAVIORS SURROUNDING COMPULSIVE GIFT GIVING

Through observation and discussion with the focal compulsive gift givers and their spouses, several common behaviors emerged.

Before examining why these individuals perform these compulsive acts, I will first enumerate what it is they do that differs from other respondents I have studied with regard to gift giving.

Use of Gifts as a Weapon

In both cases examined, the compulsive gift givers are "generous to a fault." That is, both would have more harmonious relationships with their partners, and in the case of Jane better financial stability and well-being, if they were able to curtail or decrease their gift giving. But in a real sense they cannot. They not only give until it hurts, they give in order to hurt. Under the auspices of generosity they put receivers on the defensive as well as cause discord within their families. For a recipient who tries to achieve equity through reciprocity, the overgenerous, almost-perfect gift can cause momentary delight but a long-term wound. It cannot be repaid in kind, thus leaving its receiver in an uncomfortable and irreconcilable position. Donald is explicitly aware of this process, and expresses sorrow for this after the fact, but continues the behavior.

Elevated Level of Materialism

Both of the compulsive gift givers in these case studies exhibit a level of interest in "stuff" greater than that of their spouses and others I have studied. Although Faber and O'Guinn (1989) would disagree that the extreme desire for material things is a factor in compulsive buying behavior, I am not prepared to readily dismiss our subjects' heightened level of interest in particular objects and in the retail marketplace in general. This interest, coupled with their attention to and curiosity about things that are novel or as yet undiscovered by them, may contribute to their tendency to give gifts compulsively with more frequency and extravagance than the norm. In addition, both subjects proactively seek out retail stimulation. Both admit to spending leisure time perusing catalogues at home and taking frequent walks through malls and department stores. This may be the higher level of arousal in compulsive consumption categorized by Jacobs (1989).

Presence of Other Compulsive Behaviors

Both informants mention other compulsions they experience. Jane is a self-proclaimed "neatnick." This serves as an asset to her career in retailing; she is always aware when something is out of place and immediately sets about tidying any setting. Both Donald and his wife mentioned the territoriality that he exhibits at home. He generally does not want anyone to touch "his stuff," and keeps his things separate from those of other family members. Both are forms of control, mentioned by other researchers in areas of addiction (Boundy 1993). Both subjects are also binge eaters, who afterward regret their behavior. Although both are of average height and weight, they tend to be constant dieters and worry about gaining weight.

Tendency toward Risk Taking

Similar to a finding by Faber and O'Guinn (1989) with respect to compulsive shoppers, both of our compulsive gift givers engaged in various forms of risk-taking behavior. Donald speculated in the stock market and in commodities, as well as in a series of risky business investments. Both played the lottery, smoked, and had a tendency to speed when driving. Obviously, no conclusions can be drawn from these correlations, but I include this as information that might be helpful as this area is explored in more depth.

MOTIVATIONS CONTRIBUTING TO COMPULSIVE GIFT GIVING

Several of the motivations expressed by the compulsive gift givers converged with the psychological profiles of individuals experiencing other forms of compulsions. Others, however, are directly related to the gift exchange process, which is, of course, integrated into the social fabric of daily life.

Salient Memories of Disappointments with Gifts Received

These two compulsive givers were clearly reminded of childhood disappointments as they spoke about the gifts they give. There is no evidence that they experienced greater than normal levels of disappointment as compared with other children, but they appear to have more salient memories of these dissatisfactions. Their current need to "get it right" is fed by clear memories from their individual histories when each was hurt by a gift. These experiences also taught them the power that gifts have to manipulate the feelings and behaviors of others.

Low Self-Esteem

Both Donald and Jane, despite appearing to possess many admirable social, physical, intellectual, and financial resources, evidence relatively low self-esteem. They have difficulty relating to peers as equals. Both appear to be quite self-conscious and uncomfortable in social settings. As a result, they use money in the form of purchased gifts as an attempt to buy love and acceptance. The result is transitory and superficial (Boundy 1993). Each knows this is not an effective long-term strategy toward forging true relationships, and thus their compulsive giving works to further lower self-esteem.

Tendency toward Perfectionism

Both focal compulsive gift givers tend to be perfectionists. They are viewed by both themselves and others as quite picky in their tastes, preferences, and behaviors. Both articulated a feeling that others could never know them well enough to appropriately choose gifts they would like and to adequately respond to gifts that they give. Their spouses echo this sentiment and express personal frustration with the situation. Such perfectionism gives them control of the gift exchange and the relationship itself, and undermines the trust of the exchange partners.

High Salience of Gift Giving

Our focal compulsive respondents approached the gift-giving context with elevated states of salience and anxiety. They view gift giving as an important part of their lives. They both have exalted hopes of the outcomes that will result from the exchange. They see gifts as having the ability to enhance their personal image to others (Boundy 1993), and understand the ability of a gift to change a relationship. Even though their expectations of an adequate response from their recipient are low, they approach the task with enthusiasm. Looking for a perfect gift is a treasure hunt, an adventure in which they exude confidence that they will succeed. The compulsive givers appear to devote more cognitive, emotional, and behavioral effort as well as monetary and temporal resources to the task of gift choice than do most givers on average. Giving gifts is both their vocation and avocation. They love the process, even though they know that their thrill is transitory and that regret will inevitably follow.

Rejection of Reciprocity

Both compulsive gift givers have strong feelings that their gift exchanges will never be (and can never be) equal and balanced. In effect, they are rejecting the idea of reciprocity. On a more basic level, they are also admitting they are poor recipients of gifts. Compulsive givers are not motivated by the agapic model of selfless giving. Rather, they understand that an uneven exchange brings them power and control over those who owe them. They regret their inability to form equitable exchanges and understand that they are bringing discomfort to others. However, their remorse is without a cure. They typically judge gifts they receive as inadequate, putting fault on the givers instead of recognizing their own inability to graciously receive. This lack of reciprocity in gift exchanges is an outward manifestation of the difficulty that the compulsive gift giver has in having an equitable, honest, and trusting relationship with another person.

CONCLUSION

In this attempt to explore the heretofore unarticulated world of the compulsive gift giver, I have leaned on the generosity and insight of four people who are involved in compulsive gift-exchange relationships. As I am not a trained therapist but rather a consumer researcher, I found myself treading on uncertain ground as they revealed their compulsions to me. My discipline gives me no recipes or guidance for effective intervention. My approach was to attempt to be a good listener, to allow each informant to read what I had written and to express in writing only their approved perspectives. The result from my point of view is a picture of this compulsive condition that is as honest and "real" as I (neither a mental health professional nor a compulsive giver) can understand. From my exploration I conclude that compulsive gift giving exists, and that the phenomenon requires further analysis. My hope is that this explication motivates other researchers to further clarify the area and that mental health professionals will recognize and intervene appropriately when clients evidence signs of compulsive gift giving, either in isolation or in combination with other compulsive behaviors.

REFERENCES

Beatty, S., Kahle, L., Utsey, M., and Keown, C. (1993). Cross-cultural business gift giving. *Journal of International Consumer Marketing* 6(1):49–66.

Becker, G. (1974). A theory of social interactions. *Journal of Political Economy* 82(6):1063–1093.

Belk, R. (1976). It's the thought that counts: a signed digraph analysis of gift-giving. *Journal of Consumer Research* 3:155–162.

—— (1979). Gift giving behavior. In *Research in Marketing*, ed. J. Sheth, 2nd ed., pp. 95–126. Greenwich, CT: JAI.

Belk, R., and Coon, G. (1993). Gift giving as agapic love: an alternative to the exchange paradigm based on dating experiences. *Journal of Consumer Research* 20:393–416.

Boundy, D. (1993). *When Money Is the Drug: Understanding and Changing Self-Defeating Money Patterns*. Woodstock, NY: Maverick Media Resources.

Cancian, F. (1966). Maximization as norm, strategy and theory: a comment on programmatic statements in economic anthropology. *American Sociological Review* 68:465–470.

Cheal, D. (1986). The social dimensions of gift behavior. *Journal of Social and Personal Relationships* 3:423–439.

Christmas Spending. (1998). *Special Consumer Survey Report*. The Consumer Research Center. New York: The Conference Board.

Faber, R. J., and O'Guinn, T. (1989). Compulsive buying: a phenomenological exploration. *Journal of Consumer Research* 16:147–157.

Garner, T., and Wagner, J. (1991). Economic dimensions of household gift giving. *Journal of Consumer Research* 18:368–379.

Jacobs, D. F. (1989). A general theory of addictions: rationale for and evidence supporting a new approach for understanding and treating addictive behaviors. In *Compulsive Gambling: Theory, Research and Practice*, ed. H. J. Shaffer, S. A. Stein, B. Gambino, and T. N. Cummings, pp. 35–64. Lexington, MA: Heath.

Mauss, M. (1954). *The Gift: Forms and Functions of Exchange in Archaic Societies*, trans. F. Cunnison. Glencoe, IL: Free Press.

McGrath, M. A., Sherry, J. F., Jr., and Levy, S. J. (1993). Giving voice to the gift. *Journal of Consumer Psychology* 2(2):171–191.

Otnes, C., Lowrey, T., and Kim, Y. C. (1993). Gift selection for easy and difficult recipients: a social roles interpretation. *Journal of Consumer Research* 20:229–244.

Schieffelin, E. (1980). Reciprocity and the construction of reality. *Man* 15(3):502–517.

Sherry, J. (1983). Gift giving in anthropological perspective. *Journal of Consumer Research* 10:157–168.

Sherry, J., and McGrath, M. A. (1989). Unpacking the holiday presence: a comparative ethnography of two gift stores. In *Interpretive Consumer Research*, ed. E. Hirschman, pp. 148–167. Provo, UT: Association for Consumer Research.

Sherry, J., McGrath, M. A., and Levy, S. (1992a). The disposition of the gift and many unhappy returns. *Journal of Retailing* 68(1): 40–65.

—— (1992b). The dark side of the gift. *Journal of Business Research* 28(3):225–244.

—— (1997). Monadic giving: giving gifts to the self. In *Contemporary Marketing and Consumer Behavior: An Anthropological Sourcebook*, ed. J. F. Sherry, Jr., pp. 399–432. New York: Sage.

IV Psychiatric Considerations

9

Assessment of Compulsive Buying

Donald W. Black

Compulsive buying is a behavioral syndrome characterized by excessive and inappropriate shopping and spending that creates personal distress or impairment in one or more life domains (Black 1996, Lejoyeux et al. 1996). It has been the focus of increasing attention in both the lay and the professional literature. Though widespread and problematic, clinicians are often unaware of compulsive spending behavior in their patients. While many patients will not discuss the problem unless asked, some may seek help specifically for the disorder, particularly if they have read about it or seen media portrayals. Others may present at the behest of a concerned spouse, the recommendation of a friend, or sometimes an attorney or law enforcement officer if there have been legal ramifications. This chapter reviews the clinical assessment of the compulsive buyer, and includes discussion of diagnostic and rating instruments used primarily in research settings.

THE CLINICAL INTERVIEW

The first step in evaluating patients with a compulsive buying disorder is to construct an accurate history through a careful interview. The patient's history is the most important basis for diagnosing compulsive buying. Because the assessment of compulsive buying begins with its recognition, clinicians need to become familiar with the syndrome. To help clinicians and researchers, McElroy and colleagues (1994) have developed a set of operationalized criteria (see Table 10–1, Chapter 10, this volume). Their definition recognizes that compulsive buying involves both cognitions (or preoccupations) and behaviors, each component potentially causing impairment. The criteria specify that impairment can be manifested through personal distress; social, marital, or occupational dysfunction; or financial or legal problems. The impairment criterion is now used throughout *DSM-IV*, and recognizes that symptoms in the absence of impairment fail to meet the threshold for a psychiatric diagnosis. Designed primarily for use in research settings, the criteria can easily be used for clinical purposes.

As with any psychiatric assessment, the interview should begin with a sincere attempt to develop rapport with the patient, perhaps beginning by asking the patient about herself—what kind of work she does, where she goes to school, whether she is married, has a significant other, or is single, and so on. The questions should be asked in a manner that conveys genuine interest and does not make the patient feel that she is under interrogation. After rapport is established, the questions can gradually become more detailed and specific, focusing on the patient's problems, blending open-ended questions with others that can be answered easily with a yes or no. The initial goal of evaluation is to define the buying problem through relatively nonintrusive inquiries about the individual's attitudes about shopping and spending, and then moving on to specific shopping behaviors and patterns. Once the individual has acknowledged a compulsive buying problem, she can be questioned in greater detail about the extent of the preoccupation and behavior. For general screening purposes a clinician might ask:

- Do you feel overly preoccupied with shopping and spending?
- Do you ever feel that your shopping behavior is excessive, inappropriate, or uncontrolled?

- Have your shopping desires, urges, fantasies or behaviors ever been overly time-consuming, caused you to feel upset or guilty, or led to serious problems in your life (e.g., financial or legal problems, relationship loss)?

Positive responses should generally be followed up with more specific questions about the shopping and spending behavior. For example, the clinician will want to ask when the behavior began, how frequently it occurs, what the individual likes to buy, and how much money is spent. Patients with a compulsive buying disorder may be anxious or embarrassed about their symptoms, and may need considerable reassurance before disclosing their thoughts and behaviors. Clinicians should reassure them about the confidential nature of the doctor–patient relationship.

Family members and friends can become important informants in the assessment of compulsive buyers, able to fill in the gaps in the patient's history or to describe patients behavior they may have witnessed. Patients may not always be accurate in describing the extent of their problem, but rarely are close relatives directly affected by the consequences of the behavior unable to do so.

It is important to assess the patient's psychiatric history carefully because research has shown that most compulsive buyers have comorbid psychiatric disorders (Christensen et al. 1994, McElroy et al. 1994, Schlosser et al. 1994). The presence of comorbidity may suggest particular treatment strategies or approaches as well as explanations for excessive spending and shopping that may be helpful in counseling patients. For instance, an individual's excessive shopping and spending might be attributable to a bipolar disorder, which would suggest treatment with a mood stabilizer (e.g., lithium carbonate, sodium valproate). Clinicians should take note of past psychiatric treatment, including medications, hospitalizations, and psychotherapy. The patient's history of physical illness, surgical procedures, drug allergies, and medical treatment is important, as it may help rule out medical illnesses as explanations for the compulsive buying (e.g., neurologic disorders, brain tumors) or conditions that may contraindicate the use of certain medications to treat the disorder. Because many patients with compulsive buying have histories of depression, anxiety disorders, and substance use disorders, particular attention should be focused on these conditions (Black et al. 1998).

Though the cause of compulsive buying is unknown, it is clear that compulsive buying runs in some families — families that are often troubled by depression, alcoholism, and drug addiction (Black et al. 1998). Information about the emotional and psychiatric health of the parents, grandparents, aunts, uncles, and children can help identify risk factors linked to the patient's heredity or home environment, and suggest possible diagnoses. For example, having grown up in a dysfunctional home in which one or both parents had a mental illness or addictive disorder may have contributed to the patient's compulsive buying. On the other hand, the patient may have learned inappropriate buying and spending behavior from her mother or other relatives. For these reasons family information may be helpful both in understanding the patient's disorder and in designing a therapeutic strategy for the patient.

The patient's personal and social history should be explored, including early family life; details about the home and the community; and any history of physical, emotional, or sexual abuse. Educational background, relationships, occupational history, and questions about marriage will also be helpful in evaluating the patient. Details about the patient's living arrangements, finances, and children are additional aspects of the personal history that can help fill out the overall picture of the patient's life.

INQUIRIES DIRECTED AT COMPULSIVE BUYING

The compulsive buying disorder needs to be evaluated carefully. This should begin with inquiries about when the behavior began, how it began, and what prompted its origin. Typically, patients will report the onset of the disorder in their late teens or early twenties, often at times when they began their first job, opened their first credit card or checking account, or achieved personal independence (Schlosser et al. 1994). The course of the disorder needs to be explored. Has it been chronic? Episodic? Has its severity fluctuated? Most patients indicate that the disorder is chronic, although it may fluctuate depending on life circumstances and finances (Christensen et al. 1994).

The clinician should ask the patient what she buys. Mainly clothing? Jewelry? Collectibles? Electronic goods? Does the buying occur usually in upscale department stores? Discount stores? Consignment or thrift shops? Does the patient make a habit of attending garage sales? Does the patient spend time shopping on the Internet, television shopping networks, or through catalogues? Is the shopping year-round or does it occur in sprees associated with birthdays and major holidays? Does the shopping occur when the patient is alone, or is she accompanied by a friend or family member? Is the shopping impulsive, or is it preceded by careful planning? Does the patient spend time looking through newspaper ads or catalogues? Does the patient use cash, personal checks, or credit cards? If the patient uses credit cards, how many cards does the patient have and what is the current debt? What is the patient's total consumer debt (excluding the home mortgage and car payments)?

Does the patient associate any particular emotions or affects with buying? How does the patient feel after a purchase? Does the patient have to buy, or can she be satisfied by window shopping? Has the shopping affected the patient's spousal relationship or family life? Does the patient ignore her spouse or children in order to shop? Does the patient take her children along with her on shopping sprees? Has she ever sought treatment for her shopping disorder? If so, what treatment did the patient have, and how long did it last? Was the treatment effective? Last, I always ask patients what they believe caused the disorder. In my experience all patients offer an explanation for their behavior, which may yield clues to what prompted the shopping initially and what they view as important historically in their lives.

PHYSICAL EXAMINATION AND LABORATORY TESTING

A thorough assessment of any patient generally involves conducting a physical examination and obtaining routine screening laboratories. For most persons with compulsive buying, it is unlikely that the physical examination or laboratory tests will be helpful, although they may show changes consistent with medical problems the patient may have, or her psychiatric comorbidity. For example, alcoholic patients may show evidence of liver enlargement or display palmar erythema, while laboratory testing may show evidence of liver enzyme elevations. There is no reason to administer other tests, including brain scans or electroencephalography, unless indicated to rule out specific disorders suggested by the differential diagnosis, such as a mass lesion or a seizure disorder.

While collecting the patient's history, the clinician should train his or her attention on the patient's appearance, habits, and demeanor, noting any peculiarities in dress, attitude, or speaking style. Orientation to time, place, and person, ability to reason, and memory can be assessed informally as part of a mental status examination (MSE). The MSE can help to identify patients with psychotic symptoms, severe depression or suicidal ideations, or cognitive impairment. In my experience most compulsive buyers display a normal sensorium, are well groomed and dressed, show good eye contact, and exhibit relevant and coherent speech. Some show evidence of current psychiatric comorbidity, such as major depression, panic disorder, or social phobia. Others give evidence of alcoholism or drug addiction. As a group, I have found compulsive buyers to be highly interested in their disorder. They generally show good insight and are able to describe the driven, compulsive quality of the disorder, which they feel unable to control. They may describe a feeling of anxiety that builds until it is relieved by shopping and spending. Afterwards, they may convey a sense of shame and guilt, while admitting to the pleasure they experienced while shopping and spending.

In any evaluation normal shopping and spending behavior must be distinguished from compulsive buying, though it may sometimes be difficult to draw a clear distinction. The clinician should also be aware of the inherent differences in shopping behavior of typical men and women, and understand that shopping and spending generally occur within a cultural context. In our culture shopping is typically viewed from a female perspective, a fact not lost on advertisers, who aim their advertisements mainly at women. Additionally, persons may go through periods when their shopping and spending behavior may take on a compulsive quality — for example, around special holidays and birthdays when shopping and spending are viewed as expected and normal. Persons who receive an inheritance or win a lottery may experience spending sprees or binges. The clinician needs to keep in mind that typical compulsive buyers do not confine their overspending to certain times of the year, but have a chronic, year-round problem (Black 1996, Christenson et al. 1994). The clinician needs to exercise judgment in applying the diagnostic criteria, and must be mindful of the need for evidence of distress or impairment.

DIAGNOSTIC AND SCREENING INSTRUMENTS

Prompted by the recent interest in compulsive buying, several researchers have developed instruments to help identify and diagnose this disorder. Working in Canada, Valence and colleagues (1988) developed the Compulsive Buying Measurement Scale. They selected sixteen items thought to represent four basic dimensions of compulsive buying (a tendency to spend, feeling an urge to buy or shop, postpurchase guilt, and family environment). A reliability analysis based on results from a sample of thirty-eight compulsive buyers and thirty-eight normal shoppers led the investigators to delete three items representing family environment; the remaining thirteen had high internal consistency (Cronbach's alpha=0.88). Construct validity was established by demonstrating that the compulsive buyers achieved significantly higher scores than the control group, and that higher scores correlated with higher levels of anxiety and with having a family history of psychiatric illness. A modified version of the scale containing sixteen items, each rated on a four-point scale, was tested by German researchers (Scherhorn et al. 1990). Their Addictive Buying Indicator was found to have high reliability (Cronbach's alpha=0.87); construct validity was demonstrated by significant correlations between scale scores and scores assessing psychasthenia, depression, and self-esteem. Like the Canadian instrument, the Addictive Buying Indicator was able to discriminate normal from compulsive buyers.

These early efforts led Faber and O'Guinn (1992) to develop the Compulsive Buying Scale, an instrument designed to identify compulsive buyers. They began with twenty-nine items based on preliminary work and each was rated on a five-point scale chosen to reflect important characteristics of compulsive buying. Their scale was administered to 388 self-identified compulsive buyers and 292 persons drawn randomly from the general population. Using logistic regression, seven items representing specific behaviors, motivations, and feelings associated with buying significantly were found to correctly classify approximately 88 percent of the subjects.

This instrument also showed excellent reliability and validity. One measure of reliability, internal consistency, was verified using principal components factor analysis as well as by calculating Cronbach's alpha (0.95). Criterion and construct validity were assessed by comparing compulsive buyers from the general population sample (classified by the screener) to the self-identified compulsive buyers and to the other members of the general population on variables previously found to relate to compulsive buying (Faber and O'Guinn 1989). The comparison provides good support for the validity of the screener. On each of the twelve variables examined, scores from twelve members of the general population identified as compulsive buyers were not significantly different from those of self-identified compulsive buyers. The investigators concluded that their screening instrument separates compulsive from noncompulsive buyers.

Another use of this instrument is in prevalence estimation. Based on a probability distribution, Faber and O'Guinn (1992) recommend a cut-point of 0.70 (i.e., the probability of being a compulsive buyer), which corresponds with a scale score of −1.34, a figure approximately two standard deviations above the normal population mean. Using this criterion, they classified 8.1 percent of their general population sample as being (or at risk to become) compulsive buyers. Using a more conservative probability level of 0.95 produced a prevalence estimate of 1.8 percent of the general population.

A more detailed discussion about the Compulsive Buying Scale can be found in Chapter 2 of this volume. The instrument is reproduced in Appendix A.

Christenson and colleagues (1994) have developed the Minnesota Impulsive Disorder Interview (MIDI), which is used to assess the presence of compulsive buying, kleptomania, trichotillomania, intermittent explosive disorder, pathological gambling, compulsive sexual behavior, and compulsive exercise. This diagnostic instrument is fully structured, and designed for use in research settings. The MIDI begins by gathering demographic data, and then progresses through various screening modules. It is followed by a section on family history and personality characteristics. The section on compulsive buying consists of four core questions, and five follow-up questions. The developers recommend administering their eighty-two-question expanded module to persons screening positive for compulsive buying. Expanded modules are also available for trichotillomania and compulsive sexual behavior. While the MIDI and its expanded modules have not been tested for reliability or validity, its developers report excellent interrater reliability among themselves, and believe that the instrument has good face validity (G. Christenson, personal communication, 1998).

Edwards (1993) and DeSarbo and Edwards (1996) have developed a thirteen-item self-report scale designed to identify persons with compulsive buying behavior and to rate the severity of this behavior. Each item is rated along a five-point Likert-like scale. In a study comparing the responses of 104 compulsive buyers recruited through support groups and 101 persons from the general population, the authors identified five factors constituting compulsive spending: compulsion/drive to spend, feelings about shopping and spending, tendency to spend, dysfunctional spending, and postpurchase guilt. Based on their results, the authors pared the scale from twenty-nine to thirteen items. The scale itself and its subscales showed good to excellent internal consistency as estimated by Cronbach's alpha (range, 0.76 to 0.91). The developers of the scale observe that it can be used by counselors and therapists to help identify a person's compulsive spending tendencies, as well as the severity of those tendencies, which they hypothesize to fall along a continuum from noncompulsive buying to "addicted" buying behavior. The instrument is reproduced in Appendix B.

Lejoyeux and colleagues (1997) have developed a questionnaire consisting of nineteen items that tap the basic features of compulsive buying. These dimensions include impulsivity; urges to shop and buy; emotions felt before, during, and after purchasing; postpurchase guilt and regret; degree of engagement of short-term gratification; tangible consequences of buying; and avoidance strategies. Its psychometric properties have not been examined. The instrument is reproduced in Appendix C.

AN INSTRUMENT TO RATE SEVERITY AND CHANGE

Monahan and colleagues (1996) modified the Yale–Brown Obsessive-Compulsive Scale (YBOCS) (Goodman et al. 1989) to create the YBOCS-Shopping Version (YBOCS-SV) to assess cognitions and behaviors associated with compulsive buying. The authors conclude that their scale is reliable and valid in measuring severity and change during clinical trials. For example, compulsive buyers are reported to describe repetitive problematic buying, intrusive thoughts about buying, and resistance to such thoughts. The YBOCS-SV is reproduced in Appendix D.

These investigators compared a group of clinically identified compulsive buyers and control subjects and showed that the scale separated the two groups. Interrater reliability was demonstrated for compulsive buyers ($r=0.81$), control subjects ($r=0.96$), and for both groups combined ($r=0.99$). The instrument showed a fairly high degree of internal consistency using Cronbach's alpha coefficients. The evidence for construct validity was good as well, showing that YBOCS-SV scores were the best indicators of severity of illness of compulsive buyers, not other scales that were administered, including the Clinical Global Impression Scales (Guy 1976) and the National Institute of Mental Health Obsessive-Compulsive Scale (NIMHOCS)(Murphy et al. 1982). The YBOCS-SV was sensitive to clinical change and was able to detect improvement during a clinical trial (Black et al. 1996).

Like its sister instrument, the YBOCS-SV consists of ten items, five of which rate preoccupations; five, behaviors. For assessing both preoccupations and behaviors subjects are asked about time involved, interference due to the preoccupations or behaviors, distress associated with shopping, the resistance to the thoughts or behavior, and degree of control over the symptoms. Items are rated from 0 (none) to 4 (extreme), and scores can range from 0 to 40. In the sample described by Monahan and colleagues (1996), the mean YBOCS-SV score for untreated compulsive shoppers was 21 (range 18–25) and 4 (range 1–7) for normal shoppers.

SHOPPING DIARIES

Any effort to understand and treat compulsive buyers will benefit by having patients keep a daily log of their shopping and spending behavior. In our research we have found it helpful to have patients regularly record their shopping experiences: where they shop, how much they spend, and what they buy. It may be helpful to have patients record their mood at the time, and to note whether the buying episode was prompted by anything in particular. The data collected can be used to gain a sense of the patient's typical buying behavior, as well as to provide data that can be directly monitored during a treatment trial. The data can be used to supplement (and externally validate) the rating scale scores.

The use of a daily log may be therapeutic as well. In our experience patients almost uniformly report that keeping a log is the most valuable part of their treatment. The log enables them to become fully aware of the extent and severity of their disorder;

acknowledging the disorder to a therapist is probably the first step toward any improvement. Any formal effort at behavior therapy will benefit from the use of a log, as the therapist can design an individualized program for the patient to interrupt unwanted behaviors, to help the patient learn typical cues that prompt the behavior, and to assist the patient in learning new ways to spend her time (Bernik et al. 1996).

OTHER USEFUL INSTRUMENTS AND RATING SCALES

Depending on the situation, a comprehensive assessment of the person with compulsive buying will benefit from using other instruments and scales. Researchers should begin with a structured diagnostic instrument. Several are available, including the Structured Clinical Interview for *DSM-IV* (SCID) (Spitzer et al. 1994) or the Schedule for the Assessment of Schizophrenia and Depression (SADS) (Spitzer and Endicott 1978). Both instruments are designed to be used by trained clinicians, however. The Diagnostic Interview Schedule (DIS) (Robins et al. 1981) and the Composite International Diagnostic Interview (CIDI) (World Health Organization 1990) are easy to use since they are designed for lay interviewers, but are most appropriate for large epidemiologic surveys. Axis II disorders can be assessed with the Personality Diagnostic Examination (PDE) (Loranger 1988), the Structured Interview for *DSM-IV* Personality Disorders (SIDP-IV) (Pfohl et al. 1997), or the Structured Clinical Interview for *DSM-IV* Personality Disorders (SCID-II) (Spitzer et al. 1996). The self-rated Personality Diagnostic Questionnaire-IV (PDQ-IV) may also be used to assess Axis II (Hyler et al. 1997).

Depressive symptoms can be assessed using the Beck Depression Inventory, which is useful for tapping the cognitive components of depression (Beck et al. 1961). The Hamilton Rating Scale for Depression (Hamilton 1967), or the Montgomery–Asberg Depression Scale can also be used (Montgomery and Asberg 1979). These two scales are geared to focus on the physiological symptoms of depression. Anxiety can be rated using the Hamilton

Rating Scale for Anxiety (Hamilton 1959) or the Beck Anxiety Inventory (Beck et al. 1988). Obsessionality can be measured with the Leyton Obsessionality Inventory (Cooper 1970) or the Maudsley Obsessionality Inventory (Hodgson and Rachman 1977). Somatization can be rated using the Brief Symptom Inventory or its expanded version, the Hopkins Symptom Checklist (Derogatis 1977). Hypochondriacal tendencies can be assessed with the Illness Behavior Questionnaire (Pilowky and Spence 1983).

Family psychiatric history can be assessed using the Family History-Research Diagnostic Criteria (FH-RDC) (Andreasen et al. 1977). To collect a family history of compulsive shopping, we suggest the researcher seek a history of (1) excessive or problematic shopping behavior that (2) caused the relative distress or impairment. For example, the relative may have spent time away from family responsibilities, acquired significant debts, or declared bankruptcy.

A description of other psychiatric instruments is beyond the scope of this chapter, but investigators are urged to design a comprehensive battery prior to conducting research, and to carefully match the instruments with their study goals.

ASSESSING THE COMPULSIVE BUYER: A PATIENT EXAMPLE

Heather was an attractive, slightly overweight 35-year-old woman who presented for a drug treatment study of compulsive buying. She had been compulsively shopping and spending since receiving her first credit card in her late teens. While she knew her behavior was irrational and excessive, her efforts to change had always failed. Heather's life revolved around shopping and spending, even though she worked full-time and had two young children. She often took them shopping with her, and they too expressed keen interest in shopping.

Heather's history strongly suggested a compulsive buying disorder. Her Compulsive Buying Scale score was −2.34, which indicated that her shopping and spending habits were extreme. The criteria of McElroy and associates (1994) were applied, and Heather acknowledged meeting each criterion. Administration of the SCID revealed a history of major depression and isolated panic attacks, but showed no current major depression. The FH-RDC showed that several first-degree relatives suffered major depression or were alcoholic.

Heather's disorder was assessed first with the MIDI, using the expanded module for compulsive buying. Among the information learned was that she typically bought clothing for herself (or her children), paperback books, cosmetics and hair care products, and other small items. She tended to shop at department stores and discount stores, but also bought excessively at grocery stores. She acknowledged feeling excited or even high when she made a purchase, but rarely experienced feelings of guilt. In fact, she was distressed only by the consequences of her disorder; her husband was fed up with her behavior, and they were beginning to suffer financial problems.

Heather entered the eight-week experimental drug trial. At intake her YBOCS-SV score was 26, her Clinical Global Impression (CGI) severity score was 5, and her NIMHOCS score was 7. A Hamilton Depression Rating score of 2 confirmed that she was not depressed.

A low dose of fluvoxamine (50 mg/day), was ordered and was gradually increased as tolerated to 150 mg/day. She met weekly with the researcher to discuss her shopping compulsions and other concerns. Heather was asked to bring her shopping diary to these sessions, where they were reviewed in detail. She was asked about each shopping experience listed, including date and time, duration of shopping, what was purchased, and how much was spent. The researcher also inquired about her feelings and attitudes toward the shopping and spending, and whether she felt any regret or remorse. Heather was asked about efforts she had made to disrupt or control her shopping behaviors and cognition, such as distraction techniques or efforts to close credit card accounts. As she improved, she was also asked about how she was spending the time she had previously used for shopping. We also inquired about drug side-effects, use of other medication, new illnesses, and about her general mood and level of anxiety. Heather was given an opportunity to bring up other issues or concerns that could be addressed in a supportive fashion.

By week four Heather's YBOCS-SV score had dropped to 8, and she was given a CGI improvement rating of 2, indicating "much" improvement. By week eight, the end of the trial, her YBOCS-SV had dropped to 4 and her CGI improvement rating was 1, indicating "very much" improvement. At that time her CGI severity score was 1 ("normal, not ill") and her NIMHOCS score had fallen to 2, both indicating that she had experienced substantial improvement. Heather had responded well to fluvoxamine. The weekly meetings with the researcher, though not psychotherapy per se, also seemed to have had a therapeutic effect on her. Combined with the drug treatment, by the end of the trial she reported that she thought less frequently about shopping, felt less compelled to shop, and was spending less money and less time shopping.

CONCLUSION

Compulsive buying is relatively common but rarely diagnosed or treated in mental health settings. Clinicians need to familiarize themselves with its characteristic symptoms and, as with other disorders, gather historical data, obtain confirmatory evidence when possible, and proceed with a differential diagnosis. Because psychiatric comorbidity is the rule, clinicians need to pay particular attention to the patient's mental health history. Several instruments and rating scales are available to assist in the recognition, diagnosis, and assessment of compulsive buying including the Compulsive Buying Scale, the Minnesota Impulsive Disorders Interview, and the Yale-Brown Obsessive Scale modified for compulsive buying. Patients may also be evaluated through daily shopping logs, which can help with assessment as well as with behavioral therapies aimed at interrupting the cycle of compulsive buying.

APPENDIX A

Compulsive Buying Scale

1. Please indicate how much you agree or disagree with each of the statements below. Place an X on the line that best indicates how you feel about each statement.

	Strongly agree	Somewhat agree	Neither agree nor disagree	Somewhat disagree	Strongly disagree
	(1)	(2)	(3)	(4)	(5)
If I have any money left at the end of the pay period, I just have to spend it.	——	——	——	——	——

2. Please indicate how often you have done each of the following things by placing an X on the appropriate line.

	Very often	Often	Some-times	Rarely	Never
	(1)	(2)	(3)	(4)	(5)
a. Felt others would be horrified if they knew of my spending habits.	——	——	——	——	——
b. Bought things even though I couldn't afford them.	——	——	——	——	——
c. Wrote a check when I knew I didn't have enough money in the bank to cover it.	——	——	——	——	——
d. Bought myself something in order to make myself feel better.	——	——	——	——	——
e. Felt anxious or nervous on days I didn't go shopping.	——	——	——	——	——
f. Made only the minimum payments on my credit card.	——	——	——	——	——

Scoring equation $= -9.69 + (Q1 \times .33) + (Q2a \times .34) + (Q2b \times .50) + (Q2c \times .47) + (Q2d \times .33) + (Q2e \times .38) + (Q2f \times .31)$.

Substitute your score of 1 to 5 on each question for its place in the equation. For example, if you marked question 1 as 2 (somewhat agree), use 2 in place of Q1 and multiply it by .33. When you have answered each question, add your individual scores together and subtract 9.69 to determine your overall score. If your overall score is a higher negative score than -1.34 (for example, -2.04), you would be classified as a compulsive buyer.

Reprinted with permission. Faber, R., O'Guinn, T. (1992). *A clinical screener for compulsive buying. Journal of Consumer Research* 19:459–469.

APPENDIX B

Edwards Compulsive Buying Scale

1. I feel driven to shop and spend, even when I don't have the time or money.
2. I get little or no pleasure from shopping.
3. I hate to go shopping.*
4. I go on buying binges.
5. I feel "high" when I go on a buying spree.*
6. I buy things when I don't need anything.*
7. I go on a buying binge when I'm upset, disappointed, depressed, or angry.
8. I worry about my spending habits, but still go out and shop and spend money.
9. I feel anxious after I go on a buying binge.
10. I buy things even though I cannot afford them.
11. I feel guilty or ashamed after I go on a buying binge.
12. I buy things I don't need or won't use.

Reprinted with permission: Edwards, E. A. (1993). Development of a new scale for measuring compulsive buying behavior. *Financial Counseling and Planning* 4:67–81.

* Indicates that the item should be reverse-coded.

APPENDIX C

Questionnaire about Buying Behavior

Directions: Each of the questions below contains two choices, yes and no. Please indicate on your answer sheet which choice most describes the way you act and feel. Do not leave any blanks and please respond to all questions with only one answer (yes or no).

1. Have you ever had the irresistible urge to spend money on anything at all?
2. Have you ever bought something that you later found useless?
3. Have you ever felt on edge, agitated, or irritable when you haven't been able to buy something?
4. Have you ever avoided certain stores because you were afraid you would buy too much?
5. Have you ever asked someone to go shopping with you so you wouldn't buy too much?
6. Have you ever hidden your purchases from your family or friends?
7. Has the craving to buy something ever caused you to miss a date with friends?
8. Have you ever left work in order to buy something?
9. Has one or several of your purchases ever provoked the reproach of your family or friends?
10. Has one or several of your purchases ever provoked a prolonged misunderstanding or separation?
11. Has any of your purchases ever resulted in problems with your bank?
12. Has any of your purchases ever resulted in legal problems?
13. Have you ever continued to buy things in spite of the financial and family problems your purchases caused?
14. Do you regularly regret your purchases?
15. Do you regularly feel tense or nervous before you buy something?
16. Do you regularly feel relieved after you've bought something?

17. Do you have excessive buying periods accompanied by over-whelming feelings of generosity?
18. Do you buy something "on the spur of the moment" at least once a month?
19. Do your "spur of the moment" or excessive purchases repre-sent at least 25% of your wages?

Reprinted with permission: Lejoyeux, M., Tassain, V., Solomon, J., and Ades, J. (1997). Study of compulsive buying in depressed patients. *Journal of Clinical Psychiatry* 58:169–173.

APPENDIX D

Yale-Brown Obsessive-Compulsive Scale — Shopping Version (YBOCS-SV)

1. TIME OCCUPIED BY THOUGHTS ABOUT SHOPPING. How much of your time is occupied by thoughts about shopping?
   - 0   None.
   - 1   Mild, less than 1 hr/day or occasional intrusion.
   - 2   Moderate, 1 to 3 hrs/day, or frequent intrusion.
   - 3   Severe, greater than 3 and up to 8 hrs/day or very frequent intrusion.
   - 4   Extreme, greater than 8 hrs/day or near constant intrusion.

2. INTERFERENCE DUE TO THOUGHTS ABOUT SHOPPING. How much do your thoughts about shopping interfere with your social, work, or role functioning? Is there anything you don't do because of them?
   - 0   None.
   - 1   Mild, slight interference with social or occupational activities but overall performance not impaired.
   - 2   Moderate, definite interference with social or occupational performance, but still manageable.
   - 3   Severe, causes substantial impairment in social or occupational performance.
   - 4   Extreme, incapacitating.

3. DISTRESS ASSOCIATED WITH THOUGHTS ABOUT SHOPPING. How much distress do your thoughts about shopping cause you?
   - 0   None.
   - 1   Mild, not too disturbing.
   - 2   Moderate, disturbing but still manageable.
   - 3   Severe, very disturbing.
   - 4   Extreme, near constant and disabling distress.

4. RESISTANCE AGAINST THOUGHTS ABOUT SHOPPING. How much of an effort do you make to resist the thoughts about shopping? How often do you try to disregard or turn your attention away from these thoughts as they enter your mind?
  - 0 Makes an effort to always resist, or symptoms so minimal doesn't need to actively resist.
  - 1 Tries to resist most of the time.
  - 2 Makes some effort to resist.
  - 3 Yields all thoughts without attempting to control them, but does so with some resistance.
  - 4 Completely and willingly yields to all thoughts about shopping.

5. DEGREE OF CONTROL OVER THOUGHTS ABOUT SHOPPING. How much control do you have over your thoughts about shopping? How successful are you in stopping or devoting your thoughts about shopping? Can you dismiss them?
  - 0 Complete control.
  - 1 Much control, usually able to stop or divert thoughts with some effort and concentration.
  - 2 Moderate control, sometimes able to stop or divert thinking.
  - 3 Little control, rarely successful in stopping or dismissing thinking, can only divert attention with difficulty.
  - 4 No control, experience is completely involuntary, rarely able to even momentarily alter thoughts about shopping.

6. TIME SPENT SHOPPING. How much time do you spend shopping? How much time do you spend compulsively shopping?
  - 0 None.
  - 1 Mild, spends less than 1 hr/day shopping.
  - 2 Moderate, spends 1 to 3 hrs/day shopping.
  - 3 Severe, spends more than 3 and up to 8 hrs/day shopping.
  - 4 Extreme, spends more than 8 hrs/day shopping or near constant shopping episodes.

7. INTERFERENCE DUE TO SHOPPING BEHAVIOR. How much does your shopping behavior interfere with your social, work, or role functioning? Is there anything you don't do because of the shopping?

0   None.
1   Mild, slight interference with social or occupational ac-
    tivities, but overall performance not impaired.
2   Moderate, definite interference with social or occupa-
    tional performance, but still manageable.
3   Severe, causes substantial impairment in social or occu-
    pational performance.
4   Extreme, incapacitating.

8. DISTRESS ASSOCIATED WITH COMPULSIVE SHOPPING BE-
   HAVIOR. How would you feel if prevented from shopping?
   How anxious would you become?
   0   None.
   1   Mild, only slightly anxious if shopping prevented, or only
       slightly anxious while shopping.
   2   Moderate, reports that anxiety would mount but remains
       manageable.
   3   Severe, prominent and very disturbing increase in anxi-
       ety if shopping interrupted.
   4   Extreme, incapacitating anxiety from any intervention
       aimed at modifying activity, or incapacitating anxiety
       develops during performance of shopping.

9. RESISTANCE AGAINST COMPULSIVE SHOPPING. How much
   of an effort do you make to resist the compulsion?
   0   Makes an effort to always resist, or symptoms so minimal
       doesn't need to actively resist.
   1   Tries to resist most of the time.
   2   Makes some effort to resist.
   3   Yields to almost all compulsions without attempting to
       control them, but does so with some reluctance.
   4   Completely and unwillingly yields to almost all compul-
       sions.

10. DEGREE OF CONTROL OVER COMPULSIVE SHOPPING. How
    strong is the drive to compulsively shop? How much control do
    you have over the compulsion?
    0   Complete control.

1 Much control, experiences pressure to perform the behavior but usually able to exercise voluntary control over it.

2 Moderate control, strong pressure to perform behavior, can control it only with difficulty.

3 Little control, very strong drive to perform behavior, must be carried to completion, can only delay with difficulty.

4 No control, drive to perform behavior experienced as completely involuntary and overpowering, rarely able to even momentarily delay activity.

Reprinted with permission from Elsevier Science, © 1996. Monahan, P., Black, D. W., Gabel, J. (1996). Reliability and validity of a scale to measure change in persons with compulsive buying. *Psychiatry Research* 64:59–67.

REFERENCES

Andreasen, N. C., Endicott, J., Spitzer, R. L., et al. (1977). The family history method using diagnostic criteria. *Archives of General Psychiatry* 34:1229–1235.

Beck A. T., Epstein, N., Brown, G., and Steer, R. A. (1988). An inventory for measuring clinical anxiety: psychometric properties. *Journal of Consulting Clinical Psychology* 56:893–897.

Beck, A. T., Ward, C. H., Mendelson, M., et al. (1961). An inventory for measuring depression. *Archives of General Psychiatry* 4:561–571.

Bernik, M. A., Akerman, D., Amaral, J. A. M. S., and Braun, R. C. D. N. (1996). Cue exposure in compulsive buying (letter). *Journal of Clinical Psychiatry* 57:90.

Black, D. W. (1996). Compulsive buying: a review. *Journal of Clinical Psychiatry* 57(suppl 8):50–55.

Black, D. W., Monahan, P., and Gabel, J. (1997). Fluvoxamine in the treatment of compulsive buying. *Journal of Clinical Psychiatry* 58:159–163.

Black, D. W., Repertinger, S., Gaffney, G. R., and Gabel, J. (1998). Family history and psychiatric comorbidity in persons with compulsive buying: preliminary findings. *American Journal of Psychiatry* 155:960–963.

Christenson, G. A., Faber, R. J., and de Zwaan, M. (1994). Compulsive buying: descriptive characteristics and psychiatric comorbidity. *Journal of Clinical Psychiatry* 55:5–11.

Cooper, J. (1970). The Leyton Obsessionality Inventory. *Psychological Medicine* 1:48–64.

Derogatis, L. R. (1977). Symptom checklist-90 (revised): administration, scoring, and procedures manual. Baltimore, MD: Clinical Psychometric Research.

DeSarbo, W. S., and Edwards, E. A. (1996). Typologies of compulsive buying behavior: a constrained clusterwise regression approach. *Journal of Consumer Psychology* 5:231–252.

Edwards, E. A. (1993). Development of a new scale for measuring compulsive buying behavior. *Financial Counseling and Planning* 4:67–84.

Faber, R. J., O'Guinn, T. C. (1989). Classifying compulsive consumers: advances in the development of a diagnostic tool. *Advances in Consumer Research* 16:738–744.

—— (1992). A clinical screener for compulsive buying. *Journal of Consumer Research* 19:459–469.

Goodman, W. K., Price, L. H., Rasmussen, S. A., et al. (1989). The Yale–Brown Obsessive-Compulsive Scale: II: Validity. *Archives of General Psychology* 46:1012–1016.

Guy, W. (1976). ECDEU Assessment Manual of Psychopharmacology, pp. 217–222. Washington, DC: U.S. Government Printing Office.

Hamilton, M. (1959). The assessment of anxiety states by rating. *British Journal of Medical Psychology* 32:50–55.

—— (1967). Development of a rating scale for primary depressive illness. *British Journal of Social Clinical Psychology* 6:278–296.

Hodgson, R. J., and Rachman, S. (1977). Obsessive-compulsive complaints. *Behaviour Therapy and Research 15:389–395.*

Hyler, S. E., Reider, R. O., and Spitzer, R. L. (1997). Personality

Diagnostic Questionnaire-IV. New York: New York State Psychiatric Institute.

Lejoyeux, M., Adès, J., Tassian, V., and Solomon, J. (1996). Phenomenology and psychopathology of uncontrolled buying. *American Journal of Psychiatry* 153:1524–1529.

Lejoyeux, M., Tassian, V., Solomon. J., and Adès J. (1997). Study of compulsive buying in depressed patients. *Journal of Clinical Psychiatry* 58:169–173.

Loranger, A. W. (1988). Personality Disorder Examination (PDE) manual. Yonkers, NY: D.V. Communications.

McElroy, S. L., Keck, P. E., Pope, H. G., et al. (1994). Compulsive buying: a report of 20 cases. *Journal of Clinical Psychiatry* 55:242–248.

Monahan, P., Black, D. W., and Gabel, J. (1996). Reliability and validity of a scale to measure change in persons with compulsive buying. *Psychiatry Research* 64:59–67.

Montgomery, S. A., and Asberg, M. (1979). A new depression scale designed to be sensitive to change. *British Journal of Psychiatry* 134:383–389.

Murphy, D. L., Pickar, D. L., and Alterman, I. S. (1982). Methods for the quantitative assessment of depressive and manic behavior. *The Behavior of Psychiatric Patients*, ed. E. I. Burdock, A. Sudilovski, and S. Gershon, pp. 335–391. New York: Marcel Dekker.

Pfohl, B., Zimmerman, M., and Blum, N. (1997). Structured interview for *DSM-IV* personality disorders. Washington, DC: American Psychiatric Press.

Pilowsky, I., and Spence, N. D. (1983). Manual for the Illness Behavior Questionnaire, 2nd ed. Adelaide, Australia, Department of Psychiatry, University of Adelaide.

Robins, L. N., Helzer, J. E., Croughan, J., et al. (1981). The NIMH Diagnostic Interview Schedule: its history, characteristics and validity. *Archives of General Psychiatry* 38:381–389.

Scherhorn, G., Reisch, L. A., and Raab, G. (1990). Addictive buying in West Germany: an empirical study. *Journal of Consumer Policy* 13:355–387.

Schlosser, S., Black, D. W., Repertinger, S., and Freet, D. (1994). The demography, phenomenology, and comorbidity of compulsive buying. *General Hospital Psychiatry* 16:205–212.

Spitzer, R. L., and Endicott, J. (1978). Schedule for affective disorders and schizophrenia. New York: Biometrics Research Department, New York State Psychiatric Institute.

Spitzer, R. L., Williams, J. D. W., and Gibbon, M. (1994). Structured Clinical Interview for *DSM-IV*. New York: Biometrics Research Department, New York State Psychiatric Institute.

Spitzer, R. L., Williams, J. D. W., Gibbon, M., and First, M. B. (1996). Structured Clinical Interview for *DSM-IV* Personality Disorders (SCID-II). New York: Biometrics Research Department, New York State Psychiatric Institute.

Valence, G., d'Astous, A., and Fortier, L. (1988). Compulsive buying: concept and measurement. *Journal of Clinical Policy* 11: 419–433.

World Health Organization (1990). Composite International Diagnostic Interview (CIDI), Geneva, Switzerland: WHO.

10

Diagnosis, Associated Disorders, and Drug Treatment

Toby Goldsmith and Susan L. McElroy

For over a hundred years psychiatrists have recognized abnormal spending behavior among patients. In his 1915 psychiatry textbook Emil Kraepelin included *oniomania*, the urge to make purchases, among other pathological impulses. These impulses were typified as impulsive, excessive, and uncontrollable. Six years later, in his textbook of psychiatry, Eugen Bleuler (1924) included oniomania with the reactive impulses or impulsive insanities. Following these two references to compulsive buying, however, little was written about oniomania until the late 1980s, when it began to be called *compulsive shopping* or *compulsive buying disorder* and slowly became the subject of professional interest and research.

By the early 1990s evidence suggested that the prevalence of compulsive buying might be 1.1 to 5.9 percent of the general population (Faber and O'Guinn 1992) and might be a significant psychiatric problem often resulting in personal distress, marital or family disruption, and unmanageable indebtedness or bankruptcy (Christenson et al. 1994, Glatt and Cook 1987, McElroy et al. 1989). To stimulate further investigation of compulsive buying, McElroy and colleagues (1994a) proposed preliminary operational diagnostic criteria for compulsive buying.

1. Maladaptive preoccupation with buying or shopping, or maladaptive buying or shopping impulses or behavior, as indicated
   by at least one of the following:

   (a) Frequent preoccupation with buying or impulses to buy
       that is/are experienced as irresistible, intrusive, and/or
       senseless.
   (b) Frequent buying of more than can be afforded, frequent
       buying of items that are not needed or shopping for longer
       periods of time than intended.

2. The buying preoccupations, impulses, or behaviors cause marked
   distress, are time-consuming, significantly interfere with social
   or occupational functioning, or result in financial problems
   (e.g., indebtedness or bankruptcy).

3. The excessive buying or shopping behavior does not occur
   exclusively during periods of hypomania or mania.

These criteria were based on the description of patients in earlier
studies and on the phenomenology of the twenty consecutive
psychiatric patients with compulsive buying studied by McElroy
and her associates (1994a).

Because compulsive buying shares phenomenological features
with impulse-control, obsessive-compulsive, and substance use
disorders (McElroy et al. 1994a), they patterned the proposed
criteria after the existing *DSM-III-R* criteria for those disorders.
Similar to the *DSM-III-R* criteria for obsessive-compulsive disorders (which require the presence of obsessions or compulsions but
not both), they chose to require the presence of buying impulses
(or preoccupation with buying) or excessive buying, but not both,
as the first criterion for compulsive buying. One compulsive buyer
may have distressing urges to buy while controlling her spending
behavior; another may spend excessively without experiencing
impulses to do so. These criteria would allow both patients to be
diagnosed with compulsive buying.

They chose to include shopping as well as buying because of

their findings that patients may shop excessively without buying, often as a means to limit financial problems. Similar to the *DSM-III-R* criteria for pathological gambling, kleptomania, and substance use disorders, they stipulated that excessive buying or shopping was manifest if larger amounts of money were spent than could be afforded, if unneeded items were frequently bought, or if shopping was performed over longer periods of time than intended. Unlike the *DSM-III-R* criteria for kleptomania or trichotillomania (which require the presence of impulses to steal and to pull hair, respectively), they did not require that buying impulses be present and, if present, that they be associated with anxiety or tension, or that their enactment be associated with relief or pleasure. McElroy and associates (1994a) elected to do this because some of the patients in the study on which these criteria were based denied experiencing irresistible impulses and/or tension relief.

For the second criterion they again borrowed from the *DSM-III-R* diagnostic criteria for obsessive-compulsive disorder, substance-use disorders, and pathological gambling, and stipulated buying symptoms (impulses, preoccupations, and/or behaviors) to be pathological (and thus constitute a disorder) if they caused marked distress, were time-consuming, interfered with the person's social or occupational functioning, or resulted in financial difficulties.

Today compulsive shopping is officially included among the Impulse-Control Disorders, Not Otherwise Specified in the fourth edition of the *Diagnostic and Statistical Manual of Mental Disorders (DSM-IV)* (APA 1994). In this chapter we will approach compulsive buying and spending from the view of the psychiatrist, focusing on the diagnostic considerations, its comorbidity with other disorders, and the psychopharmacological treatment of these disorders.

DIAGNOSIS

As noted above, compulsive buying disorder is included in the category of impulse control disorders. The disorders of impulse control that are listed specifically in this category include intermittent explosive disorder, kleptomania, pathological gambling, pyromania, and trichotillomania. An additional category of impulse control disorders, not otherwise specified, include compulsive buying, repetitive self-mutilation, psychogenic excoriation (i.e., skin picking), and nonparaphilic sexual addictions (i.e., compulsive sexual activity). These disorders have a common phenomenology.

The different impulse control disorders (ICDs) have different prevalence rates in men and women. Kleptomania, trichotillomania, compulsive buying, and psychogenic excoriation are more common in women, and intermittent explosive disorder, pathological gambling, and pyromania are more common in men.

According to the *DSM-IV* (APA 1994), these disorders share the inability to "resist an impulse, drive or temptation to perform an act that is harmful to the person or to others" (p. 609). Also associated with these diagnoses are significant mood symptoms that include "an increasing sense of tension or arousal before committing the act. Following the act there may or may not be regret, self-reproach, or guilt" (p. 609).

Given these symptom clusters, various researchers have sought a connection between the ICDs (including compulsive shopping) and other groups of illnesses, specifically obsessive compulsive disorder (OCD) and the mood disorders, more specifically bipolar disorders. Compulsive buying may be an ICD or a symptom of OCD, bipolar disorder, affective spectrum disorder, or substance-use disorder. The evidence for these linkages is reviewed in the discussion that follows.

The ICDs and OCD have generally been considered separate diagnostic entities despite phenomenologic similarities between the obsessions and compulsions of OCD and the irresistible impulses and impulsive actions of ICDs. These differences are outlined below.

ICD impulses and actions can be distinguished from OCD obsessions and compulsions. The former are generally considered more harmful, less senseless, and more spontaneous. ICD actions are more likely to be associated with pleasure, gratification, or relief from mounting anxiety or tension, and hence more ego-syntonic (Frosch and Wortis 1954). They are probably more likely than OCD symptoms to involve risky, sensation-seeking, or exciting behaviors. And people with ICDs are more likely to have poor insight into the dangerousness or consequences of the behaviors, lack the capacity to resist these behaviors, which they often see as rational, and lack the ability to control such thinking or behavior.

OCD obsessions and compulsions on the other hand are more frequently associated with harm avoidance, are often seen as senseless or absurd, and are frequently resisted, and there is a lack of gratification when they are performed. For the most part OCD obsessions and compulsions have been viewed as compulsive and ego-dystonic. In actuality, however, both OCD and ICD symptoms vary considerably with respect to these variables (Goldsmith et al. 1998, McElroy et al. 1993). Rather than viewing OCD symptoms as ego-dystonic and ICD symptoms as ego-syntonic, it may be more accurate to view both sets of symptoms as having both ego-syntonic and ego-dystonic features. For example, intrusive thoughts and impulses to buy can frequently be ego-dystonic. The actual buying, however, is often ego-syntonic, especially if relief or pleasure is experienced during its enactment. And following the buying episodes, the often experienced "crash" and the return of feelings of emptiness or despair are ego-dystonic.

ICDs and OCD may have some biological differences as well. Although there have been no studies comparing the biological differences among compulsive shoppers who would be diagnosed as ICD as opposed to OCD, in their review of the relationship between trichotillomania and OCD, for example, Stein and colleagues (1995) concluded that the findings of serotonergic abnormalities in trichotillomania have been inconclusive and recommended investigation of other neurotransmitter systems, especially the dopamine system. Also, when compared with OCD patients, patients with trichotillomania do not display increased neurological soft signs or differential brain glucose metabolic rates as determined by positron emission tomography (Stein et al. 1995).

Some ICDs may respond to a broad range of thymoleptic agents rather than preferentially to serotonergic reuptake inhibitors (SRI), as OCD symptoms do. Few controlled comparison studies have been done for ICDs other than trichotillomania and oncychophagia (nail biting). However, non-SRI antidepressants (e.g., tricyclics, MAOIs) and mood stabilizers (e.g., lithium, carbamazepine, and valproate) from a wide variety of classes and with different putative mechanisms of action have been reported to be effective in many different ICDs, including compulsive buying (McElroy et al. 1996). (More specific data about the effect of thymoleptic agents on compulsive buying will be provided in the section of pharmacological treatment.)

It is extremely difficult to say anything definitive about the differential diagnosis of ICD and OCD because there is so much variability in the individual symptom picture and so much overlap between the two syndromes. For example, the experience of anxiety relief and the experience of pleasure can look similar in ICDs and OCD and may vary considerably within each diagnostic category. Like OCD, ICD actions may be associated mainly with tension reduction rather than pleasure. In both kleptomania and compulsive gambling, patients have reported that there was little pleasure or gratification in their activities; they performed their stealing or gambling simply as a repetitive ritual (Allock and Grace 1988, McElroy et al. 1991b). On the other hand, we have seen OCD patients who claim to experience pleasurable feelings with their obsessions or compulsions rather than relief from anxiety, which is more commonly expected with OCD than it is with ICDs. For example, in a comparison of the clinical features in eight patients with trichotillomania and thirteen patients with OCD, the former patients reported a significantly greater degree of pleasure during hair pulling than OCD patients did during ritualizing (Stanley et al. 1992). Also, compared with OCD patients, trichotillomania patients displayed significantly fewer obsessive-compulsive symptoms, less anxiety and depression, and more extraversion.

Another point of overlap between the two syndromes is the role and nature of impulsivity in the two disorders. OCD symptoms may be impulsively enacted and associated with poor insight (McElroy et al. 1993). Indeed, *DSM-IV* uses the term *impulse* to define an obsession (APA 1994). Also, compulsive forms of ICDs, individuals with OCD and high degrees of impulsivity, and impulsive individuals with compulsive behaviors have all been reported (Coid 1991, Hollander 1993, McElroy et al. 1993). For example, the author (T. G.) knows of a compulsive buyer who has piles of toilet paper stored in several closets in her home, yet every time there is a sale on toilet paper she buys more, impulsively — "just in case." In this woman, who grew up during the Depression, anxiety is heightened by the fear of not having; this obsession is mitigated at the time of a store sale when she replenishes her overabundant stock. In addition, just as persons with OCD often display multiple obsessions and compulsions, patients with an ICD often display multiple ICDs (Specker et al. 1995). (This is further clarified in our discussion of psychiatric comorbidity in compulsive buyers.)

Phenomenologically there are other similarities between OCD and the ICDs. Both share a strong association with mood disorders (Hudson and Pope 1990, McElroy et al. 1992) and a less robust, but nevertheless similar, association with anxiety, psychoactive substance use, and eating disorders (Christenson et al. 1991a, Faber et al. 1995, McElroy et al. 1991a, 1992, Rasmussen and Eisen 1992). Furthermore, ICDs often co-occur with OCD (Christenson et al. 1991a, McElroy et al. 1991a,b). Both conditions appear to respond to thymoleptic agents (antidepressants as well as mood stabilizers) (Black et al. 1997b, Christenson et al. 1991b; Delgado et al. 1990, Fluvoxetine Bulimia Nervosa Collaborative Study Group 1992) and to behavior therapy (Josephson and Brondolo 1993). Early data also show that OCD and ICDs may share high familial rates of mood disorder and abnormalities in central serotonergic neurotransmission (McElroy et al. 1993).

It has been suggested that "although the differences between OCD and ICDs might be attributable to distinct etiologic mechanisms, many differences could be caused by variation along a bidimensional continuum of different combinations of compulsivity versus impulsivity, with 'pure' compulsive states (prototypic OCD) at one extreme, pure impulsive states (the prototypic ICD) at the other extreme, and various combinations of these pure states (mixed compulsive-impulsive conditions) located in between" (McElroy et al. 1993, p. 128).

Based on the foregoing discussion, it is easy enough to see that the ICD–OCD spectrum is broad, with much overlap, making a definitive diagnosis between the two extremely difficult. Results from the three major studies that have explored this question bear this out. In McElroy and colleagues' study of twenty cases (1994a), the compulsive buying of most patients fit the *DSM-III-R* definition of an impulse control disorder as well as the *DSM-III-R* criteria for obsessive-compulsive disorder. They concluded that compulsive buying shared features of both obsessive-compulsive and impulse control disorders and suggested that it may be a member of a larger family of obsessive-compulsive spectrum disorders, which may in turn belong to the even larger family of affective spectrum disorder (McElroy et al. 1995). In Christenson and colleagues' 1994 study of twenty-four compulsive buyers, two-thirds of the sample reported repetitive problematic buying, intrusive thoughts to buy, and re-sistance to such thoughts, though only three people described other obsessive-compulsive behavior meeting *DSM-III-R* criteria for OCD. The authors suggest that, "considering the higher rates of multiple obsessions and compulsions in OCD (Rasmussen and Eisen 1990), this latter observation would argue against classifying compulsive buying as OCD, although the possibility that compul-sive buying represents a monosymptomatic variation of OCD should still be entertained" (p. 10). And the results of a study of forty-six compulsive buyers by Schlosser and associates (1994) indicate that while compulsive buying shares many superficial similarities with OCD, including repetitive and problematic spend-ing, intrusive thoughts about spending, and resistance to such thoughts and behavior, it seems to have more in common with disorders of impulse control.

While there appears to be a common link between impulse control disorders like compulsive buying and obsessive-compulsive disorder, the similarities in phenomenology, comorbidity, abnor-malities of serotonergic transmission, and response to thymolep-tics are not enough to explain the behavior of patients with ICDs. Thus we have had to look further. It has been variously suggested that the ICDs may be a form of "affective spectrum disorder" or particularly closely related to bipolar disorder.

Affective spectrum disorders are a hypothesized family of

disorders sharing at least one common pathophysiologic abnormality with major depression (McElroy et al. 1991a, 1992, 1993, 1995, Wise and Tierney 1994). These include OCD, bulimia nervosa, and panic disorder, among others, all of which share response to antidepressants from several different classes, a high comorbidity with mood disorder, and a high familial rate of mood disorder (McElroy and Keck 1995).

It has been further proposed that ICDs may be particularly closely related to bipolar disorder, as suggested by preliminary phenomenologic, comorbidity, and psychopharmacologic observations. The relationship between compulsive shopping and bipolar disorder has not been examined specifically, but data regarding other ICDs' relationships to bipolar disorder will be presented.

As defined in *DSM-IV*, the core feature of an ICD is the failure to resist an impulse, drive, or temptation to commit an act that is harmful to the individual or to others. *DSM-IV* also stipulates that for most ICDs the individual feels an increasing sense of tension or arousal before committing the act and then experiences pleasure, gratification, or relief at the time of committing the act. The core features of bipolar disorder are periods of mania or hypomania, usually alternating or occurring with periods of depressive symptoms (APA 1994).

Although the core features of ICDs and bipolar disorder appear distinct, closer examination shows that they share a number of phenomenologic similarities.

1. The types of behavior are similar in both conditions, generally involving harmful, dangerous, sensation-seeking, and/or pleasurable actions. For both ICDs and mania these include aggressive outbursts, antisocial acts such as stealing and fire-setting, and excessive or inappropriate spending, gambling, and sexual behaviors. Particularly germane to our topic is the fact that "unrestrained buying sprees" are included in the *DSM-IV* criteria for hypomania and mania.

2. Both are characterized by impulsive thinking and behavior. Although there is no widely accepted operational definition of *impulsive*, this term usually refers to spontaneous, automatic, or

reflexive acting or thinking without reflection or conscious judgment (Stein et al. 1993, Webster's 1993). The thinking of patients with ICDs and mania is automatic or rapid and without reflection. Behaviors in both conditions are often done without forethought.

3. Both ICDs and mania are also associated with poor insight into the danger, harmfulness, and/or consequences of the enacted behaviors. Interestingly, this feature has led some investigators to describe ICDs as ego-syntonic (Frosch and Wortis 1954, McElroy et al. 1993, 1995), whereas this feature in mania has generally been referred to as poor judgment or impaired insight (APA 1994).

4. ICD symptoms are frequently accompanied by affective symptoms that resemble those of bipolar disorder. Specifically, ICD impulses are often associated with tension or anxiety similar to that which can occur with depression or mixed affective states, or with arousal that resembles the elevated mood, increased energy, and enhanced clarity of thought that characterizes hypomania. ICD actions are often associated with pleasurable feelings, variously described by patients as feeling "high," "euphoric," "a thrill," or a "rush." This high resembles the elevated mood or euphoria of hypomania or mania (Lejoyeux et al. 1995, McCormick et al. 1984, McElroy et al. 1991c, 1994a).

After performance of an ICD action and resolution of the associated high, patients with ICDs often describe the acute onset of depressive symptoms similar to those of bipolar depression, including depressed mood, feelings of guilt and self-reproach, and fatigue (Lejoyeux et al. 1995, McElroy et al. 1991c, 1994a, 1998). For example, a female compulsive shopper reported experiencing severe anxiety with her impulses to buy (which typically occurred when she was depressed), "a high like taking cocaine" with the act of buying, and then a prompt "crash" characterized by depression, guilt, anxiety, and fatigue (McElroy et al. 1991c). Indeed, patients with ICDs and comorbid bipolar disorder have described similarities between their ICD, manic, and depressive symptoms (McElroy et al. 1991b). In fact, the changes in affective state associated with the experience and enactment of an ICD impulse resemble the affective instability or mood swings of bipolar disorder and thus have a cyclic or bipolar quality.

5. Additionally, just as mania may be associated with cognitive changes including confusion and delirium, ICD symptoms are also accompanied by changes in awareness. As Esquirol (1838) noted, "the irresistible impulses show all of the features of passion elevated to the point of delirium" (Chapter 1).

Beyond the phenomenologic characteristics, there are other similarities between the ICDs (which include compulsive buying) and bipolar disorder. The course of ICDs and bipolar disorder may begin in childhood or adolescence and each frequently follows an episodic and/or a chronic course (McElroy et al. 1992, Wise and Tierney 1994). The two conditions show elevated comorbidity with one another as well as similar comorbidity patterns with other psychiatric disorders. Also, family history studies suggest that patients with certain ICDs have elevated rates of mood disorders in their families. Preliminary biological data suggest that some ICD patients have abnormalities in central serotonergic or noradrenergic neurotransmission — conditions similar to those reported in some patients with bipolar disorder. In addition, ICDs and bipolar disorder both respond to mood stabilizers and antidepressants (McElroy et al. 1996).

Of course, ICDs and bipolar disorder have important phenomenologic differences as well. Quantitatively, the affective symptoms of bipolar disorder are more intense and protracted than those of ICDs. Qualitatively, although often described as impulsive, ICD symptoms are also described as repetitive or compulsive, or as sharing features with OCD obsessions and compulsions (McElroy et al. 1994b). Manic and depressive symptoms, in contrast, typically are not associated with repetitive behaviors and thus are usually not viewed as obsessive or compulsive. In these respects, then, ICDs (or certain ICDs) may be more similar phenomenologically to OCD than to mania or depression.

The evidence linking impulse control disorders or, more specifically, compulsive buying disorder to obsessive-compulsive disorder and bipolar disorder is vast, yet incomplete. Many cognitive as well as affective symptoms allow one to make the association among these disorders. The importance of making such associations is that it encourages the clinician to view the impulse control disorders as the multifaceted entities they are. Individuals who suffer from compulsive buying disorder need extensive diagnostic evaluation. Determining where they lie along the compulsive and affective spectra makes appropriate and effective treatment all the more likely.

ASSOCIATED DISORDERS

Compulsive buying is associated with significant psychiatric co-morbidity. In a recent study by Black (personal communication 1999) the greater the severity of compulsive buying symptoms, the greater the likelihood of psychiatric comorbidity, either in the form of obsessive-compulsive disorder, substance abuse, depression, pathological gambling, and/or abnormal personality traits. Determining the extent of coexisting mental illness in patients with compulsive buying disorder is essential for adequate understanding and treatment of the compulsive buying illness. Treatment of the other illnesses may result in alleviation of the compulsive buying symptoms (Lejoyeux et al. 1995). However, without a full picture of the patient's other difficulties, symptom substitution is also possible. For example, some treatment programs encourage compulsive buyers to substitute other activities, like baking or going out to a restaurant, for shopping or buying. This could encourage people who suffer from one disorder to replace it with another, thereby promoting serial comorbidity. An understanding of which behaviors are closely related is important for optimizing treatment outcome (Faber et al. 1995).

Three recent studies review the associated psychiatric illnesses of a total of ninety patients with oniomania (Christenson et al. 1994, McElroy et al. 1994a, Schlosser et al. 1994). A summary of the comorbidity of lifetime psychiatric illness in compulsive buyers from these three studies can be found in Table 10-1. Briefly, the combined results of these studies show that half of the compulsive buyers had a lifetime mood disorder, more than one-third had

Table 10-1. Comorbidity of Lifetime Psychiatric Illness in Compulsive Buyers

Diagnosis	Christenson (1994) et al. N=24	Schlosser (1994) et al. N=46	McElroy (1994a) N=20
	%	%	%
Affective Illness			
Major depressive disorder	50	28	25
Dysthymia	16.7	***	***
Bipolar disorder	0	0	35
Bipolar disorder NOS[a]	***	***	35
Anxiety Disorders			
Obsessive-compulsive disorder	12.5	4	35
Panic disorder	12.5	17	50
Simple phobia	16.7	28	20
Agoraphobia	0	***	0
Generalized anxiety disorder	20.8	30	***
Social phobia	20.8	***	30
Eating Disorders			
Anorexia nervosa	0	0	20
Bulimia nervosa	12.5	17	25
Substance Use Disorders			
Alcohol abuse or dependence	45.8	28	35
Other substance abuse or dependence	***	13	20
Any abuse or dependence	45.8	30	40
Impulse Control Disorders			
Intermittent explosive disorder	4.2	22	10
Kleptomania	4.2	37	10
Pathological gambling	8.3	20	5
Pyromania	0	2	10
Trichotillomania	4.2	11	10
Paraphilia/sexual addictions	***	13	10

[a] All patients had bipolar type 2 disorder, with episodes of hypomania and major depression.

a psychoactive substance-use disorder, and over half had a diagnosable anxiety disorder.

In his review of compulsive buying behavior Donald Black (1996) notes that the three studies differ based on the populations studied. The groups studied by Schlosser and colleagues (1994) and Christenson and associates (1994) were recruited through community advertisements. McElroy and her colleagues (1994a) recruited patients through other clinicians at two medical centers; this clinically based population was more likely to present to their clinicians with other complaints and thus have an increased likelihood of other diagnoses.

Differences in rates of comorbid disorders could also have been affected by the screening methods used. In both the McElroy and the Christenson studies the Structured Clinical Interview for *DSM-III-R* (Spitzer et al. 1989) was used to screen the patients. The Iowa group (Schlosser et al. 1994) administered a computerized version of the Diagnostic Interview Schedule (Robins et al. 1989), which was revised to be compatible with *DSM-III-R*. Both the Schlosser and the Christenson studies also used the Minnesota Impulsive Disorders Interview (MIDI) as a screening tool to assess the presence of impulse disorders; the MIDI was developed by Dr. Christenson and his colleagues for their study (Christenson 1994). McElroy and her colleagues (1994a) used a semistructured interview to assess the presence of impulse disorders in their sample. The study by Schlosser also included an interview utilizing the Structured Interview for *DSM-III* Personality Disorders (Pfohl et al. 1987), and thus was able to report on the incidence of personality disorders in their sample.

Mood disorders were prominent among the samples studied. In the clinically recruited study from McElroy and colleagues (1994a), nineteen of twenty compulsive buyers gave a lifetime history of an affective illness; the majority of these met diagnostic criteria for bipolar I or bipolar II disorders. Many patients in this study were able to relate their mood symptoms to their buying and shopping behavior; buying impulses and behaviors typically increased during mildly to moderately severe depressive episodes and decreased during hypomanic, manic, and severe depressive episodes. Some patients reported that shopping or spending temporarily relieved their depressive symptoms and/or induced hypomanic symptoms. Indeed, several patients reported that shopping was the only activity that made them feel good. None of the shoppers in either the Schlosser or the Christenson studies were noted to have bipolar affective disorder. This was surprising, given that hypomania has been associated with compulsive shopping (McElroy et al. 1991a). However, 28 percent of those in the Schlosser study and 50 percent of those in the Christenson study gave histories consistent with the presence of major depressive disorder.

A variety of anxiety disorders were also common among the ninety patients studied. As reviewed earlier in this chapter, there appears to be a relationship between compulsive buying and obsessive-compulsive disorder. The lifetime risk of obsessive-compulsive disorder was extremely high in those studied considering the lifetime prevalence of 1.9 to 3.3 percent of OCD in the community (McElroy et al. 1994b). Lifetime rates of OCD in patients were found to be 35, 12.5, and 4 percent respectively, in the studies done by McElroy, Christenson, Schlosser, and their colleagues. Almost universally, rates of other *DSM-III-R* anxiety illnesses were also found to be elevated — including panic disorder, various phobias, and generalized anxiety disorder (Table 10–2). This is consistent with previously reported results that note a relationship between compulsive buying and anxiety (Valence et al. 1988).

Lifetime histories of other diagnoses were found to be high as well (Table 10–1). In each of the studies over a quarter of the participants were found to have histories of abusing alcohol. Many of the compulsive buyers abused or were dependent on multiple substances.

The comorbid incidence of eating disorders was also high as compared to the general population. Since compulsive buying, like eating disorders (anorexia nervosa, bulimia nervosa, and the eating disorder NOS category of binge eating disorder), is thought to have features similar to obsessive-compulsive disorder, these data are not surprising. Patients with eating disorders have also been found to have increased frequency of OCD and the reverse is true as well (Rubenstein et al. 1992, Thiel et al. 1995).

Research results have suggested that compulsive buyers and people with bulimia and binge eating disorder share a number of similar characteristics including low levels of self-esteem (O'Guinn and Faber 1989, Scherhorn et al. 1990), high levels of depression (Scherhorn et al. 1990, Valence et al. 1988) and high levels of anxiety reactions and obsessions (O'Guinn and Faber 1989, Scherhorn et al. 1990). Both behaviors may provide short-term relief from dysphoric feelings. If both behaviors emanate from similar causes and function in similar ways, comorbidity between the two disorders would be expected. In two separate studies exploring the comorbidity of compulsive buying and binge eating undertaken by Faber and colleagues (1995), results showed that obese women diagnosed as having binge eating disorder had significantly greater compulsive buying tendencies than nonbinge eaters of similar weight. These studies also showed that compulsive buyers were more likely than a matched control group to have engaged in binge eating, have more symptoms characteristic of both binge eating disorder and bulimia nervosa, and were more likely to be clinically diagnosed as having an eating disorder. (See also Barth, Chapter 12, this volume, for more information on the comorbidity of eating and shopping disorders.)

DSM-III-R impulse control disorders were well represented (Table 10–1) among the compulsive shoppers in the separate studies by McElroy, Christenson, and Schlosser that examined compulsive buyers, although not all disorders were specifically addressed in each of the studies. Illnesses including trichotillomania, pyromania, kleptomania, intermittent explosive disorder, pathological gambling, and various sexual disorders were seen in rates higher than what is believed to be present in the general population (APA 1994). This was best demonstrated in the study by Schlosser and associates (1994), which noted the presence of an impulse control disorder in over 35 percent of their compulsive buyers but in less than 5 percent of their comparison group of normal shoppers.

The personality disorders were specifically screened for only in the study by Steven Schlosser and his colleagues (1994). They used two different screening tools to develop a consensus diagnosis. Their data showed the presence of a personality disorder in well over half the patients studied. Obsessive-compulsive, borderline, and avoidant were found to be the most commonly diagnosed disorders.

During the screening and intake, as well as during the ongoing treatment, the clinician should listen carefully for symptoms that are consistent with other diseases. Awareness of the other psychiatric illnesses from which a compulsive buyer may suffer is vital to the development of the treatment plan. Comorbid illness may hinder a patient's recovery from compulsive buying behavior (for example, the patient with major depressive disorder who finds shopping the only activity that briefly elevates his or her mood) and greatly prolong the length of treatment. As previously mentioned, treatment for the comorbid illness may significantly ameliorate the compulsive buying symptoms as well.

DRUG TREATMENT

Regarding the somatic therapies, few controlled trials of pharmacological agents in the treatment of individuals with ICDs (including potential forms, with the exception of binge eating) have been conducted. Those that have been done primarily examined antidepressant or anticonvulsant agents in individuals with impulsive aggression and trichotillomania (McElroy et al. 1995). It is believed that some ICDs may respond to a broad range of thymoleptic agents, unlike obsessive-compulsive disorder, which responds preferentially to specific serotonergic reuptake inhibitors (SSRIs).

Case reports suggest that agents with antidepressant or mood-stabilizing properties may be effective in kleptomania. As reported by McElroy and colleagues (1995), ten of eighteen patients with kleptomania described a partial or complete remission in stealing impulses and behavior, usually after several weeks of treatment with doses typically effective in mood disorders.

Prior to the 1990s there was little in the psychiatric literature regarding the use of psychotropics for the treatment of compulsive shopping. In 1991 McElroy and her colleagues reported three consecutive patients who requested psychiatric treatment for compulsive shopping (1991c). Each patient met the *DSM-III-R* criteria for an impulse control disorder not otherwise specified. All three experienced significant reductions both in urges to shop and shopping behavior when treated with antidepressant medications; two of the three appeared to display complete remission of compulsive shopping on antidepressant medication, while the third displayed a partial response. All the patients reported decreases in the intensity and frequency of shopping urges and reduced shopping within one to four weeks of treatment with doses of medication typically reported effective in major depression. No antidepressant was any more effective than another; bupropion, fluvoxetine, and nortriptyline, which differ in their pharmacologic mechanism, were all associated with attenuation of the shopping behavior and the associated anxiety-provoking cognitions.

In the comprehensive examination of twenty patients with compulsive buying (McElroy et al. 1994a), the majority of patients were treated with one or more thymoleptic medications. As noted in the comorbidity section of this chapter, many of these patients were diagnosed with bipolar disorder; thus a large number of mood stabilizers (valproate, lithium, antipsychotics) were used. These same patients were treatment refractory when the mood stabilizer was withheld. Several antidepressants (bupropion, nortriptyline, fluoxetine, trazadone, sertraline, desipramine) used alone or in conjunction with a mood stabilizer were found to be effective at producing full or partial remission. In this study 77 percent of the patients receiving treatment with thymoleptic medications described a complete or partial reduction in buying impulses and behavior.

There is disagreement whether treatment of an underlying mood disorder results in amelioration of compulsive buying behavior. Lejoyeux and colleagues (1995) describe two patients who suffered from compulsive buying and major depressive disorder. Both patients stated that their buying behavior had antidepressant-like effects for them; the physicians imply that the medical treatment of the mood disorder led to the disappearance of the compulsive buying. In another article it was suggested that antidepressant treatment was markedly successful when uncontrolled buying was associated with depression (Lejoyeux et al. 1996). These same authors suggest that compulsive buying disappears in many patients in the absence of depression, and that the treatment of depressed mood could lead to a great decrease in the urge and intensity to shop (Lejoyeux et al. 1997). This idea was refuted by Black and colleagues (1997b) who noted in their uncontrolled trial using the SRI fluvoxamine for the treatment of compulsive buying in ten patients without depression that 90 percent of them reported some improvement in their behavior. They suggest that the benefit of the SRIs in compulsive buying had little to do with mood elevation, but rather with the control of buying thoughts and impulses.

As noted earlier, compulsive buying, like other impulse control disorders, has been compared to obsessive-compulsive disorder. The ritualized and repetitive nature of some buying sprees has led clinicians to use antiobsessional medications to treat this behavior. The results of the open label trial cited above (Black et al. 1997b) indicated a significant overall improvement in shopping-related obsession and compulsions of the ten compulsive buyers who received the SRI fluvoxamine. Nine of the ten patients were considered responders, that is, they had a 50 percent or greater improvement in their shopping behavior as determined by both the Yale–Brown Obsessive-Compulsive Scale-Shopping Version (Goodman et al. 1989) and the Compulsive Buying Scale (Faber and O'Guinn 1992). Black and associates (1997b) note their surprise that the symptoms and behaviors returned slowly (although not to their pretreatment level) as the patients were tapered off fluvoxamine. A randomized, double-blind, multicenter study using fluvoxamine in compulsive buying, recently completed, suggested that fluvoxamine is only slightly more effective than placebo for the treatment of compulsive buying and not to a statistically significant extent (p > 0.05) (McElroy, personal communication, 1998).

In a yet-unpublished double-blind study of the use of Luvox

(fluvoxetine) for compulsive buying disorder (Black 1998, personal communication), there was a 70 percent success rate in amelioration of compulsive buying symptoms for both the drug group and the placebo group. The high involvement of the staff with the patients as well as the construction and daily recording of shopping diaries was thought to be the most significant factor in the patients' improvement.

It is important that clinicians keep in mind all symptoms experienced by their patients with compulsive buying when selecting psychopharmacological treatment. Concurrent major depression would suggest initiating treatment with an antidepressant, and comorbid bipolar disorder would suggest initial treatment with a mood stabilizer. Furthermore, highly compulsive presentations might respond preferentially to SRIs, whereas mixed presentations (high degrees of impulsivity or bipolarity concurrent with compulsivity) might respond best to mood stabilizers with greater efficacy in mixed affective states (e.g., valproate rather than lithium) (McElroy and Keck 1995) and/or mood stabilizer combinations (McElroy et al. 1994a). Clinicians must also weigh the benefits of discontinuing an effective medication since there appears to be a risk of relapse associated with discontinuation. There is room for much more research in this area, including evaluating the efficacy of combined psychopharmacology and psychotherapy in the treatment of compulsive buying.

REFERENCES

Allock, C. C., and Grace, D. M. (1988). Pathological gamblers are neither impulsive nor sensation seekers. *Australia-New Zealand Journal of Psychiatry* 22:307–311.

American Psychiatric Association (1994). *Diagnostic and Statistical Manual of Mental Disorders*, 4th ed. Washington, DC: American Psychiatric Association.

Black, D. W. (1996). Compulsive shopping: a review. *Journal of Clinical Psychiatry* 57 (suppl. 8):50–55.

Black, D. W., Gabel, J., and Schlosser, S. (1997a). Urge to splurge. *American Journal of Psychiatry* 154 (11):1630–1631.

Black, D. W., Monahan, P., and Gabel, J. (1997b). Fluvoxamine in the treatment of compulsive buying. *Journal of Clinical Psychiatry* 58(4):159–163.

Bleuler, E. (1924). *Textbook of Psychiatry*. New York: Macmillan.

Christenson, G. A., Faber, R. J., de Zwaan, M., et al. (1994). Compulsive buying: descriptive characteristics and psychiatric comorbidity. *Journal of Clinical Psychiatry* 55(1):5–11.

Christenson, G. A., Mackenzie, T. B., and Mitchell, J. E. (1991a). Characteristics of 60 adult chronic hair pullers. *American Journal of Psychiatry* 148:365–370.

Christenson, G. A., Popkin, M. A., Mackenzie, T. B., and Realmuto, G. M. (1991b). Lithium treatment of chronic hair pulling. *American Journal of Psychiatry* 148:1566–1571.

Coid, J. W. (1993). An affective syndrome in psychopaths with borderline personality disorder. *British Journal of Psychiatry* 162:641–650.

Delgado, P. L., Goodman, W. K., Price, L. H., et al. (1990). Fluvoxamine/pimozide treatment of concurrent Tourette's and obsessive-compulsive disorder. *British Journal of Psychiatry* 157:762–765.

Esquirol, E. (1838). *Des maladies mentales*. Paris: Bailliere. (*Mental Maladies: A Treatise on Insanity*, trans. E. K. Hunt. New York: Hafner, 1965.)

Faber, R. J., Christenson, G., de Zwaan, M., and Mitchell, J. (1995). Two forms of compulsive consumption: comorbidity of compulsive buying and binge eating. *Journal of Consumer Research* 22:296–304.

Faber, R. J., and O'Guinn, T. C. (1989). Classifying compulsive consumers: advances in development of a diagnostic tool. *Advances in Consumer Research* 16:738–744.

—— (1992). A clinical screener for compulsive buying. *Journal of Consumer Research* 19:459–469.

Fluvoxetine Bulimia Nervosa Collaborative Study Group (1992). Fluvoxetine in the treatment of bulimia nervosa. *Archives of General Psychiatry* 49:139–147.

Frosch, J., and Wortis, S. B. (1954). A contribution to the nosology of the impulse disorders. *American Journal of Psychiatry* 111:132–138.

Glatt, M. M., and Cook, C. C. (1987). Pathological spending as a form of psychological dependence. *British Journal of Addiction* 82:1257–1258.

Goldsmith, T., Shapira, N., and McElroy, S. (1998). Obsessive compulsive spectrum disorders. In *Obsessive Compulsive Disorder: Theory, Research and Treatment*, ed. R. Swinson, S. Rachman, S. Richter, and M. Antony, pp. 397–425. New York: Guilford.

Goodman, W. K., Price, L. H., Rasmussen, S. A., et al. (1989). The Yale–Brown Obsessive Compulsive Scale. I. Development, Use and Reliability. *Archives of General Psychiatry* 46(11):1006–1011.

Hollander, E., ed. (1993). *Obsessive-Compulsive-Related Disorders*. Washington, DC: American Psychiatric Press.

Hudson, J. I., and Pope, H. G., Jr. (1990). Affective spectrum disorder: Does antidepressant response identify a family of disorders with a common pathophysiology? *American Journal of Psychiatry* 147:552–564.

Josephson, S. C., and Brondolo, E. (1993). Cognitive-behavioral approaches to obsessive-compulsive-related disorders. In *Obsessive-Compulsive-Related Disorders*, ed. E. Hollander, pp. 215–240. Washington, DC: American Psychiatric Press.

Kraepelin, E. (1915). *Psychiatrie*, 8th ed. Leipzig: Verlag Von Johann Ambrosius Barth.

Lejoyeux, M., Adès, J., Tassain, V., and Solomon, J. (1996). Phenomenology and psychopathology of uncontrolled buying. *American Journal of Psychiatry* 153(12):1524–1529.

Lejoyeux, M., Hourtané, M., and Adès, J. (1995). Compulsive buying and depression (letter). *Journal of Clinical Psychiatry* 56(1):38.

Lejoyeux, M., Tassain, V., Solomon, J., and Adès, J. (1997). Study of compulsive buying in depressed patients. *Journal of Clinical Psychiatry* 58(4):169–173.

McCormick, R. A., Russo, A. M., Ramirez, L. F., and Taber, J. I.

(1984). Affective disorders among pathological gamblers seeking treatment. *American Journal of Psychiatry* 141:215–218.

McElroy, S. L., Hudson, J. I., Phillips, K. A., et al. (1993). Clinical and theoretical implications of a possible link between obsessive-compulsive and impulse control disorders. *Depression* 1:121–132.

McElroy, S. L., Hudson, J. I., Pope, H. G., Jr., et al. (1992). The *DSM-III-R* impulse control disorders not otherwise classified: clinical characteristics and relationship to other psychiatric disorders. *American Journal of Psychiatry* 149:318–327.

McElroy, S. L., Hudson, J. I., Pope, H. G., Jr., and Keck, P. E., Jr. (1991a). Kleptomania: clinical characteristics and associated pathology. *Psychological Medicine* 21:93–108.

McElroy, S. L., Keck, P. E., Jr., Pope, H. G., Jr., and Hudson, J. I. (1989). Pharmacological treatment of kleptomania and bulimia nervosa. *Journal of Psychopharmacology* 9:358–360.

McElroy, S. L., and Keck, P. E., Jr. (1995). Antiepileptic drugs. In *The American Psychiatric Press Textbook of Psychopharmacology*, ed. A. F. Schatzburg and C. B. Nemeroff, pp. 351–376. Washington, DC: American Psychiatric Press.

McElroy, S. L., Keck, P. E., Jr., Pope, H. G., et al. (1994a). Compulsive buying: a report of 20 cases. *Journal of Clinical Psychiatry* 55(6):242–248.

McElroy, S. L., Phillips, K. A., and Keck, P. E., Jr. (1994b). Obsessive compulsive spectrum disorder. *Journal of Clinical Psychiatry* 55(10, suppl):33–51.

McElroy, S. L., Pope, H. G., Jr., Hudson, J. I., et al. (1991b). Kleptomania: a report of 20 cases. *American Journal of Psychiatry* 148:652–657.

McElroy, S. L., Pope, H. G., Keck, P. E., and Hudson, J. I. (1995). Disorders of impulse control. In *Impulsivity and Aggression*, ed. E. Hollander and D. J. Stein, pp. 109–136. New York: Wiley.

McElroy, S. L., Pope, H. G., Keck, P. E., Jr., et al. (1996). Are impulse control disorders related to bipolar disorder? *Comprehensive Psychiatry* 37:229–240.

McElroy, S. L., Satlin, A., Pope, H. G., et al. (1991c). Treatment of compulsive shopping with antidepressants: a report of three cases. *Annals of Clinical Psychiatry* 3:199–204.

McElroy, S. L., Soutullo, C. A., Beckman, D. A., et al. (1998). *DSM-IV* intermittent explosive disorder: a report of 27 cases. *Journal of Clinical Psychiatry* 59(4):203–210.

O'Guinn, T. C., and Faber, R. T. (1989). Compulsive buying: a phenomenological explanation. *Journal of Consumer Research* 16:147–157.

Pfohl, B., Blum, N., Zimmerman, M., and Stangl, D. (1987). Structured interview for *DSM-III* personality disorders, revised. Iowa City, IA: Department of Psychiatry, University of Iowa.

—— (1992). The epidemiology and differential diagnosis of obsessive compulsive disorder. *American Journal of Psychiatry* 53:4S–10S.

Rasmussen, S. A., and Eisen, J. L. (1990). Epidemiology and clinical features of obsessive-compulsive disorder. In *Obsessive-Compulsive Disorders: Theory and Management* (2nd ed.), ed. M. Jenike, L. Baer, and W. E. Minichiello, pp. 10–27. London: Year Book Medical Publishers.

Robins, L., Helzer, J., Cottler, L., and Goldring, E. (1989). National Institute of Mental Health Diagnostic Interview Schedule, Version III, Revised, Bethesda, MD: NIMH.

Rubenstein, C. S., Pigott, T. A., L'Heureux F., et al. (1992). A preliminary investigation of the lifetime prevalence of anorexia and bulimia nervosa in patients with obsessive compulsive disorder. *Journal of Clinical Psychiatry* 53:309–314.

Scherhorn, G., Reisch, L.A., and Raab, G. (1990). Addictive buying in West Germany: an empirical study. *Journal of Consumer Policy* 13:355–376.

Schlosser S., Black, D. W., Repertinger, S., and Freet, D. (1994). Compulsive buying: demography, phenomenology, and comorbidity in 46 subjects. *General Hospital Psychiatry* 16:205–212.

Specker, S. M., Carlson, G. A., Christenson, G. A., and Marcotte, M. (1995). Impulse control disorders and attention deficit in pathological gamblers. *Annals of Clinical Psychiatry* 7:175–179.

Spitzer, R. L., Williams, J. B. W., and Gibbon, M. (1989). Structured

Clinical Interview for *DSM-III-R* (SCID). New York: New York State Psychiatric Institute, Biometrics Research.

Stanley, M., Swann, A., Bowers, T., et al. (1992). A comparison of clinical features in trichotillomania and obsessive-compulsive disorder. *Behavioral Research and Therapy* 30(1):39–44.

Stein, D. J., Hollander, E., and Liebowitz, M. R. (1993). Neurobiology of impulsivity and the impulse control disorders. *Journal of Neuropsychiatry and Clinical Neuroscience* 5:9–17.

Stein, D. J., Mullen, L., Islam, M., et al. (1995). Compulsive and impulsive symptomatology in trichotillomania. *Psychopathology* 28(4):208–221.

Thiel, A., Brooks, A., Ohlmeier, M., et al. (1995). Obsessive-compulsive disorder among patients with anorexia nervosa and bulimia nervosa. *American Journal of Psychiatry* 152:72–75.

Valence, G., d'Astous, A., and Fortier, L. (1988). Compulsive buying: concept and measurement. *Journal of Consumer Policy* 11:419–433.

Webster's Third New International Dictionary (1993). Springfield, MA: Merriam-Webster.

Wise, M. G., and Tierney, J. G. (1994). Impulse control disorders not elsewhere classified. In *The American Psychiatric Association Textbook of Psychiatry*, 2nd ed., ed. R. E. Hales, S. C. Yudofsky, and J. A. Talbott, pp. 681–700. Washington, DC: American Psychiatric Press.

V

Psychodynamic Theory and Technique

11

Compulsive Buying as an Addiction

Ramona Goldman

The concept of addiction, once used only with reference to the abuse of alcohol or drugs, has been broadened to include a number of other conditions. Among these are overeating, declining to eat, compulsive exercising, pathological sexual activity, gambling, and an array of disorders involving the use of money. To these we must now add compulsive buying.[1] Psychotherapists are familiar with patients who consistently spend beyond their means and suffer drastic social, economic, and emotional consequences, but are unable to change their behavior. With growing frequency we see the inclination to buy more merchandise than can be afforded, more than is needed or can be used, often more than can be conveniently stored. This behavior is strongly supported by the environment. Credit is easy to obtain, and buying may be done in a variety of ways—by shopping in a store, by ordering from a catalog, by use of the various shopping channels, or online.

My own interest in this work developed after I had been doing psychoanalytic psychotherapy for a number of years. I began to

---

1. I am using the term *compulsive buying* as it is used by Susan McElroy in her article, "Compulsive Buying: A Report of Twenty Cases" (1994). Though the words *buying, shopping,* and *spending* are used interchangeably, a single term has been chosen in the interest of clarity.

notice that many of my patients, and in some cases their family members as well, had difficulty with alcohol, drugs, or compulsive eating. I sought special training and work opportunities to help me learn more about this population. As time passed, I found that many of my patients, with or without this kind of addiction, were telling me about their uncontrolled spending. This could take several forms, such as buying items for oneself, exhibitionistic check-paying in restaurants, or compulsive gift-giving, to name a few. The buying was often an important component in a particular relationship, at times representing an attempt to reenact a sado-masochistic drama or an acting out of aggression against a mate.

Beginning in the early 1980s and continuing into the present, I have heard complaints of mounting credit-card debt and complications arising from it. Most of these patients are women, and all are preoccupied with the way they are seen by others — not only physically but as regards social skills and general competence. The two areas of *appearance* and *competence* overlap. A well-chosen wardrobe that appears costly does much not only to enhance the wearer's appearance, but also to create an aura of someone in command of herself and her world. These patients continue to buy beyond their means despite mounting bills, guilt feelings, and quarrels with mates. Most of their purchases consist of clothing, cosmetics, or jewelry — tools of adornment. But even those who buy CDs, electronic equipment, and the like (most often men) seem to be trying to create an impression of themselves as people of particular tastes and sensibilities. Enjoyment of the items purchased is secondary. What is primary is the impression created by ownership.

I work from the point of view that compulsive and addictive disorders are both compensatory and defensive in nature, used both to compensate for a deep sense of emptiness and inadequacy and to defend against negative affect. The addictive involvement constitutes a flight from full awareness of these feelings, and from having them emerge undisguised for others to see. In some cases the compensatory need predominates, and I refer to these as "vulnerable" patients. In others it is the defensive need to escape aggressive feelings that is the motivating force. I think of these as the "driven" patients.

Nataraajan and Goff (1991) question the use of the term *compulsive*. They observe that some excessive buying is *im*pulsive rather than *com*pulsive, the distinguishing factors being ego syntonicity and control. I believe that each of these concepts entails some risk of inaccuracy. A given act may be both syntonic and dystonic, in sequence. Some purchases bring temporary pleasure that quickly turns to remorse. Control may be episodic as well. Borrowing a concept from twelve-step programs, we may see a person abstain from excessive buying throughout a particular day or period, yet be unable to maintain abstinence under the impact of everyday life.

While the terms *compulsive* and *addictive* are often used interchangeably, it may be useful at this point to define the sense in which I see compulsive buying as an addiction. To me, what justifies the use of the term *addiction* is the excessive nature of the buying, its use to elevate mood, and its persistence despite acknowledged negative consequences. Author Stanton Peele (1985) says, "The most recognizable form of addiction is an extreme dysfunctional attachment to an experience that is acutely harmful but that is an essential part of the person's ecology and that the person cannot relinquish" (p. 97).

Earlier, Peele (1979) had suggested that an addictive "experience" is a method of coping with life's challenges, providing escape from anxiety and tension by preoccupying the person.

For clinical purposes there is a great advantage in the use of the concept of addiction. The proliferation of twelve-step programs and the public acceptance of the term *addiction* in a variety of contexts, has begun to destigmatize eating disorders, variant forms of sexuality, compulsive gambling, and the like, in the same way that alcoholism and substance abuse have been partially destigmatized in the past few decades. To participate in a twelve-step program and publicly declare oneself an addict incurs far less censure today than in earlier times.

Many writers have seen compulsive buying as an addiction. Gerhard Scherhorn (1990) supports the use of the term *addiction* on the grounds that *compulsion* connotes pressure to do something against one's will, whereas the behavior in question "involves the extension of normal behavior into a pathological habit" (p. 159) and is more properly seen as an addiction. Regarding developmental factors, he refers to distortion of autonomy.

In this condition a subject long forced to deny genuine feelings may reach a point at which he no longer knows what these feelings really are. Thus his natural longings for personal acknowledgment and familial love are felt as wishes for impersonal material objects. This is the product of a family style in which possessions are valued over relationships, and of a society that facilitates — even rewards — excessive buying. A similar pattern prevails in alcoholism, wherein the attempt to replace the sense of inadequacy with feelings of relaxed confidence is experienced as a desire for alcohol.

Scherhorn and colleagues (1990) report on methodology and results of a study of twenty-six self-identified addictive buyers and 136 normal consumers. The purpose of the study was to test the hypothesis that the propensity for addictive buying could be traced to the aforementioned distortion of autonomy. It is noted that buying is used as one method of self-repair, and may appear as one of several forms of addiction. The authors advocate for a change in consumer education and for a supportive stance toward consumer self-help groups.

Richard Elliott (1994) reports on a study of self-identified addictive consumers in the United Kingdom. Elliott defines addiction as involving behavior that is powered by a strong urge, with the subject feeling out of control. The buying is not connected to a need for the objects purchased, but is used to repair mood, to make up for the absence of human relationships, and to meet current standards of social desirability. Neither is the buying subject to alteration in the light of reality, but continues despite negative consequences and attempts at control.

The author advocates a cognitive-behavioral approach to treatment, noting that short-term gratifications such as those provided by the addiction are more effective in reinforcing the behavior than long-term negative consequences are in altering it. Addictive shopping is presented as a form of postmodern fragmentation in which identity is expressed through affect-laden experiences.

The course of a compulsive buying addiction has been described by DeSarbo and Edwards (1996), who have empirically distinguished between two clusters of compulsive buyers, one evidencing a more addictive form of the behavior and one a more benign form. According to these authors,

> Addiction to spending occurs progressively, starting when the recreational buyer, who may occasionally shop and spend as an escape, finds the experienced "high" to be an easy and gratifying way to deal with stress or negative emotions. A crisis causing anxiety overload then triggers the individual to buy compulsively. Experiencing progressively less relief with each spending spree, the person requires "redosing" and comes to depend on shopping and spending as the primary means of coping with anxiety . . . compulsive buying may be considered a progression from normal to impulsive spending, to a means of escape from stress and anxiety, and finally to gross addiction to the experience. [p. 232]

In my experience, not every patient's compulsive buying addiction follows this course. What I have seen reflects an ongoing struggle to resist acting on the addictive impulse. A shopping binge may be followed by a period of contrition and abstinence from shopping, eventually giving way to a return to minimal excessive buying with some attempts to control the behavior. These attempts, however, are only partially successful, and at some point another shopping binge will occur that begins the cycle all over again.

Donna Boundy (1993) describes a condition wherein the addiction involves the whole experience of money, both acquisition and spending. Thus it differs from more narrowly focused writings that depict chiefly the buying process and its sequelae. Pathological behaviors reviewed by Boundy include not only compulsive spending, debting, and giving, but hoarding and underearning as well. The author cites four properties of buying addiction: obsession, loss of control, repetition despite harmful consequences, and denial. She describes each as it applies to money disorders. Types of spending are referred to as image spending, compulsive bargaining, bulimic spending, and compulsive shopping. Boundy also outlines a recovery process focusing on personal honesty, the lessening of denial, and the "amends" principles of twelve-step programs (see Donna Boundy, Chapter 1, this volume).

COMMON PROPERTIES

In my work with various addictions I have noted a group of frequently occurring phenomena. These include narcissistic vulnerability, psychological dependency, a propensity for depression, affect intolerance, generalized compulsivity often expressed through other addictions, and a large reservoir of aggression. Let us take a brief look at these.

Narcissistic vulnerability. *Narcissism* as used here refers to the level of energy used in the maintenance of self-esteem. By *narcissistic vulnerability* I mean chronic uneasiness about doing well or badly in the eyes of others, and susceptibility to feelings of abject failure and humiliation. Lacking internal mechanisms to comfort and nourish herself, the patient is easily disabled by a sense of helplessness. At such moments she grasps for a way to restore positive self-perceptions, and adopts artificial techniques of self-repair, such as compulsive buying .

Psychological dependency. This property is similar to narcissism in that it refers to reliance on the reactions of others. Glatt and Cook (1987) describe a patient who used spending as a "passport to popularity," buying expensive leather goods to demonstrate her spending power and her pretended independence from her parents. This transitory gratification was so irresistible as to obliterate moral concerns in an otherwise ethical individual, causing her, in effect, to steal from her parents. Other writers report the use of buying to elicit the friendly regard of sales personnel. In my own experience some psychologically dependent people rely on others not solely for admiration but also for the stuff of survival. Most often this takes the form of financial dependence. Because of her self-absorption, this kind of person may have developed only the most elementary of financial or work skills, and might be unable — even if she were not a compulsive buyer — to provide for herself or make a normally acceptable contribution to a household income. This could also be true if she had good work skills but was psychologically incapable of commanding adequate earnings — a "compulsive underearner," to borrow a term from Debtors Anonymous.

Whatever its cause, the inability, or unconscious refusal, to provide for herself can create conflict with a mate who resents paying her bills, or it can keep her tied to an alliance that is nonconflictual about money but has little appeal otherwise. This represents the unfolding of a hostile-dependent personality disorder. In this case the dependency on another is maintained in order to create havoc in the life of that person, either in retaliation for perceived wrongs or as a means of finally extracting nurturance believed to have been withheld by an earlier figure. The condition is self-perpetuating because the energy used in maintaining the dependency limits the patient's engagement in more life-enhancing pursuits that could promote independence.

Affect intolerance. This term refers to the inability to endure painful feelings. For these patients any unpleasant experience, especially one that is seen as evidence of personal inadequacy, brings unendurable feelings that must be replaced quickly by something else. This is one way that addictive behavior becomes activated. Using externalization as a defense, the patient drinks, eats, exercises, or shops compulsively as a momentary distraction from negative self-perceptions. This represents an attempt to feel competent and desirable, to repair mood, restore cohesion, and stimulate positive affect. The role of affect intolerance in the development of addictions has been explored in the works of Henry Krystal (1977) and Edward Khantzian (1977).

General compulsivity. Compulsivity refers to the tendency to engage repeatedly in behavior that the subject perceives as harmful and from which no pleasure is gained. The activity is sometimes associated with time spent in regret, resolutions to avoid the behavior in the future, and, perversely, making plans to engage in it once more as soon as possible. Disorders such as compulsive exercising or shopping, sometimes referred to as "nonsubstance addictions," often occur alongside alcoholism, drug abuse, and various eating disorders. Associated pathology includes major depression and bipolar illness.

Propensity to fantasy. In my experience this feature appears more commonly in compulsive buying than in other addictions. Its existence requires a significant level of denial, which gives it commonality with alcoholism and other disorders of consumption. However, I have observed that the fantasies of compulsive buyers about buying are more discreet and more retrievable to consciousness than those of alcoholics and addicts about drinking and drug use. A compulsive buyer may say, "I thought if I bought that dress I'd turn heads wherever I went." Irrational or not, this fantasy is easily recalled by the patient. By contrast, an alcoholic recalling a drinking bout does not often verbalize the expectations he had as he headed for the bar. The impulse to drink and the act of drinking, despite time elapsed between them, seem to be very much of a piece, leaving little space for any cognitive process such as reflection or fantasy.

Compulsive buyers, imagining a new acquisition, commonly see extravagant rewards attached to its ownership. In the store, fantasies allow the patient to imagine that she can easily afford the purchase — that she is a person of wealth and power or that she will become such a person if she shops like one. This is reinforced by the "dress for success" philosophy. One may hear, "For my new job I got some executive-type clothes. I want them to respect me." This is not unlike the expectations of respect that some men have in owning an expensive car. Fantasies provide the buyer with an escape from the reality of financial consequences and create an exhilarating high. Few buyers reexperience these feelings when viewing the purchases at home. At some point fantasies fade, replaced by guilt and fear of consequences. Many purchases find a secret home in the back of the closet, safe from detection. Those that make it to the unwrapping stage tend not to be valued, and may even be disparaged, as if they had taken on the negative projections of the buyer.

These properties — narcissistic vulnerability, psychological dependency, affect intolerance, general compulsivity, and a propensity for fantasy — are commonly, though not universally, found in compulsive buyers. The ego deficits of these patients resemble those of alcoholics and drug users, and I have come to regard them as a single entity. This chapter, with the use of existing literature and my own clinical experience, seeks to offer guidelines to effective treatment.

HOW THE PATTERN DEVELOPS

All compulsive behavior is accompanied by suffering yet is difficult to change. How does such a spending pattern develop? What life circumstances impel someone to adopt such an unwieldy coping mechanism as the acquisition of unneeded goods, and to retain the behavior though it requires her to neglect ordinary duties, keep secrets, and perhaps engage in sociopathic activities? A number of scenarios have been observed. Scherhorn and colleagues (1990) describe a disturbance of autonomy whereby a child is not given reinforcement for her activities or for the natural unfolding of her personality, and comes to see herself as less important to her parents than their possessions. Not feeling personally valued, she seeks to absorb the value of such possessions as she can acquire, and thus restore self-esteem. Reinforcing this is the tendency of such families to reward good behavior and achievement with money and gifts in place of affection. Faber and O'Guinn (1988) describe the impact of feeling not only undervalued, but actually unwanted by one's parents. Not uncommon with this population, this situation creates extreme susceptibility to warm greetings from salespeople, to expressions of gratitude from recipients of gifts given, and to the illusion of personal value based on spending. Any pleasurable feelings connected with buying can reinforce the behavior, laying the groundwork for an addictive involvement.

Another scenario is that of the child raised in an affluent

and materialistic family whose resources have been markedly reduced. The experience of plenty followed by scarcity brings craving for lost luxury and envy of those who still have it. As a child or adolescent the subject may not have access to discretionary money, and no pathological buying habits may develop at this time. However, the reduction of power and status of the family may be internalized, with serious consequences to self-esteem. Should the damage go unrepaired and the subject's view of herself continue to be associated with the kind of possessions she can acquire, compulsive buying may later in life become the unconsciously chosen solution to her problems.

However the life circumstances may vary, addictive buyers share one common experience: they believe that their capacities and personal attributes are insufficient to garner the regard and affection of other people.

To illustrate, let us look at a case example. This woman is the type of patient I refer to as "vulnerable."

CASE ONE

Faye was a married, 36-year-old clerical worker with a diagnosis of major depression and borderline personality disorder. She was a compulsive buyer of jewelry and clothing. Her buying sprees typically followed experiences of perceived rejection, after which she lost control and expressed strong negative emotion. She arrived for our session in a state of agitation. She said, "I'm very upset! I lost control again! I had words with my boss. Oh, I said too much!" She began to cry, and reached for tissues. "Harold is going to be furious! He'll say it's all my fault!"

Harold, Faye's husband, was a passive, long-suffering man of 45. His social inhibitions and indifference to his appearance made him unappealing to his wife, whose complaints he ignored. He worked hard, earned modestly, and despaired over his wife's spending.

Despite her tears, Faye told me what had happened.

Today had been her one-year anniversary on the job. She had expected a gift from her supervisor, because he had given one to his personal assistant on her seventh anniversary. She saw nothing unreasonable in her expectations. In a moment of fury she had called him a worm. Now she was flooded with remorse.

"You were hurt because he seemed not to appreciate you."

"Not only seemed! He said I wasn't fast enough. Now he wants me to learn the computer! I don't want to learn the computer. It makes me nervous! Why can't he appreciate me as I am?"

"Being asked to learn something new means . . ."

"I said, 'I've worked for you a whole year today and this is how you reward me.' And I started screaming, and everyone could hear me, and then I started to cry! I grabbed my coat and ran out the door and didn't go back! Oh, I must have lost my job. How can I tell Harold? How could I have done this again?"

"It seems we need to work more on your being angry and expressing your feelings without losing control."

"I wish I had gone right home, as I should have. I stopped at Lord & Taylor. Not to buy! Just to peek."

She smiled coquettishly, and went on to describe the "summer things" — items of light clothing of which she suddenly realized she had very few. She told me of several purchases, each a bargain. Then she paused, and added, "And also I bought a bracelet. It's gold, and it's beautiful. It cost $375. But that's half-price! They hardly ever have such a sale . . . it was too much for me to spend, but it was a real opportunity! And I just needed to do something . . . to buy something of value and have it for my own, no matter what!" She spoke with vigor, smiling, but now and then a look of alarm would cross her face and disappear.

This is the kind of affective split commonly seen in various addictions during times of relapse. The subject, though suffering from guilt and anxiety, has moments of exhilaration. Faye's ability to deny reality and to momentarily enjoy her purchases, despite upcoming trouble, is typical of compulsive buyers. O'Guinn and Faber (1989) and Faber and Christenson (1996) cite the liberal use of fantasy as a characteristic of these patients. Fantasy allows the subject to predict extraordinary benefits from the items bought, and to replace guilt and fear with happy expectancy.

She said, "I was in a much better mood afterward. For a little while."

"And now?"

"Well, you saw how I came in."

"When did you start feeling bad?"

"On the bus, coming here. I thought about Harold."

After this episode Faye followed a familiar procedure. First, she tore a blank check from Harold's checkbook to pay the bill when it came. She had no concern that Harold would notice a check missing. For all his angry tirades he let himself be deceived repeatedly. To use a term from Alcoholics Anonymous, he was a true *enabler*, suffering from his mate's addictive behavior but doing little to stop it — in fact, making it easy. This is common among such spouses, who are also termed *codependent*. This means that the mate of an addict may gain an unconscious reward from the role of the morally superior, burdened spouse, and is as dependent upon this role as his mate is upon the addictive involvement.

Faye grew up in a family of five children, the youngest by nearly a decade. She had a strong impression of being an unwanted birth, very likely an "accident." The family had been wealthy at one time, and Faye's mother had known no shortage of expensive clothing and jewelry. Business reverses had drained the family fortune, but Faye's mother, now a widow, managed to stay in the family home in New Jersey. By contrast, Faye and Harold occupied a modest apartment in Brooklyn. Faye kept a watchful eye on her mother's parceling out of gifts from her store of antiques and jewelry, most of which seemed to go to Faye's oldest sister. Faye assumed this was because her sister was a successful attorney and a source of maternal pride, while she, always an underachiever, held a lackluster job as a clerk.

Faye chose to overlook certain realities. Her mother, now approaching 75, needed help with her business affairs. Her oldest daughter took this responsibility. Faye could not see that this entitled her sister to their mother's generosity, just as she could not understand her supervisor's rewarding his assistant of seven years and leaving her out. This sense of entitlement permeated her thinking. As a result, she rarely got what she hoped for, and consistently felt deprived. She was often unaware of what others might expect from her. For example, she would complain of being left out of social events, but rarely extended an invitation to anyone. Having developed only the most modest of skills, she expected rewards matching those of high achievers. A poor student in high school, she had resorted to duplicity in order to pass exams. Striving desperately to gain her parents' attention, she became sexually promiscuous. When this did not get results, she left the family home, started work as a saleslady, and married Harold. It was during this time that her excessive spending developed.

Trying without success to create luxury in her life, Faye would choose expensive items of clothing and jewelry and have them "laid away" until she could pay them off. Harold never asked where the things came from because he didn't notice them. When credit cards became easily available, Faye's spending increased, as did the bills. For a number of years she could wrest occasional sums of money from her mother—a practice she kept secret from Harold. But eventually her mother warned her that times were bad, that no more gifts of money would be available, and that she must not expect a large inheritance. For as long as I knew her Faye maintained the belief that her siblings had gotten the lion's share.

The above serves to outline the themes of Faye's life: lack

of experience of feeling valued, hence the exaggerated need to own valuables; a paranoid sense of not getting enough, with denial of the measured way in which she gave to others; a chronic state of underachievement and relative lack of skills due to an inability to focus on anything except her personal needs. Compounding all of this was the lack of boundaries in her emotional expression. She could not express strong negative feelings without losing control.

At the beginning of treatment I was seen as a depriving figure — an expectable transference phenomenon. She was resistant to the ordinary demands of treatment — paying for missed sessions, not always being seen early if she arrived early, and the like. After each buying episode she would deride me for failing to cure her of her compulsion. When I suggested that her feelings of being uncared for by me were reminiscent of the deprivation of her childhood, she was pleased. She savored the word "deprivation," using it often to explain her behavior to herself. I saw that genetic interpretations were not helpful, as explaining her behavior made regressions seem acceptable. I changed my approach, and instead of interpreting her buying as a response to needs unfulfilled in childhood, I used an AA concept, that of "relapse triggers." Without using these words I helped her to identify the events and feelings that preceded undue purchases and emotional eruptions. Few references were made to the origins of these reactions. Instead, she was encouraged to reflect, "When I feel this way, I *could* go shopping." Gradually the narrow focus on her most painful current feelings allowed her to use impulse control and delay of gratification, and to increase her capacity for affect tolerance. She grew proud of her more mature behavior.

When treatment ended, Faye's shopping sprees were far less frequent and less costly than at the beginning. When they did occur she would usually tell Harold about them. At times she was able to plan necessary purchases with him, before buying.

Now let us look at another patient, one in whom both fear and aggression are closer to the surface, and who presents in a frenzied fashion. She is one of the patients I call "driven."

CASE TWO

Anita is a slim, petite brunette. A legal secretary for eight years, she is 30 years old. She entered treatment ostensibly for bulimia, alcoholism, and compulsive exercising. In my office she told me that what had worried her most in the past few months was her buying.

Like most such patients Anita is preoccupied with her appearance, and especially with thinness. In this area she flagrantly denies reality. Model-thin, she castigates herself for her imagined excess weight, declaring that she is "gross." Her boyfriend, Tony, must surely be seeking another woman. Without foundation, she accuses him of philandering, which he denies. To hold his interest she searches relentlessly for the "right" dress, the "perfect" pants.

"I really get crazy," she said. "When I get this idea in my mind, I forget everything else. It's like I get lost! I could forget an appointment, I could stand somebody up, it wouldn't matter, I could be on Mars."

"You said, 'When I get this idea in my mind.' Could you say more about that?"

"It's hard to describe. It's like being obsessed. I need, say, a pair of white pants to make the perfect outfit. Well, no, I don't really *need* them. But I feel like I do. So I go from store to store. I'll go all day if I have to, looking for this . . . *thing* that I want. And I don't always find it. But boy, do I try!"

"How do you know when you've found it?"

"If it looks the way I imagined. With pants, they have to make the line of my hip go in just the right curve or it's no good. I drive them crazy in stores. I try on so many things and don't buy them. But when I do find the right ones I make up for it, because I buy a half dozen! Really, I'm not exaggerating!

Just recently I brought home six pairs of white pants exactly alike! I thought, 'Whee! I've found them! The perfect white pants! I'll buy all they have in my size, and I'll have white pants for the rest of my life!' I was so thrilled! The people in the store thought I was a maniac. And you know what? The next day at home I tried on one pair. And they were no good! This happens all the time. I thought, 'How could I have picked these? They're horrible!'"

"What made them horrible?"

"They didn't fit! They had a bulge! They stuck way out on the side, made me look huge! I must have been blind when I was in the store. I felt so miserable! Of course I could never be seen in them! And there they are, in the back of my closet. All six pairs!"

"You didn't return them?"

"No. I never do. I can't face the salesperson. I have so many clothes I've never worn!"

I asked what she feels the shopping is meant to achieve, and what the "perfect white pants" would do for her life. "They'd change it! They'd make it perfect!"

"Or maybe they'd make you perfect."

"Yes, I think that may be the whole point. But that's impossible! I'm always saying I'll stop this, but I never do. Don't say it's crazy! I know that! I have to do it anyway!"

I asked about her indebtedness. "I owe $28,000 on credit cards! And what did I buy? Nothing. Clothes. Makeup. I'm a nut!"

As she speaks, she skips from topic to topic in a way that sometimes makes her hard to follow. She speaks rapidly, with great anxiety, like someone on the run. In an early session I asked if she had attended meetings of Debtors Anonymous. "I have," she said. "But it's no good for me. I can't get to the meetings. Between my job, seeing Tony, going to the gym — which I must do five times a week or I'm totally gross — my schedule is impossible."

Anita's frenzied activity serves to disguise her chronic, underlying depression. It also acts as a vehicle for competitive pursuits like exercising, dressing well, and vying for male attention. She says, "I'm not really in love with Tony, but if he looked at another woman I'd be ready to kill. I'm always accusing him of flirting with other women. And I fly off the handle, in a restaurant or someplace, and ruin a whole evening. I give that poor man such a hard time, it's a wonder he doesn't break off with me."

"What would you do then?"

She thought for a moment. "I'd plunge more into working out. Have the best body in town! Get so thin you couldn't see me! Then I'd have a right to spend money on clothes!"

This highlights a major motive for Anita's buying behavior. Aggressively tinged images appear often. Thinness to the point of invisibility suggests death, and having the best body implies killing off adversaries. The "best body" might deserve to be adorned with "perfect" garments. Thus the aggression that she fears in herself finds an outlet in the stores.

Anita's history contains much to explain her fear of aggression. Both parents grew up in violent families and re-enacted their childhood scenarios with little restraint. Her father, a large and bellicose man, is a person of extremes, capable of loving affection and spontaneous violence. Her mother, an outwardly passive and fearful alcoholic, would taunt her husband until he beat her. Anita managed to avoid his violence, and in fact became his favorite. Mother retaliated against Anita with verbal abuse, calling her worthless and unattractive, putting curses on her when she tried to distance herself. On the day that Anita moved out, her mother screamed after her, "You'll never be happy! You have a mother's curse on you!"

The atmosphere of the home was like a minefield. A stormy battle could erupt between the parents at any time. Anita learned to be watchful, ready for anything, determined not to be taken by surprise. This wariness is still maintained, but the focus has changed. What she fears is not physical danger but personal rejection, and she seeks safety in her attractiveness. A part of this is her scrupulous maintenance of the "perfect" wardrobe for all occasions.

The two women presented have very different external personalities. Anita, however frenzied, appears strong and competent. Faye is more childlike and appealing, though she pouts when things displease her. Internally, both women want desperately to be admired and viewed as at least equal, if not superior, to those around them. Both are susceptible to rejection, lack impulse control, and are given to addictive behavior in several areas.

In both women buying achieves several ends: it allows narcissistic self-adornment, provides an area for competition, and creates a momentary thrill at the time of purchase. It allows Anita to run from the wish to retaliate against her parents, and lets Faye console herself after a narcissistic injury.

However, the unconscious goal of the buying — that of creating wholeness and self-acceptance — is not reached. The patients are still wary, insecure, and now, additionally, in debt. It is hoped that treatment will help them build the impulse control to combat buying urges, avoid the pitfalls of other addictions, and find less toxic ways of seeking wholeness.

TREATMENT

The treatment of addiction, whether one addictive involvement or several, must be twofold. Most psychoanalytic therapists working with nonaddicted patients tend to focus on underlying dynamics, and allow manifest symptoms to change as the need for them decreases. Addiction, however, presents special challenges. The immediate consequences of an active addiction can be so drastic as to impede the treatment — as, for instance, when a compulsive buyer incurs such debt that the person paying the bills refuses to finance treatment. The therapist must encourage the patient to limit or put an end to addictive acting out so that treatment can proceed.

At the same time it must be borne in mind that addictive

behavior commonly exists in a fragile personality with poorly developed ego functions. The therapist must respond to concerns of a vulnerable person whose emotions are felt in the extreme (though not always at a conscious level), whose impulse control barely exists, whose depression may be severe despite medication, whose relationships are complicated by the subject's constant demands for reassurance, and whose unrecognized aggression presses for release. She must at the same time address the patient's urge to buy compulsively and the dire consequences of her actually doing so.

A good first step is to recommend Debtors Anonymous. Resistance may be met, as these patients tend to be secretive about their buying. Unless there has been positive experience in another twelve-step program, the patient may not comply. In this case it may be better to let the matter rest to avoid added resistance. The value of the program, for those open to it, cannot be overstated. It presents an opportunity to identify with others whose goal is solvency, a framework for ongoing commitment, and a means of helping others, without which any attempted recovery lacks substance.

Since buying, spending, and debting are not synonymous, some patients may fail to see how Debtors Anonymous can help them. Advantages of the program, despite these differences, include the reduction of isolation and a chance to be helpful to other people. The expression of altruism has been cited as a building block of self-esteem. Irvin Yalom (1985) lists altruism among the curative factors in group psychotherapy, with which twelve-step programs have much in common. Moreover, the meetings offer an opportunity to identify with others for whom solvency is a major goal. Whether the patient is one of those rare people who enter therapy with compulsive buying as the presenting problem, or instead has revealed it as an aspect of a broader pathological picture, the reduction of excessive buying must be a major objective from the beginning. This is true whether or not he or she makes use of Debtors Anonymous (for a full discussion of the use of Debtors Anonymous with these patients, see Levine and Kellen, Chapter 18, this volume).

If the patient is not already alert to the impact of her buying on her life, an early goal must be to heighten her awareness. This may develop gradually. The therapist must be alert to the patient's reluctance to share every addictive episode. It may be helpful to ask, "Did your spending help to create this problem?" and similar questions, in various situations, in order to lessen the denial. This may enhance reality testing and foster development of an observing ego.

As is common in nonsubstance addictions, a dilemma may exist regarding the setting of limits. Just as one must eat to live, so one must buy in order to function in society. Who is to say when buying is excessive? The therapist cannot make these distinctions, but must help the patient learn to make them for herself. I have found it best to focus not on the items purchased, or on the money spent, but on the motive for buying. The patient can learn to ask herself, "Why am I buying this now? What if I bought it tomorrow instead? Can I bear the waiting? What are my feelings?" and the like.

An obvious hazard is that of symptom substitution. Most compulsive buyers suffer from more than one addiction, operating serially or simultaneously. When one addiction ceases to gratify or is relinquished, another may become activated. People in inpatient treatment for substance abuse, deprived of drugs, often begin to overeat, not as a return to an earlier food problem but simply because food is available and is not monitored. In this way one addiction may follow another, each intended, consciously or unconsciously, to replace and expunge the other. Yet each involvement offers gratifications of its own, however transitory, and is not easily set aside. For example, strenuous exercise is often meant to undo the effect of overeating without the usual means of purging, but may become entrenched as another addictive behavior. In the case of Anita we saw the progression of alcoholism, bulimia, exercise, and, finally, buying as she attempted to replace fear and anger with new clothes.

Faye, described earlier, came to understand that her shopping sprees had been her answer to perceived slights, that she had been seeking ways to feel better about herself and to avoid thinking about painful experiences. As her buying episodes became less frequent, her emotional and verbal excesses also came under her control.

Given the above, the goal of treatment should not be solely to end compulsive buying, because one addictive practice may be replaced by another. A more comprehensive goal is to limit compulsivity itself. This can be approached through increased awareness of the onset of the urge to buy, of the feelings preceding, during, and after buying, and through the building of impulse control to avoid unnecessary buying. The ideal of solvency, with some measure of attainment, serves to augment progress toward this goal.

In summary, I have identified the following seven points that I consider essential to the treatment of compulsive buying:

1. Be directive in encouraging the patient to reduce or end excessive buying at the earliest point possible.
2. Recommend participation in Debtors Anonymous.
3. Consider referring the patient to a psychiatrist for consultation. Where depression is a factor, psychoactive medications may be nearly indispensable in helping the patient to progress. McElroy and associates (1989) as well as Donald Black and colleagues (1997) have given ample evidence of this.
4. Help the patient to examine those aspects of her history that make her susceptible to the buying addiction. This requires exploration of emotional states that occur before, during, and after excessive buying.
5. Use the above to identify relapse triggers. These should be clearly stated and referred to whenever appropriate so that the patient has them firmly in mind.
6. Explore the use of fantasy in buying behavior. This can be difficult, as compulsive buyers are often reluctant to share their fantasies, which they know to be ridiculous. The fantasies predict extravagant rewards from the ownership of a desired item. In treatment a growing sense of reality can reduce the power of such fantasies.
7. Express appreciation of the patient's strengths, especially those

observed in the current clinical work. The patient needs to know that the therapist sees her as an adult who is fully capable of nonaddictive buying.

The therapist should encourage exploration of the buying experience and all related experiences. She should be mildly directive when necessary, and supportive of the patient's attempts to change. Through the therapeutic relationship, the patient's negative self-perceptions can be replaced by positive ones as she gains more and more control. In time she will come to recognize her own value, to see that she has beauty and usefulness that does not depend on the valuables she owns.

REFERENCES

Black, D. W. (1997). Fluvoxamine in the treatment of compulsive buying. *Journal of Clinical Psychiatry* 159–163.

Boundy, D. (1993). *When Money Is the Drug: Understanding and Changing Self-Defeating Money Patterns. Maverick Media Resources.*

DeSarbo, W. S., and Edwards, E. A. (1996). Typologies of compulsive buying behavior: a contained clusterwise regression approach. *Journal of Consumer Psychology* 5(3):231–262.

Elliott, R. (1994). Addictive consumption: function and fragmentation in postmodernity. *Journal of Consumer Policy* 17:159–179.

Faber, R., and Christenson, G. (1996). In the mood to buy: differences in the mood states experienced by compulsive buyers and other consumers. In *Psychology and Marketing*. New York: Wiley.

Faber, R. J., and O'Guinn, T. C. (1988). *Dysfunctional Consumer Socialization: a Search for the Roots of Compulsive Buying.* Leuven, Belgium: International Association for Research in Economic Psychology Colloquium.

Glatt, M. M., and Cook, C. C. (1987). Pathological spending as a form of psychological dependence. *British Journal of Addiction* 82:1257–1258.

Khantzian, E. J. (1977). The ego, the self and opiate addiction: theoretical and treatment considerations. In *Psychodynamics of Drug Dependence*, ed. J. D. Blaine and D. A. Julius, pp. 101–117. New York: Jason Aronson.

Krystal, H. (1977). Self and object-representation in alcoholism and other drug dependence: implications for therapy. In *Psychodynamics of Drug Dependence*, ed. J. D. Blaine and D. A. Julius, pp. 88–100. New York: Jason Aronson.

McElroy, S. (1994). Compulsive buying: a report of 20 cases. *Journal of Clinical Psychiatry* 55(6):242–248.

McElroy, S. L., Saitlin, A., Pope, H. G., et al. (1989). Treatment of compulsive shopping with antidepressants: a report of three cases. *Annals of Clinical Psychiatry* 3:199–204.

Nataraajan, R., and Goff, B. (1991). Compulsive buying: toward a reconceptualization. *Journal of Social Behavior and Personality* 6(6):307–328.

O'Guinn, T. C., and Faber, R. J. (1989). Compulsive buying: a phenomenological exploration. *Journal of Consumer Research* 16:147–157.

Peele, S. (1979). Redefining addiction II: the meaning of addiction in our lives. *Journal of Psychedelic Drugs* 11:289–297.

—— (1985). *The Meaning of Addiction*. Lexington, MA: Lexington Books.

Scherhorn, G. (1990). The addictive trait in buying behaviour. *Journal of Consumer Policy* 13:33–51.

Scherhorn, G., Reisch, L., and Raab, G. (1990). Addictive buying in West Germany: an empirical study. *Journal of Consumer Policy* 13:355–387.

Yalom, I. (1985). *The Theory and Practice of Group Psychotherapy*. New York: Basic Books.

12

When Eating and Shopping Are Companion Disorders

F. Diane Barth

The mall is crowded, rather noisy . . . Mrs. Dietrich
smiles with relief. She senses that Nola too is relieved,
cheered. It's like coming home.
— from "Shopping," by Joyce Carol Oates (1992)

An article in the April 1998 *Paris Match* (Daspin 1998) described
a popular singing star as a "shopping bulimic." Leave it to the
French to coin a phrase perfectly capturing a phenomenon that is
seen in the world at large but is not often discussed in the psychological literature: a curious link between eating and shopping
disorders. Although until recently there was little research on this
subject, every therapist who works with eating disorders can
provide anecdotal reports of binge eaters who binge-shop, anorex-
ics who shoplift, bulimics who compulsively buy items they never
use, and any number of other fascinating combinations of eating
and shopping behaviors. Furthermore, although the consensus is
that more women than men have both of these clusters of difficulties, in my own practice and those of my colleagues and supervisees examples of these companion actions are frequently found in
men as well as women.

What is it that brings these two apparently different activities together? And, given the tremendous variability in the actual symptoms, why do we even suggest that the connections are anything other than coincidence? In my experience there appears to be no one-to-one association of symptoms. For example, one restricting anorexic may also severely limit herself in regard to all purchases or "gifts to myself," as one young client put it, while another shoplifts regularly and yet a third goes on frequent shopping sprees. A compulsive overeater may shop impulsively and uncontrollably; another carefully guards every penny, refusing to buy even basic necessities like toilet paper and toothpaste. To make matters even more confusing, not every person with an eating disorder also has a shopping disorder, and not everyone with a shopping problem has eating difficulties. Yet for most of us who have worked with clients with some combination of these symptoms, the association between them is apparent, if not always easily understood. In this chapter we will examine some aspects of the complex relationship between these different but often intricately linked disorders, and we will discuss some of the ways that therapists can help clients who suffer from these fascinating, painful, and often difficult-to-treat combinations.

A valuable starting point for our exploration would naturally be the psychodynamics underlying both of these disorders. However, as Pine (1985) has commented, the human condition is "endlessly complex" (p. 146). No single explanation, no matter how elegantly worded or dynamically accurate, is ever enough to fully decipher any particular aspect of our experience. To make this chapter manageable, as I am unable to cover every issue involved, I will focus on two areas of great significance that I believe hold a key to the connections between both groups of symptoms as well as their dynamic causes. These are (1) the capacity to regulate, manage, tolerate, and process a variety of emotions, and (2) the ability to use language to help in the management and processing of affects.

AFFECT REGULATION AND MANAGEMENT

Numerous authors have noted a significant connection between eating disorders and difficulties processing and regulating affects (see, for example Barth 1994, 1998, Grotstein 1991, Krystal 1988, McDougall 1989, Sackstedter 1989, Stolorow and Atwood 1992). Recently, researchers have not only validated this clinical hypothesis, but have also provided evidence that shopping and eating disorders may be linked precisely *because* of the ways they help to cope with affects (see, for example, Christenson et al. 1994, McElroy et al. 1995, Schlosser et al. 1994). Growing numbers of studies have found that compulsive, impulsive shopping and eating behaviors appear to be related to difficulty in regulating impulses and managing feelings. McElroy and colleagues (1995), for example, noted that "kleptomania, compulsive buying, and binge-eating disorder are related to mood disorder" (p. 24), and "may belong to . . . the larger family of affective spectrum disorder" (p. 25).

Using eating and shopping rituals to relieve tension and ameliorate other uncomfortable feelings is neither abnormal nor necessarily pathological. In fact, it can be quite adaptive in many circumstances, as most of us have found at one time or another in our lives. Preparing and eating food, or looking for and buying a variety of items, can help us to manage a range of affects, including soothing ourselves when we feel hurt, lonely, angry, or disappointed; relaxing us when we feel tense, overwhelmed, or overstimulated; or energizing ourselves when we feel sad, tired, or overwhelmed. In her columns on food in *The New York Times*, Molly O'Neill often evocatively captures this normal, everyday use of food to manage and/or modulate feelings. For instance, describing the experiences of the early settlers of New York State's Hudson River region, she wrote (1998), "You almost need a ritual, like a Dutch colonial tea, to live on the edge of something so beautiful and timeless, so enthralling and, ultimately, so heartbreaking" (p. 73). And again, "The mixture of beauty and, possibly, homesickness would explain their yearning for late-afternoon comfort" (of tea and cake) (p. 73).

Similarly, market research on the buying habits of successful businesswomen has demonstrated that the process of shopping for expensive items, sometimes more so than actually purchasing them, gives many women a sense of power and self-confidence. As one woman put it, "To know that I could buy these things, that the salespeople are taking me seriously and want to please me is an amazing experience. It's a time when I can feel really good about myself." These same activities can become problematic, however, when they are used as repetitive, compulsive, and undifferentiated responses to a wide variety of emotions and experiences. As in "Shopping," the Joyce Carol Oates story from which I took the quote for the beginning of this chapter, shopping and eating may provide a temporary sense of safe haven, but soon unmanageable feelings reassert themselves, requiring further soothing. Mrs. Dietrich in the Oates story turns to alcohol, but emptiness, hopelessness, frustration, and helplessness always lurk beneath the surface for her and, we suspect, for her daughter, who shows classic symptoms of both eating and shopping disorders.

When these disorders appear together, they may signal that the individual is attempting to cope with feelings she cannot process or manage. In a beautiful description of this phenomenon, Sackstedter (1989) has captured the complex interplay of the physiological and psychological aspects of unmanageable feelings. He describes a bulimic patient who "noted that when she was alone and didn't want to be and no one was available to her, she felt lonely and empty. These were first psychological feeling states, but then the emptiness became a body state . . . and she coped with that by gorging, which relieved the feeling of emptiness. She then vomited so as not to gain weight. In addition, it became clear that gorging and vomiting [were ways] to rid herself of any unpleasant feeling or thought or body state" (p. 414).

Many clients who experience something similar are not fully aware of the links between the feelings and their eating and shopping behavior. One of the first steps of the therapeutic process is frequently an introduction to the idea that the behaviors are used as coping mechanisms. Gradually, therapist and client together can begin to sort out just what kinds of feelings trigger the impulsive and/or compulsive activity. To the surprise of many therapists and clients, this is not as straightforward a process as one might imagine. Even when these clients are bright, articulate, and apparently insightful, they are often unable to make significant connections between their internal experience and their behavior.

Lianne, an extremely intelligent, verbal, and likeable young woman in her late twenties, is an excellent example of the struggles that many of us see in this work. She sought therapy because, as she put it, "I can't control my eating. I've gained twenty pounds in the past year, and I know it's bad for me." She also commented that she was depressed, but when I asked her to tell me about the depression, she could only tell me, "I must be depressed. Otherwise, why would I eat so much?" She sighed and added that she was depressed that she weighed as much as she did and that she became even worse after she ate. "I just can't stand myself sometimes." Lianne worked in finance, where she was quite successful. She very much wanted to have a boyfriend, but believed this was an impossible dream since she could not imagine anyone wanting to go out with her at her weight. In fact, to my eyes, Lianne was only slightly overweight and quite attractive when we began therapy, and even though she continued to gain weight in the early years of our work, she continued to be a good-looking young woman.

Somewhere during the first year of our work together, Lianne began to tell me about her compulsive shopping. She bought kitchen equipment, Italian pottery, exquisite dishes, elegant glasses, and other items for her apartment, even though she described the apartment as "such a mess I wouldn't ever invite anyone in to see it." She could afford her purchases, but she was ashamed that she bought "all these things that I never use." I asked her to begin to make a mental note of what she was doing, thinking, and/or feeling every time she began to think about her next purchase. I also asked her to make a similar note when she found herself eating something she did not want to eat.

The task turned out to be surprisingly difficult. Lianne had great difficulty making any connection between thoughts and emotions and her compulsive behavior. In fact, what we soon discovered was that she frequently could not tell what she was feeling. She did not know whether she felt empty, frustrated, happy, or even hungry. She could barely remember what she was doing when she began to think about eating or shopping. Her inner life was so empty that I often found it difficult to find a way to connect with her or to keep myself engaged or alert while sitting with her. I agreed with her diagnosis that she was depressed, but I found myself wondering if her depression was caused by, or causing, her sense of emptiness and disconnection from her inner and outer worlds. I also found myself at a loss as to how I could make contact with her or help her make contact with herself.

USING LANGUAGE TO PROCESS EMOTIONS

Historically, therapists have often been taught to try to help clients like Lianne "open up" and put these distressing feelings into words. But before one can do this apparently straightforward, albeit often difficult, activity, one must be able to identify and experience emotions differentially. Lianne, like many men and women with these companion disorders, often felt only her emptiness, which she filled as quickly as possible with her eating and shopping rituals. When she did on occasion experience other affects, she felt as though they had appeared from some unknown outside source. Like many clients suffering from these symptoms, she had no sense of her inner processes, no ability to conceptualize emotional cause and effect, no experience of her own agency.

These difficulties in differentiating and exploring emotions, which are not unusual for clients who struggle with shopping and eating disorders, are part of a phenomenon called *alexithymia*. First introduced by Sifneos (1967) and more recently further explicated by Krystal (1988), Stolorow and Atwood (1992), and myself (Barth 1994, 1998), alexithymia involves the inability to use language to think about feelings, to manage them, or to soothe and calm the self when they occur. For individuals like Lianne, alexithymia means that most emotions, whether positive or negative, are potentially overwhelming, disturbing, and intolerable. They cannot be digested, understood, or even talked about, and are fended off through the shopping and eating behaviors that simultaneously deaden, stimulate, and comfort.

One of the puzzling aspects of alexithymia is that it implies difficulties with symbolic thinking, which is directly related to difficulty in using language to process affects, yet it does not at all imply an inability to think abstractly or to talk clearly and intelligently about feelings. In fact, bright and articulate clients can suffer from alexithymia as much as nonverbal, less intelligent, and/or more concrete clients. The key to the capacity to use language to process affects is not intelligence or verbal skill, but the ability to use words symbolically to help metabolize emotions. And even insightful, thoughtful, and dynamically oriented individuals can fall surprisingly short in this area. This phenomenon can cause frustration and concern for therapists and clients when the exploration of apparently clear symbolic meaning has no impact on the symptoms. Many clients eagerly examine connections between eating and shopping behaviors and their childhood experiences, making fascinating interpretations of their own behavior but showing no change in their symptoms. I would suggest that this discrepancy is not the result of inaccurate interpretations, nor is it simply a matter of needing to work through the newly developed understanding, but that it is a result of these clients' inability to use their intellectual and cognitive capacities to process their emotions.

This is how it worked for Marjorie. When I first began working with her, Marjorie weighed around ninety pounds and was a little over five feet tall. Tiny, delicately built, she carefully restricted her food intake, while exercising compulsively on a daily basis. Despite — or perhaps because of — her rigid eating habits, her whole life revolved around food. She worked as a waitress during the days, and at night she baked cakes and breads that she sold to the restaurant where she waitressed. Marjorie began therapy when a two-year relationship with a man ended abruptly and painfully. As she told me, "I don't understand what happened, but I know that I've always had problems with my relationships. I need some help figuring out what goes wrong and what I can do differently." It seemed apparent from the beginning of our work together that Marjorie was bright, articulate, and capable of insight.

However, although we quickly developed a positive working alliance, and Marjorie spoke with increasing understanding of the ways she tried to control her food and her weight because she could not control the people in her life, nothing seemed to change. She remained deeply invested in her old relationship throughout the next year and a half of therapy. At the same time she focused intensely on her weight, her food intake, and her exercise regime, and she experienced tremendous, overwhelming anxiety if her weight, which she checked numerous times each day, went up as much as half a pound. Sometime during the middle of our first year together she also "confessed" that she was a compulsive shopper.

Marjorie's shopping behavior was simultaneously the exact opposite and a perfect reflection of her eating. Whereas she closely monitored every bite of food, shopping was often an extravagant spree of purchases. She ran up high credit card bills, and each purchase was carefully considered in terms of how it fit (almost all of her shopping was for clothing), how it looked, and whether or not it went with other items she either owned or was buying at the moment (as opposed to whether she could afford it). Her appearance was a precisely orchestrated act that sometimes took hours to put together. Like many women with eating disorders, she could spend an inordinate amount of time going through her closet and trying on practically everything she owned until she could put together an outfit that seemed right. Her shopping sprees often echoed her morning dressing ritual: hours spent searching for the right pieces of clothing, jewelry, shoes, bags, and so on.

Extremely articulate and insightful, Marjorie explained to me that she thought she got almost as much from the act of shopping as she did from the purchases. She regularly shopped in the same stores so the saleswomen knew and responded to her. "They like to see me coming—I'm a good customer. They know my taste, and they often put things away that they think I'll like." She felt welcome, special, and cared for, as she seldom felt anywhere else. She had also gotten to know these women, their family stories, their personal problems. "I have a relationship with them . . . even if it's a sick one." One of the problems with Marjorie's apparent insight was that it was always peppered with self-criticism, which made it impossible for her to genuinely understand and sympathize with her own needs.

Along with this extremely critical view of herself, however, was a less obvious inability to take her own or anyone else's words on any but the most concrete level. Although she clearly seemed to understand that her eating and her shopping behaviors had meaning, and that the meanings might even be related, she quickly returned to an almost obsessive delineation of her activities and purchases, accompanied by repetitive and simplistic condemnation of her behavior.

Marjorie, like Lianne, suffered from a subtle but extremely significant inability to "play" with her own images, what Benjamin (1992) has called a "foreclosure of symbolic space" (p. 56). Many clients who use compulsive eating and shopping behaviors to regulate and manage their feelings suffer from this difficulty in which, as Ogden (1986) put it, there is a collapse of the "space between symbol and symbolized" (p. 213). The resulting concretization of experience and thinking is in part responsible for their lack of sense of agency and their feelings of deadness and emptiness. Interpretations and exploration of the meaning of their feelings cannot be integrated or utilized until they have developed enough inner structure to be able to tolerate the frightening, unprocessable emotions; yet it often seems that the only way to make the feelings more tolerable is to understand their meanings. The last section of this chapter addresses the question of how therapists can help these clients build the structure necessary to allow for exploration of the emotions that trigger maladaptive behaviors.

TREATMENT

One of the tasks of any therapy is to help an individual begin to look at and think about his or her behavior as purposeful and meaningful. Clients who compulsively use shopping and eating behaviors to cope with their feelings do not develop this capacity to think about themselves through even the most brilliant interpretation of the symbolic meanings of their actions. Instead, they are best helped when a therapist can communicate genuine interest in and curiosity about what is most important to the client. In many instances this may mean an extended period of discussing the most specific and concrete details of a client's actual eating and shopping behavior. A therapist's focus on these aspects of experience often takes clients by surprise. It may arouse feelings of shame, embarrassment, guilt, and rejection; but in most cases, when a client realizes that the therapist is authentically interested, it can lead the client to actually pay attention to her or his own experience for the first time in her or his life. Gradually, through a combination of many complex factors, including the relationship with the therapist that develops as she consistently reinforces her interest in and valuing of these apparently "trivial" details, clients begin to develop and build an internal structure that includes positive self-regard, trust in another, and an ability to both observe the self and tolerate a variety of affects.

One problem that often confronts therapists is that genuine interest in the apparently inconsequential details of an individual's life can be difficult to maintain. Slade (1997) describes these feelings as she listened to a patient who binge-ate and compulsively shopped. "I have never heard the word *wallpaper* more than I heard it in her first year of treatment: she complusively shopped and returned — clothing, household items, furniture, etc. — and constantly redecorated and ultimately completely revamped her home. I consider it a therapeutic triumph that she has not redone anything in her home in the last year. The bad news is she is thinking of selling it, which raises the spectre of a new home and — more decorating!" (p. 31). This patient, like many of the eating- and shopping-disordered people I have seen or whose therapy I have supervised, had other symptoms as well. One common one is the presence of numerous somatic complaints that lead to more than the average amount of time seeing — or avoiding — doctors. Like Kohut (1971), who suggested that hypochondria is a way of trying to hold the self together, I believe that what we are hearing and seeing is a plea for someone to notice that they are suffering and to help them find a way to connect to themselves and to others. Paying attention to the details that are important to these analysands is the best way I know to help them begin to listen to themselves.

Rabinor (1991) has illustrated the remarkable impact of paying close attention to the thoughts of which these clients are most aware. By asking about the tiny details that were excruciatingly important to her anorexic client — for example, how many peas she ate, and how she decided on that particular number — Rabinor helped this withdrawn young woman begin to use language as a means for observing, communicating, and gradually thinking about her own inner experience. Sackstedter (1989) has also described the power that the therapist's interest in the so-called minutiae of daily experience can have on an eating-disordered client. And Tolpin (1983) demonstrated the many different ways that a therapist can attempt to make contact with the "experience-near" details of an analysand's life in his description of his work with a woman whose bulimia, kleptomania, and use of drugs were all attempts to cope with intolerable emotion.

I do not wish to suggest that this process is either simple or straightforward. Human dynamics are incredibly complicated, and there is no single explanation for any aspect of the treatment process. As a therapist and client explore the specific details of the client's life, they will also find themselves addressing the dynamics of the transference, the emotions that have arisen both in and out of the therapy, and intrapsychic and intersubjective phenomena of many other types. The structure-building process that occurs when therapist and client together focus on the apparently insignificant details of an individual's life becomes a powerful tool for working with these other, more common foci of therapy. As internal structure develops, it strengthens the client's ability to tolerate and manage a variety of feelings, to recognize and differentiate these emotions, and to explore and examine them in words. None of these capacities evolves in isolation, but each supports the growth of and is supported in turn by the strengthening of the others.

In the following clinical example the capacity to tolerate and manage affect developed both as a response to and in conjunction with our exploration of the details of the client's life.

> In my experience many men who have the companion shopping and eating disorders do not come into therapy on their own. Their wives or partners may seek out treatment for their own difficulties, and in the process of their therapy may learn that their husbands have parallel disorders. At times these men may go for couples therapy, often at the urging of their partners, but with no apparent recognition that they have "issues" to deal with themselves. Jack was one of these men. A tall, athletic man with not an ounce of fat on his body, Jack initially refused either individual or couples therapy, although his wife, Lyn, told him she believed that their marriage was in grave danger. Unable to make him listen, Lyn went into therapy herself. In the course of their work her therapist began to suspect that Jack had both an eating disorder and a clinical depression, and encouraged Lyn to try to get him to go for a consultation. Jack continued to refuse to seek help for himself until Lyn decided to move out, at which time he became severely depressed and sought psychiatric help. The psychiatrist prescribed antidepressants and insisted that he also go into psychotherapy, referring Jack to me.
>
> Jack saw all of his difficulties as his wife's fault. He came for therapy, he told me, only because it was a requirement of the psychiatrist, and he was considering going to his internist for the medication and forgetting about the therapy and

psychiatrist altogether. He also told me that his wife contended that he had problems in three areas: his compulsive diet and exercise regime, sexual inhibitions, and impulsive purchasing of expensive and unnecessary (at least from her point of view) clothing, sporting goods, and exercise equipment. After reiterating that this was his wife's point of view, Jack told me that he did not believe that he had any difficulties in any of these areas. "My only problem is that my wife has left me and I want her back," he insisted.

Interestingly, despite his verbalized resistance to the process, Jack was an eager, compliant client. He arrived on time for every session, associated freely and eagerly, and even made connections between his childhood experiences and current struggles. He noted that his difficulties with his wife often reflected his ongoing feeling that he could not control events in his life. He described a childhood home "filled with all kinds of junk," parents who "weren't able to change a lightbulb or make simple repairs," and a chronic worry that he would "become lethargic and lazy like them." He consciously considered his wife as his way out of the depressed family he remembered from childhood. "She's cute, she's smart, and she knows the ropes — all the things about socializing that I don't know about." Yet despite what appeared to be some genuine self-awareness and insight, Jack seemed to have little conscious understanding of the problems with his marriage or his way of functioning.

It was apparent that Jack was excruciatingly dependent on Lyn in many ways. He needed her help to regulate his emotions and to enhance his self-esteem. At the same time he was also deeply conflicted about his need for her, but he could not put either his need or his conflict into words when we began our work. Jack experienced his wife's concern about his restrictive eating, compulsive exercising, and excessive shopping as serious, unwanted criticism. "Nothing I do is right, but I don't know how to make her happy." In the sexual arena he commented that he knew he was a little unusual. He explained that he liked to take a shower before and after having sex, and that he also needed Lyn to shower before he could make love to her. "But, hey," he said, "everybody's got quirks. That's mine. It doesn't mean I have a sexual problem."

Not surprisingly, given the issues around his sexuality, Jack was unable to tolerate one of the side effects of the medication, which left him with diminished sexual appetite. I suspected that this reaction evoked feelings of insecurity about his sense of masculinity, but again, Jack was not able to discuss or think about the meanings of this experience, and therefore unable to use language to enable him to tolerate his discomfort. Able only to say that he refused to "be a guinea pig for these mad scientist drug companies," he stopped taking the antidepressants within a short time of beginning therapy with me. To protect Jack's self-esteem and the fragile relationship we were just beginning to establish, I decided not to try to push him into further discussion of the topic, but I attempted to stay alert to any openings that would allow us to explore these dynamics further. I also shared with him that I was somewhat concerned about his going off the medication, a comment that he actually appeared to experience as somewhat comforting. In general, however, our work consisted of my encouraging him to talk to me in as much detail as possible about his day-to-day experiences. What had he thought about when he first woke up that morning? What time did he get up, and what did he do? Jack was sure that all "of this endless detail must bore you to death," but I assured him truthfully that I believe that apparently insignificant detail contains all of the most important material of anyone's life, and encouraged him to keep talking.

In this way I learned about Jack's life, first in the most concrete ways, and gradually in more and more abstract dimensions as well. He spoke of the rigid rituals he followed, and he described the sense of disruption and painful loss of self that often occurred when he missed a morning workout or an evening shower. He told me of his fear of putting anything "bad" into his body, of his dread of becoming "fat and slovenly" like his parents, and, over time, of his compulsive need to purchase items that he imagined would make him feel better about himself. Again, rather than searching for symbolic meaning in his purchases or exercise routines, although those meanings were often tantalizingly available, I asked Jack to tell me as much as he could about the actual acts themselves. I asked for descriptions of the items he planned to buy, of his daydreams about those items, and his experiences before and after purchasing them. I asked about the foods he ate and the times he ate them, as well as all of the smallest details of his exercise routines.

Interestingly, Jack experienced this attention to detail as both soothing and helpful in managing a variety of affective responses that he could not always talk about. As he became more comfortable paying attention to what he called "this chitchat," I also asked him to try to begin to think back to what he was doing, thinking, and feeling just before he began to muse about any of these interests. When he started bringing in day- and sleep dreams, I used the same approach. We did not look for so-called underlying meaning, but instead attempted simply to put into words as many details as he could about these images and the thoughts that accompanied them. From time to time I asked him what he thought they might mean, and for a long time I received and accepted concrete responses, such as, "I was watching the Jay Leno show and saw something about" whatever the dream image or thought might have been, "and then I dreamed about it. That's all." Often I would then ask him to tell me everything he could about what he was doing while he was watching Jay Leno. Was he in bed or sitting on the couch? Was he eating or drinking anything? What was it? Was he by himself, with Lyn, with their dog? What did he have on? For Jack, as for many clients who struggle with these companion disorders, the experience of paying attention and putting into words these small details of his life had a powerful impact in several areas of his life, including his belief that who he was and what he did had significance, his ability to use language to represent his more abstract experience, and his ability to manage his feelings.

Over time, as he became more adept at observing himself and his environment — and finding words to communicate his observations — he began to add details about how he felt, and I treated that information just as I had every other detail in our discussions. In other words, I did not attempt to make more of any feelings than just what he told me, but I did ask for further concrete data about the experience. For example, if he told me that he was "feeling blue" while he watched the news, I asked him to describe the experience to me. Was there a physical aspect of the feeling? Could he tell me where in his body he felt it? Did he remember what he was thinking about? When did he think it had started? Did it simply appear full-blown, or was there a gradual buildup of feeling from a mild sense of something to a strong one?

Jack was not always patient or compliant in these discussions, and at times we were able to look at feelings that emerged within the therapy as I pushed for what he sometimes called "these stupid little details." He was able to tell me about feeling criticized by me, worrying that I was getting frustrated with him, and a variety of other significant transference issues. He also spoke of feeling that we were wasting time, that he was not getting anywhere, that he worried that I did not know what I was doing. In these moments we were sometimes able to take the work a little further by paying attention to the details of his experience in those moments, but Jack also found it important that I share with him my understanding of why this apparently small, insignificant information seemed so important to me. Gradually, however, sometimes so subtly that I did not realize it was happening, he began to draw connections between feelings and actions. He became more capable of observing not only the concrete details of his life, but also the more abstract, symbolically meaningful aspects of his inner world. Slowly but surely he began to use language to help him manage and regulate the feelings that had always before been managed through his compulsive eating and shopping behaviors.

CONCLUSION

Disordered eating, exercise, and shopping behaviors are often
ways of coping with and adapting to feelings that cannot be
tolerated. Most of these feelings cannot be put into words or, when
they are articulated, remain detached from an individual's actual
experience. Clients may be able to discuss their depression, anxiety, even their hopelessness and emptiness in an intellectual and
even emotional manner, but they often cannot use these discussions to actively process the affects. In therapy, exploration of the
little details of life, even if they seem almost embarrassingly
meaningless, are the places where the client really connects to her-
or himself. This process helps the client gradually begin to build
the internal structure that allows for self-observation as well as
tolerance, management, and regulation of affects. In conclusion, I
turn to one final example of the process I have been describing.

> I worked for many years with a woman who was a severe
> compulsive eater and also a compulsive shopper. Although
> her case is a very interesting one, I will focus in this discus-
> sion on only one aspect of our work. Paula, as I will call her,
> described a painful sense of emptiness in her life. With great
> shame she told me that she had no interests or hobbies,
> nothing to talk to others about, and that she could not imagine
> what we were going to discuss. In fact, what we focused on for
> some time was her eating and shopping: just what she ate and
> shopped for, when and where she purchased both food and
> items, and any other details of her eating and shopping that I
> could help her to describe. It was often hard to sit with Paula,
> who was not able to produce much interesting material on her
> own and who needed me to ask questions to help her talk.
>   Over the years we discussed restaurants, shopping malls,
> clothing, diet fads, medication possibilities, and other related
> aspects of her experience. She was embarrassed that she
> could not talk about books, films, or politics because she
> seldom read, and when she went to the movies she remem-
> bered nothing about them and had no opinions. She had no

dreams, no fantasies other than her wish to lose weight, no inner life to speak of. She felt bored and unstimulated at work, with her friends and family, by life in general. Diet groups and medication, antidepressants, group therapy, and a variety of other adjunct treatments became topics for conversation, but we seldom made any forays into anything related to "deep" meanings of her experiences. Yet gradually Paula became more invested in her life. Her friendships began to shift, as did her relationships with her family members. Work began to take on a color it never had before. Sessions became more interesting, although sometimes terribly sad, as Paula grappled with painful losses and ongoing hurts.

Paula began to read magazines, newspapers, and even books. She moved to a new apartment and hired an interior designer to help her decorate. I was fascinated when she came into a session and told me that the decorator had suggested they use her collection of antique prints as the focal point of her new living room. I asked about this collection, which she had never before mentioned. Shyly, she told me that she had always just been drawn to pictures from old magazines. She had a pile of them sitting on top of her desk, but it had never occurred to her that they had any significance, certainly not that she could frame them and hang them on her walls. "It sort of reminds me of what has happened in here," she told me quietly. "I needed you to help me see that what I'm drawn to has significance, even when it seems too small and unimportant to mention. It might be worth looking at . . . even framing. And someone else might find it interesting, too."

Many things go on in any therapeutic encounter; what I have been describing is only one facet of the process. It is one, however, that is often missed or ignored by many therapists and clients because we think of exploration of emotions as the key to our work. What we frequently do not recognize is how many of our clients are unable to access or process the very feelings they describe to us. Not only clients with eating and shopping disorders, but a surprisingly wide group of clients respond to therapy far

better when their therapist recognizes that the connection between affects and language is seldom as direct or as complete as it
sounds. Shifting the prism to the small details of daily life enhances
that connection for many of these clients, gradually deepening
their therapy in surprising and rewarding ways.

REFERENCES

Barth, D. (1994). The use of group therapy to help women with
    eating disorders differentiate and articulate affect. *Group* 18(2):
    67–77.
——— (1998). Speaking of feelings: affects, language and psycho-
    analysis. *Psychoanalytic Dialogues* 8:685–705.
Benjamin, J. (1992). Recognition and destruction: an outline of
    subjectivity. In *Relational Perspectives in Psychoanalysis*, ed. N.
    J. Skolnick and S. C. Warshaw, pp. 43–60. Hillsdale, NJ: Ana-
    lytic Press.
Christenson, G., Faber, R., Zwaan, M., et al. (1994). Compulsive
    buying: descriptive characteristics and psychiatric comorbid-
    ity. *Journal of Clinical Psychiatry* 55:5–11.
Daspin, E. (1998). Les gens. *Paris Match*, April 16, pp. 35–41.
Grotstein, J. (1991). Nothingness, meaninglessness, chaos, and the
    "black hole" — III. *Contemporary Psychoanalysis* 27:1–33.
Kohut, H. (1971). *Analysis of the Self*. New York: International
    Universities Press.
Krystal, H. (1988). *Integration and Self Healing: Affect, Trauma,
    Alexithymia*. Hillsdale, NJ: Analytic Press.
McDougall, J. (1989). *Theaters of the Body: A Psychoanalytic Ap-
    proach to Psychosomatic Illness*. New York: Norton.
McElroy, S., Keck, P., and Phillips, K. (1995). Kleptomania, com-
    pulsive buying, and binge-eating disorder. *Journal of Clinical
    Psychiatry* 56:14–26.
Oates, J. C. (1992). Shopping. In *Heat and Other Stories*, pp. 54–68.
    New York: Plume.
Ogden, T. (1986). *The Matrix of the Mind: Object Relations and the
    Psychoanalytic Dialogue*. Northvale, NJ: Jason Aronson.

O'Neill, M. (1998). Of tea and the river. *New York Times Magazine*, October 11, pp. 73–74.

Pine, F. (1985). *Developmental Theory and Clinical Process.* New Haven, CT: Yale University Press.

Rabinor, J. (1991). The process of recovery from an eating disorder — use of journal writing in the initial phase of treatment. *Psychotherapy in Private Practice* 9:93–106.

Sackstedter, J. (1989). Psychosomatic dissociations and false self development in anorexia nervosa. In *The Facilitating Environment: Clinical Applications of Winnicott's Theories*, ed. B. Smith and M. G. Fromm, pp. 365–393. New York: International Universities Press.

Schlosser, S., Black, D., Repertinger, S., and Freet, D. (1994). Compulsive buying: demography, phenomenology, and comorbidity in 46 subjects. *General Hospital Psychiatry* 16:205–212.

Sifneos, P. (1967). Clinical observations on some patients suffering from a variety of psychosomatic diseases. In *Integration and Self Healing: Affect, Trauma, Alexithymia*, ed. H. Krystal, pp. 256–267. Hillsdale, NJ: Analytic Press, 1988.

Slade, A. (1997). *The implications of attachment theory and research for developmental theory and clinical practice.* Paper presented to the Connecticut Society for Psychoanalytic Psychology, New Haven, November.

Stolorow, R., and Atwood, G. (1992). *Contexts of Being: The Intersubjective Foundations of Psychological Life.* Hillsdale, NJ: Analytic Press.

Tolpin, P. (1983). A change in the self: the development and transformation of an idealizing transference. *International Journal of Psycho-Analysis* 64:461–483.

13

The Use of Money as an Action Symptom

David W. Krueger

An action symptom attempts restitution of a missed or derailed developmental need through some substance (food, alcohol, etc.) and/or some activity (spending money, sex, a variety of body stimulations, etc.). More than remembrance through enactment, and different from actions that serve a defensive purpose, action symptoms are both defensive and compensatory. As action symptoms may temporarily regulate feelings and tension states, create the illusion of meeting a fundamental need, and serve a selfobject function symbolically, they may take on a life of their own in an addictive process.

An action symptom collapses the potential space in which feeling and fantasy (and, necessarily at times, uncertainty and confusion) otherwise reside. And each symptom, born equally of hope and fear, gives disguised voice to the feelings and needs it simultaneously conceals and reveals. In this chapter compulsive shopping and spending will be used to illustrate the process and content of money symptoms. I will also seek to demonstrate that every action symptom is a story with its own developmental history, its own psychodynamic scenario, with multidetermined defensive and attempted developmentally reparative intentions.

All of these facets are important to understand in psychotherapy and psychoanalysis.

MONEY

There are four areas of basic observations I have made that led me to focus attention on money as both symbol and reality in psychotherapy and psychoanalysis (Krueger 1986). First, money is perhaps one of the three most emotionally charged subjects in contemporary life as a carrier of feeling, significance, and striving. The other two are food and sex. Second, the theoretical, symbolic, and realistic meanings of money are important in various clinical situations. Third, some pathological processes and symptoms can manifest most vividly in the financial arena, in various money symptoms and money patterns. And finally, for some patients and couples money has come to be a tangible, external focus of emotional conflict or its enactment. For all patients money is a basic aspect of the framework and boundary that we establish and work within as therapists. The only things we exchange with our patients are words and money.

Money is imbued by each of us with conscious and unconscious equations. Money may come to represent power, security, self-worth, love, happiness, control, dirtiness, freedom, status, sexiness, worldliness, acceptance, or a host of other personal meanings. It may be used as a yardstick of achievement, immortality concretized and passed to succeeding generations. The symbolic representations and perceptions of money are influenced by cultural background, family values, developmental experiences, and emotional needs. Many of these meanings may be outside conscious awareness and grounded in early experiences. Money is an all-purpose container, a Rorschach with various emblems as cards: a check, a piece of plastic, cars, houses, jewelry, the list of the wealthiest people in America.

"How much is enough?" is rarely considered. The more that money symbolizes unfulfilled needs and desires, the less it satisfies. A fantasy that has been lost but given temporary hope by a proxy, such as money, ensures that satisfaction will only be brief.

Money Symptoms

There are many different stories involving money. In extreme cases, analogous to an addiction, each story may begin gradually to eclipse a life story, to erode or replace aspects of the self as the central theme and reference point. Money can be a character in the drama that carries hope of both self-restorative and defensive functions.

Some of the action symptoms involving money include compulsive shopping, compulsive spending, compulsive gambling, competitive spending, impulse buying, compulsive bargain-hunting, revenge spending, and compulsive refusal to spend with hoarding of money (Krueger 1992). Various combinations and expressions occur, such as competitive spending with competitive acquisition (Schor 1998).

Money Patterns

Some manifestations of these money issues occur in patterns rather than as actual symptoms. Micro-patterns, often minute, routine, and camouflaged in habit, may involve the use of money to control, to reward, as compensatory care/love, or to atone for guilt. Macro-patterns, more global configurations, may involve money in success phobias manifesting as fear of autonomy, fear of/addiction to risk, money addiction, the inability to acquire money consistent with one's potential, or the inability to enjoy the use of money (Krueger 1986).

COMPULSIVE SHOPPING AND SPENDING

Compulsive shopping and spending, action symptoms often combined with other impulse disorders, form a specific psychodynamic complex with common precursors of developmental arrest. Compulsive shopping is an overpowering urge to buy items, especially clothing, usually in a pattern of "shopping binges." The articles are not bought because they are needed, or because they are a bargain, or even out of an intrinsic desire for the things themselves. The urge, at its most intense, is a compelling desire to obtain items and is experienced as frantic and irresistible. This often leads to buying more than is needed or can be afforded, the expense at times eclipsing even children's medical needs, and is often followed by depression, disillusionment, shame, and guilt. The realization that the purchases have not filled an internal emptiness often brings on some form of self-punishment.

The distinction between compulsive shopping and the occasional shopping spree is that compulsive shopping represents an attempt at affect regulation, especially to remedy chronic emptiness and depression. The shopping binge can provide the illusion that all the emotional hunger of the past is being satisfied. Compulsive shoppers often experience an inner tension that is released only when something is bought.

For compulsive spenders the act of spending itself creates an illusion of worth, often compensating for a depleted self-worth. Frequently by using charge cards, but ranging to compulsively investing in "deals," the experience itself is pleasurable, countering emptiness or a lack of self-worth. One of my patients had become quite involved in purchasing a certain antique collectible over the Internet, spending many hours a day pursuing the euphoric experience that countered her emptiness. She rationalized that she was building a collection, disavowing how its pursuit had come to dominate her daytime hours. The act of spending made her feel in control; she was acquiring whatever she wanted. Arranging the collection perpetuated the mastery of ordering her own space, the antithesis of the lack of mastery she felt of her own feelings and, earlier, of her own body in childhood physical abuse.

Most of the patients I have worked with whose compulsive shopping or spending represented a significant symptom complex have also had other addictive processes concurrently, especially eating disorders. For some, but not all, the emotional significance of spending and acquiring possessions had been underscored by their parents, who bestowed possessions or money as well as food, substituting physical comfort for emotional nurturance. The individuals in these cases shopped compulsively as an expression of aggression and in order to confirm that significant others were willing to take care of them by giving them things as a substitute for love. The compulsive spending resulted in a need to be rescued, forcing parents or spouses to supply money to make up for the emotional support they had failed to provide. Since early childhood such individuals have often felt inadequate and as if something vital is missing in themselves and in their lives. Compulsive shoppers are engaged in an unceasing pursuit of "things" that seemingly function to fill an internal emptiness and to make them feel complete. They may turn to food, alcohol, drugs, and sex; they may forever search for the ideal companion or impressive possessions in an attempt to fashion a pseudo-identity and to reestablish a real or imagined selfobject bond.

Many of the parents of compulsive shoppers were neglected or abused during their own childhood. Loving one's children by giving them things was the model they had grown up with, and they quickly fell into the pattern by compensating for perceived neglect, separation, divorce, or some sort of abuse by showering their children with extravagant gifts.

The pattern often begins with adolescent children as parents attempt to alleviate their guilt for leading busy professional and social lives. Unable to maintain a much-needed emotional bond, they may establish their children's dependency on them by supplying cash or credit cards. The children may overspend in retaliation for the parents' neglect and to fill an emotional void; attracting the parents' attention, albeit punitively, is the net effect. For this to develop into a compulsive-shopping pattern, a significant degree of underlying developmental arrest must be present, an arrest with its roots in earliest development.

I find that compulsive shopping occurs in individuals who are very conscious of how they look and appear to others, who attempt to be pleasing to others, and whose fragile esteem and sense of self depend on the responses of others. The compulsive acquisition of clothes in particular usually follows some narcissistic injury, especially the disruption of an emotional bond with someone important. Such a disruption sets into motion a desperate need to appear attractive and desirable and a hope that new clothes will fulfill this need for affirmation.

Developmental Issues

In my book *Body Self and Psychological Self: A Developmental and Clinical Integration of Disorders of the Self* (1989), I describe pathological manifestations of action symptoms and attempts at restitution of developmental arrest. The developmental deficit in each instance involves a developmental arrest of the body self as well as psychological self; the deficit of body self includes a distorted or incomplete body image combined with a vulnerable reliance on the perception of others, especially physical perceptions. For individuals with significant arrest in their self-development, disturbances in differentiating self and other affect the individual's ability to create verbal and representational symbols of the body self and the affective self. Distinctions between the symbol and the object symbolized are incomplete; thinking is concrete in specific reference to the self, without the capacity for abstraction or representation of the body and its contents, including feelings. Lacking a basic distinction between symbols and objects symbolized (other, self, feelings, etc.), the affected individual must rely on the immediate experience of his or her own body to elicit a self-representation. The representation of self cannot be achieved symbolically, but must take place through the body-self experience. These distortions occur specifically in regard to the self, as these individuals are often quite intelligent, accomplished, and successful in other realms of their lives.

At the time of empathic rupture in a selfobject bond, or the unavailability of a necessary selfobject, the individual attempts to fill the emptiness and restore the bond. In contrast to the individual who attempts by an eating disorder to reestablish a groundedness in body-self experiences via the sensorimotor stimulation of inflicting pain, gorging with food, exercising excessively, or starving to induce hunger pangs, the individual who compulsively shops and spends attempts external enhancement of body attractiveness and desirability, hoping to address loneliness and emptiness by engaging others to validate their worth and desirability. A distinct and complete image of either the body self or the psychological self may not have been consolidated. The resultant concrete, nonsymbolic level of operation disallows the psychological distance required for movement beyond a transitional object. Symbolic equations rather than true symbols predominate (Segal 1978). Symbolic equations differ from true symbols in that they are seen and experienced as original objects rather than as substitutes or symbols for original objects. With a symbolic equation there is no "as if" quality. The individual must engage in specific, concrete, body-oriented stimulation or another form of action (compulsive shopping, spending, etc.) to achieve a representation of the need-meeting object.

An individual with a defective or incomplete body self (and thus psychological self) is motivated toward completion and restitution of that basic defect (Krueger 1989). Kohut (1971) explained these psychological transactions not on the basis of the underlying fantasy or drive, but on the structural nature of the underlying deficit. His formulations were focused on the psychological self, but can be extrapolated to the foundations of body self as well, assisting us to understand self-restitutive (or self-formative) attempts according to developmental precedents, current physiological and psychological selfobject regulation, and fantasy elaboration.

If the selfobject experiences have not been met accurately and consistently enough over developmental time to be internalized, an individual will turn to other means to seek self-organization, cohesion, tension relief, and vitality. The symptomatic use of money — to soothe, to calm, to revitalize, to establish or restore an affective experience (as others may use food) — provides the illusion of control, of an immediate and tangible effectiveness. Over time, any threat to an individual's sense of cohesion leads them to the same pattern of using money or of shopping to restore that self-cohesion (Krueger 1992).

Psychodynamic Scenarios Involving Money and Shopping

When there is a developmental deficit of affective vitalization or, alternatively, too intense a stimulation, which becomes traumatizing in itself, this action symptom scenario repeats itself in an attempt to seize control and feel effective in the only means seemingly available at the time. These patients describe their subjective experience as a feeling of being hopelessly lost, with a sense of losing form. Prior to the narcissistic injury, the selfobject had been functioning as a referent and regulator of form and boundary functions, including the experience of body intactness and shape. With the withdrawal or unavailability of that selfobject the patient precipitously loses a sense of form, because when the selfobject's boundary-regulating function ceases, she must rely solely upon her own vague or unformed self-representation that does not provide an adequate vessel for a solid, cohesive, consistent psychological self. The incomplete development of body self can be illustrated by projective drawings of the patient's own body image as distorted, prepubescent, and often fluctuating with mood. For example, when the patient feels empty or depressed after an empathic rupture with an important person, her body image drawing would be considerably more distorted, perhaps two to three times as large as when she was feeling good and calm (Krueger 1989).

The impulsive action is adopted as restitution for the disorganization precipitated by a narcissistic injury and is typically directed toward the individual's body. Actions such as bingeing, exercise, or self-mutilation (Farber 1997) are intended to stimulate or enhance some part of the body and create an acute awareness of body-self sensations. Augmenting the attractiveness of the body, such as in buying clothes or jewelry, may serve to validate worth and attractiveness via the desirability of one's body. The idealization and unconscious fantasies associated temporarily provide a vitalization and self-cohesion. That is, the often unconscious associated fantasy has a potent regulatory, restorative, and invigorating power. Focusing on fundamental body experience and sensation serves as an organizing function for a fragmented or fractured self by directing focus to the first and most basic organizer of ego experience and structure, the body ego (Freud 1923).

The individuals I have seen who compulsively shop and spend have deficiencies of self-regulation, and their symptomatic actions serve as replacement for a deficient internal regulator and a deficient integration of mind and body. Relying on other people for their supply of affirmation, enhancement, function, and esteem, they attempt to find a way to tangibly obtain the source or the promise of these emotional goods, and thereby to counter the anguish of boredom, emptiness, or deadness.

Shopping and spending are restitutive and organizing efforts designed to create or restore a perception of body boundary and integrity, and to establish contact with lost (empathically disconnected) selfobjects. An unconscious fantasy around which this activity is organized is often that once contact is made, the person within that fragile body and self-selfobject boundary will be complete, and the central organizing concept of the self as bad/defective will be transformed.

The common theme among this group of patients is the narcissistic vulnerability of certain individuals in association with a precipitating interruption in the emotional availability of a significant person who provides some essential psychological function (i.e., a selfobject). This change in the availability or relationship of a significant other can result in the internal experiences of hurt, anger, and disorganization. The narcissistically wounded individual then attempts to control something specific, concrete, and external that directly stimulates or enhances the attractiveness of some part of the body. This is a dual attempt to regulate the affect of a fragmented sense of self, and to restore selfobject functioning.

For some individuals the most salient aspect of the shopping and spending is the engagement with the sales clerk. The exclusive attention and empathic perceptiveness to the wishes of the shopper create a replacement for the disrupted bond precipitating the shopping excursion. Having developed the capacity of sensitive attunement to others, she can choose a clerk who can provide exactly the right receptivity and responses. Some of my patients have described an ongoing relationship with particular clerks, a kind of pseudoempathic bond predicated on spending money.

Another related illustration is shoplifting, the enactment of taking whatever is wanted, of creating one's own rules. While this act may be motivated by unavailable financial resources, it is more often designed to take from the shopkeeper whatever one wants, a proxy for emotionally missed "supplies" (Richards 1996).

CASE ILLUSTRATIONS

The following cases demonstrate some of the common elements of action symptom scenarios. In particular, in a narcissistically vulnerable individual, the disruption of an important selfobject bond with resultant fragmentation of the integrity of body self and psychological self, the compelling desire for affirmation of worth and desirability (to attempt restoration of what is missing via responses from others), and an attempt at effectively and tangibly giving shape and form to what is desired in order to fill emptiness and defend against hurt and rage.

Case 1

Brittany was a compulsive shopper, although that symptom was not the central issue of her troubles or the central issue in her therapy. We examined the dynamics of her impulsive and frantic shopping binges. The process and experiences she describes have been similar in many compulsive shoppers I have seen (Krueger 1988).

As a child, Brittany had several sets of parents due to an early divorce in a very extended family. When she needed money to buy something, she was intuitively able to fit the item needed with the "soft spots" of her various parenting figures, mother, father, aunt, and a grandmother who could always be tapped for "incidentals."

Going to extremes in behavior seemed an adaptive way to establish a boundary, to have someone respond to her, to contain her. She would run away from home until someone came to find her. She recalled feeling depressed all the time and wanting someone to hold her, to wrap her in enveloping boundaries. The desire to be held appeared over and over in letters that she wrote but never sent (lest she offend someone and then lose that person) and in dreams and fantasies. Concurrent with her wishes to be held and feelings of loneliness, Brittany wanted her own space. But that space never seemed outlined and distinct to her — she felt either smothered and encroached upon, or a limitless, boundless nothing. Her body self and image were as vague and ill-defined as her psychological self.

A freshman in college, Brittany felt depressed and lost. She stated, "I've wanted an unconditional love that I never possessed." She described her impulsive use of money as an attempt to possess something tangible, to make herself feel better. She said, "I felt an urge to get something new, to want more, that there's not enough. I never thought I had enough; I never thought I had plenty. I would jump up and run to the mall. I had a powerful urge to go buy clothes."

She described the urge as "an emptiness. I felt frantic, depleted, frenzied — an urge to get something more. I'd get very anxious — just like bingeing — the same feelings. Then I'd go buy some clothes. I felt like I couldn't leave without something. Even if I didn't find what I wanted, I had to leave with something."

Spending money as if there were no limit reinforced Brittany's illusion that she could have anything and everything she always wanted, the same blissful, powerful feeling she had in the middle of an eating binge. She was inside an impulse. Urge and action were fused; there was no pause, no contemplative space within which judgment could reside.

She would feel good — hopeful — as she bought an outfit.

The tag was an indication of the newness, something no one had seen on her before. Maybe she would be different; maybe the new outfit would change her. She added, "I need something there to touch, something that's tangible. I can hear but not fathom the concept of love. I can touch or grab it if it's something." The good, hopeful feeling would last until she wore the clothes for the first time. As soon as the tags were gone, the hope vaporized.

I indicated my understanding of how she wanted to give form and shape to what she wanted, something so vague and formless that she didn't understand what it was, and how compelling it seemed to make it tangible, to convert passive and helpless to active and effective. She responded, "Yes. That's why I have trouble with and want boundaries. I want to see it and touch it. Whenever I colored in a coloring book as a girl the first thing I did was to outline the boundaries very specifically." Brittany favored big, bulky clothes, which stimulated her skin and made her feel "outlined" and thus more real. Other patients want skintight spandex-like clothes that provide a tight, bound container, like being held tightly.

Like many other narcissistic individuals with vague, ill-defined body images (Krueger 1989), Brittany attempted to establish a defined body self in order to feel more real. She did this by stimulating her exterior boundaries as well as attempting to feel real internally by exercising or by filling her internal emptiness with food.

For a time her hope had settled on finding the right man by being the ideal sexual partner. Compulsive sexual activity, like purchasing clothes, was more immediate, more focused, and not vague at all. And she would get affirmation about what an unsurpassed sexual partner she was. It was the one thing she thought she could do effectively, and if she could connect with someone sexually, then he would discover how good she was. She reasoned that the one day she did not give would be the day she missed the one person who would be giving to her. She described always being up, always giving, always listening, not seeming to have needs of her own, always pleasing the man — in order not to miss that one person who would make her feel complete.

We came to understand the urge to shop in part as a need to be held, precipitated by a disruption in her connectedness with someone important to her. Now, via her enhanced self-empathy, we could reconstruct the important related experiences of her development. Clothes were a concrete way of being held, of having skin stimulation, just as food was a symbolic nurturing, all representing a valiant effort to regulate her own self-experience and affect. We came to see how this equation was furthered by family encouragement. Her mother would buy clothes for her whenever Brittany felt bad. Shopping was the transitional bridge to re-create a souvenir of the mother. Spending money was a way of giving to herself, of creating an illusion of reconnectedness with a mother who gave to her in a similar manner, who shared the same symbol of love and nurturance. The clothes were a fashionably tailored version of her earlier security blanket, imbued initially with the same magic.

Case 2

Linda, a 27-year-old unmarried woman, presented with significant depression centering on the turbulent relationship with her 40-year-old boyfriend, a wealthy, cocaine-abusing man. He essentially kept Linda as his mistress even though he was unmarried.

Linda described her depression and discontent with her life. She complained of not knowing or having her own identity and of not being ready to break away from her boyfriend to be emotionally and financially independent. She was understandably frightened because she did not have her own identity or structure for her life.

She told of her frequent feelings of depletion and emptiness, and the resulting overwhelming urge to eat, drink, or shop. She spoke of her anger at everyone who had never done things for her and her compelling drive to spend money. It was not so much the acquisition of clothes, but more the knowledge of possessing money and having the ability to spend it that afforded Linda a temporary high. An important component of her shopping was the devoted attention given by the salesperson, chosen to be someone who most resembled Linda (as a mirroring selfobject) and who seemed most caring and attuned (empathic ability). The undivided attention, the attunement to her very specific needs and desires formed a (pseudoempathic) bond highly valued by Linda, one she wanted to prolong as long as possible. The actual purchase was, for her, the anticlimax, the end of the special, invigorating attention.

Linda described her shopping episodes as an intense urge to "go into a store and get something new — even some little thing like a silver bracelet or T-shirt — but just to buy something new." She indicated that she would then end up spending several hundred dollars — up to her charge card limit — and buy an entire outfit. She especially liked to go to a particular store she and her boyfriend had shopped in, indicating, "I wanted to go in [the store] and believe that I can still go and spend the money without him. At the moment I was purchasing those items, I felt powerful, confident at a time when only a few moments before I was feeling empty and completely without power. When it hit me first — what I had done — was when they gave me the sales receipt. It was like reality hit me. I was nervous about it then and still when I came home."

She went on to recount how her boyfriend would think she looked fabulous in the outfit and how he would have to settle her bills. The shopping binge reestablished their bond. She stated, "I had to go back with him to get him to bail me out. If everything else fails, I would just have to go back to him." She would spend just enough to ensure that he would have to rescue her.

Linda recognized her shopping as an addiction and was afraid of it. At times, instead of going home she would try to think of things to buy, to gain temporary respite from being alone and feeling depressed. When she did not involve some-one else in her spending addiction, Linda felt powerful in her ability to create a situation of risk or a financial disaster and to figure some way out of it. She felt sneaky and guilty, yet excited about the risk taking.

Case 3

Allison described her urge to go on a shopping binge as a desperate yearning for something or someone, an emptiness so vague and formless that she felt baffled about its meaning and its driven nature. The compelling urge was to "hold onto something" specific, concrete, palpable. Otherwise she felt she "would burst."

Allison grew up in a wealthy family, with both parents involved in business ventures, traveling a great deal and leaving her and her three older siblings in the care of a housekeeper. Her parents gave her much materially, sur-rounding Allison with the best of everything and always bringing gifts from their extensive travels and vacations.

She reported being "programmed to believe I've always gotten everything I want." She recalled instances when she would go into her mother's closet and cuddle into one of her mother's fur coats, loving the smell and feeling secure inside as if her mother were giving her a hug.

Allison felt that buying something and charging it was like getting it free. It was as if, for that moment, she felt satisfied, without any thought of future accounting or consequence. She indicated that during a shopping binge she recognized her lack of judgment, but at the time whatever she wanted was her all-consuming focus; she was inside an impulse. Later, when she got her credit card bill, she would calculate how much she had and how much she could juggle, but inevitably that never worked because she actually never knew how much money she had. She described consciously refraining from thinking about the money she had at her disposal because she might have to restrain herself from acting impulsively. On many occasions her parents had to bail her out of trouble. When she went home to visit her parents, she would take from their house whatever she wanted: spices, toothpaste, utensils, and even at times some of her mother's jewelry. What she took was never obvious; if her mother had only one can of cayenne pepper or only one bottle of perfume, Allison would not take it. But if there were several, she felt her mother would never miss it. She took change from her father's drawer where he tossed it from his pockets each day. "On a good day I can come out with $15 in quarters." She would rationalize to herself: "I'll just take the quarters because I have to do laundry."

In recent years Allison shoplifted minor items, though she did not need to do it to save money. She shoplifted when she felt deprived, the stimulation of risk temporarily enlivening her, symbolically acquiring what her mother did not give her, such as taking cosmetics to acquire the affirmation of adequate womanhood. Furthermore, she felt she was now able to set her own rules.

She also actively collected antique tapestries, often spending tens of thousands of dollars on a credit card her father had given her for special purposes. During her psychoanalysis, we were able to examine the internal scenario of these purchases as being similar to other purchases in that they were prompted by some painful affect, often emptiness and feeling worthless. The act of spending considerable money enhanced sagging self-worth. She chose to collect and be surrounded by items of value, beauty, and permanence. The antique pieces had endured centuries, their constancy reassuring in her world of emotional impermanence.

THERAPEUTIC IMPLICATIONS

Therapy has been described as a study of the ways in which we deceive ourselves. We know from many of our patients that the loss of an illusion is more difficult than the loss of the real thing. The attempt to compensate for a porous, vague, or ineffective body self and psychological self is a central issue in therapy to be empathically understood as an attempted but aborted stab at meeting a developmental need as well as defending against painful affect. The entire psychodynamic scenario within which the symptom is embedded must be understood and addressed for effective therapeutic change.

Understanding Developmental Arrest and Defensive Functions

Therapeutic interventions for the improvement of distorted and dysfunctional body self and psychological self address integration of the two. Compulsive shoppers are guided by the responses of others and by external points of reference, so they may not even know, or have developed, a true sense of self with an internal point of reference. One young woman said "Sometimes I feel really empty. When I feel unfocused and confused, I have no image of myself. I get really scared. It's like looking in the mirror and seeing no image, and I ask myself, 'Do I exist? Where am I? Who am I?'"

These patients typically are limited in their ability to describe themselves and their feelings in a meaningful way. They constrict emotional expression and tend to describe endless details of symptoms as substitutes for feelings and to internalize experiences; they inhibit fantasy, limiting their capacity to symbolize and play (Krystal 1997). Though often quite successful, such patients describe a vague sense of incompleteness or emptiness, a feeling that something is missing. Often there is a specific external focus, ranging in presentation from a separation crisis to a specific action symptom or scenario.

Individuals with more significant developmental arrests usually have an incomplete, noncohesive sense of self. These early deficits in differentiation affect the body self and the psychological self because body-self experiences do not become symbolically represented and remain as somatic experiences. Lacking a consistent, internally regulated image of a body self or psychological self, they rely on external feedback and referents, such as other people, mirrors, or possessions and their acquisition. Narcissistic individuals have little experience of themselves as the same person over an extended period of time. Patients with profound early developmental arrests involving the sense of self do not form a cohesive body image and often exhibit significant defects of sensory integration.

Therapy for patients with early developmental arrests must address the psychodynamic scenario of the present moment in which the attempted restitutive symptom occurs, as well as the developmental deficits that underlie. The process of empathic failures experienced throughout early development may have resulted in an unconscious core organizing assumption of badness or defectiveness (Stolorow and Atwood 1992). Consistent, driven attempts at countering this core belief by unrelenting performance, and attempts at being good and loving, fail to eradicate this false self, thereby seeming to further validate its authenticity.

Such deficits in self-regulation mean that these vulnerable individuals rely on external sources to supplement deficient internal regulation. Through their reliance on others for affirmation, enhancement, function, and esteem, they attempt to internalize these sources symbolically by acquiring material goods and money, or substances such as food, alcohol, or drugs.

The desire for a more permanent solution and the wish to engage meaningfully with the therapist as well as with other people is experienced as unsafe, possibly threatening, because of the patient's assumption that such a relationship would be as unreliable as past experiences have been. The desire to be effective and to impose predictability, usually done by his or her action symptom, needs to be understood empathically, collaboratively, and nonjudgmentally. The individual cannot give up the symptom at the beginning of therapy any more than a psychosomatic patient can stop having pain as a precondition of treatment. These patients must have a new story to be inside, mutually and collaboratively created with the therapist, before they can give up their old story.

As therapists we must empathically resonate with and convey

understanding of the comfort and investment in their symptom, of its immediacy and power of tension reduction, of the difficulty and anxiety in relinquishing the power and effectiveness of the symptom to change the way they feel. Such symptoms often cannot be abandoned as a prerequisite to therapy, but they may diminish in intensity and utility over time in therapy. Consistent therapeutic attention and empathic listening must focus on the use of the symptoms: the motivation, enactment, and experience of the symptomatic act itself, and its change throughout the course of therapy.

The use of the action symptom to defensively counter an uncomfortable feeling by stopping the feeling and simultaneously engaging in the action scenario is a powerful, immediate, and effective way to make the feeling seemingly go away. Dissociation as a specific defense is central for some patients who have experienced early life trauma.

Empathic Listening Perspective

To use an empathic listening position as a way of gathering information, the therapist must place himself or herself inside the entire experience of the patient, understanding and resonating with the patient's subjective reality. Empathy does not mean being kind, sympathetic, consoling, gratifying, or commiserating. Empathy describes a listening position, a particular way of listening from inside another individual's experience that permits appreciation from that person's own frame of reference. "Listening from the inside" includes awareness of the patient's internal and perceived external systems and of the representational model the individual uses to perceive and process his or her body, psyche, and world.

Patients whose basic pathology lies in the formation and synthesis of body self and psychological self, represented by compulsive shopping and spending as well as other impulse disorders, have helped us understand the nature of empathy through their particular sensitivity to it. It is by empathic failures in their earliest development that their pathology has been created — the sense that their feelings, internal experience, and perceptions have not been listened to.

Developmentally arrested patients may view a therapist as a part or function of themselves (i.e., selfobject transference); the therapist becomes increasingly important as part of the structure of the patient's self-experience. Illustration is provided by the description of the selfobject transferences (paralleling early developmental phases) that become activated in the patient as the result of empathic listening: merger, mirroring, idealization, twinship, and alter ego. The therapist becomes the personification of the patient's own listening and experiencing process, and a developmental organizer in the growth of the patient. Through dynamic understanding of this entire process the patient develops self-empathy and self-structure as developmental growth ensues and empathy becomes internalized as part of self-regulatory capacity, ultimately obviating the need for symbolic substitutes (e.g., clothes) and action symptoms.

Neutrality

To be neutral is to remain equidistant from both sides of a patient's conflict or internal dichotomy so as to fully appreciate both components — such as a wish and fear, or wanting and not wanting the same thing — and to understand the motivations for both sides. Neutrality refers to fully and completely listening from within a patient's struggle and internal dilemma to all components without omitting focus on any aspect. Most frequently, the therapist aligns with one aspect of the patient's conflict or dilemma; for example, a common breach of neutrality I see in my supervisees is of wanting the patient to get better, and joining with the patient's attempt to overcome a symptom or maladaptive behavior. This alignment with the component of the patient's internal position to developmentally grow and to get better disregards the part of the patient's conflict that opposes growth and change. This breach of neutrality frequently creates an impasse in the treatment of the patient who seemingly does all the right things and wants to get better but remains stuck.

Fear is the guide to the desire, and both the fear and the desire must be understood. This is the essence of neutrality.

Therapy as a Developmental Experience

Psychotherapy may be conceptualized as a corrective developmental experience with the therapist as developmental organizer. The therapeutic setting contains symbolic equivalents of the mother–child relationship: consistency, reliability, empathic attunement, specific and defined boundaries, focus on the patient, acceptance of what is otherwise alienating, and a holding environment. These factors are of even greater importance in the treatment of patients with early developmental issues and arrests (e.g., narcissistic and impulse disorders) than for patients with more consistent internal structure (e.g., neurotic patients). The body self as well as the psychological self must be integrated in the developmental march of therapy.

The function of the therapist is to accurately recognize and assist in articulating affective states and to help the patient develop an internal point of reference. The capacity to articulate affective states derives from first being able to differentiate different types of somatic experience, then linking them with an affective state, and later being able to verbalize about them. Verbalization not only provides mastery via the articulation of feelings but also, more important, facilitates the accurate perception of body self and image, perception of the psychological self, and integration of the two. The blending of affective and cognitive, of the physical and the psychic self, consolidates a sense of self.

A basic aspect of the therapeutic approach for an individual coming from a severely growth-inhibiting environment and having distortions in the perception of emotional and somatic experiences and communication may be to focus initially on the accurate reading and labeling of signals, both somatic and affective. A therapeutic task may be to focus on those particular internal signals that patients may be neglecting, deleting, or distorting. Some of those signals or experiences may be quite threatening, such as the experience of emptiness or of internal disorganization. Because of this close attunement of both therapist and patient to the details of the patient's internal experiences, the patient may fear reexperiencing the disappointment and vulnerability of earliest empathic failures.

The therapist must respond empathically, developmentally, and psychodynamically to the patient, resonating with the developmental and adaptive intent of the behavior/symptom. A basic sense of causality thereby becomes established. It is the empathic immersion, resonance, and response of the therapist to the internal experience of the patient in therapy that provides a new framework of experience. The experience of effectiveness and the process of empathic attunement can then become internalized by the patient as self-empathy and resumed developmental growth. Ultimately, the individual can internalize the entire process for self-regulation from the newly developed internal center of initiative, affect, and esteem. The potential space between feeling and action, rather than being collapsed by fusion of the two, is maintained for fantasy, contemplation, and symbolism. Money and things can be recognized for what they are and for what they are not, and the action symptom is no longer a necessity.

REFERENCES

Farber, S. (1997). Self medication, traumatic enactment, and somatic expression in bulimic and self-mutilating behavior. *Journal of Clinical Social Work* 25:87–106.

Freud, S. (1923). The ego and the id. *Standard Edition*. 19:12–60.

Kohut, H. (1971). *The Analysis of the Self*. New York: International Universities Press.

Krueger, D. (1986). *The Last Taboo: Money as Symbol and Reality in Psychotherapy and Psychoanalysis*. New York: Brunner/Mazel.

—— (1988). On compulsive shopping and spending: a psychody-

namic inquiry. *American Journal of Psychotherapy.* 42(4):574–
584.

—— (1989). *Body Self and Psychological Self: Developmental and
Clinical Integration in Disorders of the Self.* New York: Brunner/
Mazel.

—— (1992). *Emotional Business: The Meanings of Work, Money,
and Success.* San Mateo, CA: Slawson Communications.

Krystal, H. (1997). Resomatization and the consequences of infan-
tile psychic trauma. *Psychoanalytic Inquiry.* 17:126–150.

Richards, A. K. (1996). Ladies of fashion: pleasure, perversion, or
paraphilia. *International Journal of Psychoanalysis* 77:337–351.

Schor, J. (1998). *The Overspent American.* New York: Basic Books.

Segal, H. (1978). On symbolism. *International Journal of Psychoanalysis* 59:315–319.

Stolorow, R., and Atwood, G. (1992). *Contexts of Being: The Intersubjective Foundations of Psychological Life.* Hillsdale, NJ: Analytic
Press.

14

Clothes and the Couch

Arlene Kramer Richards

Every morning, suit,

you are waiting on a chair

to be filled

by my vanity, my love,

my hope, my body.

In bad moments

you cling to my bones . . .

— from "Ode to My Suit" by Pablo Neruda

The enormous size of the garment industry is a reflection of how important clothes are to the women who live in them. The activities of making, shopping for, and wearing clothes provide an almost unparalleled opportunity for women to work, to express their creativity, to define themselves. For those women who experience shopping for clothes as an endless temptation, preoccupation, and sometimes torture — a never-fulfilled quest — the shopping for clothes seems to be at least as important as the wearing. How does the ordinary pleasure and necessity of buying clothes become a compulsive, driving need?

In this chapter I will consider clothes shopping in the context of a psychoanalytic understanding of women's interest in dress, discuss some issues related to how shopping compulsions develop and what they can mean, and provide clinical material to illustrate four different manifestations of this symptom. Touching as it does upon so many issues of sexuality, narcissism, safety, and power, shopping for clothing is a natural venue for symptomatology in many areas. One case that I will use to illustrate this idea appears to me to have clear aspects of sexual perversion. I will discuss it at length, because it is relevant to important work being done now on female perversions (Richards 1989, 1990, 1997) and other particularly female manifestations of sexuality.

PSYCHOANALYTIC VIEWS OF CLOTHING

Clothing has many different meanings for women, far too many even to hint at most of them here. Dressing and display are multifaceted acts. A woman can display her body temptingly as part of courtship, flaunt it aggressively to frighten and humiliate men and/or other women — or experience it privately as the comfortable center of her sense of self. Freud's comment (Rose 1988) that not even the most intelligent woman is free of the dictates of fashion suggests that the motivation for that interest is not frivolous, as some contemporary critics of Freud would have it, but has real psychological import.

There is a long tradition of clothes being taken seriously in psychoanalytic theory. But clinical interest in clothing has been hampered by societal biases and gender stereotypes, and in the recent past psychoanalysts have noticed dress primarily as an indicator of feelings and thoughts of which a person is not necessarily aware. It was a commonplace for case reports to indicate that a patient began treatment sloppily or inappropriately dressed and came to look better groomed as treatment progressed. Bergler (1953) cited many cases of what he believed to be improper or unfashionable dress as evidence of the presence of neurosis. As late as 1985 Bergmann used "femininity" of dress and adornment as an indicator of her patient's comfort with her gender identity and therefore of her mental health. But increasingly, theory and clinical observation are being applied in ways that include the importance of aggression and androgeny in female development and do not regard "feminine" as equivalent to "normal" for females.

Flügel (1930) has been an influential writer on the meaning of clothes, not only for psychoanalysts but for historians of fashion as well. He believed that clothing was used to enhance the body by enlarging salient features of it. Skirts, for instance, he noted as making the female body appear wider and therefore more powerful, especially when extended by crinolines, hoops, or bustles. He also noted negotiations over the protective functions of clothes as part of the currency between parent and child in that a mother tends to suggest to a child that he or she wear more, but rarely less, clothing (see the case of Mary, below). Bergler believed that clothing was always used to draw attention to female sexuality, and that even when apparently modest, it was used to enhance attractiveness by allaying men's fears of the unclothed female genital.

Dress is at one and the same time a clue to unconscious fantasy (Arlow 1971) and an enactment of it. Clothing can be costume as well as apparel, and as such is an actualization of the life of fantasy that keeps young children playing for hours on end and continues to operate in adults in subtler ways. (See Sally, below, and her fantasies: both the conscious one of being the wife of a rich and powerful man and the unconscious one of sadistic teasing with her parents.) Fashion can embody a fantasy of being younger or older, a cowboy or an Arab, any role of interest that is not available in ordinary life. For Freud (1908) this kind of fantasy was the kernel of creativity and the center of psychic life, not only consoling its creator for the necessary restrictions of the real world, but also providing the basis for psychological change and ongoing development. Unconscious aspects of these fantasies may play a large part in the development of compulsive shopping. Again, this is illustrated in the cases of Sally and Annie below.

Clothing demarcates the individual body. It outlines its contours, and also suggests the physical uses to which it will be put. Hollander (1994), for instance, believes that the trouser suit worn by western men since the 18th century contrasts with the skirt in that it emphasizes the possibility of activity rather than the capacity for reproduction.

But most important for my purposes here, clothes are the covering of the erotic female body. An analytic patient dreamed of looking at some silk blouses on a rack. In the dream her sister told her that cheaper blouses were just as good as expensive ones; they didn't show because they were worn under jackets and the good ones were almost as expensive as the suit itself. The patient had complained the previous day about a suit she was given by her mother. When the analyst interpreted that the patient would prefer a sexier one, her analyst hit upon a truth that changed the patient's view of herself. It countered her unconscious fantasy that her analyst had been trying to desexualize her. By allowing her to want what she believed others did not want her to have, this interpretation also helped her to feel entitled to have her own ideas about other aspects of her life. Clothing was the accessible metaphor for this woman's genital issues of sexiness, desirability, and assertion of the positive value of female sexuality. It can equally be a metaphor for protection, power, or other such important psychic constructs, and as such is a likely area for symptom development.

De Lauretis (1994) believes that clothing can function as fetish when the sense of the female body as erotic object is damaged. A fetish is a not-necessarily-sexual object, body part, or activity that is invested with profound sexual meaning, giving rise to extreme erotic excitement because it includes a strong, hidden aggressive component. As such, it itself becomes the object of desire, obligatory for sexual pleasure and taking precedence over genital sexual activity with another person. According to De Lauretis, the image of her own female body as erotic may be lost when the mother refuses to leave the father's bed for the little girl's, resulting in a woman with a permanent longing for her mother's affirmation of her worth and a need to use clothing to represent her lost, erotic, female body. Neither De Lauretis nor I imply that people are aware of such things. In most cases they are not. The psychoanalytic view is that organizing fantasies are not conscious until brought to awareness by the analytic process.

Clothes may serve women as a means of psychological negotiation with men, who also have complex but not necessarily conscious feelings about the female body as an erotic object (De Lauretis 1994). Male reactions of envy and fear of the vulva are sometimes experienced by a woman as devaluation of her feminine fullness. Sometimes a woman anticipates envy and fear and develops her own fear of being envied. Transvestites and female impersonators use feminine clothing in ways that can flatter or frighten women, but always express this envy. Clothing serves as a flexible barrier, allowing a woman to remove a bit at a time, testing whether the other will be further attracted or repelled by her femaleness. Removing clothing in stages can be part of courtship. And the changing in the dressing room is a rehearsal of the taking off and putting on of clothing that enhances the body. It both anticipates and prepares for the removal of clothing as seduction. Meanwhile, it provides the exhibitionistic pleasure of imagining oneself being seen.

Theorists from Freud through the postmoderns have suggested that a woman wants her body to be admired and desired by both men and women, just as little girls want their bodies to be admired and desired by the people they love: their parents. When she feels that it is, she may enjoy the pleasures of clothing as a way of expressing her valuation of herself. When her sense of desirability is damaged, however, and she wishes to make herself desirable again, she may turn desperately to clothing as a means to that end or even sometimes as a fetishistic substitute for the devalued body itself.

THE PLEASURES OF SHOPPING

Shopping for clothes, especially sexy ones, includes pleasures beyond the acquisition of the clothing itself. The shopping itself can be a part of feeling desirable and attractive. One woman commented that every time she tries on new clothes it feels like she's getting a hug. The physical sensation of the clothes on her skin — a pleasurable feeling that becomes less intense with familiarity — is noticed again and the sense of pleasure is renewed with new clothes. The experience of looking in the mirror also increases sensory awareness, the excitement of the newness heightening the physical sensation of something touching the skin.

There are social pleasures to shopping as well as these more sensual ones. Women shop with friends, mothers, or daughters. Someone else's seeing the new clothes can elicit the same heightened awareness that the woman above noted. An observer can respond erotically to the highlighting and/or concealing of erotogenic zones. Another person's reaction gives the wearer a mirror more faithful than the one on the wall to supplement her experience of herself. An observer provides criticism, judgment, discrimination, compliments. And there are pleasures of power — of demanding, rejecting, returning, competing, spending.

HOW SHOPPING COMPULSIONS DEVELOP

These types of pleasures are related to longings for sensual pleasure, closeness, and intimacy, and to desires for endless supplies, endless love, and endless dependency. Since possession of a garment cannot fulfill such longings, the shopping itself may become the object of desire and a shopping compulsion may develop. Yet this attempted solution is also illusory. Longings and desires of this kind are doomed to frustration, especially when their owner is not aware of them. Shopping, with its promise of a quest fulfilled, serves well to stir them up. But it has little capacity to satisfy. It inflames but cannot assuage. A salesperson may temporarily seem a dispenser of longed-for parental love and approval, but ultimately the shopper is left unfulfilled and/or guilty rather than satisfied — unfulfilled because the salesperson is not a sufficiently important object; guilty because of the stealthy nature of the covert transaction, or because the attainment of the forbidden wish requires an equally great punishment (these dynamics will be clarified in the case material below). The expenditure of large sums of money may briefly offer a consoling fantasy of control and power, but that is quickly deflated when the bills come due. To the extent that the shopper does not recognize that what she is looking for cannot be found where she seeks it, she may return to the site of a former partial success and seek it there again and again.

Compulsive shopping as a symptom has only lately appeared in the psychoanalytic literature. Schwartz (1992) has described such a compulsion in a woman with borderline pathology, Lawrence (1990) theorized a neurotic etiology, and Kaplan (1991) associated it with personality disorder of a sociopathic kind. Krueger (1988) considered shopping compulsion in terms of narcissistic psychopathology. All of these writers postulate, in the analytic tradition, the existence of unconscious fantasies that drive the quest, and they recognize the resulting paradox — that although the conscious goal may be clothing, in the unconscious quest a different object is sought.

It is my belief that this confusion of unconscious needs with the conscious wish for clothing gives rise to compulsive shopping symptoms. The complexities of these constructions are beautifully illustrated by Winestine (1985), who described a woman whose compulsive shopping was eventually traced to a childhood seduction. This had resulted in a feeling of helplessness that she attempted to overcome by shopping in fancy stores and imagining herself the wife of a powerful rich man. The patient could not afford the clothes, but she enjoyed using credit cards which she then would not pay, thus being able to cheat the bankers while blaming them because they kept extending credit to her.

It is important to recognize that the realities of wealth or wardrobe are not particularly relevant in these matters. If her resources for buying are insufficient or conflictual, shopping or shoplifting may give a woman a feeling of power, but a woman who appears to have the money to buy anything she wants still may not believe she has enough since what she really wants cannot be bought. If she experiences her needs as contemptible, the literal possession of any given object will not suffice to relieve her. If she considers clothes, accessories, or cosmetics the guarantors of beauty, yet believes she can never feel beautiful, she may understand this as not being able to buy enough. If buying things is her only experience of being loved, it will avail little against a black hole of endless unreciprocated desire. These needs are so frightening in their apparent boundlessness that a woman may provoke authority figures into setting limits in the hope of obtaining protection from her own painful longings and the powerful and menacing impulse to satisfy them (see Krueger [1988]; also Winestine, above, and the case of Elinor, below).

A word here in preparation for the case material. This driven quality can arise in any area of a person's emotional life where a commanding need is secretly going unmet. When such needs conceal aggressive wishes behind a screen of sexual or flirtatious wishes, the compulsion may take on the quality that we tend to identify as "perverse."

Psychoanalytic schools differ regarding how perversions come about, but fundamentally agree on what they are. Perversions, in psychoanalytic terms, are a form of compromise between intense sexual and aggressive wishes and the fears and moral judgments that require their suppression. They are defensive in that they keep the unacceptable wishes hidden from the person's awareness. They take the form of highly ritualized scenarios in which disguised forms of these impulses and fears are repetitively acted out. The scenarios retain the intensity of the primitive wishes, but are very tightly scripted. They allow the individual to experience the intensity fueled by aggression while avoiding the dreaded aggressive reaction from a potential partner who might have his or her own needs, both libidinal and aggressive. In return for this pleasure the perversion exacts a price: the perverse behavior itself may become a source of shame and guilt; and the possibilities of other kinds of sexual pleasure diminish. Because the perverse behavior is obligatory for arousal, it ends up replacing other forms of sexuality, coitus included, as the sole desired goal. In a "successful" perversion this complex balance protects the aggressive aspects of the underlying wishes from exposure, allowing them expression in relative safety.

Representations of (unconscious) attempts to master over-whelming childhood experiences of excitement and terror, perversions have as much to do with rage as with sexuality. The specific form of the perverse scenario for any individual is determined by his or her own particular fantasies, but all perversions depend on a sense of alienation as a shield against the power of other people. To the extent that it works, it does so by permitting, requiring, and enforcing maximum distance from the dangerous "others" who are mistakenly believed to be the source of the overwhelming feelings.

This concept has widened steadily since Freud's original for-mulation. He defined perversions as "sexual activities which either (a) extend, in an anatomical sense, beyond the regions of the body that are designed for sexual union, or (b) linger over the immediate relations to the sexual object which should normally be traversed rapidly on the path towards the final sexual aim." (1905, p. 150). That is, they indicate a deflection of interest away from the primary sexual organs and away from the goal of coitus. Freud, starting with his acceptance of Sabina Spielrein's 1911 concept of the death instinct (Freud 1920), came to consider aggression as a major source of human motivation, as important as loving or libidinal wishes within the context of the personality as a whole. Correspondingly, perversion has been seen as less motivated by loving and fear of loving, and more as a sexualized response to the sometimes intolerable intensity of these aggressive wishes toward potential sexual partners. Etchegoyen (1991) showed how per-verse symptoms could occur in people who were not sexual per-verts. He showed how the idea that aggression could be disguised as erotic excitement could clarify the perverse aspects of people who seemed on the surface to be more neurotic or even normal. Kaplan (1991) specified the concept of perversion in a way that is particularly relevant to this study. She focused on the preoccupy-ing psychological attachments to material goods and their acquisi-tion that are so common in contemporary society, and which she understands as fetishistic in nature (see above). She then proposed a connection between these preoccupations and perverse phenomena, and has extensively elaborated the uses that may be made of apparently nonsexual phenomena for perverse purposes. The difference between Kaplan's position and mine is that I see a spectrum of degree of pathology so that one person's perversion is another person's pleasure, with many degrees of fixity and restriction between the poles.

CASE ILLUSTRATIONS

Annie

Annie began compulsively shopping after her husband died. She felt that shopping for clothes was the only thing that could satisfy her. She talked to salespeople in the stores constantly, soliciting their advice on how to put outfits together and how to choose the ones most flattering to her. She enjoyed finding flaws in the things she chose, bringing the items to the salesperson and asking for a discount to compensate for the flaws. A lipstick mark on the inside of a dress or a pulled thread in a hem gave her pleasure because she could talk to the salespeople about them. She engaged them in discussions of how the clothing was made, why there were flaws in it, and whatever other reasons she could find for why she should get it for less. For her, shopping was a demonstration to others that she had been cheated and deserved reparation. She had never used shopping in this way before. It was the death of her husband that precipitated her need to console herself with material things.

She had always enjoyed having her husband look at her and appreciate her body. She talked about how helpful saleswomen were in advising her which clothes looked best on her. It occurred to me that these saleswomen were providing her with an audience like the audience that her husband once provided for her. She talked of how she did not want to be in the singles "scene." She did not want to meet new people. She had enough of that before her marriage when she was younger and had a better figure. As I interpreted her shopping compulsion as a fear that her body was no longer young and attractive enough to get her a new man, Annie's shopping symptom slowly receded. Later she began to understand that she was complaining to the salespeople about her feelings of having been damaged herself by the loss of her husband. What she was actually looking for was someone to love and someone to love her. Now that she was no longer using the symptom of shopping to get what she could never again have, the sense of being loved as a young woman, the feeling she had with her husband when they were young, she was able to look for something that she could have: a sense of being wanted and appreciated for what she was now.

The symptom was relatively easy for her to give up and replace with a new hobby: she began taking care of a group of teens who had no place to be together away from their parents. Annie began to look forward to the after-school hours when they would come to her home and watch television, play games, or bake cookies. She also found comfort in working for an organization that collected money for research on the disease her husband had died from. She met people and gradually established a new life for herself. Like most patients who are thought of as neurotic, Annie managed to achieve a new balance in her life more easily than can people like the patient I will talk about next.

Elinor

Elinor had a passion for shopping that usually ended up in her acquiring nothing. Her weekend hobby was shopping for clothing and jewelry that she would then return during the following week. She constantly yearned for clothes, and felt satisfied when she was buying them, but she hated them once she "felt trapped" into keeping them. Old clothes, "antique" clothes, were more acceptable to her. She liked knowing that the antique dealers she bought them from would not accept returns. For Elinor the only way to avoid the cycle of buying and returning was to deal with people who would not allow it.

The first phase of her symptom giving way began when she discovered that I was wearing new shoes exactly like ones she had bought the previous week. She regarded this as a triumph of taste. We liked the same things. She did not have to return the shoes even though she had been keeping them in the closet while deciding when to return them. I suggested that she think about why it was so important to her that we had chosen the same shoes. We talked about the beginnings of her pattern, and it turned out that her mother had established the pattern by encouraging her to buy several things at the same time, bringing them home to her father for his opinion, and then sending back the ones that did not meet with his approval, keeping only the one he liked best. She was harboring a childhood fantasy that she too could be returned if she were not a good enough child. She avoided making long-term commitments for a similar reason; as long as she did not choose the other person, if she could still return him, she would not be the one who was returned as not good enough.

Months after Elinor had begun to experience some relief from her continual need to shop and return things, one of her uncles died. At the funeral the uncle's daughter thanked her for coming. Elinor felt terribly sad, even as she reflected that the death of her relative would not make much difference in her own life. But although her mourning for her uncle appeared to be minimal, still she resumed shopping in a way she called an addiction. The pattern was so severe that she became extremely embarrassed at causing the salespeople so much trouble with her constant demands on their time and energy, both to sell her the things and to issue the credits to her for returning them. Sometimes she would give the clothes away to relatives or friends rather than take them back to the store where she had bought them. The symptom had been so severe before treatment that Elinor had worn the same winter coat for a decade. She could not find anything that she felt comfortable in. It was only late in her analysis that we were able to understand why a coat had such significance to her.

Trying to understand what had caused her to relapse into her old shopping ways, I suggested to Elinor that it might have something to do with her uncle's death, but she thought it had to do with her father's death. It then became clear to us that the pattern became pronounced after her father's death, and that her uncle's death had only brought it back. I interpreted that she felt her father was back with her when she bought things to return, the way she had when he was alive to approve her choices. This intervention allowed the return of memories of being taken to a large city near her hometown to buy new clothes for each new season. She and her mother would choose many things, but would return most of them.

Further analysis from this point was able to make it clear that in their shopping both she and mother had been doing and undoing — that is, acting and then undoing the consequences of the action. What was being undone related for her mother to the early death of her own father. Elinor herself, we found, had been undoing what she herself feared most, the possibility of her own mother's early death. Her identification with her mother, and fear of her loss, was concretely embodied in the buy-and-return cycle, and provided its driving force. They had participated in it together, and it provided comforting proof that anything could be undone, nothing was final, nothing was irreversible, not even death. But when death itself (her father's and then her uncle's) proved this fantasy untrue, her anxiety increased, and so did the undoing necessary to contain it. This triggered the intensified shopping-and-returning. Note that it was the apparently superficially felt death of her uncle that first alerted us to the connection of this behavior with death and loss. We were able to pursue the pattern from her uncle's death through her father's and from there to its deepest and most encompassing level, the identification with her mother and her need to undo the possibility of losing her.

This fear of loss was fueled by Elinor's unconscious rage at her parents; she feared their death because she also longed for it. Her rage at them stemmed from a sense that they had deprived her of the most important thing, their love and attention, while showering her with material objects that served only to prove to her and the world that they had the money and the power to provide these things, not to satisfy any wishes of hers. The winter coat symptom now became clearer to me. A coat is something that the world sees, it is outdoor wear. In this regard it was like her parents' gifts in that a new and expensive one would show the world that she was like her parents, exhibiting her buying power. Yet a new cheap one would not satisfy her either because it would show the world that she did not have her mother's elegant taste or her father's money. To have either was impossibly painful so she kept herself in a threadbare coat, looking, she thought, like someone who did not have what she needed, and thus shaming her parents.

This complicated set of thoughts covered up and displayed her rage simultaneously. Her rage had to be discovered over and over again as Elinor saw how she was displacing her rage onto the shopkeepers who had to take back what she did not want just as she had wished that she could make her parents take back their gifts and spend time with her instead. It is because of the intense aggressive aspect of her shopping compulsion and the substitution of shopping for the pleasures of loving another person that I see Elinor's symptom as perverse.

After several years of analysis, Elinor felt less worthless. She could relax her fear of being "returned" herself, rejected by her parents as unacceptable. She allowed herself her rage at them and was no longer so ashamed of it that she had to hide it from herself. She felt better able to cope with eventualities such as loss or death, and, feeling safer, was able to allow herself more material things as well. She became able to use clothing for pleasure rather than as a seasonal sacrifice in the service of the denial of death.

Annie and Elinor, it may be seen, used their compulsive shopping in different ways to protect themselves, in fantasy, from object loss. Lawrence (1990) has elaborated this theme provocatively. Individuals who for whatever reason find the risks of object loss too great, she says, may shift their focus away from the wish to be loved onto the love of material things. In this way they free themselves from dependency on an autonomous object whose love they desire but might lose. She also points out that a sense of psychological linkage with a concrete thing may provide a sense of shared permanence to a person who is dismayed by the evanescence of his or her own human state. She points out that the linking of oneself with concrete objects allows an individual "to transcend the death fear and impose the feeling of immortality and permanence on the ephemeral individual. In this way the object lends the individual a future" (p. 68).

Mary

Mary went shopping for clothes in preparation for each new season. She had dozens of similar outfits in a range of colors that she thought fit each time of year. She wore a dazzling array of dresses, making it clear to her co-workers that she had more than any of them. She chose dresses with the most feminine details she could find, always describing her style as "girly." She enjoyed being dressed in bright or pastel shades, wanting always to look cheerful and prosperous. From her point of view the show of prosperity was the most important purpose of her life. Her mother had been a European orphan, picked up by American soldiers and brought home as a kind of mascot by the young men who had found her starving and dressed in rags. One of them had adopted her but had been unable to keep her; his wife found the little girl unmanageable because she had temper tantrums and would steal from neighbors, friends, and family. She had gone from foster home to foster home until she married the patient's father. Her mother had always dressed herself in modest somber colors, but had taken great pride in her daughter's large, varied, and very colorful wardrobe.

Mary understood early on that her mother maintained a depressive conviction of being worthless and pitiable. She knew that her clothing in some way compensated for this for both of them. But it took the exploration of other unconscious beliefs to release her from the constant need to amass more clothes. Two other intertwined fears were connected to her constant and exhausting consuming. These had to do first with her uncertain relationship with her own femininity and sense of attractiveness to either men or women, and second with the relative value she placed on women and men.

Her sense of her own femininity was attached to her awareness of her father's attraction to her as a woman. Ambivalent about his attraction to her, at times he denigrated and disparaged her feminine charms, which led to a conviction on her part that she was unattractive. When other men responded to her as attractive she was plunged into uncertainty over whether her father really had admired her. Answering this question affirmatively allowed her to believe that he had secretly preferred her to her mother.

Her confusion about the relative value of men and women had to do with her belief that her mother, who constantly disparaged Mary's father, was the powerful and nurturing one in the family. Mary's mother required her to be loyal to her exclusively. Mary was confused by the fact that her mother remained with her father despite what the mother presented as his supposedly unacceptable behaviors.

Every time she surpassed either her mother or father in any way she felt more alienated from them. Any achievement tasted of ashes, as it made her feel that she was losing her parents' love. Yet her way of feeling better about herself was to achieve still more. The only way out of this dilemma she could find was to buy clothes. It felt good, and it did not in any way diminish her parents' achievements. In fact, it enhanced them, because it was their achievements that provided the money that bought the clothes. Mary could buy clothes to reassure herself that she was still a pretty and nice girl, still a valued part of a family that saw her other accomplishments as unfeminine and threatening.

When her doctor told her that she was entering menopause, she had the thought that she would go and spend a month's salary on clothes to cheer herself up. She then told me that before her treatment she would have actually done it, but now she could notice the impulse and think about what had triggered it. She had spent most of her life worrying about her parents, both of whom had been chronically ill since she was a little girl. Yet she had taken loans from her parents continually, never paying them back, because she needed the money for clothes. I was finally able to connect the shopping with a fantasy she had talked of years earlier of having a rich and powerful father who would always be there to protect her. In the fantasy, as long as she remained a dependent little girl, her parents would be safe from the encroachments of time. The clothes buying had maintained for her this sense of secure dependency.

In the course of her treatment she made sure to outdo me by having many more outfits than I did, by being more in step with current styles, by being more feminine in dress and grooming, and by changing her make-up so that she was more youthful looking. As we painstakingly explored her need to compete with me and be sure that I did feel bested in these ways, she taught me how she felt. As long as she was able to depend on me, as she had on her parents, as long as she needed to overspend in order to be in debt to them and to me and to the credit card companies, she was sure that none of the parties would die. She was repeating in her current life the fantasy of keeping her parents alive by depending on them and being in debt because she continually bought more clothes than she could afford. The interpretation of the dependency fantasy and how it had played out between us in the transference was what enabled her to stop the compulsive shopping.

Sally

Sally was a tall, long-limbed 30-year-old blonde. She was a saleswoman in a high-fashion optometrist's shop, and had been in analysis for several years. One of her most puzzling symptoms was her need to constantly "improve" her looks. She spent hours each morning on make-up, on selecting clothing, and on doing her hair. She was beautiful, but was convinced that she was "a dog." Handsome boyfriends made her frantic because she believed that they were always looking for a woman more beautiful than she was. She could not believe what people told her about her attractiveness. In the analysis we wondered about her belief that she was so ugly and worthless.

Sally's attitude toward her clothing reflected her attitude toward her body. She would buy many pieces of cheap clothing at a time, be interested in them for a few days, then want more. She frequently borrowed her mother's clothes and those of her friends. She seemed to be searching for another body. She was, I think now in retrospect, expressing with her clothes both a restless disappointment with her own body and a wish to be able to change it at will, having it now thinner and more childish, now fuller and more womanly.

This preoccupation was connected with the shopping, and it encapsulated some old conflicts with her mother. Sally's mother had fought vigorously against Sally's early attempts to be very thin, and the wardrobe changes that were necessary to match her changing bodily shape played into their mother—daughter drama. As Sally lost and gained weight, she complained that nothing fit her, and she used this complaint to justify buying new clothes constantly. In this she identified with her mother in the way the latter dealt with changing weight. But while her mother changed wardrobes only once a season, Sally needed new things constantly. In order to have them, she spent much of her weekends shopping. It became her hobby, her passion, her constant companion when she became a teen.

It became clear in the analysis that Sally was ashamed of the erotic aspect of buying clothing. She punished herself for the pleasure she took in it by depriving herself of the other things she "could have bought" with that money. She understood her shopping as "a release," and expressed it in highly charged language, far more fully realized than her descriptions of any of her sexual encounters with men. "I choose the store. I like the ones where they let you sit there and they show you the stuff. I can hardly afford those. They're too expensive. But I get someone to help me in the other kind. I like them to want me to want it. I like to leave them with it. I like it best when it's just a little too expensive and I can't get it."

Similarly, when the analysis had first started, Sally had reported shopping trips with both her parents that repeated a sadomasochistic pattern extending back to her childhood. She described it as an almost sexual teasing:

> When it's my birthday or something, they won't get me a present. But my Mom says I can have a new thing, whatever it is I want. So I go to a store and I find something. Then I go call my Mom and ask her. She won't let me have it. But she says: "Okay. We'll go for a walk on Saturday." My Dad comes on these trips with me sometimes. I hate it when she says "Yes" and he says "No." I hate when they both do it. She says "Yes"; he says "No." He can't stand it, but he's the one who says he wants to get me a present. They make me beg for it.

Sally's struggle of impulses came to a head after a disastrous love affair with what she called "a poor, dirty, low-class man." She became pregnant and had an abortion, which recalled to her attention a prior abortion when she was 16 years old, which she concealed from her mother. When her mother found the pamphlet on contraception Sally had gotten from the abortion clinic, she slapped her daughter and called her a whore. Sally was appalled at this, became very docile, and stopped going to nightclubs. In the ensuing years of her early adulthood she followed her mother's advice on most things, spent much of her leisure time with her mother or with both parents, and called her mother every day, sometimes several times in the course of a single day.

During this period of compliance to and intense contact with her mother, and of suppression of her own desires, shopping together was the main activity they shared. Sally described these outings as teasing glimpses of a world of luxury. Her mother would ask Sally whether she "needed" something to wear. Sally would think of something. They would go to a boutique. Mother would try on clothes, Sally would try on clothes, and each would critique the way the other looked in her outfit. Sally complained that her mother would insist on buying only the highest-priced designer clothing while restricting Sally to lower-priced items. At the same time she would make a paradoxical but oft-repeated remark that Sally found chilling but believed to be true: "Well, you will never find a man who can give you as much as I can." This statement touched on Sally's own fantasy that she was her mother's beloved but still worthy only of second-class clothes. The fantasy, we discovered as analysis progressed, had been nourished by her belief, echoed by her mother, that mother had held her marriage together for her daughter's sake, that she loved her daughter as much as she hated her husband, and that her husband, Sally's father, was a detestable man who contributed nothing to the family. This belief was so strong that Sally had real difficulty remembering that it was her father who earned all the money in the family. Over the seven years of her treatment Sally sometimes realized this and sometimes did not, in an alternating pattern.

Before the second pregnancy Sally had been exploring her relationship with her father, and had become aware that all the lower-class, immigrant, and married men she chose, including her current lover, were in the image of her father. By having an abortion, she felt she was renouncing an incestuous baby. This kind of multilayered structure is characteristic of perversion. The overt impulse of the perversion — the "stealing" of love and security from sadistic and controlling parents — was sufficiently scary to distract Sally from her much more horrifying wish for a baby, or at least a close and loving connection, with a sadistic and controlling man. The perversion protected the underlying wish, allowing it to flourish unchallenged while all of Sally's attention went into her embattled relationship with her clothes.

The analytic work on this issue led to a renewed shopping spree, although by then the shopping symptoms had begun to abate. The increase in anxiety that came up with the pregnancy wish required stronger compulsive measures to contain it. At first the spree seemed to me to be a regression or a negative therapeutic reaction. I later came to understand it as a reaction to her new attempt to make restitution for having lived on stolen goods, and to earn for herself a place in what she saw as my world. (She believed that I lived in the world of the adults, those who did not need to depend on others to sustain them.) The shopping spree defended her from depression over her abortion and the emptiness of her life of living out her mother's fantasy of her as mother's "girl." It also served to placate her self-condemnation about the fantasy of being her father's "girl" through identification with him and his power. Even though shopping reminded her that she was not the rich wife, she found it thrilling because the use of cash reminded her of the power she thought her father had when he paid for things that way. The fantasy was complex, multilayered, and changed with each deepening of the treatment. As the symptom of shopping decreased, the fantasy took one turn; interpreted, it turned protean and became something else.

Sally's mother doled out money to her grudgingly. She treated Sally as her husband treated her, and with a similar result. Sally took money from her mother's purse or bank account whenever she was desperate for cash or wanted luxury items she could not afford on her own allowance when she was not working or earnings when she had them. Money became the focal point of her guilt and her anxiety.

Early in her treatment she had paid me in envelopes of dollar bills. I worried about what this might mean, and I told her to tell her parents that I reported cash as income. She told me that she believed I looked down on them for this. She told me that they habitually bought things that they called "wholesale" or "factory extras," but which were, in reality, stolen goods. They got more than they paid for in many illicit ways, and in all of them they had to use cash so there would be no record of the transactions. I really did find that less than admirable and I had to admit it to myself and to her in order to feel comfortable asking her to trust me. Cash thus became a symbol not only of power, but also illicit power. Furthermore, it became a way that she could defy what she thought was my prissy moral code and assert her identification with her parents. Yet my assertion of principle did, I believe, act as a comforting limit set on her and on her family. She settled down into treatment after that intervention, stopped missing sessions and coming late for them, and seemed more relaxed.

Over time she stopped buying stolen goods. Since her guilt at having things that were stolen had always made her feel bad about herself, and the only way she could feel better was to have things that she believed made her look good, she had been trapped in a vicious circle. She finally got out of the circle by understanding that the things she wanted to have in order to feel better were exactly the things that made her feel worse. This was not instantaneous: she repeatedly had to go through the experience of having something illegally gotten, feeling disgusted with it, and analyzing why she felt so disgusted. There was no onetime revelatory experience that changed her life but a series of repeated understandings, each time with another nuance, each time with a bit more memory of previous times, until she finally was able to satisfy herself with something reasonable and wear it with some pleasure.

Her own resources could not provide the luxury items that went with the fantasy that she was a rich lady. She had only the fantasy that her mother's money was hers, a fantasy that echoed her mother's fantasy that the father's money really belonged to her. It turned out that her lack of satisfaction with the items she bought related to this fantasy. To suppress her awareness that the money was not really hers, she had to prove that it was by spending more. Her constant round of spending and becoming dissatisfied with whatever she had bought was both exhausting and saddening. She could not enjoy the fantasy because it was really her mother's money she had spent and her mother would inevitably taunt her with that fact. Their shopping expeditions and her mother's insistence on buying luxuries for herself while allowing Sally only low-priced clothes reminded Sally that she was not the rich wife, just the little girl who got what the mother did not want. This situation has lasted years into her analysis.

Our work over money and power was tested as we proceeded to work on matters pertaining to the second pregnancy and the renewed sprees that accompanied it. Sally's conflict over her dislike of her father was complicated by her sense that without him she had to remain her mother's "girl" forever. This fear reactivated her need to shop. Eventually, however, these impulses became manageable. Once, she felt an impulse to buy a duplicate of an item her mother had bought for her years before. This time it was from someone who had gotten it when it "fell off a truck." But she was able, to her pleasure, to resist any illicit buying, and she was even able to stop herself from buying something on the grounds that she already had it. This was something she had never been able to do before then.

Sally needed new clothes so often because she believed that her body was ugly. She was able to give up the very frequent shopping when she recognized that new clothes always seemed to offer hope of changing but did not ever really change the body beneath. Sally's analysis offers an illustration of the generalization that clothes that conceal the body beneath them also take on the body beneath them. Thus patients who hate their own bodies will hate their clothes soon after they buy them.

For Sally the erotic interaction around buying clothes was part of a sadomasochistic character disorder of the sort Arlow (1971) described as a "perverse character." Arlow defined perverse character as the substitute for perverse sexual practices. Sally's perverse character was a perverse expression of her sexuality; that is, it was a way of simultaneously experiencing sexual pleasure outside the realm of actual sexuality, and also of expressing the hate-filled and humiliating aspects of her relationships with the other people involved. In the analysis this interaction became dystonic and she became more aware of how it replaced all other forms of excitement and pleasure for her. It was confused with a mingled longing for and rage at her depriving and teasing father. Her erotic experiences with other men were tainted because they did not want to engage in her shopping, and in the teasing, demanding, yielding, and recriminating that had characterized the shopping trips with her parents. Men she encountered did not find this ritual erotic, usually experiencing it as boring or even disgusting. She mourned giving it up even as she understood that it was precluding her pleasure.

The analyzability of perversions has sometimes been questioned on the grounds that in many cases their possessors do not wish to let them go, but this is not always the case. In Sally's case she was able to establish less convoluted modes of contact, and eventually shopping became a way to relate to other people as she made a career in a retail business.

DISCUSSION

The women discussed in this chapter used clothing for "normal" purposes, but the *seeking* of it became a compulsive symptom for each one of them. They illustrate some of the many kinds of fantasies and motivations that can result from or help form a compulsive shopping symptom. For Annie shopping was a way of dealing with loss and finding an audience with whom to share her sense of being damaged. Elinor's shopping demonstrated her wish to outmaneuver the intolerable reality of death. For Mary it was a way to protect valued ties to her parents from her own conflicted ambitions to be an independent woman. Sally's shopping allowed her to displace a pattern of enraging, but exciting, teasing, and frustration away from an incestuous sexual arena to a safer place.

All four women were using the search for clothing to express old needs and wishes of which they were initially unaware, trying to fill in adulthood an emptiness they had been carrying around with them unwittingly since their early years. All of them managed to gain some peace with themselves and some control over their shopping as they became able to recognize and understand their own needs and wishes less fearfully and less judgmentally.

These women wanted more love than they had or could allow themselves to wish for. All used clothing, and shopping for clothing, to express fantasies of loving and being loved by their mothers and/or fathers. Because shopping for clothes is so predominantly a female occupation in our culture, girls often experience shopping with their mothers as the sharing of a close and acceptably erotic experience. When there are fantasies about the mother–daughter relationship or the father–daughter relationship that cannot be expressed in words, and particularly when they bear with them frightening aspects of rage and fear, they may be enacted in compulsive, and sometimes "perverse," scenarios. Rather than trying to stop the scenarios, I think that good treatment consists of gaining a conscious understanding of what satisfaction is really being sought in the compulsive behavior, and what can and cannot be satisfied by shopping for clothes. Longings for sensual pleasure, closeness, and intimacy cannot really be satisfied by shopping, and wishes for endless supplies, endless love, and endless dependency cannot be fulfilled by objects bought, so the longings and wishes are better directed toward activities that can satisfy them. When shopping enacts an unconscious fantasy of endless fulfillment, a vicious cycle of disappointment followed by a frantic search for another chance is established. When shopping is a search for something nice to wear — well, then the pleasures of shopping can be enjoyed without guilt and shame.

REFERENCES

Arlow, J. (1971). Character perversion. In *Psychoanalysis: Clinical Theory and Practice*, ed. I Marcus, pp. 177–193. Madison, CT: International Universities Press, 1991.

Bergler, E. (1953). *Fashion and the Unconscious*. New York: Brunner/ Mazel.

Bergmann, M. V. (1985). The effect of role reversal on delayed marriage and maternity. *Psychoanalytic Study of the Child*, 40: 197–219. New Haven, CT: Yale University Press.

De Lauretis, T. (1994). *The Practice of Love: Lesbian Sexuality and Perverse Desire*. Bloomington, IN: Indiana University Press.

Etchegoyen, H. (1991). *The Fundamentals of Psychoanalytic Technique*. London: Karnac.

Flügel, J. (1930). *The Psychology of Clothes*. London: Hogarth.

Freud, S. (1905). Three essays on the theory of sexuality. *Standard Edition* 7:125–245.

—— (1908). Creative writers and daydreaming. *Standard Edition* 9:143–53.

—— (1920). Beyond the pleasure principle. *Standard Edition* 18:3–65.

Kaplan, L. (1991). *Female Perversions*. Northvale, NJ: Jason Aronson.

Krueger, D. (1988). On compulsive shopping and spending: a psychodynamic inquiry. *American Journal of Psychotherapy* 42(4):574–584.

Lawrence, L. (1990). The psychodynamics of the compulsive female shopper. *American Journal of Psychoanalysis* 50(1):67–70.

Hollander, A. (1994). *Sex and Suits*. New York: Knopf.

Neruda, P. (1990). *Selected Odes of Pablo Neruda*, trans. M. Sayers. Berkeley: University of California Press.

Richards, A. K. (1989). A romance with pain: a telephone perversion in a woman? *International Journal of Psycho-Analysis* 70: 153–164.

—— (1990). Female fetishes and female perversions: "'A case of female foot or more properly boot fetishism' by Hermine Hug-Hellmuth reconsidered." *Psychoanalytic Review* 77:11–23.

—— (1997). Perverse patients and perverse analysts. *Psychoanalysis and Psychotherapy* 14:145–156.

Rose, L. (1988). Freud and fetishism: previously unpublished minutes of the Vienna Psychoanalytic Society. *Psychoanalytic Quarterly* 57:147–160.

Schwartz, H. (1992). Psychoanalytic psychotherapy for a woman with diagnoses of kleptomania and bulimia. *Hospital and Community Psychiatry* 43:109–110.

Winestine, M. (1985). Compulsive shopping as a derivative of a childhood seduction. *Psychoanalytic Quarterly* 54:70–73.

VI

Couples Treatment and Group Therapy

15

Overcoming Overspending in Couples

Olivia Mellan

I have been a psychotherapist in private practice for over twenty-five years. At first I specialized in women's issues, couples work, and conflict resolution. Since 1982 I have been giving workshops and seminars, and seeing individuals and couples who had conflicts about money. This money psychology work proved to be in such demand that I eventually wrote two books — *Money Harmony: Resolving Money Conflicts in Your Life and Relationships* (1994) and *Overcoming Overspending: A Winning Plan for Spenders and Their Partners* (1995). Creating a safe place where individuals and couples can talk about their money conflicts filled such an important need that at this point in my career money psychology work takes up 80 percent of my time and effort.

When I began this type of work, I purposely called my sessions "money harmony" work and not, for instance, "prosperity consciousness," to underline the basic tenet that we have a lifelong relationship with money. This is much like a relationship with a person, and can be either balanced or unbalanced. Unless one has a balanced relationship with money, more wealth won't fix a thing. The core of my work rests on the individual self-awareness component or, rather, working to let the patient explore for him- or herself what his or her relationship with money is all about. To this end I have designed several techniques that are described in detail in the treatment section later in this chapter.

Working with couples in conflict, I have become convinced that, whereas sex has come out of the closet, money is the last taboo for many of us. Like sex, money carries with it a heavy emotional load, symbolizing love, power, security, independence, control, freedom, and self-worth. Dealing with money matters is an integral part of most intimate relationships. Couples need to both understand and adjust to each other's money personality styles.

UNDERSTANDING MONEY TYPES

Any discussion of money problems needs to begin with an introduction to the three most common money personality types found among couples with money problems: spenders, hoarders, and bingers (Mellan 1995).

• *Spenders* love to use their money to buy whatever will bring them pleasure (this includes buying gifts for others). They have a difficult time budgeting, saving, and postponing gratification to meet a long-term goal. Overspenders have extreme spender tendencies. They often spend all the money they have, and may well be locked into a pattern of ever-deepening debt and financial crisis. Spenders have a hard time making a budget; the word *budget* makes them feel claustrophobic and straitjacketed. They need to call it a "spending plan" to be willing to take on this task at all.

• *Hoarders*, polar opposites of spenders (and usually in a relationship with them), enjoy holding onto money. They are often excellent at saving and budgeting but find it difficult to spend money on nonessentials for themselves and their loved ones. If one partner in a relationship has strong spender tendencies, the other often develops into a hoarder to restore financial balance, even if he or she wasn't a hoarder to begin with.

• *Bingers* are part spender and part hoarder—an unstable combination. They tend to save and save, appearing quite controlled and focused, until something triggers a spending binge. During this out-of-control episode, they quickly spend some or all of the money they've so carefully saved. Bingers are often unable to predict when the next urge to splurge will strike, and these binges often plunge them into serious overspending and debt. (I now consider bingers a subset of spenders, partially because I believe the spending part of the cycle is the most devastating in its effects.)

Partners involved in overspending relationships often incorporate aspects of some of these other money types into their attitudes about money:

• *Amassers* believe that greater wealth means greater power, status, or self-worth. They often put a lot of time and energy into money management. An amasser who is in a relationship with an overspender may start acting like a hoarder to prevent the depletion of his or her savings.

• *Worriers* have tremendous anxiety about their finances and expend a great deal of energy worrying about money. They take on responsibility and tight control over their finances. Most worriers are hoarders as well. When in relationships with overspenders, worriers tend to become more extreme in their money behavior, worrying and hoarding more strenuously to keep the couple from being swamped in debt.

• *Avoiders* tend to ignore, postpone, or delegate the tasks of everyday money management. They may feel nervous about handling money and afraid of making mistakes. Many avoiders are also overspenders. If an avoider forgets to pay bills and never knows where the money goes, their partner typically develops into a worrier, trying anxiously to keep track of income and outflow.

• *Money monks*, motivated by political or spiritual passions and deeply held beliefs and values, fear that accumulated wealth or frivolous spending will corrupt them. They distrust money, believing it has the power to destroy aspects of the life they hold dear. They tend to live frugally, even ascetically, and to be judgmental of other money types, especially spenders and amassers. When the money monk is in a relationship with an overspender, these judgments can cause a great deal of friction. A partner with money monk tendencies who believes the love of money is the root of all evil (and hence feels uncomfortable having too much of it), may help create a money amasser, who enjoys the feelings of success and power that come from amassing money.

In investment matters an aggressive risk-taker is usually balanced by a more conservative risk-avoider. This polarization is often gender-based, with men generally being more eager to take risks than women. When one partner is a planner, strategizing and mapping out the couple's joint financial future to the last detail, the other is often a dreamer — an impulsive, sometimes impractical, visionary.

GENDER DIFFERENCES AND MONEY

Because men and women are socialized differently, they tend to form different types of relationships with money. Despite the fact that in our culture mothers mainly raise both genders, men separate from their mothers more absolutely because of the sex difference. This leaves them with more rigid boundaries. Women on the other hand can separate with less rigidity, leaving them with more porous, flexible boundaries. Deborah Tannen elucidates these differences in her work (1990).

Men are raised to be, or at least act, self-sufficient, invulnerable, and good at handling money, though often no one teaches them how to do so. While men may appear confident, centered, and secure in their dealings with money, women are often raised to believe they won't be very good at this "money stuff," and if they're lucky some man will take care of it for them (Stanny 1997). They are encouraged to act more vulnerable, even needy. Although the world is changing, I still believe it's changing more slowly than we'd like to think. Thus many women still tend to feel less secure, more anxious, and less confident than their male counterparts when it comes to investing and managing money.

There are of course exceptions to these generalizations. Many women and men work hard to transcend their own cultural conditioning (or were lucky enough to be raised in families that did not limit them in this way). For many others, extricating themselves from their upbringing is not an easy task. Thus, despite our best efforts, many men and women have internalized these traditional separating norms on some level. So, when it comes to money, they are living in separate worlds.

Men and women have different burdens and different fears when it comes to money. Men fear getting laid off, injured at work, or dying young and leaving their families in financial trouble. Most women have "bag lady nightmares," and are gripped with the fear that they will lose everything and be totally unable to support themselves. This overwhelming fear comes from years (centuries, I suppose) of chronic financial dependency on men, and the knowledge that women are still paid less than men for the same work. Half of all marriages end in divorce. It is well known that most women fare significantly worse after divorce, while men's financial condition characteristically improves following divorce. Most women will outlive their husbands, so even if they don't divorce, they will need to take care of themselves in their old age. Women who inherit wealth have even more bag lady fears — their money has come to them magically, through no work of their own, and it seems that it can disappear just as magically.

Men feel the provider role as a heavy burden, even if they are not the chief wage-earner. Women feel the burden of the "second shift" — being all things to all people — wife, mother, career woman, caretaker of aging parents, and so on. Both burdens are equally real. It is important for men and women to develop compassion for the burdens of the opposite sex, and to communicate this compassion.

When it comes to power and decision-making, men tend to function more as autonomous decision-makers. Women, raised to be accommodating and cooperative, seek mutual, shared decision-making. Men find it natural to go out and buy the big-screen TV or the new sailboat without consulting their mates. Women feel hurt and excluded: "How could you do this without me?" Men's response (remember, they're raised to see the world as hierarchical): "What are you, my mother? I don't have to ask you for permission."

This difference is exacerbated if the man makes more money

than the woman in a relationship. Many men who are the chief breadwinners feel they should have prime decision-making authority about how money is spent. Even when the women are better at managing the day-to-day finances, men who make more tend to believe this. But if the woman makes more money, she tends to want democratic, shared decision-making. This is one place where I feel the women's way works best: with shared decision-making comes more intimacy, better communication, and more mutual respect.

But in many other ways, men and women need to find a way to span their differences, to learn to communicate with empathy and compassion across the bridge of their different cultures.

For example, where most women are "feeling types" who seek the "harmony of the whole," most men are Jungian "thinking types," wanting to make decisions in a more linear, rational, or logical manner. Thus, when it comes to discussions about money, women want to talk about the process, the feelings, how they make decisions, what their goals are. Men want to talk about the "facts." They're each half right. As a therapist, I believe that the feeling-type talk has to come first. Only after thoughts and feelings are shared in a nonblaming, respectful way can the couple come to clear decision-making and negotiation about the facts of their money life.

How the money is kept in a relationship reflects what are often unconscious differences regarding the tasks and challenges of intimacy for men and women. For the man, one of the greatest challenges of intimacy is to learn to merge, to get connected and stay connected. Thus a man's desire to merge the money may well be a loving expression of his yearning for a fuller connection with his partner. On the other hand, a woman's primary challenge in intimate relationships is to learn how to preserve her healthy sense of autonomy in the midst of intimacy. Wanting some or all money to be kept separately is a symbol of this healthy separateness, which enables her to connect with her partner from a deeper, more solid place (Mellan 1994).

Notarius and Markman (1990), who have spent years examining happily married versus distressed couples, report that it is not the extent of difference between the members of a couple that determines their degree of marital contentment, but how they "sit with" these differences. Thus, if men and women can be educated to understand these different challenges and the valid needs that arise from them, win-win compromise solutions become possible. For example, a couple could merge some money for joint expenses and joint savings and investment, and keep the rest separate. Or they could merge most of the money, but the woman could keep a small portion separate. Solutions do not have to be symmetrical to work well. But they do need to honor and reflect the deep, often gender-related needs of each member of the couple.

Money Conflict in Context

Why is it that many couples lack the skills necessary to facilitate productive money discussions with their partners? To begin with, most of us grew up in families where our parents didn't talk about money. When I say this in my workshops, someone will usually counter: "Not so—in my family, we talked about money all the time." But if I ask what that talk was like, the type of response I usually get is, "My dad worried about not making enough or having enough, and he chastised my mother for spending too much." This is not what I mean by talking about money. Most people grow up with no clear idea of their family's true economic status and no clear idea about how financial matters were handled or financial decisions made.

We tend either to imitate our parents' way of dealing with money—often careening back and forth between two opposing money styles—or we make vows never to be like a particularly negative model and strive to become the opposite. For example, if Dad was a reckless overspender, the son or daughter might become a supertight hoarder, neglecting to enjoy any immediate pleasures in life for fear of becoming a spender like Dad. If Mom was a constant worrier, the child might become an avoider, not dealing with any of the details of his or her money life to get away from the worry and money demons that plagued the family of origin. In either case, whether we imitate one or more parental models or make vows never to be like Dad, Mom, or Aunt Tillie, we are not free to evolve our own healthy money style and money personality, reflective of our own values and our own integrity.

When couples come together, a curious and predictable phenomenon occurs. After twenty-five years of specializing in couples therapy, I've said this so often that others now call my belief "Mellan's Law." Quite simply, I believe that if opposites don't attract right off the bat — and they usually do — then they will create each other eventually, each member of the couple modifying his or her habits to balance the other's behavior. This polarizing dance of opposites is the norm, not the exception. The reactions involved run the gamut from mild to extreme, depending on how convinced each member of a couple is that the partner's actions will endanger the financial health and balance of the relationship. Although the couple may remain solvent (an outcome by no means guaranteed), balancing acts like this are often achieved at the cost of tremendous internal friction between two radically different money types — literally "duel" personalities (Mellan 1995).

In most couples' relationships in which there is polarization around money, we find one spender and one hoarder. Often, in the same couple, the spender is also a money avoider (not paying attention to the details of his or her money life) and the hoarder is a worrier. This double-whammy marriage is extremely common. Moreover, as time goes on, the polarization will tend to deepen, intensify, and rigidify, with one member attacking the other for his or her differences.

In our society we cannot talk about overspending in a vacuum. We live in a culture in which the media and our vast advertising industry, as well as the constant pressure on us to keep up with the (imaginary) Joneses, encourage consumerism and overspending, creating desires for objects we never knew we needed until we saw those ads. We do not learn to save. What I call "money harmony" — a state of balance in which money is just dollars and cents, a tool to accomplish some of our life goals — and not love, power, security, control, or self-worth is difficult to achieve. As life goes on, moving toward money harmony becomes more and more vital to everyday happiness and to a couple's intimacy.

TREATMENT OF THE OVERSPENDING COUPLE

My therapy work with overspending couples focuses on using structured communication as a depolarization tool. Communication between partners is enhanced by their ability to listen to and appreciate each other's viewpoints. Instead of arguing over which partner is carrying the more onerous burden, each partner needs to take the time and develop the empathy necessary to acknowledge the real and separate burdens they carry. This is the only way they will make their joint lives work, both financially and emotionally (Mellan 1994).

If a partner feels attacked and judged during a discussion, open communication will be aborted and no resolution will be possible. To create an environment conducive to productive money talks, a couple must first learn how to listen and respond to each other effectively and empathetically. The couple must learn to create an environment in which they both feel safe enough with each other to be fully honest without worrying that what they express will be used against them.

What a Spender Needs to Do to Change

First, of course, a spender needs to acknowledge that he or she has a problem with controlling impulses to spend money. Second, he or she needs to identify "points of temptation" and "slippery places" — times, emotions, and places that trigger a spending binge or episode. Then the spender needs to strategize ways to avoid these temptation points and slippery places — with help. I encourage spenders to seek individual therapy, at least weekly, and to join Debtors Anonymous or some similar support group (hopefully free like DA, or at least low-cost) and to attend at least one meeting a week to support their new actions and attitudes. These efforts can

be supported or undermined by the behavior and emotional response of a partner in an intimate relationship. My job is to make
sure the relationship is a supportive one.

How a Nonoverspending Partner Can Help

It can be tremendously helpful for a caring partner to offer solid
support to an overspender. For this to happen, it is useful to
evaluate the influence of the relationship on the overspender's
compulsion. An increase in the compulsion to spend since the
relationship began may signal that the problem may be due to
factors within the relationship. Perhaps the nonoverspending partner is overly controlling, or excessively money-conscious and
hoarding, possibly triggering the spender's increased compulsion
to spend in rebellion. If there are problems with workaholism,
intense intimacy fears, isolation, or sexual or communication
problems in the relationship, the overspender may be spending
money to create some sort of temporary happiness or solace that
the relationship is not providing.

If a partner's overspending has improved within the context of
a relationship, then the other partner may be exerting a healing
influence. By being loving, open, and vulnerable, the partner
functions as a "money mentor" to keep the overspender on track in
the "recovery" process. Indeed, this can be crucial to the recovery,
helping (in a nonpunitive way) to find solutions to a partner's
compulsion to spend.

If the overspender's patterns of consumption and spending
have been unaffected by the relationship, this probably indicates
that the addictive behavior is more deeply rooted. It may stem
from long-lasting emotions and traumas such as childhood deprivation and feelings that may include emptiness, incompetence,
anxiety, depression, and lack of self-worth or lack of self-love.

In any case it is important for the partner to learn how to be
compassionate, yet detached from the overspender's compulsion.
If the overspending is severe, the partner may have to separate his
or her finances from those of the overspender to safeguard the

household from the ravages of overspending. The partner also needs to view the compulsion or addiction as an illness, which does not need to overwhelm the partner's total identity or the whole life of the couple or family.

Many partners fall into patterns of rescuing overspenders regularly until they become sufficiently resentful or burned out from the attempt. Therapists can teach partners of overspenders how to be aware of when and how they start falling into patterns of codependent thinking or enabling behavior, and help them devise strategies to insulate them from this trap. Then, healthy compassionate detachment can be cultivated, and intimacy and even healing between partners can develop over time. The overspender's partner can practice not feeling defeated or hurt when the partner slips. Progress is often one step forward, half a step back.

Because everyone hates to be labeled as the "crazy" or "sick" one in a relationship, it is imperative for the spouse or partner of an overspender to be willing to confront his or her own imperfections, and to share these struggles in an open, vulnerable way with the struggling overspender. This is sure to help the partner feel less alone, less judged, and, ultimately, safer to grow and to take on this painful compulsion or addiction.

Myths That Impede Couples' Healing

In my work with overspenders I've uncovered four myths that often derail partners from providing the type of support their overspending partners need.

- *"True love can conquer all"*: This is the belief that if the partner of the overspender just loved him or her enough, the overspending would miraculously disappear.
- *"I can fix what's wrong and make my partner stop hurting"*: The overspender's partner worries that he or she is causing the partner to overspend. For example, "If I didn't work so hard, my partner wouldn't feel so alone and take refuge in spending." While it's true that overspending-prone partners often spend more when they feel lonely, abandoned, angry, or unfulfilled, in many cases the

deep roots of this behavior indicate that it's likely to continue even if the immediate source of dissatisfaction is remedied. Although it may be very helpful for the overspender's partner to be attentive to the needs of the overspender, it is the overspender who must engage in active work to deal with and resolve the causes of the problem.

- *"It's useless to try to help"*: The partners of overspenders may be extremely helpful and supportive if they work together with their partners to understand this compulsion and to identify some of the sources of emptiness and deprivation that serve to fuel it.

- *"If I get too close, we'll end up struggling in the tar pit together"*: While this is true on some levels, there are ways to find a balance in which the overspender's partner may help without becoming too enmeshed in the overspender's progress. If the partners of overspenders take on too much of the burden of their partner's journey to healing, the overspenders may be unable to develop the strength they need to heal. Avoiding this pitfall is a difficult task because often a caring partner's response is to try to make life less painful and difficult for the overspending partner. This can result in enabling behavior and rescuer fantasies.

Helping Overspending Couples Learn to Talk about Money

Overspenders and their partners can learn how to set effective limits together, so that one party doesn't feel responsible for the other's "cure." Supportive detachment and sensible self-protection on the part of the partner help to create the insulation needed to safely work with the overspending partner toward healing the compulsion without regularly falling into either rescuer or attacker behavior. There are times when partners of overspenders will slip into destructive patterns of communication and action. Couples in overspending relationships can learn to be aware of this behavior when it arises and should take steps to prevent escalation. Such couples can better work together to facilitate healing when they have a realistic idea of what to expect, and when they know how to offer each other real, solid support. They need to get to the point where they can mutually agree to set financial limits, taking care to avoid the trap of the nonoverspender's taking full financial control and policing the overspender. Keys to healing, for overspenders and their partners, involve effective communication, shared power, and mutual respect.

I give exercises to couples related to goal-setting. I ask each member of the couple to construct a list of short, medium, and long-term goals. They both agree on how long a short, medium, and long-term period will be. To make sure the lists are not impulsively driven, I ask the couple to do the exercise two or three times over the course of a month so they see which goals they can trust. They then share the lists, often in my presence, using the structured, respectful communication techniques I have taught them, and try to combine them, using a spirit of compromise to arrive at a list of mutually satisfying short, medium, and long-term goals.

All clients who see me are invited to write (or role-play in my office) a money dialogue early in our work together. In a money dialogue a client generates a conversation (written or spoken) between him- or herself and his or her money — back and forth, until it winds down and comes to closure for now. For example, money might say, "Treat me with more respect," and the client might say, "I'll try, but that's going to be really hard." Then money might say, "I'm not asking you to respect me all the time, I'm just looking for more than I've got now." The client might then answer, "Okay, now that you put it that way, it doesn't seem quite as hard."

Then at least three voices comment on the dialogue — mother, father, and any other strong influences, past or present, such as a spouse, an ex-spouse, or an authority figure from school. The dialogue ends with a commentary from God, Higher Power, or the voice of inner wisdom. This meditation on one's relationship to money provides awareness tools to help clients see where they are, where they've been, and where they need to go to reach what I call money harmony. I invite members of a couple to do this assignment before looking at how their money personalities and money styles interact for better or for worse.

Establishing guidelines for money discussions helps couples

develop the tools they need in order to have productive money talks, and gives them the skills they need to communicate effectively with each other. The first guideline should be an agreement that both partners will not use trustingly confided information against each other in this money talk. Partners also need to agree that information learned during money discussions will not be used as ammunition for future fights. Finding a time to have money talks when stresses are low (not when children are around, or when taxes are due, or the week they buy a new house) will maximize a positive outcome.

Money talks should begin with warm-ups that help to launch open communication by creating a warm and caring atmosphere. Warm-ups begin with each partner verbalizing the positive aspects of the other's attitudes and/or behavior around money. Partners of overspenders are often afraid to express admiration for their partners' spending out of fear that this will reinforce and increase the overspending. More often, however, when this positive message is communicated, spenders feel less judged and freer to admit their fears about their spending behavior without feeling their partners will take their disclosure as an opportunity to criticize. For example, if the partner of a spender says, "I admire the care you put into buying presents for us, and the way you beautify our home," you may hear the spender say, "Thanks, but I feel I have no sense of control. . . ." I have them practice these warm-ups at home with each other until the sharing comes naturally and creates a positive cycle of appreciation, validation, and willingness for both to look at their own limitations.

It is important for partners to remind themselves and each other that their partner's assets outweigh their faults. Sharing their fears about their partner's spending behavior in ways that stress the positive creates an environment in which overspenders no longer fear the loss of their partner's love and respect. Partners of overspenders must learn to approach each money talk with curiosity, vulnerability, and openness about their own money attitudes and behavior. If overspenders' partners feel themselves superior, the overspender may feel preached at and condescended to, compromising the couple's real need for deepening intimacy and mutual sharing.

Partners should practice using "I" language when talking about money to minimize or even eradicate the blame implied in "you" talk. For example: "I feel scared that we will not have enough money for our children's college fund," rather than, "If you keep spending money this way, our children will never be able to go to college!" Similarly, couples need to be reminded — and eventually need to remind themselves — that they are not enemies but allies working together to help each other.

Although couples may have fallen into accusatory habits with each other, a therapeutic coach can encourage them to start assuming the best of each other, and to give each other the benefit of the doubt in building a positive communication base. Rather than, "How could you spend so much money on that CD player when you know we're supposed to be putting money into our vacation fund?" the partner of an overspender can say, "I know how important music is to you, but I'm concerned that we won't have enough money to take the vacation we planned if we keep this CD player. Do you think we can work out a way for you to be satisfied with your stereo equipment and still be able to save enough money to have a nice vacation together?" Assuming the best will reduce defensive behavior between partners.

I also help couples learn to listen patiently to their partners. If they find themselves feeling rushed, agitated, or angry in the midst of a money discussion, they can agree to separate for a few moments, or to take some deep breaths until they are ready to resume responsible, empathetic, and respectful communication. Before negotiating new spending habits or money management, it is essential that all feelings and thoughts on the matter are aired by both partners. If the emotional load is not lightened first, negotiations will break down and lead to a hardening of ingrained behavior and character stances.

Throughout my career, I've been teaching couples a structured communication technique developed by Isaiah Zimmerman, a clinical psychologist in Washington, D.C. This format helps

couples communicate clearly and respectfully — even when discussing the most emotionally charged material. Couples sit back
to back so they can focus individually on communicating their
thoughts and feelings deeply and honestly without censoring as a
result of seeing the other's facial expression. I instruct the couple
to keep each communication short and to the point so it does not
become a tirade or monologue. There is a no-interruption rule so
conversation can be kept to a standard of respectful listening. Each
member of the couple gets a chance to be both the sender and the
listener.

To begin, one partner announces that he or she has a message
and reveals the nature of that message up front, selecting from four
main channels of communication: (1) the "upset" channel (Zimmerman [1975, personal communication] called this "attack" or
"unequal"), which includes negative, stirred-up thoughts and feelings of any kind; (2) the thoughts and feelings channel, which
includes neutral or positive thoughts and feelings; (3) the empathetic listening/feedback channel; and (4) the negotiation channel.

If a partner feels angry, hurt, resentful, disappointed — stirred
up in any way — he or she should use the "upset" channel, by
saying, "I'm upset." If a partner simply wants to share a neutral or
positive thought or feeling, he or she uses the thoughts and feelings
channel and should start by saying, "I have a thought [or feeling]
that I want to share."

After announcing the channel of the communication, the first
speaker, the sender, asks if the partner is ready to listen. Willingness to listen with an "unrebutting mind" is crucial. If the listener
is feeling defensive, I instruct the partner to say No instead of Yes.
If the listener does say No, he or she needs to take the initiative to
continue the dialogue, either by asking for time to share upset or
negative feelings to release what is blocking the listening capacity,
or by postponing discussion to a specific time.

If the listener says "Yes," he/she is ready to listen with an open
heart and mind, then the sender communicates the message and
announces when it is finished. After each person has shared upsets
(I assume there will be some "upsets" built up where there is

money tension or other couples' conflicts), I encourage the couple to move on to the third, most crucial channel, called "verification" and "feedback." One states "I want to verify what you said. Are you willing to listen?" which leads the other to play back as empathetically as possible what the partner has just shared in the "upset" channel.

After verifying, instead of ending with a simple "I'm finished," the verifier asks, "Did I hear you as you wished to be heard?"; *not* "Did I hear you accurately?" This is because one of the most important reasons for playing back or verifying what was heard is to communicate the spirit of the content as well as its literal meaning. The sender responds by saying "Feedback . . . Are you willing to listen?" If the answer is yes, then the sender tells the listener what fraction or percent he or she felt was heard well and empathetically. I added a percent reporting because often couples tend to tell each other what the partner left out, without giving an overview of how well they heard the whole message. "You heard about 75%" is very important to say before focusing on what was left out.

Finally, after many cycles of upset messages and verification/feedback, couples are ready to move on to the fourth and final channel: negotiation. This is the only action channel. To use this, the sender says, "I have a negotiation: Are you willing to listen?" and if the listener says "yes," then the sender offers something before asking for something in return. The only things that can be negotiated are actions and behaviors. Feelings *cannot* be negotiated. A partner can ask a mate not to yell, but can't ask a mate not to be angry. Both partners need to know that they have the right to feel whatever emotions are gripping them.

If the listener accepts the negotiation, he or she shares that acceptance with the sender. If the listener doesn't accept the negotiation, he or she can go into the "upset" channel and respond critically, or into the thoughts and feelings channel and respond neutrally or positively in some way, or can offer a counternegotiation in his or her own negotiation channel.

In any of these cases, when one partner identifies and announces the nature of the message and asks for willingness to listen, the other partner will feel respected and apprised of where the communication is headed. Though this format may sound unwieldy at first, with coaching it really is quite simple. Within the structure of this exercise a great deal of psychological territory can be traversed. As long as there are firm boundaries and no interruptions, and each person takes full responsibility for the intent and content of messages, a climate of safety is created. Nothing is worse than sneaking an "upset" message into the "neutral" channel. I teach my clients this important concept by suggesting: "When in doubt, be upset. Warn your partner when you're about to share something that is difficult to listen to" (Mellan 1995).

Eventually, couples can integrate some of these concepts and channels into their communication outside my office. Some of the techniques are useful for all couples, not only those who have money problems. For example, much more respect and safety would be created if, instead of coming home and dumping complaints about work on a spouse unannounced, the complainer expressed a desire to complain and asked whether the other was ready to listen. The same is true for money talk.

Practicing the Nonhabitual

A core concept of "money harmony" work is the transformative power of "practicing the nonhabitual," or doing what doesn't come naturally. Since I believe that all couples' creativity, flexibility, and deep intimacy come from practicing this concept, I help each member choose one action a week (related to their money attitudes or money behavior) that constitutes practicing the nonhabitual. Obviously, for the overspender, the nonhabitual involves actions such as putting money in savings or investments, keeping cash in an envelope and not spending it, getting rid of credit cards, avoiding "slippery places" such as malls or particular stores in which one tends to overspend, and so on. For hoarders it involves spending money on oneself or loved ones for immediate pleasure purchases. For avoiders it involves taking on tasks one usually avoids, at least one a week.

I urge clients to reward themselves for their new actions or attitudes in a way that doesn't undermine their progress (spenders can't reward themselves by spending a lot of money, or hoarders by hoarding). I also recommend that they monitor their progress by writing down or speaking into a tape recorder how it feels to act differently.

I once extended this couples assignment with a new, more active role-play technique I call "A walk in each other's shoes" (Mellan 1995). These are the ground rules:

- The overspender decides what to shop for.
- The item should be something both members of the couple would like to have.
- The couple should set aside forty-five minutes to one hour to shop for the item.
- During this time period the partners should switch money roles while they shop.
- The couple should be instructed to interact with each other while they shop, each one playing the other's usual role seriously, with positive intent, without spoofing or criticizing.
- When the trip is over, each member of the couple should share how it felt to be out of his or her usual role, playing the role of the other.

This exercise proved successful through my work with Mark and Rosemary, a couple engaged to be married and having serious conflicts about money.

CASE ILLUSTRATIONS

Mark and Rosemary: An End to Conflict

Mark, an out-of-control shopaholic, would become entranced once he walked into a department store. He wanted virtually everything, like a kid in a candy store, and without regard to money, bought whatever he wanted. Rosemary was a super-hoarder, at the opposite extreme. She was hesitant to spend money on necessities such as livingroom furniture, and was terrified of not having enough money to sustain herself. During our interview, Rosemary spoke of memories she had of her family having to go on welfare, and her determination never to be in a situation like that again. Mark spoke of his childhood as the son of a loving single mother who "lived on the edge and never seemed to notice it," a description that perfectly described him as an adult. When this couple became engaged, they decided to merge their money in a kind of "trial by fire" experiment that was eroding, if not destroying, their otherwise loving relationship. As a result, Rosemary was panicked by Mark's spending habits and Mark was frustrated by Rosemary's tendency to hoard.

The couple agreed to do the role-reversal exercise with me. Rosemary's assignment was to role-play being a spender like Mark, and he would role-play being a hoarder like Rosemary. The goal was for them to experience being in each other's shoes. We decided that the three of us would go to Macy's to look at two items that Rosemary did not feel she could afford to buy, a videocassette player and a couch. I coached them and then we went for a forty-five-minute shopping trip.

Rosemary, in Mark's usual role, walked around in a frenzy, wanting to buy everything she saw. Mark kept saying things like, "We can't buy this today. We have to go home and check our budget." "We didn't agree to look at CD players and make-up!"

When the exercise ended Mark was awed: "No wonder she worries about money so much; I refuse to set any limits at all!" Rosemary said, "No wonder he loves shopping so much. It's really seductive . . . like a chemical high! I was in a trance-state in the store!"

After our postshopping trip discussion, I encouraged them to seek ongoing money therapy to continue the progress they'd made. I urged Mark to start attending Debtors Anonymous meetings. The couple also agreed to let Mark begin taking more responsibility in managing his money.

Six months later I interviewed this couple again. They were delighted that their tension and conflict about money had all but disappeared. Mark said that he and Rosemary had been able to help each other transform their behavior. They used my 1994 *Money Harmony* book, working on each chapter and doing the suggested exercises. Mark talked about the deep changes in his behavior following our experience at Macy's. He had changed in three important ways, he told me: "First, I began to see things from Rose's perspective, I saw what my overspending had done to her. Second, I became more aware of the way I thought about money and treated it, and realized what was compulsive about my behavior. Third, I've gotten much more involved in our finances. I know how much money we have in our accounts now, and it's nowhere near as much as I used to think we had."

When I spoke with Rosemary she told me that now she was capable of treating herself to little things she desired without feeling guilty. Mark's new ability to control his spending behavior allowed her to become less of a hoarder. Rosemary also spoke of some practical steps they took to take care of themselves while working toward money harmony. Rosemary said simply, "We separated our money. We each have our own checking account and our own set of credit cards. That one step took away 80 percent of the stress we used to have about money."

Further down the road, Mark had a temporary slip and fell "off the wagon," money-wise, when their planned wedding was canceled due to hurricanes in the Caribbean. He was so devastated that he went into the stores and spent a lot of money on clothes again. But once the road is paved, it's easier to walk on it again, which is what Mark and Rosemary are doing now.

As Mark and Rosemary's success story suggests, money harmony between overspenders and their partners can be achieved through hard work and mutual commitment to the resolution of money conflicts. This process takes time, patience, and motivation. Even with their resolve to work through money conflicts with their partners, partners of overspenders may become frustrated and confused by the time and effort it takes for the healing process to occur.

Unfortunately for overspenders and their partners, no quick fix or magic bullet exists. Spending issues cannot be resolved by simply setting stricter spending limits or having one partner maintain more financial control. For the overspender, admitting to a problem with spending often comes hand in hand with feelings of shame and denial, like coming face to face with an addiction. Understanding the shame and denial experienced by compulsive spenders and appreciating the difficulty inherent in working through these issues is crucial for their partners.

Here's another inspiring story that showed me how powerful and gratifying work with overspenders and their partners can be when there is good will between the couple and commitment to do the work all the way.

Hector and Christine: The Power of Love and Respect

Hector and Christine, both in their forties, knew that if they were to have the children they wanted, they ought not to wait. But after six years of marriage Christine found herself hesitant to make this commitment, worried about her uncertain financial future with the spendthrift husband she loved. Hector was affectionate, charming, and impulsive. A technological wizard whose corporate job paid $70,000 a year, he didn't seem to care how much he made — or how much he owed. Month after month he ended up juggling bills and overdrawing their bank accounts.

Christine could hardly have been a greater contrast. A talented potter, she regularly asked too little money for her work. Furthermore, she was reluctant to spend anything on herself. After her inexpensive Timex wore out, she went for months without replacing it. When Hector bought her an expensive replacement watch for her birthday, she felt totally overwhelmed and unworthy of such a beautiful and costly gift.

Hector and Christine had read *Money Harmony* and recognized themselves as a spender/avoider and a hoarder/worrier couple. This difference in their money styles was the only significant source of tension in their relationship, but it was serious enough to prompt them to seek therapy, and to make Christine unwilling to move forward on trying to have a baby with her overspender husband.

To understand their attitudes better, we looked at their family backgrounds and past influences, a step that proved very enlightening. The son of immigrants from Puerto Rico, Hector had grown up with no role models to show him the value of frugality, saving, or setting limits. His father, who had worked his way into a well-paid position as a researcher, enjoyed spending money on extravagant whims to show the world he had achieved status and success. His mother, a schoolteacher, had felt so guilty about leaving her three children with a babysitter while she was at work that she tended to buy them everything they desired. Thus it was almost inevitable that Hector, the baby of the family, would eventually develop into an overspender and an avoider.

Christine, too, was just one generation away from poverty. Her father had been the only one of ten children in his farm family to go to college. Though he had become an engineer with a decent income, he behaved as if he were still very poor. Christine's mother, who had stayed home to raise Christine and her five siblings, never got enough money from her husband to meet all the family's needs. She scrimped, saved, and worried, and Christine in turn became a scrimper, saver, and worrier.

As different as Christine and Hector were, the saving grace this couple possessed was an extraordinarily loving and solid relationship. So when I asked each of them to write a money dialogue and practice the nonhabitual, they were ready to take action.

Hector agreed to write down all his debts and to begin keeping a list of everything he spent money on. Christine wrote down her money worries and bought some small items for herself, noting her feelings about this unfamiliar self-indulgence.

By the next session both reported that their tension and worry about money had already eased to some extent. As Hector reviewed his family history and recorded his expenditures, he began to realize the extent of his overspending problem. Immensely relieved by his new awareness, Christine lovingly supported his first small steps toward more balanced behavior. When he toyed with the impulse to buy something fairly extravagant, she found ways to suggest less costly alternatives. For example, when they went out to a restaurant for dinner, Hector's usual habit was to order an appetizer, an entree, wine, and dessert. When Christine now suggested they just order an entree and either wine or dessert, he willingly agreed. Hector learned to cut back on spending at lunch, too. Instead of going out with friends every day and picking up the entire tab, he began to bring his lunch to work four days out of five. Christine, on the other hand, was encouraged to spend small amounts of money on things she ordinarily wouldn't let herself enjoy.

Little by little Hector made significant and sustained changes in his behavior. He put together a schedule for paying off his debts and has kept to it faithfully. Once they were well on the road to recovery, Hector and Christine tapered off to monthly therapy sessions during which they set new tasks and goals for themselves as each of them continued to move toward the middle. Then they stopped coming to see me, confident that their new habits were fully anchored and that they could continue the work on their own.

After a few years, Christine called to refer someone to me for a speaking engagement. She thanked me for the fine work we did together. And I discovered, to my great joy, that the couple had just given birth to their first child, and are happy, financially depolarized, and serene.

By understanding the roots of their money behavior, learning to communicate more effectively with each other, practicing the nonhabitual, keeping track of their expenditures and their emotions, and aligning themselves with their individual and couples short-, medium-, and long-term goals, they created their own success story.

CONCLUSION

Each relationship has unique qualities. It takes time for couples to develop new ways to communicate with each other, and to learn to practice depolarizing behaviors. Eventually, with the help of a therapist, they can develop and internalize these new skills. They should be reminded to be patient with themselves and each other, and to remember their roles as each other's allies. Remind them, too, that conflict and frustration is an inherent part of this healing process. But with practice and commitment, enhanced intimacy is not only possible but probable. Money harmony is a realizable goal, and once couples are on this path, money is no longer a barrier that impedes closeness—it becomes a tool to help achieve it.

REFERENCES

Mellan, O. (1994). *Money Harmony: Resolving Money Conflicts in Your Life and Relationships*. New York: Walker.

—— (1995). *Overcoming Overspending: A Winning Plan for Spenders and Their Partners*. New York: Walker.

Notarius, C. I., and Markman, H. J. (1990). *Controlling the fires of marital conflict: constructive and destructive strategies to manage anger*. Paper presented at the Maryland Psychological Association/Foundation (1990–1991) Post-Doctoral Institute Workshop, Columbia, November.

Stanny, B. (1997). *Prince Charming Isn't Coming*. New York: Viking Penguin.

Tannen, D. (1990). *You Just Don't Understand: Women and Men in Conversation*. New York: Ballantine.

16

Group Cognitive Behavioral Therapy for Buying Disorder

Melissa Burgard and James E. Mitchell

This chapter describes a form of group cognitive behavioral treatment (CBT) developed to treat individuals with compulsive buying disorder. The manual was developed by James Mitchell, M.D., and his colleagues (1993) while he was in the department of psychiatry at the University of Minnesota. As with most treatment manuals designed to be used in clinical trials (Fairburn et al. 1993), this form of group CBT has a preset schedule and a preset agenda. The treatment consists of fourteen meetings over a period of eight weeks. There are two meetings a week for the first six weeks, and one meeting a week for weeks 7 and 8. This form of therapy focuses both on factors that maintain the problem buying behavior and on strategies for controlling buying problems. It does not focus on the individual group member's personal problems or histories other than as they relate to buying behavior. Why or how the buying problem started is addressed only superficially; current factors that precipitate or maintain the behavior are more the focus. Each group member is expected to take responsibility for change and to take an active role in the group. The therapist serves as a guide and provider of information, and group members provide support and encouragement to each other. Members are also expected to complete homework assignments and read materials regularly as assigned. The goals of the treatment are set forth prior to its beginning. They include interrupting the buying disorder behaviors, establishing a healthy purchasing pattern, identifying and restructuring maladaptive thoughts and feelings associated with shopping and buying, developing healthy coping skills and communication patterns, and implementing relapse-prevention techniques.

Prior to beginning the group, each potential member is assessed briefly for any other psychiatric comorbidity, and certain individuals for whom group CBT would not be appropriate are excluded (e.g., persons demonstrating suicidal thoughts or self-damaging behaviors, or those with current misuse of alcohol or drugs). Individuals who are not deemed appropriate for this form of treatment are referred to treatment more suitable for their more pressing problems. Participants are educated in advance regarding the strict need for confidentiality of the material discussed in group.

Built into this program are two evening meetings that involve family and/or friends of the participants. The first is an informational meeting that is open by the member's invitation to people in their support system. The group members do not attend this meeting. The purpose of the meeting is to provide information to the members' support system, and to answer questions about buying disorder and its treatment. The purpose of including and educating friends and relatives is to encourage the development of an environment that will help facilitate the patient's efforts to overcome her or his buying disorder. The second meeting is a support meeting that both the group members and the members of their support system attend. The purpose of this meeting is to help the participants and the members of their support system communicate more openly about individual needs and conflicts. The first family and friend informational meeting is during week 2, preferably concurrent with the fourth group meeting held separately. The second is during meeting 8 in week 4.

The following is a brief outline of each meeting and the week in which it occurs.

We now turn to a description of the material covered in each group session. Each description is followed by a brief clinical illustration.

GROUP SESSION 1

Group Session 1 provides an overview of the treatment program. Educational materials regarding the clinical characteristics, complications, and associated conditions of buying disorder are presented. Members are encouraged to choose a shopping partner to accompany them on any shopping excursions in the weeks ahead.

This session also includes a discussion of the many reasons why the buying disorder is difficult to overcome. For example, when stopping the excessive buying behaviors, individuals may experience unpleasant affects. Also, as one cannot avoid shopping or buying, the behavior can't be avoided altogether but must be controlled. Most members will have had multiple previous failures in attempting to stop their behavior. They usually fear they will fail in this treatment program as well. The therapist should point out that there are good reasons for patients to be hopeful that they will be able to successfully stop excessive buying and shopping. We point out that the program is based on treatment concepts that have helped many others recover from problems similar to excessive buying, but also emphasize the fact that recovery involves much hard work. Treatment, including the regular completion of homework assignments, needs to be a priority. Members are then asked to sign a contract to make a commitment to change and to make treatment the number one priority in their lives while they are active in the program.

At this stage in treatment group members are strongly encouraged to begin to decrease their excessive buying behaviors. Problem buyers can be reassured that they can decrease their behaviors if they are properly motivated, well prepared, and offered the support they will need.

The treatment program overview also includes an explanation of the role of the group in changing problem buying behavior. Group treatment can provide sufficient structure and support to allow individuals to interrupt the chronic, habitual nature of the behavior. It will also promote reduction of the shame that accompanies the behavior, increase the number of individuals in their environment who can offer support, and permit group members to increase their own self-esteem by providing support for other group members.

Material is presented on the clinical characteristics of buying disorder, the epidemiology and diagnostic criteria for the condition, and the negative consequences of buying disorder, including cognitive and emotional, social, and behavioral problems. Psychosocial factors, including social and cultural contexts, and psychological factors, such as self-worth, ability to cope with stressful situations, and mood, are reviewed in order to further group members' understanding of buying disorder.

A final goal of Group Session 1 is for group members to choose a shopping partner. Many people with this problem tend to shop alone and a shopping partner can offer social support for the individual as she or he shops. In the next eight weeks of the program the members are encouraged to go shopping only with someone else, a spouse or significant other, perhaps, who is willing to help them remain in control in a positive, nonjudgmental way. The group member and the shopping partner are to agree before the shopping trip on where they are going and what they will buy. If a change is to be made in the itinerary, they are told to be flexible, but the shopping partner needs to agree on such changes.

Toward the end of Group Session 1 the therapist goes over the homework assignment for the members. This consists of completing purchasing records that include daily monitoring of the times of day they shop and the items they buy, the amount of money they spend, and the thoughts and feelings that are linked to their shopping and buying. They are asked to indicate whether items are "necessary" purchases or not. They are instructed to bring completed records to the next meeting.

> Jill is a 36-year-old mother of two who has experienced problem buying since the age of 18. During her assessment for group treatment, it was determined that she met the diagnostic criteria for compulsive buying disorder, including having irresistible impulses to buy as well as a sense of loss of control, social and occupational impairment due to excessive buying, and financial consequences. Jill also had a history of alcohol abuse and major depression, both in remission. Jill realized she had a serious problem with buying at the age of 29, when her credit card debts were "out of control." She was currently seeking treatment due to her increasing debts (more than $10,000), and threat of divorce from her husband. Jill seemed somewhat anxious during the first session, but was able to

discuss her problem thoroughly and offered support to other group members.

GROUP SESSION 2

Group Session 2 focuses on identifying problem behaviors and their consequences, identifying reasons for and against changing unhealthy buying habits, and preparing the group members for what to expect as they change their buying behavior.

At the beginning of Group Session 2, members should be asked to take out their completed purchasing records. These are examined in the group, a goal being to identify whether buying episodes are out of habit or in response to specific cues or triggers. The records can be used both to evaluate the current purchasing patterns, and to compare the records to what would be considered "normal" or responsible shopping. Members are asked to identify and characterize their own excessive buying and buying-related behaviors (e.g., impulse purchases, multiple purchases, shopping without an item in mind, credit card abuse, returning items, storing or hiding items, or buying to please or impress others). Group members are also asked to identify when they are most at risk to engage in problem buying behaviors, such as time of day or in response to specific feelings, such as anger. In discussion the group is asked to explore the consequences of the problem buying behaviors.

Some possible reasons for and against changing unhealthy buying habits are then briefly reviewed, and members are asked to complete a "pros and cons" worksheet prior to Group Session 3. Reasons for stopping may include excessive debt or conflict at home. Reasons against stopping may include the sense of excitement one experiences when buying.

There is also discussion on what members can expect as they change their buying behavior. As buying behavior decreases, individuals can expect to experience changes in thoughts and feelings. A brief list of possible changes is offered, such as increasing anxiety and depression. It is pointed out that these changes can be mild to troublesome. If such changes present a problem for group members, they are asked to bring these concerns to the group's attention. Group members can be reassured that the unpleasant thoughts and feelings will decrease as they learn healthier responses.

> Although Jill completed shopping records and signed her treatment contract, she disclosed that she was having trouble deciding on a shopping partner. She didn't think her husband would be supportive enough, and was leaning more toward asking her good friend Nicole. The other group members were supportive during this decision process. During this session, Jill also characterized her excessive buying behaviors as credit card abuse and buying items to impress others.

GROUP SESSION 3

Group Session 3 focuses on the cognitive model of buying disorder looking at cues and consequences in more detail. An attempt is made to have each member look specifically for possible cues that trigger problem buying behaviors, including social, situational, physiological, and mental cues. Members discuss the consequences that result from their buying episodes. Once individuals have identified specific cues and consequences (both positive and negative), they are encouraged to begin to develop strategies to disrupt the pattern of cues and consequences. One strategy is to take control of the cue by breaking the relationship between it and the buying response. This can be done by rearranging or avoiding cues, and by changing the response to them. For example, it is possible to restructure the environment to remove the cue by restricting the stimulus field that triggers the behavior, such as avoiding certain stores altogether. Another way is to strengthen the cue for a desired behavior as opposed to problem buying. For example, bringing along the shopping partner may strengthen the cue for responsible rather than compulsive buying.

Several suggested methods can also be given to assist in changing the response to cues, such as building in a pause or delay in the response. For example, when struck by an urge to buy compulsively, the member would agree to wait an hour before leaving for the store. Another method is suggesting alternative behaviors to cues, such as replacing a maladaptive behavior with a competing behavior that is adaptive (e.g., putting a paycheck in the bank rather than going shopping).

An extremely useful technique to make the undesired behavior unlikely or impossible is to eliminate credit cards, and to carry only a limited amount of cash. Although many individuals are reluctant to do so, it is best for them to have someone else (e.g., shopping partner) keep *all* of their credit cards for now.

It is also important for the participants to develop a list of alternative behaviors that they employ for times when they have a sudden impulse to shop (e.g., go for a walk, write a letter). Members should start to compile their list prior to Group Session 4. Members are also encouraged to continue to monitor their purchasing by keeping purchasing records.

Homework can include identification of the cues and consequences frequently associated with their problem buying and writing down strategies they can use to rearrange cues to change responses (i.e., to minimize the occurrence of problem buying). Members should be reminded to invite someone to the family/ friend informational meeting to be held concurrent with Group Session 4.

> In completing her homework assignment from the last session, Jill compiled a list of "pros and cons." Her reasons for stopping the unhealthy buying habits included excessive debt and conflict with her husband. Her reasons against included feeling noticed and attractive in the new clothes she wore to work. She also decided that her friend Nicole, rather than her husband, would be the most supportive shopping partner, and invited her to the informational meeting. She was able to identify advertisements for clothing in the newspaper as a prominent cue.

GROUP SESSION 4

Group Session 4 focuses on changing cues, and on cash management. It is important to review with participants the discussion of cues and consequences of excessive shopping from the prior meeting and have them discuss cues and consequences they may have identified in their homework. Point out that when people have problems with compulsive buying, they often describe themselves as acting impulsively and feeling their behavior is out of control. The need to decrease the availability of money (or the equivalent) to spend by not having access to cash or credit can be stressed. Participants should be encouraged again to destroy their credit cards during this session or, if unwilling to destroy them all, to entrust the ones they "need" to their shopping partner to keep for emergencies. It is important to point out that this can be frightening and painful, but will be extremely helpful in limiting excessive buying since credit cards are a powerful cue for most individuals with these problems. This should be discussed with the understanding that the decision to give up credit cards is one that will vary from person to person.

If at all possible, it is helpful to have a financial counselor meet with the group. Several suggestions can be made regarding cash management. It is useful to have members keep track of how much money they spend — including petty purchases — for a few weeks in order to assess where and on what they are spending their money. The group leader may suggest putting 10 percent of their net income into savings, setting up an escrow fund for periodic payments for things like car insurance, using automatic payroll deposit and savings deposit in which paychecks are deposited automatically into their bank accounts, and using automatic bill payment in which bills are paid automatically from the checking account on a certain date.

A useful strategy is to have participants leave their checkbooks at home when they plan to go shopping, and for them to carry only as much cash as they can afford to spend. A good suggestion relative to credit cards is to pay off any remaining balance every month. If credit cards are a problem, but they need to carry one after they leave the program, they can consider reducing their credit limit. Another suggestion may be not to buy nonessential items until they've made satisfactory payments on their debts. Members also can be instructed to consider putting any tax refunds into savings immediately, and to balance their checkbooks every month.

Group Session 4 is also used to educate participants about healthy spending practices — using money in a thoughtful and responsible way for past, present, and future purposes, and allocating it in ways that reflect priorities to enable them to live the kinds of lives they want to. First, there is thoughtful spending for past purposes, that is, gradually paying off the bills they have already accumulated. Second is thoughtful spending for present purposes, meaning spending the right amount of money, neither too much nor too little, on life's necessities such as shelter, clothing, and food. Third is thoughtful spending for future purposes — setting aside the right amount of money for future needs, such as emergencies, retirement, and educating children. Obviously, the right amount of money for each purpose will vary from person to person, and will also depend on income and obligations as well as values. However, it is important to point out that all — income, obligations, and values — are influenced by what money means to her or him. For some people money can mean success. For some it may mean a sense of security. Group members should be encouraged to examine what money means to them.

Planning ahead can also be a useful stimulus control technique. Toward the end of Group Session 4, give the homework assignment to plan the next weekend in order to eliminate high-risk situations and to increase the frequency of alternative healthy behaviors. It may also be useful to point out that the weekend plan should not be a list of things to be accomplished, but rather activities that can be done in moderation that will result in providing balance and structure in the day. This can include some shopping or buying with their partner if they need to make specific purchases. They should also be encouraged to include at least one activity in their day that they enjoy, and one opportunity in which they can experience a sense of accomplishment and success. It is also important to set aside time to relax and unwind from a busy week or a stressful day, and relaxation techniques such as a hot bath or listening to music may be helpful in their weekend plan. Exercise can also be discussed. Self-rewards can be built in, such as pleasurable activities or other rewards after accomplishing a goal. At the end of the weekend they should review their plan to see if they followed it. They should look particularly at activities that were associated with feelings of accomplishment or success, pleasure or enjoyment, discomfort or tension. By doing this they can assess if there is anything that happened during the weekend that they would want to see changed (enhanced or avoided) in the weekends ahead.

> Jill decided to give up all of her credit cards except one, which she chose to entrust to her husband for safekeeping. She discussed in group that the credit cards were a cue for her behavior, the consequence being excessive debt. Most group members agreed with this, and also decided to give up credit cards.

GROUP SESSION 5

Group Session 5 concentrates on the responses — thoughts, feelings, and behaviors — that are part of the cognitive view of the maintenance of the buying disorder (see Figure 16–1). It is a good idea to begin by reviewing these in detail. Cues or triggers precipitate responses, and then there are consequences for the responses. Cues can trigger external and internal responses. External responses are behaviors that can be observed by others; internal responses are thoughts and feelings that are usually private, often more difficult to identify, and also more difficult for others to observe. This can lead to a discussion of how thoughts about a situation or cue are linked to feelings and behaviors.

A good example of this system is one that illustrates how different people react to the same cue. A person who doesn't have a buying disorder may pass by a shop and think, "Maybe I'll take a

FIGURE 16-1

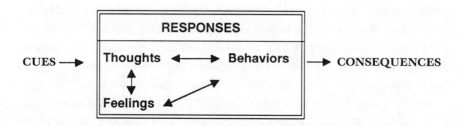

look before I go home." Someone with a buying disorder may think, "I've had a rough day, I'm passing this shop, I think I deserve some new clothes. I'm going to go shopping in order to feel better." It is also a good idea to examine the related feelings, since feelings can be determined by thoughts. The person without a buying disorder in the above scenario may feel relaxed and happy while browsing in the shop whereas the person with a buying disorder may feel tense and out of control. There are no right or wrong feelings; feelings are just feelings. Everyone experiences different feelings throughout the day, but it can be suggested that members need to look at the feelings they are feeling most intensely, since they may be causing a change in their behavior.

A discussion of automatic thoughts and maladaptive styles of thinking can be helpful in preparation for the next session, in which cognitive restructuring is covered. Automatic thoughts are thoughts in response to certain situations that come automatically — for example, driving a car from one place to another, but not remembering how you reached your destination. Obviously it is necessary to think in order to drive, but in that particular situation you are not aware of the behaviors and thoughts associated with driving. They came automatically. It is also useful to review the different styles of maladaptive thinking. Several styles of thinking typically lead to problem buying responses and contribute to buying behaviors. One example is *overgeneralization*, or deriving a rule based on one event and applying it to other situations. Using words such as *always* and *never* can sometimes be indicators of overgeneralization (e.g., "I am *never* going to be able to control my shopping"). Second is *catastrophizing*, or embellishing a situation with surplus meaning that isn't supported by objective evidence, or seeing certain situations in an extreme way (e.g., "I've made more purchases than are on my purchasing plan. I'm a failure"). A third example is *dichotomous thinking*, sometimes called *all or nothing* or *black-or-white* thinking (e.g., "I have already gone over my budget, I may as well buy these extra things"). *Self-fulfilling prophecy* is making predictions about the outcome of one event and acting in ways to ensure it will come about (e.g., "I will always be in debt"). *Over-reliance on the opinions of others* can also be considered an example of a maladaptive style of thinking (e.g., "The saleswoman told me this dress was meant for me — I'd better buy it").

At the close of the session it should be mentioned that it is important for the members to begin to recognize their particular maladaptive styles of thinking and to begin challenging thoughts they recognize as maladaptive. It may be helpful to ask them to list some maladaptive thoughts that they frequently have in relation to their buying disorder in preparation for meeting 6. Another homework assignment is a Restructuring Thoughts Worksheet used to identify a cue or situation that leads to a problem shopping response, and how they are responding to it, that is, how they are feeling, what their thoughts are, and what behaviors are triggered by this cue. They can then consider the consequences, both positive and negative. An example of the Restructuring Thoughts Worksheet using the example discussed in the following session is shown in Figure 16–2.

> During this session Jill and the other group members discussed what went right and wrong in their weekend plans. In particular, Jill had planned not to go shopping as she usually did on Saturday afternoon, but to go to a movie with her husband instead. She was upset that this part of her plan did not go as intended as her husband was called into work. She was angry and frustrated and decided to go to the movie by herself, but as she drove by the mall right next to the theater she felt anxious and had an urge to stop and shop,

FIGURE 16–2. RESTRUCTURING THOUGHTS WORKSHEET

CUE	RESPONSES		CONSEQUENCES
	Thoughts	**Behaviors**	
Bad day at work	*There is no way I can control myself once I have the urge to shop*	*Shopping at lunch*	*Guilt* *Shame* *Feel bad about self* *Hide purchases* *Lie to husband*
	Feelings		
	Stressed *Overwhelmed* *Upset*		

which she did. When Jill deviated from her plan she told the group she felt she would never be able to stop the excessive buying. The group helped her come up with alternative behaviors she could use in this situation next time, and encouraged her to keep trying.

GROUP SESSION 6

Group Session 6 includes an examination of thought restructuring. The therapist can introduce basic cognitive restructuring techniques to help participants begin to restructure thoughts linked to problem buying behaviors. A brief review of the previous session (becoming aware of thoughts, feelings, and behaviors that are triggered by a particular cue and result in specific consequences) is useful since this is the first step in cognitive restructuring.

The second step is to teach the members to evaluate the thoughts they have in such situations to determine whether they are accurate and reasonable. One method is to challenge maladaptive thoughts by questioning them. Three primary questions will assist participants in doing this.

1. What is the evidence to support or refute this thought?
2. What are the implications of this thought? In other words, what if this thought is really true?
3. What are the alternative explanations (thoughts) that are possible?

For example, "There is no way I can control myself once I have the urge to shop" can be challenged using the questioning method. "What is the evidence that supports this thought?" None. "What is the evidence that refutes this thought?" The evidence is that there is no indication that the participants can't control themselves. They've been able to control the urge to shop in the past.

"What are the implications of having this thought?" can be answered by looking at the evidence that the thought has not always proven to be true. The individual has been able to be in control sometimes when he or she has had the urge to shop. Also, if the person is having a very hard time with the urge that particular day and feels in danger of shopping, he or she can do something else — take a walk, call a friend.

"What are the alternative explanations of this thought?" The person may be having a particularly hard day at work or may have had a fight with his or her spouse. This may explain why he or she is thinking so negatively.

Using this method, individuals can decide what is a reasonable thought to have about themselves once they have reached a reasoned conclusion about why they may have had the negative thought to begin with.

Another method used to evaluate thoughts is to set up experiments that test for accuracy of the thoughts. One example of a thought that could be tested by experimentation is: "I couldn't possibly survive without my credit cards." To test this thought the member may actually give up credit cards for a certain period of time. It is likely he or she would survive during this test, and in fact find out that this is not an accurate thought. Some of the thoughts tested, however, may be found to be accurate. In this case it may be helpful to evaluate the implications of the thoughts.

The third step in cognitive restructuring is for individuals to change their thoughts based on new information uncovered through their questions and testing. The fourth step is to evaluate how these revised thoughts would change the associated feelings, behaviors, and consequences. At the close of Group Session 6 the therapist can go over homework assignments to complete prior to Group Session 7. The Restructuring Thoughts Worksheet, the assignment from the last session in which they listed cues, thoughts, behaviors, feelings, and consequences, may be used to further practice restructuring thoughts. Members can challenge thoughts that they wrote down in that assignment using the three questions (i.e., "What is the evidence?" "What are the implications?" and "What are alternative explanations for the thought?"). They can then come up with revised thoughts, feelings, behaviors, and consequences. By doing this, members will be able to practice the cognitive restructuring that is the core of changing maladaptive thoughts.

> The group used Jill's thought from the last session ("I will never be able to stop shopping") and identified it as an example of overgeneralization. They worked together to challenge the maladaptive thought by questioning it. Jill discovered there was more evidence to refute this thought than to support it. She mentioned that her husband said he was very proud of her for trying so hard and that she and Nicole had agreed to go shopping, but went to the park with the kids instead.

GROUP SESSION 7

Group Session 7 concentrates on an examination of "cues and chains," and is used to build on the cognitive behavioral approach the patients learned more about during the previous session. The therapist can give a brief review of the three components of behavior. The cue leads to responses (consisting of thoughts, feelings, and behaviors) that lead to specific consequences — the basic cognitive model of maladaptive shopping behavior. This figure can be built on now by looking at chains. The occurrence of a behavior often involves more than three components — much of the time consisting of a series in which each part represents one link in a long behavioral chain. For example, a cue triggers responses such as thoughts, feelings, and behaviors that may then become cues that trigger another set of responses, and so on until the final consequences occur. Members are encouraged to write out a behavioral chain as a helpful strategy for understanding how a particular behavior came about. An example of a chain should be given so that the members understand that the series can start one day and the consequence can occur several hours or several days later. An example: a chain was started by the cue of criticism from a boss, which was followed by driving by the mall, which led to an urge to shop and then actual shopping, which led to guilt and shame, which led to a consequence of lying about the purchases. This can lead into another chain.

It is important to stress to participants that determining their chains of behavior can assist them greatly since they can learn to break the chain early in the cycle. The earlier the chain is broken, the easier it is to prevent the occurrence of buying behavior. The strategies for behavioral change that were taught in the previous lectures (rearranging cues, changing responses to cues, rearranging consequences, and restructuring thoughts) can be used to break the behavioral chain, and can be reviewed during this session. Examples to help members decide what technique can be used to break the chain can be discussed.

At the close of the session participants should be encouraged to continue to self-monitor their shopping behavior and also to do a homework assignment of identifying behavioral chains of their own. In addition, they can identify places they could break the chains and assess strategies they may use to do this. Participants should be reminded to invite family members and/or friends to the next session. Some may be reluctant to do this, and it is important that the therapist and possibly other group members try to persuade them to bring someone. By educating friends and relatives and answering their questions, the program can help them to provide members with an environment that can facilitate their efforts to overcome the buying behavior.

> During this session Jill was able to identify a behavioral chain as an example for the group of something that had happened in the recent past. It had started with an argument with her husband about her spending habits. This led to her feeling very bad, which led to her plan of returning the credit card purchases she had made. In going back to the store, she ended up buying a whole new outfit instead of returning her other purchases. Jill told the group how this made her feel even more guilty, which led her to lie to her husband and hide her purchases from him. The therapist agreed this was an excellent example of a behavioral chain.

GROUP SESSION 8

The focus of Group Session 8 is family, friends, and social support. Hopefully the participants have brought family members, friends, or someone else from their support system to the meeting. Research studies can be reviewed, including work that indicates that people who have a buying disorder tend to report that one or more of their family members have a past or current problem with depression. The members and other participants can discuss ways in which they think the buying disorder affects them.

Participants can also describe how the process of making changes due to treatment are affecting their family system and their friends. Members are encouraged to describe how their families and friends can be more supportive to them, being as specific as possible. Family rules, or the silent assumptions of a family system, can be discussed. These are often established outside the family members' awareness. Participants are asked to list some of the family rules concerning money, shopping, clothing, credit cards, debt, and budgeting. They may recognize these rules by looking at "shoulds" (i.e., "what *should* we be doing?").

Another aspect of the family that can be examined during this session is family roles and the expectations of each family member. Each person in a family is an individual who plays many different roles — wife, daughter, sister, mother, husband — and each role has a different expectation. The participants need to discover what their roles are in the family and what these roles mean. What do the other family members expect of them? What labels do family members put on them? How do their family roles relate to the buying disorder?

> Instead of her friend, Jill brought her husband to this meeting. He indicated that he noticed a change in her shopping behavior and that it was having a positive impact on their relationship. Some of the group members, including Jill, listed ways in which their family and friends could be supportive to them. Jill pointed out that when her husband got angry with her for shopping, it made her feel hurt and angry. This would lead to stress and often precipitated another bout of shopping to relieve the stress. They agreed to discuss his concerns directly and quietly in the future.

GROUP SESSION 9

Session 9 concentrates on self-esteem, which can be defined as the way in which individuals evaluate themselves. Self-esteem is one aspect of self-concept, a more general term for how individuals define themselves. Self-esteem is important because it may play a large role in the buying problem. Many individuals with buying problems have low self-esteem and tend to evaluate themselves in a negative, self-critical manner. Specifically, they exaggerate their weaknesses and minimize their strengths. Self-esteem problems often contribute to buying problems, since many individuals end up shopping to make themselves feel better or as a form of self-punishment. Following excessive spending, individuals often end up feeling even worse about themselves, which may contribute to even lower self-esteem. Members can be taught that the techniques they learned to use for evaluating the accuracy of their thoughts can also be used to challenge and test the thoughts that contribute to low self-esteem. The first step in doing this is to identify the types of cognitive errors they tend to make in evaluating themselves. Examples of such errors related to low self-esteem are provided, and labeled as the kinds of thinking errors they have learned in the previous sessions. For example, some may tend to overgeneralize by thinking, "I'm no good. I'm a failure." They may catastrophize by thinking, "I can't do it. I'll never do it right." They may minimize by thinking, "I did it well but I could have done it better." They may use dichotomous or black-and-white thinking by thinking, "If I don't do well at one thing, it means I'll never be successful." Finally, they may engage in "mind reading," which can be described as, "Everyone thinks I'm a loser." After the patients have identified the types of errors they make in evaluating themselves, they should challenge and test the accuracy of their thoughts (e.g., by asking, "What is the evidence?" "What are alternative explanations?" "What are the implications of these thoughts?" "Are there ways of testing the accuracy of these thoughts?"). In addition, they can examine the type of language they use in evaluating themselves.

Members should complete a Self-Concept Inventory as a homework assignment in which they write down descriptive comments about their physical appearance, how they relate to others, how others see them, their performance at school or work, their mental functioning, their friends, and their romantic life. By doing this they can specifically look at the language they use in evaluating themselves, and analyze these comments. Members should be encouraged to include both positive and negative comments. The second step in examining the language is to go through the inventory, separating the comments pertaining to their strengths and weaknesses, and rewrite these comments. For strengths they should use synonyms, adjectives, and adverbs to elaborate. For weaknesses they should attempt to use nonpejorative, accurate words, specific rather than general language, and to find exceptions or corresponding strengths to their weaknesses. The third step is to write a new description including the revised strengths and weaknesses. The last step is to remember their strengths.

Suggestions are given, for example, to write them down on index cards and read them several times each day for daily affirmations, or to place reminder signs in their home or at work to cue them mentally to repeat their affirmations, or to use active integration in which each day they would select three strengths from the list and remember situations from the past that exemplify those strengths.

> Jill realized that she was very critical of herself and had been for as long as she could remember. She shared with the group a time when she was in junior high and was on the track team. She came in second in a race and was extremely disappointed that she didn't win. She identified this as minimizing.

GROUP SESSION 10

Session 10 deals with assertiveness. Assertiveness and assertive behavior are the responsible expressions of feelings and thoughts that do not violate one's own or others' rights. Assertiveness may be used to expand one's choices in a variety of situations and to develop communication with others. Assertive behavior is described as the direct and honest statement, communicated both verbally and through body language, of what one does and does not want. Members can discuss examples of passive, aggressive, and assertive thoughts, feelings, and behaviors in response to specific cues, and evaluate the consequences. The therapist should provide examples. Use the story of a boss asking them to do something. An example of a passive thought is, "I don't want him mad at me." Feelings of anxiety and fear may accompany this thought, and the individual may behave passively. The consequence may be feeling angry and frustrated. An aggressive thought in relation to this cue may be, "How dare he ask me to do that!" This may lead to feelings of frustration and anger and cause the individual to behave aggressively. The consequence may be to storm away and feel increased anger. An example of an assertive thought may be, "I do not have time to do that today, I need to tell him I will need extra time in order to get this task done." A feeling of satisfaction and relief may accompany this thought, which would lead to assertive behavior and the possible consequence of more respect from one's boss. It is important to point out that using assertive nonverbal communication is also essential in getting your assertive statement across. A nonverbal statement can consist of eye contact, for example, or body posture, voice tone, and position of hands and feet. The group may discuss examples of such communication for passive, assertive, and aggressive behavior.

The therapist may recommend that members practice assertiveness skills with another group member and then receive feedback on their verbal and nonverbal presentation. Another suggestion is to practice in front of a mirror. The more one practices, the easier it is to be assertive in real situations. Toward the end of Meeting 10 members should be asked to continue their self-monitoring and complete another Restructuring Thoughts Worksheet. They should be instructed to fill in a cue, either recent or anticipated, and then pretend to use a passive response patterned to that cue, such as passive thoughts, feelings, and behaviors. They should then complete the worksheet as if they are using an assertive response pattern, analyzing the change in thoughts, feelings, and behaviors that would come about from that assertive response pattern compared to the passive one.

> Jill completed her homework assignment of the Self-Concept Inventory. She indicated that it was very helpful, especially when identifying her own strengths. Jill pointed out that another reason this assignment was useful was because people just don't take time to evaluate their strengths, and this gave her a reason to do so. She discovered several things about herself that she had not been paying attention to. She characterized herself as a "good mother" and a "thoughtful, helpful friend to Nicole."

GROUP SESSION 11

Group Session 11 focuses on stress management and problem-solving skills. These are skills that will be helpful in day-to-day activities so that group members can learn to deal with the difficulties that typically precipitate a shopping event.

In the popular press stress is seen as the enemy, but in reality stress is a natural phenomenon and essential to life. It is how individuals respond to stressful events, and in particular what they tell themselves about a stressful event, that determines whether they experience stress in a healthy or unhealthy way. This information may be useful for group members when they begin to evaluate their attitudes about stress, how they perceive "stressors," how they *choose* to respond to (or cope with) these stressors, and how the consequences of stress affect them.

The first component of stress is the stressor or the demand. This could be of major proportions — such as moving or loss of a significant other — or of minor proportions — such as completing an assignment. Most people recognize and accept the significance of major stressors, but minimize the significance of the minor ones, although repetitive minor stressors can accumulate and take on major proportions. It is important for members to recognize their stressors. The second component is the stress response, which involves thoughts, feelings, and behaviors that are triggered by the stressor. These can be either positive or negative responses.

Information on how to manage stress should follow the discussion of stress and its components. Effective coping is managing the stressor and the stress response (the thoughts, feelings, and behaviors) in such a way that the results or consequences are positive — balanced and healthy.

Two tasks involved in managing stress — *problem solving* (dealing directly with the problem) and *stress management* (minimizing stressors and managing the stress response) — should be introduced. It's important to point out that sometimes members will need to deal with the problem first, then manage their stress response to the problem. At other times they may need to handle the stress response first and the problem later. More often than not they will do both tasks concurrently, first dealing with the problem until the stress response gets them out of balance (negative consequence), then managing the stress response until they are back in balance (positive consequence). They will then be in a position to return to the problem.

Problem solving involves identifying feelings and behaviors, defining the problem, deciding what one wants, establishing goals, generating possible solutions and evaluating each alternative, and choosing the best alternative. The best alternative should then be implemented. After implementation, the individual should verify the consequences or the actions and determine if she or he is satisfied with the results. If the answer is no, she or he can go back and reevaluate the choices and choose the second-best alternative.

Stress management involves several components. The first consists of assuming one's general well-being and developing regular, healthy habits. This includes eating three adequate, nutritionally balanced meals a day, exercising regularly (but not overdoing it), getting an adequate amount of sleep, listening to one's body and relaxing when needed, providing time for pleasant and rewarding activities in the day, and arranging some quiet time for peaceful solitude, as well as avoiding excessive use of alcohol and caffeinated beverages. One can then focus on organizing oneself by setting priorities, structuring one's time, learning to use one's time efficiently, setting realistic and practical goals, and making decisions (learning to identify alternatives and to evaluate pros and cons).

Stress management also calls for establishing friendships so that one can be emotionally involved with others, be exposed to different perspectives or ways of thinking, validate one's feelings and check out perceptions with people whose feedback they can trust and respect, have access to information and other resources, and have the opportunity to practice specific skills and receive support and encouragement. Stress management also means controlling one's environment by avoiding too many changes at one time.

Managing thoughts and feelings (or emotions) is another component of stress management. This can be done by diverting one's attention or detaching oneself by becoming mentally involved in other activities, examining one's expectation or thoughts about one's ability to cope with this situation (i.e., "Are my thoughts reasonable and accurate?"), or examining the words one uses, such as *should* and *must* that are usually associated with unrealistic expectations.

The final step in stress management is to manage behaviors and feelings (physiological responses). One may unwind or do short relaxation exercises, meditate or go for a walk, or work off the stress by exercise, gardening, or being involved in an activity. At the close of Group Session 11 the homework assignment can be for members to identify a stressor in their lives, choose a technique to cope with or reduce the stressor, and then describe the results of their experiment. They should also continue to self-monitor their shopping behavior and the use of purchasing plans for their purchasing.

> Jill found the Restructuring Thoughts Worksheet easier this time than she had several weeks before. She was able to identify a recent cue and then complete the worksheet as if responding passively and assertively. Jill realized that she responded passively to many cues, but was now trying to respond more assertively, and was practicing using an assertive response pattern.

GROUP SESSION 12

Group Session 12 provides information that will assist the members in long-term cash management. Instead of offering lists of goals from which individuals are to select the most important, as many financial planning books do, we suggest an alternative that will assist members in coming up with their own financial goals. This process has three steps. The first step is to set the scene in order to identify what one really wants. This is the key to the process. A useful organizing strategy is to have spending categories, which may include groceries, rent or mortgage, telephone, transportation or car payments, home upkeep, child support, health care/health insurance, home and car insurance, property and income taxes, recreation, relationship enhancement, debt repayment of bills, and replenishment of savings/investments.

Once members have identified what is important for them in each of the spending categories, the second step is for them to translate what is important into dollars per month, and how much of their monthly take-home pay they will need to allocate to each of the categories. This can be given as a homework assignment. In addition to the above steps, it is helpful for them to compare the new spending plan to past practices. One way for them to do this is to go through their checkbooks line by line for the preceding six months and write down how much they actually spent each month on each of the categories.

> Jill found last week's lecture and homework assignment very enlightening. She identified a major stressor in her life as her job. Since she had gotten a promotion in her office and changed supervisors, her job had become very stressful. Often after a stressful day at work she would stop at a clothing store on the way home and shop. The salespeople knew her there and were helpful and friendly when she walked into the store. She decided one way to manage this stressor was to join a gym that was close to her job. That way she would be able to stop there on the way home from a stressful day at work instead of going shopping. She could either take a sauna or exercise, or both, to assist in managing the physiological responses to that stressful situation.

GROUP SESSION 13

Group Session 13 is used to provide information regarding relapse prevention. A relapse is said to occur when a patient goes back to the full-blown syndrome and gives up on recovery. A lapse, or slip, as it is also called, is a temporary recurrence of the behavior. This session reintroduces high-risk situations and identifies hoarding behaviors. Group members need to have realistic expectations about lapses and relapse, and need to prepare for occasional setbacks, even after prolonged periods of "abstinence" from excessive buying behavior. They may be precipitated by emotional stress, inadequate attention to high-risk situations, or feelings of anger or anxiety. Several suggestions are given to help members prevent a lapse and a potential for relapse, including following purchasing plans, avoiding the use of credit cards, and practicing stress management skills regularly.

At the beginning of treatment it was suggested that members avoid high-risk situations. At this point it is recommended that they begin to incorporate such situations into their life by practicing exposure. It can be suggested that they start with the least feared situation, and plan to expose themselves at first only with help (e.g., accompany a friend to a high-risk store). The importance of structure and sufficient support should be stressed to ensure success. It is important that they assess their thoughts and feelings following this, and possibly discuss them with their friend. They should be aware that certain feelings (such as anger) or certain thoughts ("I will lose control") may make it difficult to attempt exposure to a new situation, and they may need to delay the exposure until they feel in better control.

Hoarding is buying things one does not need and then storing them, sometimes still wrapped, and not using them. Members are encouraged to evaluate the types of items they may hoard by specifically looking at the number of items, their value, and where the items are stored or hoarded. Members who engage in this type of behavior are told that it is time to "clean house" by getting rid of the items. Several suggestions are offered. They can simply throw them out. If the items are valuable, they can be given to a worthy charity for a possible tax deduction. They can take the items back to the store, or they can give them away.

> Jill decided, from reading the material for this session, that she did not engage in hoarding the way it was described, since she tended to wear the clothes she would buy. She did recognize that she kept an entire closet full of clothes she no longer wore, even though they were not worn out. This was some-

thing that upset her husband, who felt the space could be better utilized. She decided to clean house, as suggested, by packing up the items she no longer wore and donating them to a local charity. She thought her husband would be happy with this decision because of the deduction they could take on their income taxes and the extra closet space that would be opened up.

GROUP SESSION 14

Group Session 14 continues a focus on relapse prevention, specifically, long-term planning for lapse and relapse. Group members should be encouraged to discuss scenarios of a possible relapse, and describe what they would do in each scenario to prevent a relapse. They may also write out a detailed plan (step by step) they can carry out if relapse occurs.

To avoid relapse members must continue to practice the skills they have learned in the group — problem-solving techniques, stress management skills, alternative behaviors, challenging maladaptive thoughts, improving self-esteem, and rewarding oneself for accomplished goals. They will need to maintain a support network of family and friends or support groups. They will also need to continue to develop a healthy, positive, and balanced lifestyle.

The important thing for participants to remember is to have realistic expectations and goals that are not set too high. They can expect and prepare for slips, and if slips occur they can learn from them.

Jill and the other group members were nervous about the end of the group meetings, and of the possibility of relapse. Jill exchanged phone numbers with some of the members and they agreed to be part of each other's support networks. As the group broke up Jill said that she had done a "nice job" in the program, and how helpful it had been in terms of helping her get her buying on the right track. She also decided one goal she would set for herself in the next few months was to read a book on assertiveness that the therapist had recommended. Jill had been abstinent from excessive buying for the prior four weeks, but realized she still needed to prepare for and be realistic about possible setbacks.

CONCLUSION

This treatment manual was developed to address a perceived need for finding ways to treat compulsive buying since little empirical work has been done concerning this behavior. Most of the treatment concepts were taken directly from group therapy models used for individuals with other types of compulsive or impulsive behavior, such as women with bulimia nervosa or binge eating disorder (Fairburn et al. 1993, Mitchell et al. 1993). Thus far, a group using this manual has been conducted only once, and included eight individuals. All were females, ranging in age from early thirties to late fifties. They were recruited through an advertisement in the newspaper. Systematic data on frequency of target buying behaviors pre- and posttreatment were obtained. These data, along with data from subsequent groups, will be published in a later report. The overall impression, however, was that most of these individuals experienced substantial improvement in the frequency of problematic buying behavior.

Several issues emerged during the group sessions that will need to be addressed in later programs:

1. It became apparent early on that many of these individuals did not have a clear sense of what constituted problem buying behaviors and what was normal buying behavior for them. These behaviors seemed to exist on a continuum. Therapists working with these individuals would be well served to delineate these different modes of buying carefully for each patient early in treatment.

2. The plan for each individual to have a shopping partner was not fully realized in the group, and several members never established such a relationship. If this is a strategy to be employed in the future, a separate session or sessions early in treatment to include the individuals in the group and their shopping partners are recommended.

3. A number of individuals in the group had other problems; not uncommon were problems in interpersonal relationships, mood problems, or problems at their place of work. Therapists conducting such a group need to remember that for the group to remain time limited and focused, they must be willing to some extent to suppress exploration and discussion of these other problem areas, and instead keep the individual participants focused on the problem buying. It can be suggested that the individuals may need additional therapy during or following their involvement in the group to deal with these other issues. The amount of material that can be covered in a limited number of sessions is fairly small, and therapists who allow individual group members to devote much time to other issues in the group sessions will find they will be unable to complete the material.

4. There was considerable financial heterogeneity within the group, ranging from individuals who were barely scraping by on welfare to two group members who were clearly quite well off, and the differences in the problem buying between these socioeconomic extremes were rather striking. For example, one woman in the group would impulsively buy expensive jewelry, clothes, and furniture, while another woman was having financial difficulties from buying inexpensive trinkets. One might consider, given an adequate number of potential group members, stratifying on socioeconomic variables and conducting separate groups for those with greater financial constraints and those with more wealth.

Overall, this was an interesting, enlightening population to work with and the experience in the group was encouraging enough to suggest that further work should be done using this group model with this population.

REFERENCES

Fairburn, C. B., Marcus, M. D., and Wilson, G. T. (1993). Cognitive behavior therapy for binge eating and bulimia nervosa: a comprehensive treatment manual. In *Binge Eating: Nature, Assessment, and Treatment*, ed. C. G. Fairburn and G. T. Wilson, pp. 361–404. New York: Guilford.

Mitchell, J. E., Pyle, R. L., Pomeroy, C., et al. (1993). Cognitive-behavioral group psychotherapy of bulimia nervosa: importance of logistical variables. *International Journal of Eating Disorders* 14:277–287.

17

Psychoeducational Group Therapy for Money Disorders

Leonard Brazer

It is a bit ironic to be writing a chapter in a book about treating "money disorders" (Boundy 1993) when at present the *Diagnostic and Statistical Manual of Mental Disorders (DSM-IV)* (APA 1994) doesn't recognize their existence. This sort of phenomenon is not new to the mental health/addiction professions. For many years the treatment of alcoholism was conveniently concealed under the guise of depression until insurance reimbursement became available. While this information does little more than date me, I hope it serves as a reminder of a mistake that does not need to be repeated.

TREATMENT OVERVIEW

I have been leading outpatient treatment groups for people with money disorders for the last nine years. During that time I have treated over 500 patients. Approximately seven out of ten have been female. Most are compulsive shoppers, spenders, or debtors, although there have been a fair number of people who were codependent with money (i.e., someone who either buys compulsively for others or enables a compulsive buyer) and to a lesser degree compulsive hoarders. Treatment begins with a comprehensive evaluation that includes:

- A detailed money history
- A psychosocial assessment
- A mental status exam
- A compulsive buying scale

After the evaluation is completed and discussed with each patient, he or she is given an overview of the structure and goals of the program.

The six-week outpatient program meets once a week for three hours. The first ninety minutes of treatment is psychoeducational in nature, and consists of a didactic lecture that provides information and teaches concrete skills necessary for recovery.

The six lectures are entitled:

- *Living Recovery: Debtors Anonymous and the Twelve Steps*
- *Money Disorders: The Disease Concept*
- *Debt Repayment: How to Deal with Creditors*
- *Resentment, Anger, and Depression: Relapse Prevention — The Warning Signs*
- *Who Am I? Increasing Self-Esteem*
- *Spending Plans: The Road to Solvency*

Each lecture is tied to a general set of goals for recovery and solvency. The lectures also teach concrete skills necessary for recovery.

The next ninety minutes are spent in a more traditional group psychotherapy session. An attempt is made to have the group process consistent with the topic of that evening's psychoeducational lecture. Often someone in the group is having some kind of a crisis related to his or her money disorder. In these circumstances I try to set aside some time before the group therapy portion ends for the person with the crisis to talk about it and get help from the group.

In addition to the psychoeducational lectures and group therapy sessions, I occasionally offer individual, marital, or family counseling based on the specific needs of the identified client. Any new client can begin the program at any point.

A number of clients have asked to continue to come to group therapy after the initial six–week period has been completed. An aftercare group is in place for those who wish to continue in treatment.

PSYCHOEDUCATIONAL LECTURE SERIES

I: Living Recovery: Debtors Anonymous (D.A.) and the Twelve Steps

Goals:

To attend D.A. meetings on a regular basis
To become involved in D.A. and to establish a supportive social
    network (find a sponsor and numerous contacts)
To join a home group
To understand and work the steps of D.A.

At the core of long-term, ongoing, comfortable recovery is self-help. D.A. does for people with money disorders what A.A. does for alcoholics. While the philosophy, steps (see Appendix I), and spiritual journeys of the two twelve-step programs are similar, D.A. also has a number of notable differences from A.A. (e.g., pressure relief meetings, spending plans, etc.). Most of this information is available in a D.A. newcomers' package. For more information about D.A. see Levine and Kellen, Chapter 18, this volume.

It is my belief that the integration of self-help and professional help produces a synergistic effect, which is unobtainable when the two are used in a mutually exclusive fashion. An important task of treatment is to get someone to D.A. in the first place. For some clients this is relatively easy. They know of self-help through the treatment and recovery of other addictions they may have, and are readily agreeable. Approximately 35 percent of our population is cross or polyaddicted. Some anecdotes from patients suggest that they find D.A. to be like "graduate school," a metaphor born of the extensive task of recording flexible spending (which we will discuss later).

For others D.A. represents the first attempt at self-help. As with other addictions, our clients' imaginations regarding self-help are quite vivid. It is not uncommon for clients to feel loathing initially, or to feel as though they are at a revival meeting. However perceived, I try to validate the individual's thought process and then make them return. *Therapy*, from the Greek, means comrades engaged in a mutual struggle. It couldn't have been more aptly named for some ever-resistant patients who are convinced that D.A. is not for them.

The lecture entitled "Living Recovery: Debtors Anonymous and the Twelve Steps" helps facilitate attendance at D.A. During this lecture I provide information that is historical, outlining the inception of self-help established by Bill W. and Dr. Bob. I trace the development of A.A., N.A. (Narcotics Anonymous), and G.A. (Gamblers Anonymous), noting that it was not until 1971 that the first D.A meeting was held.

I present the twelve steps of self-help and demonstrate how debt replaces the concept and theme of alcohol in the original steps. I also find it helpful to explain the spiritual aspects in the program, and to point out that these are spiritual and not religious issues in recovery. I speak about powerlessness, unmanageability, and the vagueness about money that may be the common denominator to both. It is important to stress that D.A. needs to become integrated into one's lifestyle but not become the be-all and end-all of living. With advanced understanding some of the anxiety and resistance is minimized.

I encourage compulsive shoppers and spenders to attend D.A., and let them know that D.A. is not just for people who have problems with debt. While these people may not have issues with debt, their shopping and spending have created problems. D.A. can help them gain clarity about their spending through accurate reporting, and provide the support they need to deal with inappropriate spending. Despite my most convincing arguments and techniques, sometimes there is still resistance to attending D.A. When all else has failed, I make treatment contingent on attending D.A. meetings, insisting that all group members begin to attend meetings by the third session.

I also identify characteristics of a healthy sponsor (e.g., consistency between words and actions) and the difference between a sponsor and contacts (a personal guide versus someone to speak with). Having said all this, the work is then up to each client. Going and doing, one day at a time, are the watchwords.

I use a handout to help clients see that each step is tied to the development of a healthy characteristic regarding money and recovery (see Appendix II).

II: Money Disorders: The Disease Concept

Goals:

For the client to understand the disease concept of addiction
To reduce the client's shame and guilt
To lessen the client's denial
For the client to understand the need for total abstinence from debt

This lecture bombards the group with information that for the most part they were previously unaware of. Most feel a sense of empowerment and become motivated to deal with the issues of recovery that lie before them. I explain the disease concept of addiction and discuss the work of Jacobs (1989). He states that addiction is a disease that includes a dependent state, acquired over a period of time by a predisposed person in an attempt to cope with or alleviate a chronic stressful situation.

During the course of the lecture there is debate over whether a money disorder is an addiction just as there is debate over whether addictions are diseases. Until someone comes up with a definitive answer to either or both questions, I err on the side that says that money disorders are addictions that are best explained by understanding the disease concept.

To help achieve these goals I use a handout (see Appendix II) that lists and describes the characteristics of a disease and of a dependent state. Dependent states can be physically or psychologically induced.

People who tend to become addicted have an abnormal physiological resting state that seems to be determined by genetics and relates to arousal level. Most people with money disorders have a low arousal level; they are easily bored and need a great deal of stimulation to be engaged in life. Thus shopping or spending, whether in a mall, supermarket, on TV, the Internet, at a garage sale, or in catalogues, provides relief from the boredom they feel when in their typical resting state.

An atypical psychological experience relates to psychosocial development. A dramatic or traumatic event or series of events that has lowered an individual's self-esteem is an atypical psychological experience. For many with money disorders, money and self-esteem were equated. The stimulation of shopping or spending alleviates the chronic stress or dysphoria felt by many people who have this combination of an abnormal physiological resting state and atypical psychological experience.

If it happens that the shopping or spending makes someone forget about his or her problems (disassociation), or makes him or her feel that he or she is special (altered state of identity), this will encourage the repetition of obsessional thoughts, leading to urges and more compulsive behavior. Tolerance will increase, creating progression of the disease and a need to continue to shop or spend in spite of knowing how self-destructive it is.

In presenting and reviewing this information, I find that most clients are willing to accept that there is something wrong with the way they are spending or have spent their money. Identifying that they have a treatable disease and are perhaps psychologically dependent on what they do sounds reasonable to them.

It is necessary to explain that people with addictions are initially in a state of denial about their disease. This denial prevents identification and recovery. Unlike alcoholism, drug addiction, or even eating disorders — which all have recognizable symptoms — but similar to pathological gambling, the course of the illness often remains invisible to others for a long period of time. As such, it seems the walls of denial become more and more difficult to permeate and the rationalizations for the behavior more convincing. In fact, if one's objects of choice are clothing, the worse the addiction is getting, the more likely it is that there will be secondary reinforcement of the spending behavior in the form of praise and compliments from other people.

In an effort to change the mind-set that elicits shame and guilt, both of which are barriers to recovery, I offer the following explanation: "You didn't ask for the biopsychological predisposing factors that in effect caused your dependent state. By the time you became aware of your money disorder, you were probably out of control. Recovering is a different story. Like diabetics who have no control over what will happen to them when they ingest sugar, and must take full responsibility for not ingesting it, you too need to take responsibility for this dependent state that came about through no fault of your own."

To help clients understand this need for total abstinence from nonsecured spending, I tell them that nonsecured spending seems to precipitate the loss of control associated with buying things you wouldn't have if you had to use cash. It also precipitates binge spending, and that's why debt consolidation, bankruptcy, and shifting balances from a credit card with a high interest rate to one with a lower rate make the problem progressively worse, not better. It only creates room for new debt."

To summarize, presenting the group with information regarding addiction and the disease concept helps them understand that they are not responsible for their predisposing factors, but that they are responsible for their behavior, especially in recovery. This will hopefully lessen some of the shame and guilt, empowering the individual to face the patterns of denial that he or she employed to rationalize, justify, or minimize the progression of the addiction. Having developed a new cognitive set from this data, the client may better understand the need to remain abstinent from all nonsecured spending, given the nature of the illness.

III: Debt Repayment: How to Deal with Creditors

Goals:

To reduce clients' anxieties in dealing with creditors or collection agencies

To provide information regarding clients' rights and responsibilities outlined in the Unfair Debt Collection Act

To help clients understand how creditors can collect

Calls from creditors or collection agencies usually evoke shame or guilt. They also create high levels of anxiety for people with money disorders, and they become a part of their daily living. With the exception of one client who had a knack for doing wonderful impersonations, which he used on the phone to avoid dealing with creditors for a long time, most are overwhelmed by this process. Their responses to creditors run the gamut from unrealistic compliance to angry defiance; neither works particularly well. The inevitable consequences prevail. However, there are laws protecting consumers and there are things one can do to deal effectively with creditors or collection agencies. I explain that they have rights and responsibilities when dealing with creditors or collection agencies, which are outlined in the Unfair Debt Collection Act, and we discuss these in detail.

I suggest that clients make the first move in contacting the creditor, especially before the debt is turned over to a collection agency. This increases the likelihood of cooperation from the creditor. Being honest and humble with a realistic explanation and plan for repayment can alleviate a lot of hassle before it starts.

I also tell the client that his or her family is the number one priority and must not be deprived of its needs so that debt can be repaid. It is then a good idea to prioritize and decide which debts are most important, and I suggest that if there are debts to the IRS it is a good idea to pay them first.

I strongly suggest that no matter what overtures a creditor or collection agency might make, clients should not turn an unsecured debt into a secured one (e.g., a second mortgage to pay off credit cards), because it can give them more room to start to debt again.

Given this information, it is important to convey that clients are responsible for their debts. Some will interpret the aforementioned information as an affirmation that they have been victimized and therefore not responsible for making restitution or dealing with their creditors.

I tell clients emphatically that a creditor *can* take them to court for the debt they were unable to pay, that they are *not* immune from legal proceedings, and that if a creditor takes legal action against them, the creditor will invariably win. I make sure that clients realize that (1) a creditor is able to apply attachments to bank accounts (savings, checking, and certificates of deposit), income (salary and wages), real estate, and vehicles, and (2) a creditor who receives a judgment can garnish up to 10 percent of their wages.

Finally, I tell clients that a judgment is worth only as much as the paper it is written on if it cannot be converted into money. This again is not said to enable. If a collection agency is being very unreasonable or if clients' ability to recover is jeopardized, there are things they can do to "judgment-proof" themselves. I suggest to clients that they check with a competent attorney to do this.

IV: Resentment, Anger, and Depression: Relapse Prevention Warning Signs

Goals:

To identify a generic cycle of relapse
To identify their individual "build up to spending syndrome (catch their BUS)

The goal of all addiction treatment is to prevent relapse. The fourth lecture is presented in hopes of minimizing that likelihood by helping group members learn about the "build up to spending" syndrome. This term refers to those behaviors that are likely to trigger a relapse. It is important to convey that relapse, involving a single debt or a binge, is as serious to the individual with a money disorder as a drink is to a recovering alcoholic. Ultimately, "slips" will lead one right back to the same chaos that the client experienced before stopping compulsive shopping.

I believe that frustration triggers the relapse cycle. Irrational thoughts or intense feelings lead to poor planning, the wish for immediate gratification, or the setting of unrealistic goals, all of which lead to frustration. Frustration typically leads to anger, but not before the individual attempts, in an anxious or impulsive way, to remove the obstacle that's in the way of fulfilling a goal or meeting a need. Often this fails, and one begins to feel angry, annoyed, or agitated. If at this point in the cycle an individual suppresses the anger, choosing not to address it directly, it typically turns into some degree of depression.

These feelings of frustration, anger, and/or depression continue to grow in strength if no solution is found. When one begins to feel the depression, the world becomes narrower, and thoughts about shopping and spending begin to invade the psyche. The options of dealing with the urge to shop or spend become more limited. It is here that the obsession urge-compulsion cycle is strengthened. The relapse cycle looks like this: frustration leads to anxiety, which leads to anger, which leads to depression, resentment, feelings of inadequacy, deprivation, shame, guilt, or self-pity. Self-pity seems to be where compulsive spenders "earn" the right to relapse, leading to their escape of choice. This cycle can become an automatic subconscious response. "I didn't get what I wanted, so I relapsed" may occur in the blink of an eye.

Breaking the cycle means examining the initial frustration. I emphasize that one must continuously reevaluate immediate goals and needs and determine the difference between "wants and needs." Becoming aware of oneself and establishing an optimal range of stimulation can help to determine healthy limits (i.e., set achievable goals and reduce the likelihood of relapse).

At this point I explain to the group, "Thoughts and feelings combine to produce behaviors, and both thoughts and feelings are necessary for behavior. When feelings are in control of thoughts, we will invariably begin to set ourselves up for relapse. I believe there is a normal range of feeling. I'm not sure I can define it, but I'll demonstrate it with this example. If someone crashed into my new car, I'd be angry. That's normal. If my anger leads me to pick up my brand new tire iron to rearrange the person's anatomical structure, then that level of feeling is outside the range of normal, acceptable, or appropriate behavior." When shoppers become desirous of a purse or a blouse, the strength of their feelings about it may distort whether it is a need or a want and it will typically make them think they need to have it. Thus the thought that it might be nice to have it, but that it is not necessary, becomes a dim and distant memory. As their feelings exceed the "normal" range, they behave under the influence of those feelings, as if psychologically intoxicated.

The easiest way to begin to control behavior is by dealing more rationally or realistically with thoughts. Albert Ellis (Ellis and Harper 1975) offer keen insights regarding the use of rational thinking to correct unrealistic expectations of self and others and I recommend his *A New Guide to Rational Living*. So much of relapse prevention comes down to clear thoughts, coherent plans, and establishing realistic goals, all of which minimize urges. The fewer the number of urges one can experience, the greater the likelihood there is of preventing relapse. I can't imagine people getting well or staying well for long when they experience urges continuously.

V: Who Am I? Improving Self-Esteem

Goal:

To help improve self-esteem by establishing a more realistic self-image

To increase adult ego state functioning
To identify dysfunctional messages about money

Most, if not all, people with money disorders tend to be unrealistically negative about themselves. Shopping and spending provide indulgences that serve to anesthetize these feelings. In fact, purchases can temporarily boost self-esteem through compliments from other people. The euphoria is short-lived, and the dissonance between outside messages and the messages one has about oneself leads to confusion.

This lecture employs concepts from transactional analysis (T.A.) to help the patient alleviate this confusion.

I describe the four life positions (Berne 1964).

1. *I'm OK, You're OK*
2. *I'm Not OK, You're OK*
3. *I'm OK, You're Not OK*
4. *I'm Not OK, You're Not OK*

I'm OK, You're OK represents a healthy life position. People with this life position are accepting, genuine, and caring. They have healthy attitudes toward money and no illusions or associations that money can buy love, self-esteem, or belonging. Money does not elevate their status in any way.

The other three life positions are all unhealthy. *I'm Not OK, You're OK* is a victim's position. This person has developed unhealthy attitudes regarding money and in particular has difficulties with the mechanics of money. His or her purchases are typically self indulgent; limitless collections of objects of choice are accumulated in an attempt to remove bad feelings about him- or herself. "I can't keep track of my expenses; I was never good at math; no one ever taught me how to balance a checkbook" — these are kinds of statements you'd hear from these people. People who take this life position often assume little to no responsibility for their spending or debt and blame it on feelings of helplessness and worthlessness.

The individuals who take the life position of *I'm OK, You're Not*

OK are the rescuers of the world. They have learned to use money to take care of other people. Sometimes their purchases are attempts to buy others or control relationships.

Finally, there are those who take the position *I'm Not OK, You're Not OK*. These people are the persecutors in the T.A. framework. These people tend to be fearful of letting go of money and become motivated to hoard it. They are the hardest to treat because they are negative and distrustful of themselves as well as others.

People in these three unhealthy life positions must learn that there is a better psychological place to be. Identifying their life position and linking it to certain ego states aids in that learning process. In the healthy life position (*I'm OK, You're OK*) the adult ego state is functioning. Rational and logical thought processes, awareness of one's environment, assuming responsibility for oneself, good problem-solving skills, and assertiveness best describe the adult ego state's functioning. There are no pretensions about money. The adult ego state makes rational discriminations between spending on one's needs and wants.

Our unhealthy beliefs about money are derived from the child and parent ego states. There are two types of parent ego states and two types of child ego states. Someone in a nurturing parent ego state tends to be intimate, protective, and caring; someone in the critical parent ego state tends to be rigid, perfectionistic, sarcastic, and negative. Someone in the spontaneous or free child ego state feels accepted and acceptable, and someone in the adaptive child ego state feels that he or she has to perform. The natural parent ego state and the spontaneous child ego state tend to occur in the same person. It is unlikely that this person will have a money disorder. The critical parent ego state and the adaptive child ego state also tend to occur in the same person. This person is likely to have a money disorder.

The healthy adult ego state usually mediates between the demands of the child ego state and the restrictions of the parent ego states. When the adaptive child is needy, money and possessions take the place of the healthy nurturing that was lacking. Underdeveloped and immature, it becomes demanding of itself and others. The ensuing negative self-image, born out of rigid, demanding, and otherwise unobtainable goals, leads to the pursuit of external sources of self-esteem.

When someone in a critical parent ego state is feeling guilty, he or she will try to buy things for others to alleviate that guilt. Critical parents can unwittingly instill the notion of "money equals love or success" by using money to reward good grades or sports achievements. These internalized messages set the groundwork for future money dysfunction.

I leave the group with the thought that the only antidote for escaping dysfunction with money is the development of a healthy adult ego state. Rational and logical thoughts lead to good money mechanics and "clarity." Awareness helps one discriminate between the child's wants and needs. Assertiveness can set limits on these. Good problem-solving skills can lead one to constructive outlets other than strategies that involve purchasing. Being responsible means that "no one else can make me repeat the shopping or spending unless I want to."

VI: Spending Plans: The Road to Solvency

Goals:

To establish clarity with money
To develop a comprehensive spending plan

When I first started working with people who had money disorders, I was unaware of what I was about to experience. Making a spending plan and following it is, in and of itself, not terribly difficult. The intervening emotional blocks, however, make this task near impossible for some. I should also say here that Mundis (1988) provided me with an incredible amount of helpful information. I recommend his book to all who enter our program. After reading Mundis, I became a human guinea pig for the program by making my first comprehensive spending plan. It was a sound decision, both personally and professionally. For anyone who hopes to be successful in understanding compulsive shoppers, the insight you will receive from recording expenditures and integrating them into a spending plan will prove invaluable.

The spending plan lecture provides an overview of the mechanics that clients need in order to begin their journey toward solvency. I try to simplify the process as much as possible, and I provide printed recording sheets for clients to use.

The lecture begins with an explanation of what debt is and what it is not. Debt is any form of nonsecured payment, where an individual buys without using either cash, a "good check," or collateral in the purchase (e.g., house, car). The question of debit card use often comes up. While I believe that in principle this is no different than the use of a check, for some it is too familiar to be safe. The actual use of a plastic debit card early on can serve to trigger anxiety for the recovering individual. Obviously, in these cases I recommend abstinence.

I also try to explain the difference between reasonable, problematic, and compulsive debt. *Reasonable debt* means being free of any problem with debt. It is the equivalent of social drinking or recreational gambling. Most people with a debt problem can recognize it as such, correct the situation that created the debt, or obtain some insight that makes them stop. However, there are those who are compulsive with debt, refuse to recognize the compulsion, and continue to accumulate debt in spite of negative consequences. The compulsion becomes a repetitive set of behaviors that are harmful to the individual (Mundis 1988).

I explain that there are three categories of expenses that most, if not all, people have: fixed expenses, indebtedness, and flexible expenses. *Fixed expenses* are those that occur with regularity and ostensibly cost the same amount each month. The simplest example of a fixed expense is a rent or mortgage payment. Fixed expenses include, but are not limited to, utility bills, insurance payments, and child support.

To create a spending plan, the first task for the compulsive spender is to identify what these fixed expenses are and how much they cost per month, and then to record all of that information. Of all three categories of expenses these seem to be the easiest to identify and record because, to the money disordered individual, they represent the most "legitimate" expenses. We also discuss how to record fixed expenses that vary month to month, such as the telephone bill.

The next category of expenses I address are those that involve indebtedness. Indebtedness is made up of two subcategories: loans (unsecured) and credit card debt. There are various types of loans. In recording these, I ask clients to include the name of the creditor, the total amount of the loan, when it will be paid off, and what the monthly payment is. Credit card debt, obviously, is what is owed to credit card companies. I ask clients to list all their credit cards (store cards, gas cards, phone cards, any other credit cards), their most recent balance, the finance charge per month, and the minimum payment per month, and to leave a blank column for an "actual" payment. Compulsive debtors have much resistance to this section. Their mechanics are shrouded in many layers of denial. Because this part of a spending plan can be overwhelming, I often schedule individual counseling sessions to accomplish this task.

The final category in our spending plan is flexible expenses, which consist of anything outside the categories of fixed expenses or indebtedness. Flexible expenses typically vary from month to month and may occur in some months and not in others. They include eating out, entertainment, personal hygiene, gifts, vacations, medications, car expenses, and therapy, among many others.

One of the recording sheets provided has a column for categories of flexible expenses. I suggest that clients record the cost of items as quickly as possible after a purchase is made. Some save receipts and record them daily.

When clients have accumulated all of these numbers, the total of their fixed and flexible expenses is added to the minimum payments per month in their indebtedness column. The sum is subtracted from net income per month. If there is a positive number, they have a surplus. If a negative number remains, they have a deficit. While none of my clients has ever started out with a surplus, I do believe that someone can have a surplus and still have a money disorder.

It is important to stress that it is the individual in treatment who must do this work. When the person is married or cohabitating, the spouse or significant other may in many cases sabotage the client's efforts. In this situation a family or marital session can be helpful. I also explain that my ideal for a family (marriage) is three checkbooks, three savings accounts, and three mechanisms for investment — one for each spouse and one for the couple. I suggest that clients contribute to the family expenses based on their percentage of the family's net income. I also make it clear that they need to be responsible for dealing with their own debt repayment. Clients can then allocate the rest of their money to their personal expenses, savings, or investments. Complex as it seems, it reduces resentment and resistance and increases each member's financial independence.

I again emphasize the need for abstinence from nonsecured spending. It is the only way a spending plan will work. When deficits exist, some hard decisions are involved. My belief is that fixed expenses that are necessities come first. By examining their indebtedness and their flexible expenses, clients may be able to reduce these payments enough to cover their bills without having to feel severely deprived. I suggest initially that rather than eliminating expenses, they try to make cuts in flexible expenses across the board. All this recording, computing, and thinking is a tedious task. I try to be empathic and emphasize that achieving clarity will be enormously empowering.

Much of the work is based on individual spending patterns. A description of all the possibilities is an enormous task and beyond the scope of this text. Again, I suggest referencing Mundis (1998). In addition, Karen McCall's financial recovery work, (Chapter 19, this volume) provides another extremely comprehensive look at spending plans.

GROUP THERAPY

As mentioned earlier, a ninety-minute group therapy session takes place after each psychoeducational lecture. The major goal of the

six ninety-minute therapy groups is to help clients establish abstinence from debt and to learn how to lead a debtfree, balanced
lifestyle. Six ninety-minute group therapy sessions dealing with
what are often long-standing patterns of shopping, spending, or
debt are hardly sufficient to accomplish the aforementioned goals.
It is a start, however, and as long as one begins to scratch the
surface and some degree of hope in the clients is attained, the
efforts are not in vain. Each group session is an attempt to provide
corrective emotional experiences consistent with the psychoeducational material previously presented. I try to employ an action-
oriented technique to achieve the goal for that evening's group. If
time remains following the action-oriented technique, it can be
used for troubleshooting about specific crises that have occurred
during the day or the week.

GROUP FOLLOWING "LIVING RECOVERY" LECTURE

In the meeting following the "Living Recovery" lecture, my goal is
to have the group identify examples of powerlessness and unmanageability that were created by their shopping, spending, or debt. I
want the participants to begin to feel or experience that what they
were doing was typical of others with the same problem, but not
normal. I distribute a handout that has clients list examples of
powerlessness and unmanageability in a variety of categories,
including dangerous and destructive behavior; preoccupation with
shopping, spending, and debt; social life; spiritual life; business
and work life; financial life; family life; and physical condition. I
ask all participants to review what they've written. This exercise
helps them deal with the first step of D.A.

After a relatively short review, this material can be used in a
number of therapeutic ways. Each group member can share one
example from each category listed. Group members can pair off
and discuss their examples. It is important to have a process with
the group so that after each pair speaks, you can ask a group
member which item was the most shameful, or guilt producing,
or embarrassing and ask the other members if they can identify

a similar situation. I then ask a person who identified with the first speaker's example to share his or her most shameful, guilt-producing, or embarrassing item.

The exercise is simple and powerful, and often moves group members from their cognitive state to a much more visceral level. It is a good exercise for group cohesion as well as for identification.

GROUP FOLLOWING THE "DISEASE CONCEPT" LECTURE

Following the "Disease Concept" lecture, I introduce the group to the "Get Got Game." I saw this demonstrated about fifteen years ago by a group of peer counselors who were working with adolescent alcohol and chemically dependent individuals and was floored by its effectiveness. I have used it in many incarnations thereafter, with many different populations.

To begin, place all the chairs for the group in a large circle. Then remove one chair and ask the person without the chair to stand in the middle of the group. The person in the middle is "gotten." The rules of the game are simple. "Gotten" asks the group a question. Group members who identify with the question must leave their seats and find one that has been vacated but is not immediately to either side of the one they just vacated. If only one person vacates a seat, "gotten" takes it and the other person has been "gotten."

I demonstrate the first couple of questions prompting "gotten" (i.e., I ask the group if any of them have ever purchased something with a credit card that they wouldn't have purchased if they had to pay cash for it). I then have the members who identify get up, move, find an appropriate seat and prompt the next "got" (i.e., "Have you ever hidden credit card bills from another person?"). If no one identifies, "got" has to ask another question of the group. After a couple of successful tries, I tell the group it's time to play at full speed. I tell them to have their question ready if they become "got," to ask it quickly, and I tell the other group members to change seats quickly. Invariably, the game feeds on its own momentum and becomes rowdy at times. As long as no one gets hurt,

I'll continue the game for about ten minutes or until exhaustion, whichever comes first.

There is much to process and deal with subsequent to this rather benign game. The first level involves asking the group what happened. They usually talk about the laughing and giggling. They also usually identify that they are feeling more excited or "pumped up" than they were before the game started. I explain that this is because of the flow of adrenaline and the endorphins that have been released. In this instance they accommodated their atypical physiological resting state by creating "action" that was not harmful to them. In the course of their disease they attempt to achieve this state through harmful shopping and spending. I also ask if during the game anybody was actually focused on the consequences of his or her problems. Invariably no one was, the message being that in a state of activity and involvement it is nearly impossible to be thinking about one's problems. It is important to incorporate healthy "activity" into recovery. Healthy actions can be physical activity, community service, and going to meetings (and interacting rather than sitting passively in the last row near the door), among many others.

We also process the identifications with the questions that were asked. First and foremost, I explain that they just painlessly continued the process of lessening their collective and individual levels of denial. Typically the kinds of questions asked include: "Has anyone ever had an urge to go shopping after just getting paid?" "Does anyone shop more now than previously?" "Did anyone ever neglect paying a bill in order to have more money to shop with?" These reflect the characteristics of a dependent state (e.g., obsessions, compulsions, urges, tolerance, withdrawal, progression, negative consequences). As the dust begins to settle, I try to have all the participants talk a bit more about what they just identified with.

GROUP FOLLOWING "DEBT REPAYMENT" LECTURE

The "Debt Repayment" group therapy session combines work on assertiveness with role-playing. The composition of the particular group may dictate which area needs to be emphasized. I begin with some simple warm-up exercises for the group. In one exercise two group members engage in a conversation, but they can only use one of two words to communicate: "yes" or "no." Each member pretends to be convincing his or her partner of something. The other group members are asked to observe and stay aware of what they are feeling during this process. Allowing two to three minutes for this interaction is sufficient. According to the size of the group this can be repeated with other members who can use the same two words or others such as "good" and "bad," "true" and "false," "me" and "you."

We then process what went on. We talk about inflection, tone, nonverbal behavior, and how each dealt with the frustration that arose, each trying to convince the other that his or her partner should say the opposite. I explain that assertive responses involve eye contact with the person they are speaking with. In addition, speaking in a moderate tone of voice rather than screaming or whispering is important in order to convey an assertive message. I then introduce the concept of speaking from the first person and we practice "I" messages through role-play. Group members observe each other and provide feedback about the efforts of the other group members who are doing the role-play.

We then create various situations in which participants have to convey the strength of their convictions, saying "yes" when they mean "yes," or "no" when they mean "no." Learning this skill is vital to their recovery. Scenarios we have developed include saying no to a salesperson or to a friend whom they had previously shopped with. We have role-played scenes in which participants take a phone call from a persistent or obnoxious creditor, incorporating what they need to ask of the creditor and how to respond to the resistance they may encounter.

I explain that I believe everyone has the capacity for assertive verbalizations and behavior. Like any other learned behavior, one must practice to become proficient. I also try to incorporate these fundamentals in all subsequent groups.

This group is typically quite engrossing, and many times the group forsakes the "crisis of the week" to continue to deal with the here-and-now experience.

GROUP FOLLOWING "RESENTMENT, ANGER, AND DEPRESSION" LECTURE

Following the "Resentment, Anger, and Depression" psychoeducational lecture, the group therapy session focuses on cognitive change that can prevent relapse. As outlined previously, frustration often sets up the relapse cycle. I explain to the group that we are going to be working on correcting two major sources of frustration. One source emanates from our irrational thoughts; the other is unrealistic goal setting — goals that are either too easy or too hard to achieve. Both sources can lead clients through the relapse cycle and ultimately to repeat self-defeating patterns of behavior (e.g., charging items with insufficient funds, or not recording expenses).

I begin by asking group members to identify unrealistic messages they have heard about money or their relationship with money (e.g., money doesn't grow on trees, you'll end up in the poor house, money can buy you happiness, marry for money, etc.). These messages are typically identified by the group as unrealistic.

After this we move on to discuss the irrational thinking that leads to unrealistic goals and self-defeating behavior, which results in money dysfunction. For example, "If I'm out for dinner with others I might feel it necessary to pick up the check." This usually brings up issues related to a lack of love and attention, and to feelings of not belonging. Group members will often share stories about how they were given gifts instead of love, and money as rewards for achieving either in sports or in school.

I challenge the irrational thought that people will like them if they pick up the tab or buy someone something expensive by asking them to think about the most meaningful gift or present they ever received. Often clients think about hand-made gifts, or cards they received from a child. In many cases someone's child made a plaster of paris hand or a ceramic dish or a card that says,

"I love you." "How much did it cost?" I inquire. "Did you only love him or her for $1.50's worth?" By now there tend to be some rumblings of disagreement, but the message becomes clearer. Money and love are not equated. I try then to get back to the restaurant and the bill. "Will others really like you if you pay for them?"

Another irrational thought that is good to mull over with the groups is: "If someone buys me a present, I have to buy him one of equal or greater value." This leads to an unrealistic goal that often involves nonsecured spending to achieve. Again I challenge and confront the thought. Exaggeration can drive the point home. For example, "Let me see if I understand this. If someone bought me a car, then I'd have to buy her a house?" Group members usually agree that this is crazy thinking. Reduce the stakes and use more likely examples. Everyone in the group will have irrational thoughts that they can challenge by doing this exercise.

GROUP FOLLOWING "WHO AM I?" LECTURE

Following the "Who Am I?" psychoeducational lecture, the group therapy session attempts to answer that question. This group begins with a simple projective exercise. I have each member list five people, using initials, they are very fond of or to whom they are attracted. I then have them list one adjective to describe the characteristic that best initiates the attraction. We repeat this by identifying five people they are absolutely turned off by. They also list a single adjective that describes those people. When everyone has completed the exercise, we begin to process the responses. All members share their responses. When everyone has had a turn, I explain that these characteristics also represent the positive and negative perceptions they have about themselves. Most are surprised and have various degrees of insight. I then look to see if any of these characteristics tap into the "wants" of their child ego state or set up conflicts with their parent ego state, to see if these connections are also set up by shopping and spending. If so, I explain that as healthy adults we need to integrate the positive and negative characteristics, accepting both sets as part of who we are. In the group members can present what they perceive to be one of their positive or negative characteristics. The other group members will provide feedback that either validates or discounts their perception. The group will suggest alternative ways of dealing with that characteristic if it is one that leads to shopping.

Another experiential exercise I use is to have group members play the role they most identify with in the drama triangle (i.e., victim, rescuer, or persecutor). They can then select two other members to play the roles they didn't identify with. The three are positioned as points on a triangle and act out a scenario that relates to inappropriate shopping or spending. The person who is doing the work begins with a message to the others that is reflective of their chosen role. For example, if a person is a victim, they might say, "My boss really took advantage of me today so I feel I need to buy something to make myself feel better." The scenario, of course, involves a "BUS" (build up to spend). The rescuer will then respond with some enabling statement (e.g., "You poor thing. Let's go look at earrings"). The persecutor may then chime in telling them how stupid they both are. I let them converse for a while and when any of the three verbalizes a statement from one of the other roles (e.g., if a rescuer is unsuccessful and begins to persecute), he or she is to change positions with the person playing that role. I have the group members who are not participating think of which role they most identify with and talk about that with the group. If any of the participants chooses not to play any more (indicated by an adult ego statement) — which is the only way to get out of the triangle — that person selects a group member to take his or her place in the triangle. Group members can help any one of the participants by pointing out an irrational thought, modeling an assertive statement, or suggesting a healthy technique to solve the dilemma without shopping or spending. There are countless themes that emanate from this. We process these dramas and try to relate them to the particular money disorder of each of the group members.

GROUP FOLLOWING THE "SPENDING PLAN" LECTURE

The only group therapy session that doesn't have a preset agenda following a psychoeducational lecture is the one that follows the "Spending Plan" lecture. Inasmuch as the lecture schedule was randomized, it is extremely likely that one person may be starting group therapy this night and one may be completing the program. If one of the group members is completing the program, with that person's permission we may use the group to demonstrate how to integrate what they recorded and begin to formulate a spending plan. As we walk through the spending plan, each individual is requested to participate. With careful observation one can begin to see group members' strengths and weaknesses regarding this work. Some may be anxious about their math skills. Some may be enthusiastic about the process, and some extremely resistant. The fact that this is a therapy group allows the therapist the opportunity to observe all of this and process it right then and there. This cuts down on the group's anxieties about being able to formulate and work with a spending plan and builds the support necessary for them to follow through on their own.

CONCLUSION

The fact that these groups have spent a minimum of eighteen hours together over the course of six weeks makes it imperative to deal with separation. Although certainly not as profound as it is in long-term groups, many clients feel a sense of loss at the end of the program.

A number of people in the program have said that this program was the first thing in their life that they had started and actually completed. This is a telling and powerful statement that can be threatening to new group members who aren't at all sure they have what it takes to finish. It is important for the therapist to both recognize the magnitude of this accomplishment, and at the same time underscore the need for participants to continue the work they began in the program.

We have a nice way of ending the program, which is optional for all members of the group. Those who choose to participate make donations of their excess clothing to various charitable organizations in need. The members who are ready to do this report that this event constituted a line of demarcation between their lifestyles of debt and overindulgence and their newfound emotional abundance and balance.

So there you have it. Solvency or, at the very least, on the road to solvency in six weeks. I urge anyone who reads this to realize that this is but one approach to dealing with recovery from money disorders. My clients who complete the six-week program express positive feelings about the experience.

New programs, as this book bears witness to, are beginning to sprout as these problems become more and more widely recognized. I hope my experience will prove helpful to those who are already working with people with money disorders and for those therapists who may want to begin to do this work.

APPENDIX I

THE TWELVE STEPS

1. We admitted we were powerless over debt — that our lives had become unmanageable.
   (*Honesty — Reality*)
2. Came to believe that a power greater than ourselves could restore us to sanity.
   (*Hope*)
3. Made a decision to turn our will and our lives over to the care of God as we understood Him.
   (*Faith*)
4. Made a searching and fearless moral inventory of ourselves.
   (*Courage*)
5. Admitted to God, to ourselves, and to another human being the exact nature of our wrongs.
   (*Integrity*)
6. Were entirely ready to have God remove all these defects of character.
   (*Willingness*)
7. Humbly asked Him to remove our shortcomings.
   (*Humility*)
8. Made a list of all persons we had harmed, and became willing to make amends to them all.
   (*Self-Honesty*)
9. Made direct amends to such people wherever possible, except when to do so would injure them or others.
   (*Self-Discipline*)
10. Continued to take personal inventory and when we were wrong promptly admitted it.
    (*Responsibility*)
11. Sought through prayer and meditation to improve our conscious contact with God as we understood Him, praying only

for knowledge of His will for us and the power to carry that out. (*Patience, Perseverance*)

12. Having had a spiritual awakening as the result of these steps, we tried to carry this message to other debtors, and to practice these principles in all our affairs.
(*Love, Respect, Service*)

APPENDIX II

I. CHARACTERIZATIONS OF DISEASE

A. A disease is *descriptive*. One can trace the course of a money disorder from "normality" to "being totally out of control."
B. A disease is *predictable*. It gets worse under stress.
C. A disease is *progressive*. The more you use nonsecured spending, the more you have to.
D. A disease is *primary*. A money disorder is the problem. It is not a symptom of an underlying disorder. It must be treated first before you deal with the damage it has created.
E. A disease is *permanent*. It can't be cured. It can be put into remission, but will never be gone.
F. A disease is *terminal*. It can kill you if you don't take treatment seriously. Given the number of psychosomatic symptoms money disorders creates, it can shorten one's life span.

II. CHARACTERISTICS OF A DEPENDENT STATE

A. *Obsession:* A thought or unwanted thought that one has (re: spending) that seems to lead to urges to spend. Sometimes many obsessions are present.
B. *Compulsion:* Behavior or series of behaviors engaged in to rid oneself of thoughts or urges to spend.
C. *Tolerance:* The need to shop, spend, or debt more to achieve the emotional effects that were once achieved by lesser amounts of shopping, spending, or debt.
D. *Progression:* The need to shop, spend, or debt more and more often to prevent withdrawal.
E. *Withdrawal:* A symptom-specific syndrome that occurs when one ceases to engage in shopping, spending, or debting (e.g., anxiety, agitation, or depression).
F. *Negative consequences:* In spite of realizing that shopping, spending, or debting is detrimental or causing harm, one continues to do it.

III. INTEGRATION FORMULA

A	+	B	=	C
Someone with an abnormal physiological resting rate	who has also had a prolonged	atypical psychological experience that either lowered self-esteem or equated money and self-worth	leads to	a state of chronic stress that can lead to (1) dissociation and (2) an altered state of identity in order to cope.

REFERENCES

American Psychiatric Association (1994). *The Diagnostic and Statistical Manual of Mental Disorders (4th ed.)*. Washington, DC: Author.

Berne, E. (1964). *Games People Play*. New York: Grove.

Boundy, D. (1993). *When Money Is The Drug: Understanding and Changing Self-Defeating Money Patterns*. Woodstock, NY: Maverick Media Productions.

Ellis, A., and Harper, R. (1975). *A New Guide to Rational Living*. North Hollywood, CA: Wilshire.

Jacobs, D. F. (1989). A general theory of addictions: rationale for and evidence supporting a new approach for understanding and treating addictive behaviors. In *Compulsive Gambling Theory Research and Practice*, ed. H. J. Shaffer, S. A. Stein, B. Gambino, and T. N. Cummings, pp. 35–64. Lexington, MA: Lexington Books.

Mundis, J. (1988). *How to Get Out of Debt, Stay Out of Debt, and Live Prosperously*. New York: Bantam.

VII   *Treatment Adjuncts*

18

Debtors Anonymous and Psychotherapy

Betsy Levine and Bonnie Kellen

The goal of this chapter is to acquaint therapists with Debtors Anonymous by explaining its basic concepts and tools. Our intentions are for the reader to (1) understand when and why referring a patient to D.A. may be appropriate, (2) feel educated enough about the program to effectively introduce it to the patient, and (3) understand the kind of ongoing input that D.A. provides. In addition, the therapist may be able to cull useful concepts and methods from those of D.A., integrating them into his or her own treatment modality to enhance the treatment of patients with money disorders.

Patients may come to therapy already in Debtors Anonymous, or they may enter D.A. in the course of their treatment. As is the case with all referrals to twelve step programs, if a therapist refers patients to D.A., some patients will accept the therapist's suggestion and go to a meeting immediately. Most, however, will have some degree of resistance that requires the therapist to do some preliminary work with them.

We will first provide a brief summary of the philosophy and principles of the Debtors Anonymous program, followed by an explanation of some of the tools of the program. Three vignettes of psychotherapy clients who benefited from referrals to D.A. are included, each with different character structure and life circumstances. Much of our writing is in the language and conceptual set of the D.A. program in order to familiarize the reader with that framework.

DEBTORS ANONYMOUS PHILOSOPHY

D.A. is a twelve step Program based on the Alcoholics Anonymous model. This is a behavioral model. At its core is the concept that debting is an addictive disease and that solvency is the solution. Solvency is defined as not incurring any new unsecured debt, and is D.A.'s equivalent of A.A.'s sobriety. The D.A. program provides both a conceptual framework and explicit tools for managing what has been unmanageable. The plan is to first stop the out-of-control money behavior, then follow specific recommendations that will increase clarity, reduce shame, and end financial panic.

UNDERSTANDING THE TWELVE STEPS
OF DEBTORS ANONYMOUS

The Debtors Anonymous steps are directly derived from Alcoholics Anonymous, the only changes being the replacement of the words "alcohol" and "alcoholics" with the words "debt" and "debtors." Steps are typically "worked" with a *sponsor*, a member of the program whom the new D.A. member asks to help with recovery. A sponsor is someone the new member has heard share his or her own problems and whose recovery and attitude he or she respects. The sponsor is "farther along the path," with at least a year's solvency and experience going through the steps himself.

Admitting powerlessness over debt and acknowledging how unmanageable this has made one's life constitute the first step in D.A.'s program of recovery. Going to a D.A. meeting is to some degree a first step in and of itself. Unless someone attends a D.A. meeting at someone else's insistence, and firmly denies having money problems, attending a meeting is, to a certain extent, an acknowledgment that he feels out of control in this area. The program suggests the next goal be to stop incurring new unsecured debt.

The second and third steps deal with "a power greater than ourselves," introducing the concept of "God as we understand him." Belief in and reliance on a higher power are seen as crucial aspects of recovery from the addictive disease.

Spirituality is a central aspect of D.A. In twelve step programs addiction is viewed as a misguided attempt to manage all issues and problems by oneself. This is attributed to "spiritual bank-ruptcy," a lack of any significant spiritual, and often moral, anchor. Addicts experience themselves as a cross between the all-powerful king and the disempowered baby, and thus set off on an ill-fated journey of compulsive behavior, attempting in this way to control everything they encounter. In twelve step language this is the "insanity" of the disease. Acknowledging the existence of a "higher power" and turning oneself over to its care lead to being "restored to sanity."

Since addicts have felt that the addiction was essential to their psychic survival, it has gone on even in the face of mounting evidence of negative consequences. If they can begin to see them-selves as not needing to control everything and everyone around them, not needing to manage all feelings and manipulate all situations themselves, they can more readily give up the addictive behavior.

A higher Power is described as "God as we understand Him." For some this is the god of their formal religious background; others reject this version and develop another concept of a higher power. Some use the acronym G.O.D., which stands for Good Orderly Direction. Others see their higher power as related to the collective wisdom of the group. Still others see it as a combination of an external source and the reflection of that source in an aspect of themselves. Most important is that people define a loving higher power in a way that works for them.

One spiritual belief system underlying much of the D.A. pro-gram is that of an abundant universe with an ongoing flow of abundance and prosperity. The universe is experienced as a safe place where, if one works for it, one will be given what one needs. This is very comforting to people who have felt desperately out of control and afraid about money.

For some new D.A. members it may be difficult to relate to this spiritual component. Some therapists with clients attending D.A. may find this concept incompatible with their own particular treatment (or personal) philosophy. It can be reassuring to know that there is no need to take in this aspect of the recovery process right away. The rate at which one does "step work" is highly individual. Some new members focus initially on the specifically money-related aspects of the program. On the other hand, many find it empowering to believe in a benevolent force in charge of their lives and financial recovery.

For dyed-in-the-wool atheists or agnostics, the recommendation is that they keep an open mind, not letting this block their receptiveness to the rest of the program. There is a slogan used in D.A. for such circumstances: "Take what you want and leave the rest."

At some point D.A. members continue working the steps. In the fourth step they take a "moral inventory" of themselves, including their financial history. They list the positives and negatives of their personality and behavior, how they have affected them and others in their life. They then write out their financial story, including a list of their outstanding debts. Then, as a fifth step, this is "turned over"—read to their sponsor or some other respected person. This is considered admitting their wrongs to a higher power, themselves, and another person. It is a way to let go of shame over past actions and behaviors, establishing them firmly in the time before recovery. Recovery is seen as a fresh start.

The sixth and seventh steps involve acknowledging one's "defects of character" and asking one's higher power to remove them. This speaks to a process of looking at harmful behaviors and defenses, and of being ready and willing to let them go and to act more morally.

The eighth step is listing those one has harmed and becoming willing to "make amends" to them. The ninth step is actually making those amends, a process one works on with a sponsor. Amends in D.A. may take the form of verbal apology, or may be actual financial debt repayment. If there is no way of making direct amends without hurting oneself or others, an indirect compensation for the past misdeed is devised. The point is for the member to end up feeling he or she has a clean emotional slate.

The tenth step is a daily inventory, a commitment to ongoing self-examination and honesty. The eleventh step involves integrating prayer and meditation into one's life to maintain contact with one's spirituality. These steps can be more or less formal, depending on individual preferences.

The twelfth step is about using the principles of recovery in all areas of life, as well as "carrying the message." D.A. members help others by participating in meetings, assisting others in working on their own recovery, and sometimes by helping those outside the program who still suffer from compulsive debting.

THE TOOLS OF RECOVERY

The "tools" of the D.A. program are specifically tailored to financial recovery. They are used in addition to the twelve steps, and provide explicit techniques and structures for dealing with money and achieving and maintaining solvency. Rather than explaining them all in detail, we will examine those we think will be of most interest to therapists.

Abstinence

Abstinence means not incurring any new unsecured debt — debt that is not backed up by some form of collateral. A mortgage acquired to buy a house, for example, is secured by the house. If the purchaser doesn't pay the mortgage, the bank takes the house. The important thing is that the person does not end up owing more money. Debting can take many forms; for example, using a credit card, not paying bills when due, taking a loan from family, or borrowing a few dollars from a friend.

If one abstains from incurring new unsecured debt for one day, he is "solvent" for that day. D.A. members count days, months, and years of solvency as A.A. members count their time of sobriety. In the first ninety days one is considered to be a beginner and at high risk of relapse as recovery is very new.

Meetings

Meetings are places where members can see and support one another as well as support newcomers. "The fellowship" refers to the community-support aspect of the program, and meetings are at its core.

A typical meeting is an hour to an hour and a half in length. There is a traditional structure that varies somewhat from meeting to meeting. This lends predictability and some sense of ritualized tradition. Often a meeting starts with the Serenity Prayer, adopted from A.A., and sometimes the reading of the steps. Each group is self-supporting, passing the basket and usually collecting approximately a dollar per person to make the rent.

Groups rent space in a public institution, usually a church, school, or hospital. A leader is elected for a three-month term. This person meets criteria set by the group, including having at least a certain minimum time of solvency and having "worked the program" in other specific ways. Some groups have more specific leadership requirements — for instance, needing to earn a certain percentage of income from self-employment in order to lead a meeting with a self-employment focus.

Record Keeping

Members "keep numbers," which include a daily spending record of income and expenditures as well as a record of past debts and the retirement of any portion of that debt. The most basic aspect of record keeping is a daily spending record, a literal record of all income and expenditures in the course of a day. Usually members have a small notebook containing their daily numbers. Some enter checking account information only in their check registers; others keep that information in the same record book as other daily numbers. The daily records are compiled into a monthly spending record, allowing an overall picture to develop. This is an objective database of information, and helps cut through the denial that is so key to addictive behavior. Clarity is essential, as it counteracts what the program calls "terminal vagueness."

Spending Plans

With the help of more experienced D.A. members, one develops an *ideal* spending plan. This type of spending plan does not take into account income or debt, but is a structure for creating a vision for the future. In an ideal spending plan the member outlines what he or she wants and needs, and adds up what that will cost. This helps conceptualize a future where the member's spending will be based on more money. It is a way of coping with the feelings of deprivation which may arise as he or she stops debting and faces the need to delay gratification. The ideal spending plan also provides concrete motivation to increase earnings. If it will take 50 percent more money for the member to live the way he or she would like to live without debting, he or she can work on earning 50 percent more income.

Using this information as well as the records of current spending and income, one creates a *realistic* spending plan delineating a reasonable allocation of the money one has and the categories in which it should be spent. Looking at the spending record, one can see the person's values, lifestyle, habits, and responsibilities. A spending plan is not a budget — which would imply fixed, rigid, nonnegotiable categories — but rather a comprehensive plan to accomplish a goal: having the best possible life under the present financial circumstances. Inherent in this are the concepts of flex-ibility, options, and choices, which differ from person to person.

The basic premise is that a current spending plan should define a solvent, abundant, and responsible allocation of the resources available. A plan for debt repayment is also included. The empha-sis is on improving one's life, not on deprivation and punishment. If, for example, music lovers want to allocate money each month to buying CDs, they can. If they want to allocate 20 percent of their income to buying CDs but claim not to have enough money for health insurance, their D.A. support system would probably ques-tion that decision.

Except with a member who has trouble meeting even basic expenses at this time, a spending plan includes categories for savings — for example, for taxes that aren't automatically de-ducted, for retirement, and for developing a prudent reserve. This is a savings account specifically designed for safety, so that even in case of financial reversals, one will have a cushion and not have to debt.

Anonymity

This is referred to as the spiritual foundation of all twelve step programs. The principle of anonymity is that one can attend meetings and speak openly, and neither one's attendance nor one's disclosures will be revealed. This is a group norm designed to create safety. Last names are not used in meetings. Typically, members introduce themselves by saying, for example, "Hello, my name is Jane, and I'm a debtor." Some may say "a debtor and an underearner," or "a compulsive shopper," or another such specifi-cation. Anonymity levels the playing field. No matter what one's occupation or outside circumstance, the principle of anonymity speaks to the fact that in terms of D.A., all are recovering debtors. Another aspect of anonymity is that the well-being of the commu-nity comes before individual preferences, putting "principles be-fore personalities."

Pressure Relief Meetings

All members of D.A. ask two other members to be their "pressure people." The suggestion is that there be one man and one woman, based on the idea that two presumably quite different perspectives will result. A meeting is set up for the member and pressure people to devote a set amount of time to reviewing the member's financial situation. The member brings his or her daily and monthly spending records, as well as an idea of the issues he or she wants help with. This information is used to develop goals. The member and his or her pressure people develop an action plan of things he or she wants and/or needs to do.

Members have pressure relief meetings once a month or less frequently. In a time of crisis someone might schedule a pressure relief meeting every week for a while, but this is unusual.

Awareness

Part of the D.A. program is maintaining awareness of the pervasive nature of debt and overspending in our culture. While those who attend Debtors Anonymous have clearly gone further than the norm, members view awareness of the cultural acceptability of incurring debt as essential to their recovery. In D.A. it becomes clear that a "just charge it" culture can be very dangerous.

Debt Repayment

Patients we refer to D.A. are often in what they experience as overwhelming debt. In the program more experienced members can give guidance on how to structure a debt repayment plan. The recommendation is that members maintain their current life and allocate only a specific amount of current income to the repayment of debt. The principle is that one does not live for one's creditors.

Dealing with Creditors

Members are helpful to one another by giving advice on how to deal with creditors. They exchange stories about going to court, dealing with the IRS, and other such difficult issues.

While beginning to repay debts is considered essential to recovery, solvent D.A. members do not do this at the expense of their current life. In D.A. the goal is not that recovering debtors do penance by living in deprivation, but that they make consistent, manageable financial restitution to their creditors. Working within this organizing principle, D.A. members are often able to offer their creditors a surprisingly detailed rationale for a slow, steady debt-repayment plan. This allows for empowered, functional negotiation.

CLINICAL VIGNETTES

To demonstrate the fact that D.A. and psychotherapy can be a powerful combination in recovery, we offer the following vignettes.

The Narcissistic Debtor

The following is the story of a man with a grandiose, narcissistic personality and how a combination of individual therapy and D.A. can help further psychological growth.

> Bruce is a 60-year-old trading executive. His younger years were marked by ADD and daily marijuana use, both of which continued throughout his adulthood. He had been highly successful professionally as the CEO of a securities firm and a respected officer of the local stock exchange. He and his family lived well, but always above their means. Known for his optimism and sunny disposition, he was able to invest aggressively and take risks without fear. Always a jock, he applied vigor and team spirit to his professional life.

His buoyant optimism and love of action led him to open his own firm, into which he poured all his assets. He was soon shocked to realize his business was losing money. After borrowing from every source available, he finally declared personal bankruptcy. The IRS seized his house and most of his possessions. A divorce followed, as his wife was neither willing nor able to tolerate the situation.

A personable man, Bruce soon began making new friends. His old friends were disgusted with him since he did not repay his debts to them. A new job, with a modest expense account, allowed him to continue overspending and maintain a false front of financial stability.

Before long he had a girlfriend. Bruce didn't want her to know his real situation, so he bought her three dozen roses at a time. One dozen was not enough. He bought four expensive watches at a time because they were "a good deal." He refused to save. Saving or spending modestly went against his grain; he still believed he would make a lot of money in the future. His new girlfriend eventually saw through his grandiose behavior and left him. She saw how desperate his financial situation was and wasn't willing to stay with a man she felt was a financial risk.

At this point Bruce became depressed. He was referred to both D.A. and a psychotherapist by his medical doctor, who understood that his financial situation was central to his depression.

Bruce's depression eased as he entered D.A. and treatment. The new sense of community was energizing to this extrovert. Previously, his identification with other bankrupt professionals ("There are a lot of guys like me") had been identification with a shameful secret fraternity. Now it saved his life. As he met recovering people with whom he identified, he could see there was a viable way out of the shame.

Bruce went to therapy once a week, realistically assessing that he couldn't afford to come more often. D.A. was very helpful to him. He kept a record of his spending, and his planning became reality-based. Although it was a struggle for him to give up his grandiose acting out, therapy helped Bruce tolerate making these changes.

He came to understand his financial behavior in a new way. He saw that what he had formerly described as "playing big" reflected an unwillingness to realistically assess risk. It had been based on fear of suffering an intolerable loss of self-esteem if forced to live more moderately. Bruce's worst fear had been to see himself as what the program calls "one among many." His grandiosity made living modestly, what he called "being boring," more frightening than going broke. Thus he felt he had to "spend big" and take risks.

Bruce got a sponsor with a history much like his own. It was a powerful relationship. Unlike his therapist, his sponsor was allowed to identify with him and "call him on his stuff" in a playful "can't bullshit a bullshitter" way. Through working the steps of the program, which entailed doing written work about his debting and spending, he came to understand his financial history as a reflection of "spiritual bankruptcy," of having "made money his higher power." He saw that his "character defects" had developed as a defense against desperately low self-esteem.

His therapy was enriched by his new insights. The work with his therapist was largely focused on understanding and grieving the childhood history that had set up these dynamics. With the support of the D.A. program he addressed both underlying issues and concrete, present-day behaviors. Bruce integrated D.A. and psychotherapy in an effort to make a fresh start.

In recovery, Bruce kept records of his "numbers," both spending and income. He stopped using credit cards. With the help of pressure relief people he made a spending plan that outlined reasonable, balanced expenditures in each of his spending categories. No longer could he "blow it all" on three dozen roses. One dozen would have to do.

His focus shifted to having a good, well-rounded life, and he realized that although he was anxious to make money, he had to take time for other things. He made sure he had time to exercise, attend D.A. meetings, and have a social life. For the first time, he was able to see his worth as a person as more than the size of his bank account.

The Codependent Debtor: Enabling a Compulsive Shopper

This patient's inability to set financial limits became most apparent in the course of his divorce from a compulsive shopper. Issues around shame and codependency were explored in his therapy and in his recovery in D.A.

John had been married to Lynn for eight years and they had one child. John had been sober in A.A. since before they met. He had a moderate-paying job as a schoolteacher. There was never enough money for Lynn, who had come from a wealthier background and felt entitled to "better things." Having a job was beneath her, and she felt that buying "nice things" was her right.

When they divorced, the financial discussions were bitter. Lynn wanted John to continue paying for everything. She wouldn't accept that with limited resources and two homes to support, things would have to change. There hadn't been enough for her tastes in the first place, and now that she was experiencing emotional pain, the last thing she wanted to do was cut back. John was afraid he would lose his relationship with his daughter if he didn't satisfy Lynn.

It soon became clear that the financial agreement they'd made was untenable. John couldn't make it on his share of his paycheck. He relied on credit cards to make up the difference, and as their balances rose, so did his anxiety. He walked everywhere to save carfare; he considered stopping therapy. John had given up hope of ever having enough money to have a decent life for himself. If he complained to Lynn, her suggestions were that he should change his profession or take a second job. His depression and hopelessness deepened.

Things became clearer as John and his therapist explored

his intrapsychic and interpersonal issues about money. What emerged was a picture of how John had allowed Lynn's overspending to continue in order to maintain the relationship. Before they met, John had taken pride in living on as little as possible. He didn't need much and liked it that way. He had been able to take care of himself and also to have some savings. While married, he had "gone into a little debt." Lynn had shopped compulsively, spent beyond their means, and complained about his income.

When they divorced, things got worse. Because these issues hadn't been addressed while they were still together and he felt guilty leaving, John agreed to a financial settlement that left him strapped. Supporting two homes was a strain. It seemed impossible to him that Lynn's spending could change. The way things were felt painful but nonnegotiable.

John's therapist encouraged him to join D.A. to get some clarity about his financial situation. Since A.A. had long been a part of his life, he was willing to give it a try. John felt a tremendous sense of relief when he admitted that he was powerless over debt and that his life had become unmanageable, which meant taking the D.A. first step. He came to understand that his debting stemmed from codependency. He began to label Lynn's shopping as an addiction, and realized he had avoided confronting difficult issues between them by enabling her.

His new peers in D.A. supported John in taking care of his own needs, too. He began to call himself a "financial anorexic," the D.A. term for someone who takes inordinate pride in having few financial needs and is more comfortable living in deprivation. The anorexia metaphor allowed him to have an observing ego about the lengths to which he'd gone in terms of self-deprivation. He realized that although his style of dealing with money might have been workable before his marriage, it had interacted disastrously with Lynn's overspending. He had acted as though he had no needs and she had acted greedy.

In D.A. John developed a spending plan outlining what he

could realistically afford. As he accepted his financial reality, he was able to disentangle his finances from his estimation of himself as a man. He identified his feelings of inadequacy and shame, and worked in therapy to uncover their historical roots. He realized he had fallen into his pattern with Lynn so easily because much the same dynamic had existed between his parents.

Working the D.A. program helped John develop ego strength. As he came to believe that he deserved enough money to live comfortably, he was able to recognize Lynn's demands as unreasonable. He could then set effective limits with her and put a stop to her insults regarding financial matters.

John and Lynn's lawyers negotiated a more reasonable financial agreement in keeping with John's current situation. John continued to develop ways to have meaningful and satisfying contact with his daughter. It became clear to him that his time and his love were far more important to her than his money. Lynn got the message that if she wanted more money than John could provide, she would have to get it from other sources or earn it herself. Her compulsion to shop was brought into dramatic relief by these new limits, a revelation that made her more uncomfortable. Eventually, Lynn entered treatment as well.

The Compulsive Shopper Who Wants to be Rescued

This young woman's dependency needs were expressed by over-spending in an unconscious attempt to be taken care of.

Susan is a 32-year-old single woman who came to therapy complaining of feeling hopeless. She had never had a relationship with a man that lasted more than a few months. Her friends were getting married, and she was worried about never being able to settle down. She described herself as "always broke," and had had a series of office jobs lasting from a few months to two years. She knew she needed to make changes in her life but didn't know what to do.

Susan came from a lower-middle-class family and was raised in the suburbs. She was the youngest of three siblings, and the only girl. She had been raised with the idea that it was important to "marry well" and have "a better life." Working was conceived of as an interim measure before marriage.

Susan became depressed after the third of her close friends got married. A relative suggested she enter therapy and Susan agreed. Her therapist was chosen largely because she had a new practice and could take Susan on for a modest fee. The initial treatment plan was to begin once-a-week psychotherapy and consider medication if the depression did not diminish. Susan was opposed to taking medication, which she considered a sign of weakness.

Susan's initial focus in treatment was her difficulty finding a boyfriend. She dated, but was constantly comparing men to the image she came to call "the prince." They unfailingly came up short, and Susan would stop seeing them. She became aware that she made unreasonable demands early in her relationships, needing her dates to be financially generous and to make her feel "taken care of," and feeling sorely disappointed when they didn't meet her exact expectations. It became clear this was a pervasive pattern.

When she entered treatment, Susan was living with a friend on a couch in the living room and her welcome was wearing thin. She had moved there after losing her apartment for nonpayment of rent. She was able to make ends meet only by borrowing money from her family every few months. At some point her family had said "that's enough," and Susan was furious.

Vocationally, Susan's history revealed a pattern of taking low-paying jobs and then sabotaging them with frequent absenteeism. In therapy she first raged about being taken advantage of, feeling underpaid and abused by her employers. She slowly began to take responsibility for her pattern.

She had been accepting low-paying jobs and resented them, then acted out her discontent and got fired.

At the same time one of Susan's favorite activities was shopping. She didn't spend much, she insisted. It was just "really relaxing" to go shopping. With detailed questioning, however, it became clear that Susan actually spent just enough to be unable to pay her bills. Part of her anger at her employers came from feeling that she should at least be paid enough to "buy nice things." The idea that necessities like rent came first and luxuries like jewelry came next was foreign to her. The therapist urged her to attend Debtors Anonymous in order to get some sense of balance and to establish financial priorities. Susan was annoyed by the suggestion, saying money was not her main problem and that she preferred to talk one to one with her therapist. The discussion of D.A. was tabled, brought up by the therapist only when financial problems were discussed in session.

Susan's financial situation continued to decline. By the time she started therapy she was no longer paying rent to the friend she lived with. The woman had suggested Susan save her money so she could afford to move out. Susan was guiltily aware that she had not been saving the money as promised, but had been spending it on things like clothes and makeup. She was in no better shape financially than she had been a year ago.

Initially, Susan paid for her sessions each week. About six months into the treatment she started missing payments and building a balance. At this point the therapist insisted Susan go to D.A. as a condition of continuing therapy. She also insisted Susan pay her fee weekly, knowing this patient could easily build a huge balance in an effort to have the therapist "take care of her" without being paid.

The therapist's countertransference was a mixture of caring and annoyance. She felt responsible for the well-being of the depressed patient and aware that the patient's financial and dependency needs were being enacted in the transference. But she also felt manipulated and at risk of being used, and she knew it was important to set firm limits.

Susan reluctantly went to D.A. She started "counting days of solvency," and hence paying her weekly fee on time. As she became more motivated to function consistently, it became clear that some of her difficulties stemmed from depression. She started on antidepressant medication, which helped curb her anger and anxiety. She was less overwhelmed and thus less likely to overspend or to act out at work. In D.A. Susan identified herself as a debtor, compulsive shopper, and underearner. She started seeing how her desperate wish to be taken care of had caused her to manipulate family, boyfriends, and friends for financial support. She realized that her fear of not being able to earn an adequate living had been a self-fulfilling prophecy. Susan had submerged any impulse to take initiative in favor of angrily demanding that others take care of her. While earning modest salaries, she had shopped compulsively and overspent on luxuries. People who at first were willing to rescue her ultimately got fed up and said "no." This cycle had led to escalating depression, partly from shame and from anger turned inward.

Susan heard many similar stories in D.A. and was able to develop a vision of a better future. She felt she could earn a living, pay her bills, have a stable life, and shop within reason. She could support herself and learn how people loved her in other ways. She could date without the pressure of having a secret, desperate financial agenda.

The changes in her outlook influenced her relationship with her parents. Her father was proud of her and understandably relieved not to have to bail her out. Her mother was worried that Susan would lower her standards and "make a huge mistake" by becoming involved with a man of whom her mother wouldn't approve. Susan could actually laugh at this thought—and then reassure her mother.

After two years in therapy and a year and a half in D.A. recovery, Susan's gains were impressive. She had a new secretarial job with a 50 percent increase in salary and was looking into paralegal training. She had a spending plan that detailed appropriate spending in the areas of clothing, makeup, jewelry, and the other things for which she used to shop compulsively. She abstained from shopping as an activity in and of itself, painfully aware of how often she had gone shopping instead of dealing with some issue or feeling.

Susan ended up living with a roommate in an apartment where each had a bedroom and each paid half the rent. She had a savings account, which she called her "prudent reserve," so she would no longer need to ask her family for money in case of an emergency. Her relationship with her parents had improved as her inappropriate dependence on them diminished. Susan was now able to date more comfortably. She could see how her need for men to rescue her had limited her choices and her ability to start a relationship. Susan was pleased with her independence and the changes in her life. She had developed self-respect. She and her therapist both felt that these gains could not have been achieved this rapidly, if at all, without the synergy of therapy and D.A.

DISCUSSION

Debtors Anonymous offers an enormous service to people with money disorders and can be quite synergistic with therapy. One of the benefits of attending D.A. is that it is an act of mobilization, a powerful step in fighting passivity, denial, and inertia. Someone trapped in an addictive cycle is on much stronger footing if he has at least begun to address his problem.

The fact that D.A. offers gradual steps allows the patient to at least get started, at "whatever level he's at." There is no pressure to take immediate action, and it may take awhile for the program to take hold. However, even being part of the community is therapeutic. It provides an opportunity to find new role models, develop increased perspective by listening to others' stories, and tap into a ready-made support system. There are opportunities for resocialization and relearning in many areas.

D.A. offers a well-thought-out plan to target specific money-disordered behaviors, breaking problems into component parts and providing a graded task hierarchy for mastery. This is accomplished within a large support system experienced at dealing with similar issues. Those with long-term recovery act as role models, encouraging newcomers in abstinence from acting out. The tools and steps taught in the program aid the newcomer with self-monitoring, planning ahead, and delaying gratification.

Compulsive debting, overspending, and underearning are some of the patterns identified in the program. Debtors who have been on the brink of eviction for nonpayment of rent learn to pay their bills on time. Compulsive spenders who have amassed large credit card bills charging expensive vacations learn they can take a vacation. They just have to have the money for it, in cash, and not take it from some inappropriate place like the money for next month's basic expenses. Compulsive shoppers who may have bought five sweaters at a time develop the impulse control to buy only one; they develop the capacity to feel the feelings that come up when they "pass" on the others. Underearners who have never felt they could afford to "indulge in luxuries" learn they can save $10 a month, and when they have $30, they can have a facial.

THE DISEASE CONCEPT AS IT APPLIES
TO COMPULSIVE SPENDING

One of the major differences between D.A. and A.A. is the substance that must be given up. The alcoholic in recovery stops drinking entirely. The debtor in recovery stops debting, one day at a time.

The debtor must learn moderation and develop a paradigm of appropriate versus inappropriate spending. In D.A. one doesn't use credit cards. One doesn't borrow without collateral. One doesn't "spend other people's money" in any way. There are specific guidelines and an underlying value system with which to tackle this complicated disorder.

For the therapist working with compulsive spenders, it can be remarkable to observe their transition from impulsive to planned spending. One understanding of the role of planned indulgence is that knowing one can eventually have a desired object reduces the driving compulsion to have it now. The compulsion often relates to an unconscious belief that if the person doesn't get that thing now, in a furtive, stolen way, he'll never have it through any legitimate means. It's analogous to the alcoholic's last drunken night on the way to the rehab, or the overeater's binge as she says, "I'll start my diet Monday."

When a therapist makes a referral to D.A., not every client will be ready to jump in immediately. Some may require extensive "socialization for recovery." This might include providing a rationale for the patient's going to D.A., at least a rudimentary explanation of the program, and perhaps a booklet of information.

There are of course some patients with money disorders for whom D.A. will not be appropriate. Most people are quite capable of doing excellent, challenging recovery work with the support of their peers, but the therapist must assess whether the patient can tolerate a structured, somewhat emotionally confrontational process in a setting that does not provide professional support. Examples of inappropriate referrals might be a patient who is currently suicidal, or someone too paranoid to tolerate a nonprofessionally led group. These patients would have to be further stabilized before they could safely make use of D.A. On the other hand, some very disturbed therapy patients have been known to benefit from and greatly enjoy the sense of community, normalization, and structure available in twelve step programs. In the program they find themselves one among many, even though they may have felt like outsiders in other settings.

Financial recovery especially lends itself to combining psychotherapy with the twelve step modality. For the patient with a money disorder, recovery entails so much concrete, detailed work that an individual therapist would be hard pressed to meet all the patient's needs. The D.A. program allows patients to acknowledge their problem, then provides a comprehensive structure within which they can do their recovery work. The therapy is enriched as patients' insights deepen and they stop acting out with money.

D.A. helps clients manage emotions as well. Self-management, along with the support of a recovering community, helps tame guilt, shame, anger, anxiety, and depression. Debilitating indecisiveness and self-criticism are slowly molded into focusing and a task orientation. Members become better able to decatastrophize anger and anxiety, and have increased opportunities for mastery and pleasure.

Most people don't find that D.A. conflicts with therapy. Meetings and program supports help with money behaviors and management, leaving plenty of room for other work to be done in psychotherapy. The possibility of splitting exists, however, as it does when a patient becomes involved with any significant person or organization outside the therapeutic dyad.

The therapist's theoretical viewpoint will dictate his or her understanding of this dynamic. Some questions to consider: Why is the split occurring now? How does this reflect the treatment dynamics in general? Are idealization and devaluation prevalent themes in the patient's life? Is this primarily a one-person issue, or is it being cocreated within the dyad?

Either the patient or the therapist may perceive a conflict between therapy and D.A. For example, the patient's D.A. support system gives advice that may seem in conflict with therapeutic aims. A patient may find that the program offers more direction than the therapist does and wish that the therapist, too, would make helpful suggestions. Along with a discussion of the differences between psychotherapy and twelve step work, one might explore this as an expression of the patient's relational needs. Expressed wishes might include the desire to be taken care of, guided, and nurtured, or the desire to have acting-out behavior contained. Detailed exploration within therapy will clarify the intrapsychic and interpersonal issues involved. It's all grist for the mill.

In the course of getting solvent, the patients may decide they can't afford therapy. If this is explored on both concrete and dynamic levels, the appropriate response will become clear. If the urge to terminate is more about avoiding therapy issues than about real financial constraints, this can be brought into the open and worked through. If the urge to terminate is about real financial constraints, that is another matter. Assessing and respecting their own financial limitations is something many debtors have never done, and is a key to their recovery. There certainly are money-disordered patients who shouldn't spend money on therapy or should be in therapy for only a limited time for realistic financial reasons. In such cases the therapist might view D.A. as a good available alternative, encouraging patients to return to professional treatment as soon as their finances allow.

THE SPIRITUAL COMPONENT OF D.A.

This aspect of D.A. is an alien concept to many therapists, who were trained to be blank screens in the area of religion, and to separate religion and psychotherapy. D.A. is a language, a culture, and a theoretical framework. Therapists would do well to try to understand it, remembering that twelve step programs have proved effective and sophisticated in their results.

There are numerous benefits to twelve step spirituality. The idea of a safe and abundant universe is calming and counteracts paranoia and anger. Being open to receiving from an abundant universe is an expansive attitude that increases one's openness to opportunity. The twelve step process of taking a moral inventory and making amends to those one has harmed cuts through denial, guilt, and anxiety, creating the space for a fresh start.

Spirituality is also a way of getting outside the individual's locus of control. A key element of twelve step programs is the paradox that recovery comes only after the individual accepts a lack of control, admits defeat, and surrenders. Someone or something else is in charge, and participants acknowledge that, left to their own devices, they are powerless over their compulsive behavior. These people have "hit bottom," and have to admit they have lost in order to win.

Once in D.A., the patient learns that money is not a "higher power." The fellowship is a ready-made community, a family of a sort that cradles newly recovering debtors and provides them with a holding environment. The program teaches them that the universe is a safe place, and that if they work for it they'll be given what they need, although a feeling of well-being may not come in the form they were expecting. This straightforward work ethic is in marked contrast to the manipulations involved in compulsive debting.

CONCLUSION

As therapists who are treating people with money disorders, we do not need to be financial planners, but we should not be vague about these kinds of problems. By educating ourselves about the intricacies of such problems, we avoid becoming enablers or glossing over the symptoms altogether. In the treatment of money-disordered patients, psychotherapy and Debtors Anonymous have proven to be an effective combination, facilitating both an exploration of dynamics and active behavioral recovery.

RECOMMENDED READING

Treating the Alcoholic: A Developmental Model of Recovery (1985) by Stephanie Brown, published by Wiley, and *Passages through Recovery: An Action Plan for Preventing Relapse* (1989) by Terence T. Gorski, published by Harper/Hazelden, may be useful for those interested in further reading about the integration of psychotherapy and twelve step programs. Although these readings were written about Alcoholic Anonymous, they can be adapted to Debtors Anonymous.

Jerrold Mundis's book, *How to Get Out of Debt, Stay Out of Debt, and Live Prosperously* (1988), published by Bantam Books, is of use for learning about the Debtors Anonymous program and its application.

19

Financial Recovery Counseling

Karen McCall

Since 1988 I have been working with clients who suffer from money disorders — including compulsive spending, compulsive debting, compulsive underearning, and problems managing inherited wealth — within a counseling framework I call "financial recovery™."

My method is to deal with the whole person: while supplying the tools and teaching the skills clients need for managing their money effectively, I also address the underlying family-of-origin and spiritual issues that helped shape, and may continue to fuel, the client's money behaviors. In what follows I've tried to give a detailed overview of the way I see these problems, how I do the work, and how I integrate the financial recovery process with psychotherapy and other support services.

MONEY TALK: A MUTUAL BLIND SPOT

As I drafted my thoughts for this chapter, I was acutely aware that many of my more extraordinary cases, and the illustrative material I wanted to use, involved clients who were themselves therapists. I thought to myself — not for the first time — that this could certainly help explain why the subject of money is often not raised in a therapeutic context.

A good case in point is a therapist I'll call Julia.

Julia came to see me because her "money troubles" were causing her great anxiety. A recovering alcoholic, Julia told me that she "didn't feel okay as a person or as a therapist." A woman whose message growing up had been to "marry well," Julia had developed into a person who had no way of judging what was enough. Julia reported that "saying 'no' to myself just feels so punitive and makes me feel poor," and said she had various ways of tricking herself into thinking she could afford the compulsive purchases she made.

Julia had few clients at this point. Unable to focus on her practice, she would see a client, then rush out to shop until it was time for her next session. There was no quality energy going into her work, which fed her already low self-esteem and contributed to her feeling, deep down, that she didn't deserve to have a successful practice.

Although her income had dropped dramatically, Julia still had periods when she felt flush. She would experience an inordinate exhilaration at receiving a sizable check from a client's insurance company; and if a client paid her in cash, she thought of it as an unexpected bonus that she could use for "play money."

Julia was a fairly isolated person, and did a lot of her compulsive shopping on weekends, much of it for jewelry or for art objects that she could place in her office (these she rationalized as business expenses). Among the most emotionally rewarding aspects of her compulsive shopping were the relationships she formed with the artisans and shopkeepers from whom she made her purchases. This was also a trap for her because, as she said, "Once I had formed that relationship, it was impossible for me to walk away without buying something."

After we had been meeting for two months, Julia came to her session looking dazed and disoriented. She was astonished and very anxious at the well of feelings she was beginning to tap into as a result of our financial recovery work, especially the depth of her shame. For the first time in her life, she told me, someone else was "really seeing her," and she felt exposed. She described the experience as having evoked a deep, paralyzing humiliation that she realized stemmed partly from her compulsive shopping and its attendant chaos, but that had extended itself into every aspect of her physical, psychological, and professional world.

I can remember being deeply moved as she talked: here was a woman whose profound sense of shame was causing her world to become smaller and smaller, to severely restrict how much of herself she let others see, how much she let others into her world. Little wonder that she was unable to deal effectively with the money-related issues that arose for, or with, her own clients.

Julia's story illustrates one of the most important truths I've seen in my ten years in business as a financial counselor: both clients and the professionals who serve them often have trouble talking about money and the role it plays in the client's inner and outer lives. Sometimes discussion of a client's relationship to the uses of money is excluded from the therapeutic process because the client simply never mentions money as an issue. In other situations the trouble can be that a client offers clues about his or her relationship to money but these threads are not picked up by the therapist (sometimes due in part to the therapist's own relationship to money) for integration into the therapeutic process.

Marilyn, for example, a woman in her early forties, told me that one day she went to her appointment with her therapist filled with remorse: she had just spent $500 on a small handbag to carry to the opera, when as an out-of-work writer she needed to conserve her cash for necessities like rent and food. Marilyn had lamented to her therapist for many months about her financial situation. She was really living on the edge in terms of her ability to pay rent, and to buy food and other necessities, and this, she said, made her feel "less than" her friends who were able to afford fairly lavish lifestyles.

About the small gold evening bag, her therapist suggested that, with all she was going through, maybe she deserved to have something pretty — reinforcing Marilyn's sense of entitlement but missing an opportunity to confront her on her self-defeating money behavior.

A friend of mine, Bob, provided me with a story that illustrates a third scenario. Bob had entered therapy for food-related issues. The work was very productive, but as his food issues began to clear up, his personal finances started veering out of control. First it was late payment of his car loan, then a bounced check or two, then finally nonpayment of his rent. His checking account was closed and he got into legal troubles for failing to pay court-ordered child support. Finally, the pressures from his money worries became so acute that Bob resumed his pattern of out-of-control eating. The cycle repeated itself several times until Bob's therapist made the comment that Bob's behavior with money seemed connected with, and very similar to, his behavior with food. It was an emotional breakthrough for Bob.

His therapist told Bob that he felt his specific money problems were outside the boundaries of the work they could do together, but recommended that Bob begin attending meetings of Debtors Anonymous, where he found the tools and support system he needed to transform his long-standing dysfunctional relationship to money.

Bob was very lucky: he had a therapist who was a skilled observer, able to "connect the dots" between seemingly very different behavioral issues but wise enough to acknowledge — both to his client and to himself — the limitations he felt in trying to treat Bob's money behaviors.

Whatever the individual sets of circumstances are, however, over and over again I find that the difficulty in raising the subject of money lies on both sides of the therapeutic relationship.

Author Barbara Stanny (1997) observes, "It's not just . . . clients who have a hard time talking about money. Three major surveys of psychotherapists revealed that money matters were the most difficult subject for the therapists themselves to discuss with their patients" (p. 149). Describing a survey on the subject of money sent out to members by the American Psychological Association, Stanny goes on to say that "few [recipients of the survey] bothered to send it back. The money survey had the lowest rate of return of all their sponsored polls. 'Either therapists believe that money is not a worthwhile research variable,' concluded one APA official, 'or money is part of the new obscenity in which we talk more freely about sex but never mention money'" (p. 149).

Why is money so conspicuously absent from the range of emotional and behavioral issues that are dealt with in the therapeutic relationship? With the anxiety caused by self-defeating money behaviors often one of the issues that sends clients into therapy in the first place, how can it be that the topic of money is dealt with sporadically—when it is dealt with at all? Why, as another of my clients who is a therapist put it, do the therapist and the client so often "collude in keeping money's power over our lives in the dark?"

Part of the problem is that we're all victim to whatever old taboos we first learned at our parents' knees. Margaret, a middle-aged woman who was raised on an eighteenth-century plantation in South Carolina, still believes with absolute certainty that "polite people don't talk about sex, money, or politics."

Society at large has also made its contributions to our belief systems about money. Both ancient and contemporary religious writings put forth the idea that "money is the root of all evil"; our everyday language includes such self-fulfilling idiomatic expressions as "I'll get what I want if I have to beg, borrow, or steal . . ."; and in nearly every facet of modern life we see evidence of the widely held conviction that "money talks."

But whatever the causes—and there are many—compulsive consumer buying and other money disorders have become one of our society's most compelling and challenging social ills.

Whether a client's presenting problems are centered on compulsive shopping or other money disorders, both the downward spiral of the disorder and the upward trajectory of recovery have very specific benchmarks (see Table 19–1).

Table 19-1

The Progressive Nature of Compulsive Spending and Recovery

The Downward Spiral

Financial	Emotional		
Stashes unopened mail; asks friends for small loans; lets checkbook go to pot; ignores necessary payments	Denies there's a problem	Has old belief system replaced by sure sense that there is enough	Rebuilds credit history; moves to housing that works; lives fulfilling life based on personal vision
Floats checks toward end of pay period; increases use of credit cards for non-essentials; bounces checks; is unable to pay off credit card purchases	Tells self, "It's only temporary"; vagueness increases Magical thinking and feelings of entitlement occur	Has growing sense that there is enough	Gradually reduces debt load; resolves legal disputes; cleans up back taxes; develops lifestyle choices
Uses cash advance from one credit card to pay off another; misses one or more rent/house payments	Grandiose behavior arises to cover growing fear; there are illusions that there will be enough soon — big check coming in	Feels empowered	Spends according to spending plan; secures health and car insurance; saves for periodic expenses

460

Financial	Emotional		
Experiences financial deterioration	Contemplates suicide so family gets insurance	Gains increased feelings of self-esteem	Explores appropriate employment; finds supportive earning environment; feels increased clarity about financial life
Consolidates loans or refinances to pay debt; promises others not to debt again	Thinks of relief; promises self not to debt again	Begins to regain self-esteem and the beginning of hope	Makes honest assessment of compulsive spending and other money behaviors; identifies bottom-line behavior
Begins using credit cards again; financial deterioration accelerates; family conflict intensifies	Loses control; cycle begins again	Moves out of "victim" role	Contacts creditors to open communication; learns to ensure basic needs are provided; writes money autobiography
Misses work to "figure it all out"; lets insurance lapse; owes back taxes; has credit cards revoked; is sued for bad credit	Depression increases; self-esteem is impacted; denies problem; feels self-loathing	Learns it's not a moral issue	Creates a spending plan; becomes aware of areas of deprivation; opens mail; maintains checking account awareness

Financial	Emotional		
Sells assets and personal belongings; gets evicted or foreclosed; wages are garnished; bankruptcy; loses jobs due to money; undergoes periods of homelessness; loses personal transportation; borrows or steals to survive	Experiences hopelessness/despair; has increased feelings that there is not enough and there will never be enough	Comes out of fog/denial; develops ability to connect consequences to behavior	Stops debting in any form; uses available resources for assistance (therapy, Debtors Anonymous, Credit Counseling)
	Feels defeated; surrenders	Feels defeated; asks for help	
		Emotional	Financial

Upward Trajectory of Recovery

Stages of Financial Recovery Work

From an emotional and intellectual point of view, financial recovery work generally has four distinct stages:

1. Establishing Clarity

Most of those who come for counseling feel that their financial lives are out of control, a feeling compounded by the fact that these clients lack the tools and skill sets that would allow them to handle money in a way that serves them. Handling a checkbook, using credit cards appropriately, saving for periodic expenses, long-term savings, repayment of debts, how to make choices — almost everything about the way they earn and use money is a mystery as far as new financial recovery clients are concerned.

This first phase of financial recovery work is focused on helping clients come out of the "money coma" or "financial fog" (other words for denial) that so many financial recovery clients describe. We identify their current financial situation: how much they earn and spend, whether they have any savings or investments, how much debt they have.

I also ask what the debt consists of. Sometimes the client's debt will be due to a luxury vacation, the purchase of a car, or some other tangible purchases. Nine times out of ten, however, clients will have no idea how much they actually owe.

As we attempt to create clarity about clients' situations, I also look at their current behaviors. Do they keep a running balance in their checkbook, for example? Do they reconcile their bank statement when it comes? How do they use credit cards? If they are self-employed, do they pay their quarterly taxes? If they have employees, are they current with federal- and state-mandated withholdings?

Clients describe a profound sense of relief during this phase of work. Even if the news is worse than they imagined, clarity gives clients not only knowledge, but a new sense of purpose: once they begin facing the truth, they can make *choices*. For most clients it is also the first time they have allowed another person to glimpse this part of their lives (and/or the first time the task of setting their financial life in order has been viewed with a supportive, rather than a judgmental, attitude), and this, too, contributes to feelings of relief. It is the beginning of hope.

2. Gaining Deeper Understanding and Introducing the Tools of Recovery

After clients have a picture of where they stand financially, I want to learn more about their early family experiences with money so that I can be sensitive to some of the emotional components of their relationship to money.

For example, if a client was badgered as a young girl about every single penny she received and what she did with it, my knowledge of this will help me be sensitive to her potential resistance to record keeping, where we track every penny. This part of the process is very revealing, as clients begin to see that their money behaviors are not the result of their "being stupid" or "having a lazy streak," but rather the natural outcome of the early spoken and unspoken messages they got about money.

The emphasis with clients now is on learning some practical, hands-on tools for shaping a more effective relationship to money. Among these are the Spending Plan, the Action Plan, and a log for tracking daily expenses by category.

As they work with the tools and their financial situation begins to change, of course, myriad feelings will usually surface. Many clients report feeling angry that they were not taught about money or how to use it. They may see for the first time that they were overindulged with material possessions as a substitute for affection, or that they were neglected completely by the adults around them. They understand for the first time how the love and nurturing they so craved then are needs they are trying to meet today through their patterns of compulsive spending.

Because of the feelings that come up for clients — including the anxiety that accompanies the attempt to change long-standing patterns of behavior — it is at this point (if a client is not already in therapy) that I will often refer clients to an appropriate therapist and/or to Debtors Anonymous.

There may also be times I refer clients to other twelve step and/or recovery programs. This is because regular review of the client's record keeping and spending plans sometimes will reveal additional treatment issues that should be addressed. I may find inordinately high (or low) spending on food, for example, which might be evidence of an eating disorder. There may be expenditures related to drugs, alcohol, sexual behavior, or gambling that — especially when the client attempts to disguise these expenditures by folding them into another category — also raise a red flag for me and indicate that the client needs some specific therapeutic intervention. If a client has a full-blown addiction, it's essential that this be addressed before we go much further in the financial recovery work.

3. Stabilization

Up to this point in the process, we've been focusing on gaining awareness and on putting in place the practical tools and techniques that will allow clients to take care of themselves more appropriately. By practicing daily record-keeping and using a monthly spending plan as a guide, clients are experiencing a new relationship to earning and using money, and one of the things I consistently see at this point is a significant increase in self-esteem at even the smallest successes.

Now the task becomes one of gaining a fuller knowledge of the "empty" areas in a client's life, and exploring ways for the client to fill the voids that were once paved over with compulsive shopping or other self-defeating money behaviors.

Clients learn to see that there is usually enough to meet their needs if they change the spending choices they make. For example, cutting down on the number of times they eat in a restaurant during the month will give them money for badly needed car repairs. Their attitude begins to shift: they are learning to address their needs no matter what their financial situation.

4. Recovery

Having experienced a different and more productive relationship to money, clients begin to feel empowered to make different choices in their lives. They are ready now to make financial recovery the foundation for a life.that is enriched physically, emotionally, and spiritually.

Often during this phase the client's inner journey once again comes to the fore. Financial and emotional resources are being "banked" and put to use in appropriate ways rather than squandered, and clients typically experience a lot of powerful feelings as they begin to tackle longed-for — but once unimaginable — goals: changing careers, reevaluating relationships, transforming lifestyles.

Where money, or the lack of it, has been the main identified obstacle to success, now clients, having addressed their financial behaviors, often begin to explore possibilities that may not have occurred to them when they were mired in financial difficulties. As one therapist who regularly refers clients to me reported, "When clients transform their self-defeating money behaviors, it really fast-tracks the therapeutic work from that point on" (McCall 1998).

A KEY TO THE WORK:
LEARNING TO SEPARATE "WANTS" FROM "NEEDS"

Underlying each of the four stages of the financial recovery process is another important piece of work: helping clients understand the difference between a *want* and a *need*. A want is a wish, a desire, something we hope to have in our lives. A need is more fundamental — groceries for the table or warm clothes in winter, for example.

Compulsive spenders are often in the habit of deferring these and other basic needs like receiving regular medical and dental care, keeping a car safely maintained and properly insured, having a savings account, and creating the time and space for regular relaxation. If needs are neglected, however, over time they become deprivations, and usually lead not only to a serious deterioration in a client's physical well-being, but — by supporting the client's sense of low self-esteem and feelings of "not being worth it" — a downward emotional spiral that makes any meaningful recovery impossible.

Revealing deprivations can slow down compulsive behaviors: with money behaviors, just as with the food we take into our bodies, when basic needs are met, craving will usually disappear.

I work with exploring the issue of want versus need in two ways. First, each of my clients receives a Wish List and a Deprivation Inventory. I ask the client to think of everything she or he would like to buy, and then to write each item on either the Wish List or the Deprivation Inventory.

At this suggestion I often see the client stop cold, not able to determine where an item should be placed. Many times clients will place all the items on one list, and it is sometimes many months before they learn to distinguish between a want and a need. Once this is accomplished we move on to discussing ways of balancing clients' spending so that their needs are met in a way that also allow them to build toward acquiring some of the items on their Wish List.

If clients have gone for many years without taking care of basic needs, their deprivation list can be quite long and the prospect of change daunting. I usually suggest that they start reducing their list of unmet needs with a single action step. If it's the beginning of the rainy season, for example, I might encourage a client to buy a new set of windshield wipers for his car to replace the worn-out set he's had for three years, or to purchase a pair of warm, woolly mittens or socks if she has nothing to keep her hands and feet warm. Then the client can begin putting a little aside each month to meet the larger needs.

For compulsive shoppers, most of whom learned early in life to equate having things with being someone, understanding the difference between desire and deprivation can be a wrenching and confusing experience. As clients' self-esteem continues its downward trajectory, they are often tempted, in an attempt to feel better, to buy something on their Wish List. While this may feel good in the short term, it will never have the more authentic and lasting effect that addressing an item on their Deprivation Inventory will provide.

Assisting clients in healing their deprivation is one of the major tasks of financial recovery work.

THE PROCESS OF FINANCIAL RECOVERY

The First Phone Call

My work begins with the first phone call a prospective client makes to my office. The first thing I try to do is "qualify" the caller to see if he or she is an appropriate candidate for financial recovery work. I do an abbreviated assessment of the potential client's current financial situation; if he or she is calling about credit repair or bankruptcy, I make sure he or she understands that these are not part of the initial process in financial recovery work, although they may become part of the solution later on. (Without a desire to change the behaviors, these solutions are merely quick fixes and will not have lasting results.)

Another key part of the first phone call is a discussion of fees, because this is where I usually get my first look at prospective clients' relationship to money. Do they have a problem negotiating fee? Are they silent about money? Does the caller start "bickering" with me over my hourly rate? (I am occasionally willing to adjust my rate if it's necessary, provided that the client agrees to revisit the subject with me on a monthly basis so that we can continue to match what the client pays with his or her financial picture.)

Still a third topic that I always raise in the first call is the issue of canceling an appointment. I allow clients to cancel a session without paying my fee only if they make the request no later than two full business days before their scheduled session (carefully defined emergencies are excepted).

This closes the "escape hatch" that a client will often try to create by canceling an appointment the night before our session because he or she didn't do the homework. If a client comes in unprepared, we simply do the work together. Having boundaries around the cancellation of an appointment keeps the client in the process and often helps control a client's potential for slipping back into old behaviors — or giving up completely.

The First Appointment

Although I normally have an agenda in terms of what I want to accomplish during a client's first appointment, there are times when I do choose to shift gears. A case in point is Barry, an entrepreneur who came to me after an impulsive, rapid, overexpansion of his business (a larger-scale example of compulsive buying) had left him almost penniless. We had hardly finished greeting one another when Barry sat down and the torrent of words began. It was a tremendous relief for him to begin talking about his situation, and to feel that he no longer had to bear the weight of his "secret, shameful behavior" alone.

This kind of situation aside, however, a first session is generally spent with my doing a detailed assessment of the client. I want to find out:

1. *Where the client is today*: What is the client's current financial situation? What are her earnings, her savings, her debt? Is there a long-standing pattern of compulsive shopping or other money disorders, or is a specific event the source of the problem? Where is the unmanageability residing?
2. *Where the client has been*: What does the client remember about growing up? My focus is on having the client describe his specific experiences during these years. Did he have money of his own as a child and, if so, was he allowed to make choices about how to use it? Did the mother go shopping, then warn the children, "Don't tell Dad!" Did Dad give the children money but whisper, "Don't tell Mom"? Did the parents teach their children any money management skills? Are their other forces at work in

the family — alcoholism, eating disorders, depression, abuse? What were the client's "secret deprivations" as a child?

3. *Where the client wants to go*: What does the client hope to get out of financial recovery work? Has the client attempted to do anything about her financial situation before and, if so, what? I ask, "Knowing yourself as you do, what do you think your biggest challenge will be in doing this work?"

If a client's current situation is one of crisis (legal or otherwise), of course we address this. But my goal is always to assist clients in putting seemingly urgent issues into perspective and to remove the paralysis that often will have new clients in its grip.

It's important during the first appointment to set clear goals. Otherwise, I'm setting up both the client and myself for failure. It's equally critical to make sure clients understand that when there have been long-standing patterns of self-defeating money behaviors, there will be no quick fix. Often, though not always, it takes three to six months just for clients to get their arms around their situation, so I encourage them to think of the work in terms of months or years instead of weeks.

In the beginning I see clients twice a month (once at the beginning of the month and then mid-month). After three to six months, depending on their financial recovery progress, we move to once a month and then to a bimonthly schedule of appointments. Eventually clients may come in only once a quarter.

After recovery has taken root it's not unusual to have clients come in once or twice a year for a number of years. These sessions are used either for checkups or to discuss large purchases or life changes that involve financial concerns — work that is valuable (and fun) for clients, and tremendously rewarding to me as I see how they have continued to build on the original recovery process.

It's important to end the first appointment with clearly defined action steps to take between appointments. I introduce clients to a daily record-keeping system that gives them not only greater financial clarity but more financial choices. If possible, we get an accurate checkbook balance (this sometimes involves calling the client's bank while we are in session). My goal here is to begin building awareness of the choices the client is making and their consequences.

We are beginning to establish bottom-line behaviors so that clients have some reference point for evaluating their behaviors with money. Homework from the first appointment is to start writing a comprehensive money autobiography to help clients expose the inner forces that drive their behavior with money.

This can be an especially powerful process for couples. I have counseled clients who have known each other for years and who, through this process, come to understand for the first time why their partners respond the way they do to money issues. The two are then often able to move from simply reacting to each other to developing their capacity to respond in an empathic and understanding way.

The Second Appointment

During the second appointment we begin work on creating a spending plan. This plan focuses on defining the client's needs and on balancing those needs with other expenditures that must be made (debt repayment, for example). The spending plan, which has many layers, is divided into categories of spending ranging from "Food" and "Transportation" to "Gifts" and "Spiritual Life." Each category is further broken down into individual line items.

Compulsive shoppers and those with other self-defeating money patterns are used to concerning themselves only with the money they will have to spend this month, not about anything that might be coming due in future months. As we create the spending plan, we write in planned expenditures for the current month for each basic spending category. We also identify, however, periodic expenses like automobile registration, tax payments, and holiday spending that will occur in subsequent months. We prorate these periodic expenses over a year, putting into the spending plan the amount that will need to be set aside each month to meet these obligations when they come due.

If clients have no savings, I encourage them to start building some. I will often have clients save for a short-term goal: when this success — a planned-for purchase — is experienced, a client's self-esteem and sense of motivation can skyrocket.

As we work on the spending plan, I continue to evaluate how clients are — or aren't — taking care of themselves. How long has it been since the client has been to the doctor or dentist? How long has it been since a woman had a pap smear or mammogram? Is auto insurance current? Clients report feeling nurtured by this process; it may be the first time anyone has actually asked them how they are taking care of themselves.

Using the Deprivation Inventory and the Wish List, I help the client identify actual and perceived areas of deprivation. Again, it's important that clients understand the difference between a want and a need. This knowledge will help them set appropriate priorities for the use of their emotional and material resources. Even more important is the fact that confusing desire with deprivation can be a powerful trigger point for a compulsive shopper.

It is easy for compulsive shoppers to rationalize or justify any purchase as something they "need." If they are unable to recognize rationalization and justification when they arise, they are setting themselves up for yet another round of compulsive spending, because we can never get enough of what we don't need.

When we identify areas of unmet needs, these needs — and the steps clients must take to address them — are written down on an Action Plan. Sometimes work on an action step will need to be delayed because of financial limitations. In these cases I encourage the client to think of ways of meeting a particular need that costs little or no money. More often, however, clients discover that their needs are unmet not because of monetary restraints but because of the emotional bind they are in. This can be a liberating moment. Clients begin to see the spending plan as a tool, a map for the month's spending, rather than as a tiresome, restricting exercise.

Third and Subsequent Appointments

Clients create each month's spending plan at the beginning of the month, but we also have a mid-month appointment to see how expenditures in each category are stacking up, discussing what worked and what didn't work, and comparing what was spent against planned expenditures. It's a little like sending an astronaut to the moon: the journey from here to there is long enough that you generally need to do a mid-course correction to keep yourself on target.

If planned expenditures in one category have changed dramatically — the need for an unexpected car repair, for instance — we then adjust planned expenditures in one or more other categories so that the client's monthly totals will be in line with the original plan. This mid-course correction also helps keeps clients grounded in reality. By staying with the process (not abandoning the entire spending plan, for example, just because one or two categories are off), clients gradually come to see themselves as being in charge, rather than as victims of circumstances they didn't create.

For our next appointment at the end of the month I encourage clients to add up what they have spent in each category for the month. If they don't do this, I take time during our session to add the figures with them. In early recovery the spending plan by month's end may look like it was planned by one person and implemented by another. Sometimes this is because the client had no idea what things actually cost. Other times it's because the client was simply unable to monitor his or her spending.

Another part of the end-of-the-month process is taking a look at what, if anything, clients repaid on their debts, what the new balance for each creditor is, and whether they added any new unsecured debt (credit card or other consumer debt that is not backed up with any kind of collateral) during the month. We again review the monthly plan, discussing what worked and what didn't work, and comparing what was spent in each category to what was planned. The client and I will also discuss what feelings came up for the client during both the planning process and the actual spending in various categories during the month.

Invariably, what occurs is that clients feel relieved to have somebody with them in the process of examining their spending — somebody asking, without judgment, the important questions: "When you spent $500 on clothes, but had $100 planned, what was your process?" Or, "I see you decided to get a new car stereo this month instead of buying the new tires we discussed. What was the thinking you used to make your choice?"

Now we've created a spending plan, done a mid-month check, summarized with an end-of-the-month review, and discussed the feelings created by the process. We're ready to begin work on the next month's plan, and the cycle starts anew. Each month the process will deepen, with the client experiencing more awareness, increased self-esteem, and a newfound ability to make choices.

JACK'S STORY:
FINANCIAL RECOVERY COUNSELING IN ACTION

A 41-year-old professional freelance writer, Jack was highly successful, with fifteen years of experience writing speeches and doing special projects for the top executives of many major corporations. He was especially valued by his clients for the "heart" and personal values he brought to his corporate work, and he himself felt that this was an important part of what he could offer clients, and what set him apart from his competition.

Jack was making about $85,000 a year, had a small but pleasant apartment in the city where he did most of his work, and drove a five-year-old car that was paid for. He entertained only occasionally — in fact, he said he didn't have many real friends and went out infrequently — and usually vacationed at his parents' summer home, which cost him nothing to use and was only a short drive away.

Yet Jack was always broke because of his compulsive shopping. His money went for designer clothes and jewelry, although instead of wearing the latter he kept it locked up in his safe deposit box. He had no savings, but bought expensive crystal and table linens for the rare occasions when he had people to dinner. He also did a lot of what he called "here-and-there" spending on nonessential items.

At this point Jack was living from check to check, and had

begun floating checks to cover basic needs like food and rent — scrambling to get the next client check to the bank before the bad checks went through. He was using credit cards for nonessential purchases, and took cash advances from one credit card to pay off another. He'd also hit upon what he thought was a great scheme for putting some extra cash in his pocket: he would frequently go out to lunch with as many business associates as he could round up, then insist on putting the tab on his credit card and having his table mates pay him for their portions in cash.

Jack was an "episodic" shopper whose spending binges were often triggered by seemingly unrelated incidents that arose from emotional needs of which he was generally unaware.

For example, while on a Sunday afternoon excursion into one of his city's trendiest, liveliest neighborhoods, Jack chanced to glance into the window of an antiques and collectibles shop, where his eye was caught not by the merchandise but by the extremely attractive woman behind the sales counter. Jack entered the store, ostensibly to browse. But, lonely and isolated, his real goal was to meet and (he hoped) exchange "vital statistics" (single, etc.) with the woman who had attracted his attention.

As she showed him around the shop, the woman, Michelle, took special pains to point out to Jack some African stoneware she had for sale. She explained that it was rare that she ever had examples of this particular style because decades of political strife in its region of origin had kept the artisans from their work. Jack left the store without buying anything, and soon forgot all about both Michelle and the rare stoneware.

Later that week, however, Jack was at a party — one of his rare social outings — where he met a woman who, as it happened, lived in Africa. By way of making conversation, Jack mentioned his visit to the antiques store, and that he had seen some interesting stoneware there. The woman was quite impressed that Jack was familiar with the work of the African artisans she knew so well, and suggested that she could buy some things for him and deliver them on her next visit to America. Puffed up with grandiosity and suffused with what he later described to me as "a warm feeling of belonging," Jack agreed to this plan, never dreaming that the woman would make good on her promise to bring him back the very expensive stoneware items.

Of course she did follow through on what she thought was their agreement, and it was only with great difficulty and embarrassment that Jack extricated himself from the financial and ethical predicament his compulsive buying decision had caused.

By the time Jack came to see me, his compulsive shopping had gotten him into quite a serious situation. He was losing sleep worrying about how to pay off his credit cards, was considering taking out a loan to consolidate his debts with one lender, and found himself, over and over, promising himself that he would "not do it again." He was a classic illustration of the emotional cost of compulsive spending.

His desperation to get new clients (more fees) and to hustle new work for existing clients (because he could then ask them to "rush" his paycheck) had begun to affect the work he had once so enjoyed. Projects now became only a means to an end, and his clients merely the providers of the next meal or rent payment. His situation had led him to accept projects from clients whom he did not respect and with whom he could not work effectively, and this began to affect both his confidence and his self-esteem. Worse, negative word-of-mouth from these clients began to get back to his good clients, who began to wonder if he would be able to complete new projects for them.

Jack told me that he occasionally took workshops and went to lectures to further his personal and professional growth, and also bought books and tapes that he used to enrich his inner life. He said he had a therapist, but because of his financial difficulties had arranged to see her only once a month. In our second session, when Jack and I began to work on a spending plan, none of his basic expenses seemed out of line. In fact, it looked as if Jack should not only have been quite comfortable living on his income but that he should have been able to put a significant amount each month into a savings account.

When we got to specifics of his current spending, however, it turned out that Jack was taking up to three personal growth workshops a month, was buying three to five of the latest self-help titles (hard cover) from his favorite bookseller, and had been spending extravagantly, ordering books over the Internet. As Jack and I worked together, he came to see that his compulsive "spiritual consumerism" had been a way of compensating for everything he felt was missing in his life, especially close and authentic human companionship.

He realized that the workshops he took, while valuable, gave him only a temporary feeling of having a community; his frequent visits to his neighborhood bookstore gave him a fleeting feeling of connection and friendship with the store's proprietor and sales staff. He saw that instead of nurturing him, his overspending on personal growth was actually depriving him of many basic things, including peace of mind.

We developed a spending plan that allowed Jack to meet his basic expenses, including repayment, over time, of his taxes and other debts. We pared his workshop commitments to a more realistic schedule of one workshop every six weeks or so. I also suggested that he reinstate his weekly visits with his therapist: the feelings and issues that were coming up for Jack in the course of our work were complex and quite painful, and I felt strongly that he needed more therapeutic work to help him process these feelings in a productive way.

I felt at this point that it might be helpful if his therapist and I talked to one another, and I asked Jack to consider it. He initially felt threatened by the idea — his former scattershot approach to healing himself had meant that no one service provider had a complete picture of Jack's situation and his alarming behaviors. But now, he said, he saw a coordinated set of treatment plans as evidence that others cared about him and his well-being — something he had rarely, if ever, experienced in his life.

At his next therapy session he asked the therapist for a release form that would authorize her to speak with me, signed it in her presence, and brought me a copy. His therapist and I had two consultations over a two-month period, and these conversations were enormously useful to both her and me in our mutual effort to help Jack stay in the process of recovery.

Today Jack has shed his undesirable clients, and has once again begun to enjoy his work. He has regained his confidence and self-esteem, and begun making real friends for the first time in many years. As he continued to work with his spending plan, he had the benefit of his new awareness, and was able to see that if he watched his compulsive shopping, he actually didn't need to work as many hours as he'd been putting in.

This in turn opened up the possibility of a career change that he had long dreamed of making. He started to take college classes that counted toward a degree in career counseling, a field in which he now combines his business savvy and interpersonal skills with the personal, inner journey that is so much a part of his more authentic self.

WHAT IF A CLIENT RELAPSES?

In the early phases of financial recovery, as with any other recovery process, it's not uncommon for clients to relapse. I actually expect it.

Sometimes it's fairly simple to identify and confront the behavior that constitutes a relapse. There are clients who from the beginning have great difficulty sticking to a plan. One woman, for example, went to a large department store to buy a tube of lipstick and came out with $700 worth of cosmetics and perfume. Another reported that, after learning that her former husband had just taken a European vacation with his new bride, she bought a new car. Though this was not an item on her Deprivation List and there were many needs on her list that had not been met, she told me she felt she "needed" that car.

More subtle, but still fairly easy to spot, are situations in which the issue is not the actual compulsive spending but the trigger that sets up the compulsion. A client may agree not to use credit cards, for example (in fact, this may be easy since her cards are probably at their limit anyway), then come to a session having rationalized their use "just one more time."

> One such client, Anne, had come to me well aware of her problems with compulsive shopping; she knew she could not stop the behavior on her own, and she was tired of trading off the temporary sense of well-being she got from shopping for lasting peace of mind.
>
> While Anne made a good living as the assistant manager of a local retail store, by the end of each month she was always scrambling for money. It had been clear to me from the beginning that even though she paid her credit card bills in full and on time each month, this was a client who should not be using credit cards. It was equally clear as we did Anne's spending plans that if she could forgo using the cards for even a month (her monthly bills from credit cards alone took a huge bite out of her paycheck), she would see that she actually had enough money to take care of her needs and still buy a few items each month.
>
> But Anne — like an alcoholic who cannot drink "just a little" on a special occasion — couldn't use her credit cards "just a little." As she put it, "With me, it's all or nothing."
>
> She came to a session one day having racked up $1,400 on her credit cards in a single day while shopping for clothes to wear on a blind date. Anne reported that she had felt an urgent need to "look really, really good" for this man, and that the new clothes bolstered her confidence. (Ironically, the clothes she had bought for the date proved inappropriate for the event

they attended, and she ended up wearing an ensemble that was already in her closet.) In working with her therapist, Anne had developed a sophisticated awareness of how she had been using compulsive shopping as a buffer between her and her overpowering sense of inferiority.

This, however, was a turning point for Anne. She finally accepted that, for her, credit cards simply would not work. I was impressed with the progression of her willingness at this point; it sometimes takes a great deal of courage for clients to give up the crutch that has supported their compulsive spending.

Together Anne and I identified some bottom-line behaviors that she agreed to, including:

- Being aware of her projected monthly income (part of her compensation was commission)
- Always knowing where her money went (she became willing to track her expenditures by writing them down, to the penny, each day in her expense tracking log)
- Keeping her checkbook balanced
- Making sure the balance of her reconciled bank statement agreed with her checkbook balance
- Keeping track on a monthly basis of how much she owed and what it was costing her in interest.

Anne and I further agreed that if any one of these lines was crossed between our sessions, she would call so we could nip potential slips in the bud and keep her financial recovery on track.

While not using credit cards was at times inconvenient for Anne (she traveled frequently on business), she began to plan ahead for handling such expenses as hotels and rental cars with cash or with a debit card that took the cash directly from her checking account each time it was used.

There are times when sorting out what does and does not constitute a relapse is more complex.

Rod, an executive assistant to the head of a midsize corporation, was also in school working toward a degree in architecture — a long-time dream for him. One day Rod told me that he had begun to suffer terribly from lower back pain. His job involved heavy computer work, and he spent many hours at his keyboard. Nights he was at his drawing board until late doing highly detailed drawings and plans. Both these activities, he knew, were big factors in his back problems.

Rod told me that while he knew he needed to do something differently to address his injury, he felt he couldn't give up working on his computer — it was paying the bills; and he couldn't give up the detailed architectural drawings that were a part of his course work. Rod mentioned that in traveling to do various tasks for his boss, and to and from campus at night, he was doing quite a bit of driving, and that his older model car was not ideal from the standpoint of ergonomics. At this point, to Rod, buying a new car — though he could ill afford it — seemed like a logical solution that would allow him to begin taking better care of himself.

Such situations can be tricky from the standpoint of effective counseling. I was empathetic about Rod's injury, of course. I also pointed out, however, that up to this point he had not considered a new car to be a priority, and suggested that to make a major purchase at this particular time would move him further away from his life goals.

Together we explored finding a planned way to meet Rod's need, and developed an action plan that included an investigation of low-cost clinics, and also sharing his situation with his boss. His boss made a temporary change in Rod's job duties, and Rod was able to give up several hours a day of computer work. We also created a category in his spending plan that allowed him to put aside money each pay period for a series of acupuncture treatments, which Rod had read was providing significant relief for people with his particular problem.

CONCLUSION

This work has been a profound and moving experience. As clients continue to gain awareness and to master the practical tools to create more stable and fulfilling lives, they blossom. They cease being vague and confused about how to take care of themselves, literally growing up before my eyes into adults who are able to take responsibility for their actions and make productive choices about their lives.

There has never been a time when giving attention to compulsive spending and other money disorders has been more critical, not only in our private lives but in the lives of the state, the nation, and the world. One has only to pick up a newspaper or turn on television to find evidence of the terrible price our world is paying for the financial choices its peoples and their societies are making. The concomitant epidemic of "spiritual bankruptcy" is perhaps even more devastating.

The good news is that financial recovery has finally begun to gain recognition as a legitimate treatment issue. Hospitals, treatment centers, and even corporations under the aegis of their Employee Assistance Programs — from all quarters, programs and policies are springing up to try and address the issue of financial recovery in a meaningful way.

The task now for professionals who are actively working with these clients is to join together to coordinate the efforts being made on clients' behalf so that we make a significant and lasting difference. If we can do this, we are reaching not just a single individual — not just those who have directly sought our help — but a much broader arc. The image called to mind is that of casting the proverbial stone into the pond, then watching as it makes itself felt in ever-widening circles.

The particular blessing I find in doing this work is that, even after all this time, each client leaves me both the changer and the changed.

REFERENCES

McCall, K. (1998). *Financial Recovery™ Workbook*. San Anselmo, CA: self published.

Stanny, B. (1997). *Prince Charming Isn't Coming*. New York: Viking Penguin.

20

Simplicity Circles
and the Compulsive Shopper

Cecile Andrews

Americans are denounced again and again as a shallow, materialistic, and status-seeking group of people. But the truth may be that we are instead a lonely people starved for affection and attention. Much of the research on compulsive or addictive shopping seems to indicate that it is not the *stuff* we want, but the *sensation*. It's not another blouse or a new sweater so much as a friendly smile and a compliment. It's not a new VCR we need, but another way to find self-esteem and a sense of belonging. To help people deal with their compulsive shopping, we need to help them find new ways to deal with the stresses and anxieties of our commercialized, competitive, consumerist society.

. There is a tool that can help — the voluntary simplicity study circle, a form of adult learning and social change that I have been working with for the past several years. In 1989, in my position as director of continuing education at a community college, I offered a workshop on the subject of voluntary simplicity. Only four people registered and it had to be canceled. In 1992 I offered the workshop again, and this time 175 people came. What was the difference? The publicity was the same. Time had passed and perhaps people's lives were growing increasingly stressful. But the only measurable difference was that in 1992 I offered people the chance to get involved in simplicity circles.

Ultimately, because the demand for information on simplicity and simplicity study circles was so great, I resigned from my full-time job. Since 1993 I have spent my time working to spread the concept of the simplicity study circle.

WHAT IS VOLUNTARY SIMPLICITY?

Voluntary simplicity is an age-old philosophy that has been a constant theme in American history. It can be seen with our founding fathers and mothers, and resurfacing later in the days of Thoreau and Emerson, during the Great Depression, and in the 1960s. It has once again captured people's imagination as we struggle to build lives of high fulfillment and low environmental impact. Our lifestyles of rushing too much, working too much, and consuming too much are killing people's spirit and ruining the planet.

Voluntary simplicity is not — as one young person thought — a life of self deprivation. It is a turning away from activities that have failed to deliver satisfaction and contentment — activities such as shopping and scrambling up the career ladder — to activities that bring true joy and meaning — creativity, community, and the celebration of daily life.

It is people taking stock and trying to live with balance, moderation, and harmony with nature. It is people learning to live consciously and making their own choices. It is a movement that questions the American definition of success that is measured in terms of wealth and status; it is a redefinition of "the good life."

WHAT ARE STUDY CIRCLES?

Study circles are small groups of people engaged in democratic, participatory, egalitarian learning and personal transformation. Study circles have a long and honorable tradition. They are used with particular frequency in Sweden where, in the nineteenth century, study circles transformed a poor uneducated group of peasants into citizens of a country that is today among the most committed to saving the environment. Sweden has been called a study circle democracy because two-thirds of Swedish adults participate in study circles, exploring every sort of issue.

SIMPLICITY CIRCLES

In 1992 I brought the two together, and through the help of several organizations, simplicity circles are growing in popularity. But can these circles also help compulsive shoppers? Let me give an overview of this form of personal and social change and then show how simplicity circles may help compulsive shoppers meet the needs they so desperately seek in the shopping mall. This is not to say that I have found a cure for compulsive shopping. As the research indicates, there may indeed be biological causes for compulsive shopping as there are with addictions to alcohol or drugs. But I hope to show how some compulsive shoppers might benefit from simplicity circles.

Small Group Form of Learning

First, a simplicity study circle is a small-group, participant-directed form of learning and social change that is noncompetitive and nonauthoritarian. The substance of the circle is conversation focused on learning from personal experience and from each other. The circles help people:

- Discover wisdom through analysis of the personal story
- Engage in critical and visionary thinking by linking the personal and the political
- Experience transformative change through concrete personal action and group reflection

Three Basic Elements

1. Each session centers on a question that is relevant to people's lives, a question that everyone can answer from his or her own experience. People discover their own truths by telling their own story instead of by reading a book.
2. The insights of the personal story are linked to an analysis of public life. People learn to think critically by discovering how their personal issues are affected by forces in the larger society. This approach encourages people to work for social as well as personal change — an experience that is liberating and exhilarating because it brings meaning and community to people's lives.
3. After reflecting on personal and social issues, people take concrete actions. They begin to see themselves as capable of making real change, both in their personal lives and in the larger society. Each subsequent session begins with a "check-in," with people reporting the results of their prior week's actions. This approach to action and reflection gives a study circle energy and life and keeps it from being abstract and boring.

The Format

People usually commit to spending ten weeks in the circle, meeting weekly and using the curriculum found in the last section of my book, *The Circle of Simplicity: Return to the Good Life* (1997). Each session begins with a question that can be answered from the life of the participant. People may do some reading, but the point is for people to analyze their own experiences.

Questions for each of the weeks are listed below.

Session One: Why are you here? What is going on in your life that attracts you to the subject of voluntary simplicity? How do you define voluntary simplicity? What are you already doing to simplify your life?

Session Two: What negative educational experiences have you had?

Session Three: What is something you bought that you regret buying? Why did you buy it?

Session Four: What is something you love to do?

Session Five: Think of something you love to do that someone would pay you $10 for.

Session Six: When in your life did you experience community?

Session Seven: What in our society discourages community? How could we encourage community at work?

Session Eight: What are some of the foolish things you have seen people do when they were rushing? For instance, things people do in their cars.

Session Nine: What are some of the ways you would like to change your work situation? How have you changed your work situation?

Session Ten: What societal change would bring about a reduction in people's greed?

The questions focus on consumption, finding your passion, building community, living mindfully, and transforming work. Only one session is allotted to dealing with spending habits. I think that for most people the answer to the problem of extreme consumerism is meeting their real needs instead of the artificially created needs. When people are involved in their particular passion, feel a part of a community, and are taking steps to transform their work lives, they have no desire (and certainly no time) to go shopping.

Let me illustrate how this works. One of the sessions focuses on "community." The question for the session is, "When in your life have you experienced community?" People respond with their personal stories — always generating a great deal of excitement. From their stories emerges a definition of community. Next, people discuss the question, "How does society limit or undermine your experience of community?" People begin to think critically as they analyze the forces in our society that destroy community, things like television, shopping, long work hours. Finally, people go around the circle and tell the group what concrete steps they will take during the coming week to increase their sense of community. People decide to do such things as walk more, have a potluck supper, or start reconnecting with old friends. When they return the following week, they go around the circle and report on their results. It doesn't matter if they succeeded or failed — either way, they get support and ideas about what to do next.

Simplicity Circle Outcomes

I have found that this approach generates some basic outcomes:

1. *Development of self-trust*: We have a society in which people have no trust in their ability to make decisions. In our educational system we learn to turn to the experts and authorities. Simplicity circles help people learn to trust their own experiences.
2. *Development of critical thinking*: Television encourages us to act without reflection, to buy without stopping to think. By linking their personal stories to societal issues, people begin to see how they are manipulated and can find ways to resist.
3. *Creation of a safe place to talk*: We live in such a competitive society that people rarely feel they can offer their opinions without someone verbally assaulting them. As Deborah Tannen (1998) points out, we are a highly argumentative culture. Even in ordinary discussions the goal is often to prove that you are right and others wrong. Many people retreat from such combative discussions and remain silent. In simplicity circles people don't argue about right and wrong; each person is encouraged to find his or her own way to live.
4. *Creation of a sense of acceptance and recognition*: Because the circles focus on the personal story, people get to reveal their true selves. So often in today's society we argue about ideas, never getting to talk about personal issues and emotions. When people are listened to, their true selves grow and blossom.

NEEDS OF COMPULSIVE SHOPPERS

How can this approach help compulsive shoppers? Research reveals that compulsive shoppers are often shopping not for things but emotional gratification that gives them a sense of worth, a feeling of community, and a sense that someone cares. When that salesperson smiles and tells them how lovely they look, compulsive shoppers are distracted from a sense of loneliness and low self-esteem. When that salesperson listens to them, they feel — at least for the moment — that they have worth.

Furthermore, compulsive shoppers are often trying to escape negative situations. In the mall there's no one arguing with them, it's always clean and bright, and there are no unpleasant people around demanding things.

And at last there is someone they can please. They see the look of pleasure when they write their check. They've made someone happy. And what a sense of power — hand over that credit card and you can have anything you want. (And, of course, if that card is maxed out, there's always the one you got in the mail yesterday.)

And while they're there, they can indulge in the fantasy of their new popularity and beauty. Soon they'll look like models, and who will be able to resist them? Reluctantly they leave the exciting mall to return to their messy houses, crabby families, and dull lives.

Now not everyone fits this profile, but studies have found that many compulsive shoppers are searching for self-esteem, affection, feelings of power, and a way out of what some people feel to be a meaningless life (Elliot 1994). Simplicity circles, then, can help these people meet the immediate needs of acceptance and recognition and at the same time help them design strategies to resist consumerism.

How Circles Can Meet the Needs of Compulsive Shoppers

Positive attention and supportive human interaction: We live in a society that is so rushed that it increasingly has little time for human interaction. The study circle *is* human interaction. You get to talk to people about real things. How often in everyday life do you talk to people about your passion, about community, about spirituality? By using the "circle" format of discussion — people take turns going around the circle — each person gets a chance to talk. In our competitive society it is often only the quick and the articulate who get a chance to speak up. When people know they will have a turn, everyone relaxes, and they all get to say what they want.

Building Identity: Compulsive shoppers not only have low self-esteem, they have a lack of personal identity (Faber 1992). They are unable to answer the question "Who am I?" Indeed, the way they answer it may be through shopping. They can say "I am a person who can find good bargains" or "I am a person who always knows the latest fashions." One of the most effective ways to develop a concept of identity is to have a chance to develop your personal value system and to find your particular passion, subjects covered in the simplicity circles.

Further, they can experience their true selves; because the conversation is designed to be noncompetitive and nonjudgmental, people feel free to express their true selves.

Boredom: Compulsive buyers often shop to relieve themselves of feelings of an internal deadness (Benson, personal communication). In simplicity circles people use their personal stories as the basis of their interactions, and because of this the conversations are often lively, with people becoming articulate and often very funny. In particular, people can freely express emotions and feelings. Too often conversations in the workplace or the classroom require that you speak with objectivity — that is, hide your emotions. Having a place to speak about their feelings can be quite enlivening to compulsive buyers.

Reflection: One of the goals of simplicity is to help people feel fully alive. People can feel fully alive only when they are meeting their true needs and engaging with real life. People need time for reflection and awareness to become aware of their true needs. The circle allows for this experience of reflection, an experience that impulse-driven compulsive buyers don't often have.

Practical strategies: Not only does the circle help people meet psychological needs by giving them an experience of community and caring, it also helps them develop strategies to reduce their shopping. People describe how they get rid of their credit cards and pay only cash, how they find ways to avoid impulse shopping, and how they become more aware by writing down their purchases. They learn ways to avoid the constant pressure to consume by watching less television, stopping catalogues and junk mail, and developing friends who value low-consumption lifestyles and who tend not to focus on personal appearance through clothes or cosmetics. When people are given practical techniques, they are given hope that they can indeed change.

Let's take a look and see how this worked with one specific woman.

MANON'S STORY

At first, when Manon told me her story, she began by telling me that her money problems were caused because she was a child of the depression. Not only did her family have no money, she said, but money was never discussed—it was taboo. It was something she knew nothing about. Then, when she married at age 23, she went "from the frying pan into the fire." For eighteen years her husband handled all the money, giving her money only for food. Out of that allowance she clothed her children and herself with second-hand clothes.

All her furniture was bought second-hand when she first married and was never replaced in eighteen years. Her home was "a wasteland." It was barren of rugs and she covered some orange crates with curtains to use as a makeshift dresser for her children's clothes. Her husband was "a miser."

(Only somewhere in the middle of her story, when I asked if she had ever worked, did she tell me she was a very successful motion picture cartoonist, working on the animation in several notable films.)

When she was 43, she got a divorce and discovered credit cards, and she started to furnish her house with credit. For the first time she bought new things. She got rid of all the "broken-down things" and bought beautiful new furniture, a new stove, and a new refrigerator. She started buying new clothes for herself and her kids. She wanted to do something really wonderful and she heard about a Viennese opera ball, so she bought a beautiful opera ball gown. She "felt like Cinderella" and "spent money wildly."

Within a year or two she declared bankruptcy.

"But," she said, "I didn't learn anything. I kept spending." In 1992 she declared bankruptcy again, and within the year she sold her house. It was a big house (she had gotten it from the divorce), but she had refinanced so many times that she cleared only $15,000.

She finally started to suspect that she had a problem. She didn't like hearing the words "compulsive spending," but she began to suspect that might be what was wrong. She started attending Debtors Anonymous, but she hated it.

So then she began to read — *Money Demons* (Forward and Buck 1994), *Can't Buy Me Love* (Coleman 1992), *The Money Drunk* (Bryan 1992). And she finally decided she needed therapy for her compulsive spending. She had gone into therapy after her divorce because she "felt like a failure," but now she began to have therapy for her spending.

Then, a few years ago, she discovered the voluntary simplicity movement and a year ago joined a voluntary simplicity study circle. When she first heard of the simplicity movement, she thought, "Wow, I'd love that!" And she never, never misses her circle.

The circle is important to her, she says, because she feels that she is part of a wider movement, that she is "part of something larger." Hearing people's stories about dealing with money validates her own struggle with money. "I don't feel so much like a wild creature out there struggling all alone."

The circle helps her, she says, because she is constantly

reinforced for living within her means, and constantly reminded of the importance of sticking with her budget. She
knows that each week she'll be talking about it. Because
everyone is there for a different reason, she has begun to see
how her personal problems are connected with wider issues
like the environment and the global quality of life. This gives
her a sense that what she does really matters.

Other stories inspire her and give her new ideas. One
couple, she said, began about 5 years ago to worry that one of
them might lose their job, so they decided to live on only one
income. Well, neither of them lost their job, and, in fact, they
were promoted. But they continued to live on one salary. Now
they have so much money saved that they feel they will never
be anxious about money again. Another couple had lived in a
large, expensive house and decided they wanted something
simpler and moved to a smaller house with space for a garden
and for animals.

As Manon describes these stories, you can hear the excitement in her voice. She is also proud to tell her own story,
proud to be part of a movement.

As I said when I began, Manon blamed her problems on
the fact that she was a child of the depression. But after she
finished her story, I asked her if she felt there were any other
reasons for her issues around spending. Her response was:

"Well, when I was divorced and began spending, for the
first time I learned to give myself love."

"Was your husband a loving person?" I asked.

"No, he absolutely was not! Ask my children. They'd have
some stories to tell you!"

"But it doesn't sound as if your childhood family was
abusive," I observed next.

"Well," she said, "I had only my mother. My father abandoned us when I was 6. In her way my mother must have
loved me. I always felt I had to escape her, though, and I
finally did. That's the reason I got married."

Once again, the psychological roots of the compulsive
shopper are revealed. Manon certainly is a person who suf-

fered from emotional starvation, if not abuse, both in her childhood family and her adult family.

Manon also continued therapy throughout this period, so it is difficult to determine the exact role of the circle. However, she feels the simplicity circle played a central role in her improvement.

It certainly sounds to me as if the circle has given Manon a new sense of affection and being cared for. Because the conversation is noncompetitive and nonjudgmental, a sense of caring and support always emerges in these circles. Being listened to and affirmed for her actions gives Manon a new sense of herself. That she is a part of a movement that helps both people and the planet makes her feel more worthwhile as a human being, with an important role in life. Certainly the circle and the simplicity movement have given her a new sense of purpose and excitement in her life. There is no need to shop to fill empty days.

Finally, she begins to see herself as more than just a sick person, a woman with a problem. She sees her problem as part of a larger societal issue, making her feel less neurotic. Because others in a simplicity circle are not necessarily compulsive shoppers, the compulsive person gets to see positive, healthy role models.

CONCLUSION: A GROWING MOVEMENT

Compulsive shoppers who participate in simplicity circles will find themselves part of a growing movement. Simplicity circles are spreading across the county and around the world. Women who participated in the early women's consciousness raising know that participating in a historical movement can be an exhilarating, transformative experience. In the often-quoted words attributed to Margaret Mead: "Never doubt that a small group of thoughtful, committed citizens can change the world. Indeed, it is the only thing that ever has."

REFERENCES

Andrews, C. (1997). *The Circle of Simplicity: Return to the Good Life*. New York: HarperCollins.

Bryan, M. (1992). *The Money Drunk: 90 Days to Financial Sobriety*. Chicago: Contemporary Books.

Coleman, S. (1992). *Can't Buy Me Love: A Guide to Recovery from Compulsive Spending and Money Obsession*. Minneapolis, MN: Comp Care.

Elliott, R. (1994). Addictive consumption: function and fragmentation in postmodernity. *Journal of Consumer Policy* 17:159–179.

Faber, R. (1992). Money changes everything: compulsive buying from a biopsychosocial perspective. *American Behavioral Scientist* 35(6):809–819.

Forward, S., and Buck, C. (1994). *Money Demons: Keep Them from Sabotaging Your Relationships — and Your Life*. New York: Bantam.

Tannen, D. (1998). *The Argument Culture*. New York: Random House.

Conclusion:
What Are We Shopping For?

April Lane Benson

Shortly after her 90th birthday, Lillian Susskind visited her favorite store to replenish her wardrobe. Cane in hand, she hobbled in, then cheerfully selected and tried on several outfits. When she was ready to pay for her purchases, she placed her cane on the counter, freeing her hands to find the correct amount of cash.

Elated by her fabulous bargains, she took her shopping bags and marched proudly toward the exit, forgetting her cane. An astonished cashier, cane in hand, ran after her, shouting, "Madame, this is Loehmann's — not Lourdes!"

— Nemy 1998.

Shopping makes for easy jokes. This one hints at shopping as panacea, a magical elixir that promises more than it could ever deliver. Retailers seize any opportunity to prey on this fantasy. One of the most fashionable stores in New York City unabashedly mailed postcards to its customers inviting them to a "psychotherapy sale," urging them to bring their emotional baggage to fill with mood-enhancing bargains. "Get in touch with your inner shopper," the store beckoned.

Whether it's Lillian Susskind or the ditzy blonde struggling with armfuls of boutique bags, whether it's the panting bargain hunter, poised and ready to leap, or a tongue-in-cheek postcard, shopping stereotypes are quick fodder for a laugh. We've all seen the bumper stickers that boast "When the going gets tough, the tough go shopping" and "Shop 'til you drop!" — or, for the classically inclined, "Veni, Vidi, Visa." All this comedy underscores a strongly mixed cultural message: shopping, however alluring, is silly and superficial, as is anyone who passionately pursues it.

So it's easy to be anxious about shopping. Even as our marketing-intensive culture has elevated retail seduction to a high art, shopping is simultaneously discouraged and devalued. Given the omnipresence of shopping humor and negative shopping stereotypes, it's little wonder that compulsive shopping is often such a shame-based symptom. Yet many people experience an excitement in shopping, even a joy, that is too deep to be trivialized. What, then, are we to make of this double message? How can shopping be both laughable and vitally important?

Shopping, like eating, can be compulsive or perfunctory or a way to escape painful feelings; under the pressure to consume, ceaselessly applied by marketing professionals and the media, it often is. But we laugh at the jokes for more than their mirror of our temptable selves. At some level we also recognize unseized potential. Shopping humor — like much other comedy — exploits what may be a subliminally understood gap, in this case the distance between shopping gone bad, as in compulsive shopping, and the actualizing possibilities of search.

As a practicing psychologist, I have the privilege of listening in on many life stories. A resonant theme in even the most dissimilar of these lives is the ongoing search for who we are, what we need, where our place is in this world. I believe that reframing shopping as a process of search, a vital activity that reaches far beyond its traditional associations with buying or having, can aid in this quest for identity and meaning.

IS *SHOP* A FOUR-LETTER WORD?

Early in my study of consumer behavior I attended a national conference on eating disorders. Catherine Steiner-Adair, one of the keynote speakers, asked the audience what we thought were the two major activities traditionally pursued by women to deal with life's ups and downs. The silence was palpable. She then answered her own question: "Dieting and shopping." Her statement was instantly acknowledged throughout the room, first by a saddened hush, then with murmurs of agreement all around. This response reinforced my belief in the importance of shopping and spurred me to examine the stereotypes more closely. I subsequently uncovered several misconceptions, a complex shopping mythology, that rely on contextual prejudices and reflect an extremely narrow view of the shopping process and of shoppers.

Perhaps the hardest of these misconceptions to deconstruct is the equation of shopping with getting and spending. But to regard the shopping process as nothing more than material consumption is like thinking of food as solely nutritional or sex as wholly for procreation. Shopping and consuming are not the same thing. A consumer consumes, takes in and uses up, rather than produces. That consumer might be conscientious or wasteful, picky or indiscriminate, but the act itself is clearly about taking something as one's own. Shopping is different. If it weren't, why, then, the chase? When our patients head to the store, aren't they generally in search of something more fundamental than the sneakers or throw rug on their shopping list? Isn't their enterprise more about social interaction, or time to themselves, or relief from some negative internal state, or even the prospect of a visual feast?

Another misconception lurks beneath the smile — sometimes the sneer — in a lot of shopping humor: shopping is meaningless. It's this notion that amuses us, for example, when the car bumper in front of us announces "Born to Shop," and we speculate a little condescendingly on the lifestyle of the driver. How, after all, can so ordinary a task as shopping bear the heft of birthright? We respond, in other words, to the deflated balloon of the sticker's language: "Born to," hinting at the grandiose, collapses to "shop," the epitome of the mundane. But commonness does not preclude meaning any more than rarity guarantees it.

The final misconception is that shopping — and compulsive buying — is a woman's thing. The truth is gender-neutral. Capitalism, exploiting the "aspiration gap" (Schor 1998) that is so significant a feature of our culture today, has been a pernicious enabler to both men and women. Perceptions, though, because they are affected by both paternalism and the different calculus each gender applies to shopping, are often at odds with this equity.

Men and women differ in how they shop and what they shop for, and they articulate very different attitudes about the process. A persuasive 1990 study (Scherhorn et al.) of compulsive shoppers found that women — who tend to be other-oriented and relationship-centered — bought clothing, jewelry, and cosmetics, objects related to appearance. Men — who tend to be self-oriented and activity-centered — purchased high-tech electronic and sports equipment, primarily functional goods. The sexes not only buy different things, they relate differently to what they have. Several studies in the United States and England suggest that women value more their emotional and symbolic possessions, while men favor functional and leisure items (Csikszentmihalyi and Rochberg-Halton 1981, Kamptner 1991, Wallendorf and Arnould 1988). Women also gave more emotional and relationship-oriented reasons for valuing their possessions; men had a more functional, instrumental, activity-related rationale for their choices (Dittmar 1989).

Historically, of course, shopping as we traditionally understand it — shopping for goods, shopping to buy — was one of the few areas of validation available to women, an extension of their gatherer role in primitive societies. While men went out to hunt, women concentrated on tasks and responsibilities based close to the hearth. Over the centuries, the hunter/gatherer division of labor became value-laden, and the woman's place, now not only practically speaking but morally as well, was in the home. Carolyn Wesson (1990) describes this subjugation and the compensating mechanisms that grew up around it: "Until quite recently, women had to follow a set of rules as constricting as a whalebone corset. [They] had to go underground and express any negative feelings in acceptably feminine ways. When angry they grew quiet, withdrew sexually from the husbands, dreamed of revenge — and made clandestine trips to the local emporium" (p. 13).

The same tradition paints men as consumers and collectors but not shoppers. This sleight-of-name is personified by the commonly seen bumper sticker that reflects male acquisition: "He Who Has the Most Toys When He Dies Wins." This is the legacy of paternalism, imputing different values to two kinds of shopping, making the male action respectable and slightly refined — and not calling it shopping — while the female act appears self-indulgent and unimportant.

Call it what you will, the fact is that both genders are subject to serious abuses when it comes to buying behavior. Doubters would do well to review the recent news of several compulsive spenders: former Justice Department official Web Hubbell, once a law partner of Hillary Clinton, forced to resign for embezzling money to support a lifestyle he could ill afford; Garth Drabinsky, cofounder of a huge entertainment conglomerate and, according to *The New York Times*, "A Man of Outsized Acts and Spending," ousted from his post (Weber 1998). Then there's the New Jersey collector, reported earlier in the *Times*, who embezzled $12,000,000 to support his antique-clock habit — and wound up getting twelve years (Smothers 1997).

If many of our confusions about shopping are socially based, there is an economic double message as well, a sort of psychological war between consumption and production. On the one hand, as producers of goods and services we must sublimate, delay, and repress our desires for immediate gratification; we must cultivate the work ethic. On the other hand, as consumers we must display a boundless capacity to capitulate to desire and indulge in impulse; we must hunger for constant and immediate satisfaction. The regulation of desire thus becomes an ongoing problem: we find ourselves continually besieged by temptation while socially condemned for overindulgence.

This powerful double-bind, which looks upon the act of consumption with the disapproving countenance of the work ethic, promotes the kind of double life we hear so often from our patients, especially the ones who have also been dieters: ascetic by day, wildly indulgent on evenings and weekends. All the more important, then, that we help them embrace the self-actualizing possibilities of shopping as search, facilitate the transformation of their need for ever more meaningless goods and services into meaningful ideas and experiences. Conscious shopping, shopping as a process of search, is not about buying, it's about *being*. It's an experience of learning and living that has little to do with spending money. We engage in it all the time, in corners of our lives where unit prices don't apply.

CAN SHOPPING EVER REALLY MATTER?

> The material environment that surrounds us is rarely neutral; it either helps the forces of chaos that make life random and disorganized or it helps to give purpose and direction to one's life.
> — Czikszentmikhalyi and Rochberg-Halton 1981

Shopping, whether for a mutual fund, a pair of pumps, or a political candidate, is a way we search for ourselves and our place in the world. Though conducted in the most public of spaces, shopping is essentially an intimate and personal experience. To shop is to taste, touch, sift, consider, and talk our way through myriad possibilities as we try to determine what it is we need or desire. To shop consciously is to search not only externally, as in a store, but internally, through memory and desire. Shopping is an interactive process through which we dialogue not only with people, places, and things, but also with parts of ourselves. This dynamic yet reflective process reveals and gives form to pieces of the self that might otherwise remain dormant. By deconstructing and reconstructing what the shopping process is all about, we can help patients develop a consciousness about shopping—a respect for their own search process and an attunement to their individual searches. By encouraging patients to take a painstaking look at what they're really shopping for, we help them untie the knot that binds shopping and buying so tightly together. Then they can slowly begin to open themselves up to the opportunities for growth that shopping may afford.

Helpful here is another expansion, that of the concept of materialism. To fully understand the role it plays in our lives, I suggest to patients that, as with shopping, they stretch out the way they view it. We *are* living in a material world, and material things matter. But what's "material"? The piles of cutting-edge inventory at the local Sharper Image store — is this material? The chipped blue coffee mug one can't start the day without — is this material? What, then, about the "material" a comedian creates and refines for her stand-up routine? When a patient and I talk about shopping, we are talking about a process of search that can go on in an infinite number of spaces. In the same way, I suggest, we can start to think of material in an infinite number of ways. Material — what we're shopping for — includes more than tangible objects; it can embrace information, ideas, and experiences that money can't buy.

Csikszentmihalyi and Rochberg-Halton (1981) discuss materialism in a way that underlines this. Exploring the bad–good dichotomy of materialism, they broaden the concept to include two distinct types. *Terminal materialism* is the "runaway habit of possession," acquiring for the sake of acquisition. But when the materials we possess serve goals that are independent of greed and provide a means for the fuller unfolding of life, this is *instrumental materialism*. We might say that terminal materialism is nothing more than a pile of dusty, unused musical instruments taking up space in somebody's attic, whereas instrumental materialism is the conscious act, whether by James Galway or a curious second grader, of blowing air into a flute and bringing it to life.

"Money," says an Arabic proverb, "is an excellent servant but a terrible master," and compulsive shoppers epitomize this, often poignantly. As the economist Robert Linder (1970) has pointed out, acquiring objects and maintaining them can so fill up a person's life that there is no time to use the things acquired. When such a pass is reached, the adaptive value of objects is reversed; instead of liberating psychic activity, the things bind us to useless tasks. The former tool turns master into slave. Instead of mindlessly exhausting resources in their more-is-better philosophy, patients need to realize that the relationship between well-being and consumption is not necessarily linear. Less is often more.

The person who comes to see shopping as search, whose perspective on materialism expands beyond the tangible, is far less likely to resort to self-destructive symptomatology. Such people gradually pass up wild rides on the consumer merry-go-round; they use a different vehicle to satisfy their basic human needs for stimulation, activity, attachment, affiliation, and self-expression. The act of shopping, when viewed as a process of search, can help the people we work with become mindful of themselves, of those around them, and of their larger contexts in the world.

Some searches, to be sure, are more exalted than others — seeking a philosophy of life is loftier than, say, hunting a delectable carton of strawberries — but the mundane may often be as important as the rarefied. The searching we are born doing, as essential to us as breathing and blinking, doesn't happen exclusively on grand tours of our souls; it is happening all the time, every day. It happens when we are running errands, making breakfast, doing the laundry. We comb the cerebral lexicon for just the right word. We examine a dozen pumpkins before choosing the "right" shape and size. We seek out the doctor whose experience, hospital affiliation, and bedside manner we feel most comfortable with. These searches are working drafts of the living autobiographies we're constantly writing — our patients and ourselves.

IS SELFHOOD FOR SALE?

To understand how and why shopping can promote self-cohesion, self-continuity, and self-esteem, we need to take a look at what motivates shopping behavior and what psychological functions it can serve. From the moment of birth, our "selves" develop to initiate, organize, and integrate our various motivations; conversely, our motivations organize our selves. Each of us is a single, unitary self, but we express many self-images, personae, identities, and roles. These many possible selves reflect who we've been, who we are, who we'd like to become; they suggest what we wish for and what we fear.

Trying on selves for size is a lot of what we do when we enact the tasting, sifting, and considering that I'm calling shopping. We make decisions about those selves we want to approach—the selves we "buy," in the colloquial sense—and those we want to avoid. When we purchase a particular car or perfume, when we select a destination from a travel brochure, some possible self rather than the current one is imagined and temporarily embraced. Who will we be to ourselves and the world if we choose the Miata, who if we go with the Bonneville? And what if we opt for a Harley?

It's important to see that conscious shopping, shopping as search, is a dynamic process whose evolution begins in infancy. (In this sense we are indeed born to shop.) From the earliest days and weeks of life, infants explore; they shake bells or rattles, for example, and move mobiles hung in the cribs. Such behavior is not directly or immediately connected with their caregivers. Rather, it manifests the exploratory-assertive, one of the five fundamental motivational systems that, in Lichtenberg's taxonomy (1989), account for all human behavior. Infants, in other words—like the adult shoppers they will become—are seeing what's out there and learning what they can do with it. This exploration brings them an experiential sense of aliveness. The infant who learns to cause her rattle's sound has developed competence; making it sound again brings her pleasure, the intrinsic experience of success. One may well argue that the exploratory-assertive activity of infants is less related to the search for stimuli than to the experiencing of aliveness, of vitalization, that comes with efficacy.

Such pleasure at finding ourselves "at cause in the matter," whatever the matter, is hardly limited to infancy and childhood. There are obvious parallels between, on the one hand, an infant's exploratory activity and resultant vitalization, and, on the other, a shopper's search and postpurchase satisfaction (the "high" that many compulsive buyers cite). These parallels help to explain why, for many buyers, the object purchased is far less important than the feelings that attend the transaction. In this respect shopping resembles another exploratory-assertive activity that is central to most lives, work; in work, too, the dominant affect is efficacy and competence pleasure — the feeling of mastery, power, control.

A brief shopping story illustrates the satisfaction of being "at cause." A woman I work with, an episodic compulsive buyer, bought an ivory silk dress that needed a belt. After several unsuccessful attempts at locating what she wanted, she became convinced that she "just needed to rotate my head in a different direction." She stopped looking for a belt. Instead, she let herself be drawn to color and fabric. Quite soon, she found a wire headband, wrapped in ivory silk, with ivory roses fashioned at each end. She twisted two headbands together, wrapped them around her waist, and *voilà!* — an original and beautiful belt. The exhilaration she felt was quite striking; she had exercised a talent she'd hardly known she had. In the ensuing months she continued to explore this creative new part of herself — and her compulsive buying slowed. Applying her talents had enhanced her self-esteem in a way that simple acquisition could not.

Although the shopping impulse can flow purely from the exploratory-assertive motivational system, it may derive as well from a second element in Lichtenberg's taxonomy, the attachment-affiliation motivational system. When this happens, when shopping gives us intimacy pleasure as well as efficacy and competence, it becomes a form of play, with its own special vitality. Again, the roots go back to infancy. Much of a baby's alert time is spent in interaction with caregivers, where feedback from its mother's face and voice generates positive emotion. The mother's responses and their mutual exuberance mark the success of its efforts. Over time there develops an inner experience of competence at being able to advance the state of intimacy, and this augments the pleasure into play.

When *we* shop, salespeople and companions — shopping buddies, friends, spouses, or children — function in much the same way: interaction with them meets our need for attachment and affiliation. Many of the case illustrations in this book have demonstrated the significance of the shopping companion, both as a symbolic transference figure and as a real provider of mirroring and idealizing responses. My own discovery of the actualizing process of search, as I mentioned in the preface, was fueled by the healing maternal role provided by a particular store and my long-term relationships with the people who worked there.

Robert Prus has studied the influences and interpersonal dilemmas that arise from shopping with companions (1993). His research, which focuses on the social processes involved, describes both the difficulties and the benefits. He notes that companions can provide technical knowledge or expertise, can advise on the appearance or appropriateness of items, and can function as a forum for reflecting on purchases — all of particular importance to the compulsive shopper. He observes as well how some shoppers lose their sense of self-direction once they've opened themselves to a companion's influence. Prus's summary emphasizes that the needs of attachment and affiliation move shopping toward a quest for identity and meaning:

> Shopping is very much an exercise in reflectivity and intersubjectivity. Simultaneously an experience in distancing and sociability, shopping represents an interplay of autonomy and self-direction on one hand and interaction and interdependency on the other. [E]ach shopping episode emerges as a lesson for the self, both in dealing with others and in managing frustrations, developing preferences, and reconciling oneself to one's circumstances. [p. 106]

ARE CONSUMER AND CULTURE CODEPENDENT?

For as long as we've been able to document civilization, consumer and culture have been bound together. Wallendorf and Arnould (1988), who explored the relationship, conclude that attachment to things may be a culturally universal function, symbolizing security, expressing the self-concept, and signifying connection to society. Boxer (1998) puts it another way: "How you shop is who you are. Shopping is a statement about your place in society and your part in world cultural history. There is a close relationship, even an equation, between citizenship and consumption" (p. B7). And consumption supports the culture, allowing it to survive and grow. Broad-based buying fuels our American economy, which has produced the highest standard of living yet achieved on the planet.

But any relationship can become exaggerated, begin to spin out of control. The dramatic rise in compulsive buying is one of many signs that we are witnessing such a phenomenon today. In an economy that has been markedly successful over the last few decades, we see a progressively escalating rate of bankruptcies and an alarming decrease in human satisfaction. A vicious work-and-spend cycle has taken hold. Americans work more than they ever have, save less, and spend *much* more: average spending in our culture rose anywhere from 30 to 70 percent between 1979 and 1995 (Schor 1998). And shopping has skyrocketed. Paco Underhill (1999) sums up the explosion in dramatic absolutes: ". . . the economic party that has been the second half of the twentieth century has fostered more shopping than anyone would have predicted, more shopping than has ever taken place anywhere at any time" (p. 31).

Nor is it merely the quantity of shopping that has changed. Just as important is the change in quality, in the nature of the experience. Falk and Campbell (1997) argue that today's malls function as a safe, even a sacred, space, a substitute for church or town square. Boxer (1998) sees them as modern city-states, each one separated from the outside world, a place where people make choices, render opinions, and socialize with others. These views, according to Goss (1993), set shopping as "the dominant mode of contemporary public life" (cited in Falk and Campbell 1997, p. 3). Statistics support the notion. The average American spends more time at the shopping mall than anywhere else outside of home or work, a whopping six and a half hours per week — and that includes only the time spent inside stores (Bloch et al. 1991).

All of this involves the hardly incidental concurrence of two developments, one socioeconomic, the other technological. Beginning in the 1960s, America witnessed a boom in wealth, with consumption reaching new highs. By the '80s, as Juliet Schor (1998) has demonstrated, there had arisen an extremely wide gap between very rich and very poor. Because the people at the top of the income spectrum spent more on luxury goods, the acceptable consumption levels for the people just below them shifted upward, leading to increased spending for this group, and, in domino fashion, for each group below.

Simultaneously, television allowed the universal display of this new wealth, making possible for the first time a globalized desire for things. Keeping up with the Joneses, the classic dynamic of competitive spending, began to look very different. The Joneses used to be the people next door, unlikely to have an income and lifestyle significantly different from our own. But now the Joneses became people who lived far away and led very different lives. We compared our lives with "Lifestyles of the Rich and Famous"; we watched sitcoms, even those portraying blue-collar workers, that painted an unrealistically upscale existence. People, no matter where they were in the economic spectrum — but especially the middle class — began comparing themselves to the top of the income distribution.

As early as the '60s Herbert Marcuse had recognized that advertising and the media were stretching out reference groups vertically, that the new consumerism had drastically widened the aspiration gap between who we were and who we wanted to be, keeping our feet firmly planted on the consumer escalator. In *The One Dimensional Man* (1964) Marcuse warned about "people [being] manipulated through the media and advertising into believing that their identities will be enhanced by useless possessions" (reported by Nava 1992, p. 188). The ad men, of course, saw this brave new world differently. Betty Friedan, in *The Feminine Mystique* (1963), quotes one: "Properly manipulated . . . American housewives can be given a sense of identity, purpose, creativity, the self-realization, even the sexual joy they lack — by the buying of things" (cited in Nava 1992, p. 188).

Marcuse foresaw what the ad men did not, that more may well be less. Studies document a profound decrease in human satisfaction from a peak in the late '50s to the uncertain and anxious present. Virtually all the data converge on Paul Wachtel's apt phrase, "the poverty of affluence," title of his important 1983 book.

Quite simply, superabundance has proved unfulfilling, and people for whom it is a priority experience an unusual degree of anxiety and depression as well as a lower overall level of well-being (Kohn 1999). Today we are living in "the era of the empty self," where we treat alienation and the loss of community with "the lifestyle solution" — by buying what the advertisers tout (Cushman 1990, cited by Elliott 1994).

Rob Shields (1992) locates and describes this fluid, uncentered postmodern climate: "In shopping malls and markets the world over, new modes of subjectivity, interpersonal relationships, and models of social totality are being 'tried on,' 'taken off,' and 'displayed' in much the same way that one might shop for clothes" (p. i). Bombarded by chaos — crashing planes, ethnic cleansing, even 14-year-olds who blow up their schools, friends, and selves — we seek security through what we *can* control: the things we own.

All signs point, then, to a codependency between consumer and culture, destructively and inextricably linked, the quintessential Japanese finger pull. For this ill, no quick fix. But there is always hope in consciousness. Two centuries ago philosopher Denis Diderot foreshadowed the dissatisfactions of the consumer elevator in his essay "Regrets on Parting with My Old Dressing Gown." The elegant scarlet robe that replaced its shabby predecessor and so delighted him initially set in motion a chain of replacements; in the end their owner found himself "seated uncomfortably in the stylish formality of his new surroundings, regretting the work of this 'imperious scarlet robe [that] forced everything else to conform with its own elegant tone'" (Schor (1998, p. 145). *Plus ça change, plus c'est la même chose.* We too must recognize the full cost of the consumer/culture codependency — and begin returning that relationship to health. One can look with amusement at the peacock dragging its fine feathers in the dust, encumbered with the evolutionary weight of its power of being. Can we not see the compulsive shopper showing the same drive, on a psychological rather than biological level?

Sanders (1998) supposes that "our evolutionary history has shaped us to equate well-being with increase, to yearn not merely for more offspring but also more of everything. If this is truly the case, we can't just decide to feel good about living with less. We can, however, shift the focus of our expansive desires. We can change the standard by which we measure prosperity" (p. 49).

Mindful shopping can help us change that standard, at least individually. By seeing the shopping process as a dialogue of self and soul, as a search for the external reflections of interior substance, we can step off the escalator of consumption and put both feet on the ground. Balanced there, in control, we can select rather than seize. When Yeats remarked that education is not the filling of a pail but the start of a fire, he had in mind the distinction between mechanically gathering up knowledge and creatively shaping the imagination. Mindful shopping — shopping as conscious exploration of self — is similar: not the filling of a bag but the start of a very rich search.

REFERENCES

Bloch, P. H., Ridgeway, N. M., and Nelson, J. E. (1991). Leisure and the shopping mall. *Advances in Consumer Research* 17:298–305.

Boxer, S. (1998). I shop, ergo I am: the mall as society's mirror. *New York Times*, March 28, Sec. B, pp. 7, 9.

Csikszentmihalyi, M., and Rochberg-Halton, E. (1981). *The Meaning of Things: Domestic Symbols and the Self.* Cambridge: Cambridge University Press.

Cushman, P. (1990). Why the self is empty. *American Psychologist* 45:599–611.

Dittmar, H. (1989). Gender-identity-related meanings of personal possessions. *British Journal of Social Psychology* 28:159–171.

Elliott, R. (1994). Addictive consumption: function and fragmentation in postmodernity. *Journal of Consumer Policy* 17:159–179.

Falk, P. and Campbell, C. (1997). Introduction. In *The Shopping Experience*, ed. P. Falk and C. Campbell, pp. 1–14. Thousand Oaks, CA: Sage.

Friedan, B. (1963). *The Feminine Mystique.* New York: Norton, 1983.

Goss, J. (1993). The magic of the mall: an analysis of form, function, and meaning in the contemporary retail built environment. *Annuals of the Association of American Geographers* 83(1): 18–47.

Kamptner, N. L. (1991). Personal possessions and their meanings: a life-span perspective. *Journal of Social Behavior and Personality* 6(6):209–228.

Kohn, A. (1999). In pursuit of affluence, at a high price. *New York Times*, February 2, Sec. F, p. 7.

Lichtenberg, J. (1989). *Psychoanalysis and Motivation*. Hillsdale, NJ: The Analytic Press.

Linder, S. B. (1970). *The Harried Leisure Class*. New York: Columbia University Press.

Marcuse, H. (1964). *The One Dimensional Man: Studies in the Ideology of Advanced Industrial Society*. Boston: Beacon.

Nava, M. (1992). *Changing Cultures: Feminism, Youth and Consumerism*. Thousand Oaks, CA: Sage.

Nemy, E., with Alexander, R. (1998). Metropolitan diary. *New York Times*, November 2, Sec. B, p. 2.

Prus, R. (1993). Shopping with companions: images, influences, and interpersonal dilemmas. *Qualitative Sociology* 16(#2):87–110.

Sanders, S. (1998). The stuff of life. *Utne Reader*, November/December, pp. 47–49.

Scherhorn, G., Reisch, L. A., and Raab, G. (1990). Addictive buying in West Germany: an empirical investigation. *Journal of Consumer Policy* 13:155–189.

Schor, J. (1998). *The Overspent American: Upscaling, Downshifting, and the New Consumer*. New York: Basic Books.

Shields, R., ed. (1992). *Lifestyle Shopping: The Subject of Consumption*. London: Routledge.

Smothers, R. (1997). In a passion for antique clocks, executive embezzled $12 million. *New York Times*, October 1, p. 1.

Underhill, P. (1999). *Why We Buy: The Science of Shopping*. New York: Simon and Schuster.

Wachtel, P. (1983). *The Poverty of Affluence: A Psychological Portrait of the American Way of Life*. New York: Free Press.

Wallendorf, M., and Arnould, E. J. (1988). My favorite things: a cross-cultural inquiry into object attachment, possessiveness and social linkage. *Journal of Consumer Research* 14:531–547.

Weber, B. (1998). A man of outsized acts and spending. *New York Times*, August 11, Sec. D, p. 6.

Wesson, C. (1990). *Women Who Shop Too Much*. New York: St. Martin's Press.

Index